MODERN MYSTERIES,

EXPLAINED AND EXPOSED.

IN FOUR PARTS.

I. CLAIRVOYANT REVELATIONS OF A. J. DAVIS.

II. PHENOMENA OF SPIRITUALISM EXPLAINED AND EXPOSED.

III. EVIDENCE THAT THE BIBLE IS GIVEN BY INSPIRATION OF THE SPIRIT OF GOD, AS COMPARED WITH THE EVIDENCE THAT THESE MANIFESTATIONS ARE FROM THE SPIRITS OF MEN.

IV. CLAIRVOYANT REVELATIONS OF EMANUEL SWEDENBORG.

BY

REV. A. MAHAN,

FIRST PRESIDENT OF CLEVELAND UNIVERSITY.

"There are more things in heaven and earth, Horatio,
Than are dreamed of in your philosophy."

FOURTH THOUSAND.

BOSTON:

PUBLISHED BY JOHN P. JEWETT AND COMPANY.

CLEVELAND, OHIO:

JEWETT, PROCTOR AND WORTHINGTON.

NEW YORK: SHELDON, LAMPORT AND BLAKEMAN.

LONDON: TRÜBNER AND CO.

1855.

CAMBRIDGE:
ALLEN AND FARNHAM, STEREOTYPERS AND PRINTERS.

INTRODUCTION.

PERHAPS we cannot better introduce the reader to the treatise before him, than by giving a short statement of the circumstances which led us to adopt the views therein developed in regard to Spiritualism. Since the year 1850, our residence has been in one of the grand centres of this movement, and where, consequently, the mysterious phenomena were continuously pressed upon our attention. Believing it to be our duty as a religious teacher, and an instructor of youth, sufficiently to acquaint ourself with any influences which are abroad in community, and are operating there with great power to give form and direction to the intellectual, moral, and religious sentiments of the public, to be able to speak intelligently in respect to the same, as occasion may require, we accordingly turned our thoughts more or less upon the mysterious phenomena under consideration. One of the circumstances which first impressed our mind was the utter incompatibility of the fundamental characteristics of these facts, as reported even by spiritualists themselves, with the supposition that they are the *intended* results of intelligent minds who are communicating with us from the heavenly or infernal world. By no laws of mind known to us could we account for the facts, by a reference to such an origin. When they were referred to good spirits, our reply was: good spirits cannot falsify as these do; for these falsify, when spirits, if present, cannot but know the truth; profess knowledge, when they must know themselves ignorant, and make positive affirmations, when they must know that they are only guessing. Good spirits cannot thus act. When they were referred to bad spirits, our reply was: these spirits do not lie like men in the flesh, nor as any spirits would do whose conduct is governed by any laws known to us. There is a certain "*method*" even in lying, wherever it appears, and here is lying which has no such method, nor any method at all which can properly be ascribed to spirits aiming at some intelligent end good or bad. When individuals told us, that they had had communications with their spirit friends, our reply was: the spirit here speaking says some things, that that of your mother, if present, might, and no doubt would say. Your mother, however, when alive and with you, never falsified as this spirit does, and would not thus falsify, if now present. We therefore rejected the *ab extra* spirit hypothesis, as wholly incompatible with the facts.

We were first led to refer the facts to tricks of the mediums. Soon, however, we were confronted with phenomena wholly incompatible with such a supposition. We met, for example, with evidences which we could not resist and maintain our integrity, of the reality of physical manifestations of a very startling and impressive character. We ourselves personally witnessed such facts as we could account for, by no reference to conscious or unconscious muscular action. We also met with individuals of the first intelligence and integrity, and who utterly repudiate the spirit theory, who had themselves witnessed such phenomena. In the Congregational Society's Rooms in Boston, for example, an orthodox Congregational clergyman, of unquestionable intelligence and integrity, affirmed to us, in the presence of several other clergymen, that on one occasion he saw a medium place her hands gently upon a marble-topped table, no other person being near; that after holding them there awhile, the object began to move after her around the room, that he himself got under the table, and taking hold of its legs, attempted to hold it still, and that he was, with the table, drawn quite a distance over the floor, all his efforts to the contrary notwithstanding. From many others we received precisely similar and equally credible statements. We found, then, that we had to admit the facts, or take the ground that no strange events can be established by testimony. How then could we ask the world to believe in Christian miracles? We found equally valid evidence for the reality of the facts of Spiritualism, as far as the *intelligent communications* are concerned. We found ourselves necessitated, therefore, in moral honesty, to admit the facts, and then to seek an explanation of them on some mundane hypothesis, as their character precluded any other supposition than their exclusively mundane origin.

As we reflected upon the facts under consideration, we were forcibly struck with this suggestion, that they seemed evidently to imply the existence in nature of a *polar force* not yet distinctly recognized in philosophy, a force having, when developed, very strong attractive and repulsive power; a force, the direction of whose action, when certain conditions are fulfilled, accords with mental states, and is determined by the same; a force, finally, through which the mental states of one mind may be reproduced in others, and thus embodied, as in these communications. The existence of precisely such a force seemed demanded by the facts, whether we supposed it governed, in the production of these manifestations, by spirits in the body or out of the body. We were also deeply impressed with the obvious correspondence of these manifestations, physical and mental, with the phenomena of mesmerism and clairvoyance, on the one hand, and those of another class which from time to time have, in all ages, startled and troubled mankind, and which philosophers now refer to a power in nature denominated the Odylic Force, on the other. This led to a careful examination and classification of each of these classes of phenomena, and to an equally careful comparison of the results thus obtained with the spirit phenomena, physical and intellectual.

The following are some of the conclusions to which we were thus conducted: 1. There is in nature a force having the identical properties above specified, and which we denominate the Odylic Force. 2. This force is identical with the cause of all the mesmeric and clairvoyant phenomena, on the one hand, and with the immediate cause of these manifestations, on the other. 3. By a reference to the properties and laws of this force as developed in the spirit circles, and to its relations to the minds constituting the same, we can account most fully for all the spirit phenomena, of every kind, without the supposition of the presence or agency of disembodied spirits. Consequently, the hypothesis of Spiritualism is wholly unsustained by any valid evidence whatever. 4. The entire real facts of Spiritualism demand the supposition, that this force in the production of these communications is controlled exclusively, for the most part unconsciously, by the minds in the circles, and not by disembodied spirits out of the same. 5. We finally found, what we did not at first expect, that we had developed facts and principles which gave an equally ready and satisfactory explanation of the phenomena of witchcraft, necromancy, fortune-telling, etc. etc., phenomena which from time to time have been the wonder and terror of mankind in all ages. 6. Other consequences of equal and far greater importance seemed undeniably to follow from our facts and deductions. The results of our investigations, the reader will find embodied in the following treatise. Before putting our thoughts in type, however, we first, after fully satisfying our mind upon the subject, submitted our facts and arguments to a large number of the first thinkers, clergymen and laymen, in the country, and requested their careful inspection of, and candid judgment on the same. We are gratified to say, that we have yet to meet with the first individual who has thus heard, and with us, admits the facts of Spiritualism, that has not expressed the belief, that the mystery that has hitherto hung around these manifestations is now satisfactorily explained, and who has not expressed the earnest wish to have this work presented to the public. Thus assured and thus encouraged, we throw our thoughts abroad upon the public mind, that their merits and demerits may be adjudicated upon.

As we have intended to produce a work which would stand the most rigid test of criticism, we have been exceeding careful in the induction of facts. We have rejected all that came before us, in the reliability of which we were not perfectly assured, that full confidence might be most reasonably reposed; and if we have, in a single instance, overdrawn a single feature of any fact adduced, it has been contrary to our honest intentions.

The other topics discussed, are now so connected, in the public mind, with the spirit movement, that none will question, we think, the propriety of introducing them, as we have done, into the same treatise. With these suggestions, we leave the work with the public.

THE AUTHOR.

JULY, 1855.

CONTENTS.

PART I.

CLAIRVOYANT REVELATIONS OF A. J. DAVIS.

PART II.

PHENOMENA OF SPIRITUALISM EXPLAINED AND EXPOSED.

CHAPTER I.

HAVE WE VALID EVIDENCE THAT DISEMBODIED SPIRITS HAVE ANY AGENCY IN THESE MANIFESTATIONS?

SECTION I.

SECTION II.

THE ODYLIC FORCE.

SECTION III.

SECTION IV.

CHAPTER II.

TENDENCY OF SPIRITUALISM.

SECTION I.

SECTION II.

SECTION III.

CHAPTER III.

MISCELLANEOUS TOPICS.

SECTION I.

PART III.

EVIDENCE THAT THE SCRIPTURES ARE GIVEN BY INSPIRATION OF THE SPIRIT OF GOD, AS CONTRASTED WITH THE EVIDENCE THAT THE SPIRIT MANIFESTATIONS ARE FROM THE SPIRITS OF MEN.

CHAPTER I.

ARGUMENT FROM EXTERNAL MIRACLES. MIRACLE DEFINED.

SECTION I.

SECTION II.

CHAPTER II.

ARGUMENT FROM PROPHECY.

SECTION I.

SECTION II.

CHAPTER III.

ARGUMENT FROM INTERNAL EVIDENCE.

CHAPTER IV.

OBJECTIONS ANSWERED.

OBJECTIONS RELATIVE TO INTERNAL EVIDENCE.

OBJECTIONS BASED UPON WHAT IS FOUND IN THE BIBLE.

PART IV.

CLAIRVOYANT REVELATION OF EMANUEL SWEDENBORG.

MODERN MYSTERIES.

PART I.

CLAIRVOYANT REVELATIONS.*

WHEN any new and very gross absurdity is commended to public regard, men of real science, theologians especially, pass it by, under the impression, that should they expose the imposition, they would appear to the public in the repulsive light of "answering a fool according to his folly." It is this fear, we think, rather than a prudent regard to the public welfare, which has shielded modern "spirit revelations" from that degree of scientific scrutiny requisite to unmask the imposture before the world. Whatever may be thought of the subject in general, the writings of the individual whose name stands at the head of this article seem to demand a critical examination. The volume to which we have referred, consisting of 782 octavo pages, purports to have gone through no less than eleven editions in this country. It has been reprinted

* "The Principles of Nature; her Divine Revelations, and a Voice to Mankind; by and through Andrew Jackson Davis, the Poughkeepsie Seer, and Clairvoyant. In three Parts," etc.

in London; and how many editions it has gone through in Great Britain we have not been informed. It has also laid the foundation for that "spirit" movement which now controls the religious, and, to a great extent, the scientific faith of vast multitudes in this country and in Europe. We shall therefore make no further apologies for an attempt at a somewhat critical examination of the philosophy and character of this great primal production of modern spiritualism.

The self-asserted claims of our author are very wide sweeping, and very peculiar. In the state in which his revelations are given to the world, he claims to be possessed of a power hardly less than omniscient, in regard to the past, present, and, to a great extent, future history and condition of the universe. "His philosophy," says his scribe, "is only that which is involved in the laws and principles which control the universe and mankind unerringly, and his theology is only that which is written on the wide spread scroll of the heavens, in which every star is a word, and every constellation a sentence." "And *whatever* truths," says our seer, "have entered the minds of investigators, they will see the same reflected," (in these revelations,) "which will be a source of inward gratification. There will also be a consolation derived from the things contained in the revelation, consisting in the reflection that the dross and impurities of systems and theories have become purged off, or rather repulsed by the truth, which is positive and eternal." What the stern Mohammedan did with the celebrated Alexandrian library, the world, if our seer's claims be admitted, should now do with all the books of all investigators of truth, since the world began. "*Whatever* truths," (the italics are our author's,) "these works contain, is found in this revelation, and found here, as it is not found in those works, in a state of total freedom from all dross and impurities. What use is there then for any such works? Let them be given to the flames. Then these revelations contain not only the truth, but the *whole* truth. The revelation, our author affirms, "will progressively reveal every visible and invisible existence, until it arrives at the highest sphere of perfection, and then will retrace the links of development back to the original cause and foundation of all things." What investigator, from this time forth, will have the audacity to write another book, when *all* truth pertaining to the visible and the invisible, and that in its origin and progress, is here revealed in a state of total freedom from all admixture of error?

The *manner* of our seer claims a passing remark in this connection. Everywhere he speaks "as one having authority, and not as the scribes." The only foundation that he lays for our faith in his revelations, is the fact, that in the state of clairvoyance in which these revelations are given forth, this Poughkeepsie seer has an *impression* that things are thus and so, and is *impressed* to say it. Simply and exclusively because he is thus *impressed*, in the state referred to, we are to believe that "the material universe is a *vortex*," and "that the earth, when comprehended as an entire whole, is a *stomach;*" that the world had a beginning, and yet that it revolved around the sun from eternity; [after describing the process of the creation of this and all other planets, he tells us, page 430, that the modern philosopher, who discovered the fact, that the earth revolves around the sun, "*discovered* the truth; but that the truth had existed the same from all eternity;"] that Jesus Christ was laid in a manger, not at his birth, as the sacred writer affirms, but at a subsequent period, and that he lay there not over forty minutes by the watch; that the Bible, instead of "bringing life and immortality to light," enshrouds this whole subject in clouds and darkness; that it does not "present any proper conception of the constitution, character, greatness, omnipotence, and majesty of the divine mind;" nor "teach that holy virtue, morality, and refinement which should receive the name of religion;" that, in short, it has been a source of injury rather than good to the world, possessing not even the humble merit of preparing the way for the sublime revelations of the Poughkeepsie seer, etc. Take a single example of his manner. "Previous to this journey, [the flight into Egypt,] a necessary circumstance compelled Mary to lay her child in a manger, in which place, I am distinctly impressed, he lay not more than forty minutes." Thus we are to throw away our Bibles, and believe any thing that may be commended to our regard, for one reason only, namely,— Andrew Jackson Davis, in a state of clairvoyance, has had an impression; he is "*impressed* to say;" is "*distinctly impressed.*"

Permit us here to invite special attention to the argument on which, exclusively as we understand, the high claims of our seer are by him and his associates based. In his natural state he appears, it is affirmed, as an uneducated young man; without learning, without science, without high ideas, or an unusual amount of language. In his clairvoyant state, he has the most wonderful visions, and naturally embodies these visions in the sublime language found in these Revelations. The inference based upon these asserted facts is, that these visions must be the pure embodiment of eternal and immutable truth; that his "philosophy is only that which is involved in the laws and principles which control the universe and mankind unerringly; and his theology is only that which is written upon the wide spread scroll of the heavens, in which every star is a word, and every constellation a sentence." Take away the facts above named, and all grounds for the conclusion that such is the character of the revelations of our seer, disappear at once, and that totally. Now, we say that a grosser *non sequitur* never danced in the brain of Enthusiasm, Superstition, or Fanaticism, than is involved in the above argument. Granting the facts in all their force, how do we know that these visions are the revelations of truth? How do we know that they are not the exclusive creations of an over-excited and disordered imagination? and therefore the embodiment of error, and not of truth? The fact that our seer has no such visions in his natural, and that he has them in his clairvoyant state, presents not the shadow of evidence that these visions are true; unless it can be shown that in a state of clairvoyance the mind sees nothing but truth. If it is not the exclusive character of the visions of universal mind in this state, how do we know that it is the character of those of our Poughkeepsie clairvoyant in the same state? Should it be said that the visions of our clairvoyant are of a higher order than those of others; does this, we ask, prove an infallible criterion of truth? To what degree of sublimity must the fallible rise to become infallible? The claims of our Seer are too shallow, we should think, did not painful experience evince the contrary, to command the faith even of children. The fact that so many quite sensible people have made shipwreck of a divine faith upon such a visible snag as this, evinces to our mind the melancholy truth, that much of the thinking of this age has little of sound reason or logic in it.

In the case of our seer, however, we have the opportunity to test his claims by an infallibly "sure word of prophecy." He professes to give us, with no intermixture of error, a knowledge of "every visible and invisible existence." Suppose that we can convict him of the grossest conceivable absurdity and error in his philosophy, and statements in regard to the visible; his pretended revelations pertaining to the invisible, we shall have no occasion to investigate. We have here indicated the train of thought which we design to pursue. We have little to do with our author, as far as the invisible is concerned; but confine ourselves almost exclusively to what he is "distinctively impressed" in regard to the visible. Hence we shall pass over unnoticed the first part of these revelations, the part which relates to the *principles of nature*, and confine ourselves almost exclusively to the second part, in which he gives us his theory of creation, and a professed history of the progress of events from the beginning to the present time. In the progress of our remarks, we intend to show that the theory of creation set forth in these revelations, is self-contradictory and absurd, and its truth impossible, and that in his statements pertaining to known facts, our seer shows a degree of ignorance, recklessness, and error which has but few parallels. We shall then give our impressions in regard to the moral character of our revelator, from facts which have come to our knowledge.

As a philosopher, our seer is an absolute materialist. In one place, he tells us, that "it is a law of Matter to produce its ultimate, Mind." In another, he says, that to him, "all ultimates are matter." Again, "I would, moreover," he says, "have all understand, that I consider (because I perceive) that all things, whether tangible or intangible, are material." Once more, "I use the terms 'spiritual,' 'celestial,' and 'heavenly,' as representing distinct degrees of material refinement.'"

As a materialist, our seer is an equally absolute necessitarian, or fatalist. His sentiments on this point are fully set forth on pages 463, 464, where he affirms that "it is impossible for any rational mind to conceive of such a thing as 'freewill.'"

Consequently he holds to the existence of spirit and of God, in no other form than as an ultimate, a development of matter. On this point our seer has, throughout, the merit of self-consistency. He pretends to hold to no other form of spiritual existence, or manifestation, but that under consideration.

In testing the validity of his theory of creation, we are to take matter as originally given in theory, and then, from the known laws of this substance, see if we can deduce from it, in accordance with the principles of that theory, the facts of the universe just as they are. In regard to the original condition of matter, we will let our seer speak for himself.

"In the BEGINNING, the Univercœlum was one boundless, undefinable, and unimaginable ocean of LIQUID FIRE! The most vigorous and ambitious imagination is not capable of forming an adequate conception of the height, and depth, and length, and breadth thereof. There was one vast expanse of liquid substance. It was without bounds inconceivable, — and with qualities and essences incomprehensible. This was the original condition of MATTER. It was without forms, for it was but *one* form. It had no motions; but was one eternity of motion. It was without parts; for it was a whole. Particles did not exist; but the whole was as *one* particle. There were not suns; but it was one eternal sun. It had no beginning, and was without end. It had not length; for it was a vortex of one eternity." [He has just told us that it had length inconceivable. Strange logic that also; that because it is "a vortex of *one* eternity," that it therefore has not length. "A vortex of *one* eternity!" How many other eternities are there? "A vortex of one eternity!" What a palpably intelligible idea.] "It had not circles; for it was one infinite circle. It had not disconnected power; but it was the very essence of all power. Its inconceivable magnitude and constitution were such as not to develop forces, but omnipotent power!"

"Matter and power," he goes on to say, "were existing as a whole, inseparable. The *matter* contained the substance to produce all suns, all worlds, and systems of worlds, throughout the immensity of space. It contained qualities to produce all things that are existing upon each of these worlds. The *power* contained wisdom and goodness, — justice, mercy, and truth. It contained the original and essential principle that is displayed throughout immensity of space, controlling worlds and systems of worlds, and producing motion, life, sensation, and intelligence, to be impartially disseminated upon their surfaces as ultimates!

"This great centre of worlds, — this great power of intelligence, — this great germ of existences — was one world! — corresponding to a globe visible; for it was *but* one, — containing the materials and power to produce all others. It had *wisdom* equal to matter to plan them and direct their infinite movements. It had goodness equal to the extent of its substance, to give perfect harmony and distributive usefulness to all parts of this infinitude. It had justice; but only to be manifested in proportion to developments of suitable mediums upon these subordinate spheres, or forms of the *great* sphere. It had mercy, lenity, and forbearance, to be developed as corresponding with like developments in sensitive and intelligent beings. It contained *truth eternalized*, like its own nature. So the whole of these principles were joined in one vast vortex of pure intelligence."

"The great original mass," he tells us, "was a substance containing within itself the embryo of its own perfection. It became pregnated by virtue of its own laws, and was controlled, guided, and perfected, by virtue of its own omnipotent power." From eternity up to a given period, as he subsequently informs us, while it contained in itself the laws and principles of progression, it had not progressed. "It contained the *power* of progression, but had not progressed."

Such, according to our seer, was the original condition of matter prior to creation; a condition in which that substance had, up to a certain period, continued from eternity. How were the worlds and the systems of worlds originated from this "mass of liquid fire?" Around this mass, he tells us, was an atmosphere extending infinitely in all directions. The mass itself, at length began to evaporize light, heat, and other materials adapted to the formation of suns and worlds. The substances thus evaporated were borne upward by the atmosphere referred to, and "became at length a nebulous zone [a zone, as we are informed in these revelations, corresponding to the rings of Saturn] surrounding the immensity of space!" Such is the language of our seer. A tolerably large zone that, — a zone which surrounds the immensity of space. "By constant action and development of the particles thus subjected to the motion of attraction, repulsion, and the law of condensation ; by a repelling of that which was averse to the process of condensation, and an attracting of that which was of like affinity, and suitable to become a part of the same mass, the formation of worlds was first instituted." Suns were first formed, and from these planets, etc. Thus one circle or ring of suns and worlds was commenced and perfected, — or in the language of our seer, " The *first* great ring of converging formations was thus commenced and completed."

Subsequently, " after an unimaginable length of time," by a process precisely similar to that above described, another nebulous zone, either within or without the first, and which, our seer has forgotten to inform us, was formed, and from it another circle of systems, of suns and worlds " was instituted." Thus five such circles have already been " instituted," and a sixth is now in process of being " instituted," but is not yet complete.

We have thus given a full, and as all who have seen the original will admit, a fair and correct statement of our seer's theory of creation. The way is now prepared for some remarks upon this theory.

1. The first step, or great fact, in this process demanding our attention, is the *formation* of Deity. All spirit, as we are taught in these revelations, is an ultimate of matter. God, as a spirit, as given in the theory under consideration, is no exception to this principle. He is an ultimate of the original condition of matter, which was such as " to develop for us omnipotent power," " power containing wisdom and goodness — justice, mercy, and truth." The whole of these principles, joined " into one vast vortex of pure intelligence," constitute the God of these revelations. And how was this ultimate of matter, this " vortex of pure intelligence," this " omnipotent power," this " great positive mind " pro-

duced, or, in the language of our seer, *developed?* By a vast amount of matter in such a state of intense heat, as to constitute "one boundless, undefinable, and unimaginable ocean of liquid fire." Matter to a certain amount, and heated to a certain degree of intensity, being given, and, as the necessary result, we have developed a God, — "a great positive mind," possessed of "omnipotent power," and all possible perfections. If we had a smaller amount of matter heated to the same degree of intensity, we should have a God still, a lesser one to be sure, but still a real "positive mind." We should have just as many Gods, as we could have masses of matter thus heated. These are the necessary, undeniable consequences of the fundamental principles of this theory. This is the theology of "Andrew Jackson Davis, the Poughkeepsie seer and clairvoyant," the only theology we are told that is written upon "the wide spread scroll of the heavens, where every star is a word and every constellation a sentence." We, for ourselves, have endeavored to read this scroll; we have attentively looked at the stars, and the constellations too; but we have been able to find no such theology there. Before we should surrender our faith in

> "That dearest of books that excels every other,
> The old family Bible that lies on the stand,"

to embrace such a theology as this, we should ask considerable time for sober reflection.

The theology of our seer has one merit, to say the least, that of entire originality, as far as our knowledge extends. The idea that matter, heated to a certain degree of intensity, will generate, or develop, mind, "positive mind," and that "one boundless," [not so boundless, but that it may still be surrounded by six, and an infinite number of other circles of suns and worlds,] "undefinable, unimaginable ocean of liquid fire," would generate, or develop the great positive mind, namely, God, — such an idea never danced in our brain, till we met it in these "divine revelations." And what would become of this "great positive mind," should this "ocean of liquid fire" once burn out? an effect, which, from the laws of matter, must occur, in the progress of the eternal future. This mass, however large, must be finite and limited, and in perpetually giving off from itself the materials for the formation of unnumbered suns and worlds, must, at length, totally burn out, and consequently wholly cease to give off such materials, or it must become totally evaporated. There is no escaping this conclusion. Where then will be our fire-begotten, or fire-developed, and consequently fire-sustained divinity? If this theology is true, the universe must soon be without a God, without any "great positive mind."

2. To our limited capacities, there is another fundamental error in the theology of our seer. No cause can generate or develop an effect greater than itself. This is a first truth of science. Now this "ocean of liquid fire," as a cause, must, as we have already seen, be in its nature limited, finite. It is so, according to the positive teachings of our seer; for he affirms, that this very ocean is already surrounded by six circles of suns and worlds. How then can such a cause develop "omnipotent power?" The idea is just as inconceivable and impossible as the supposition, that a globe two feet in diameter actually fills and occupies infinite space. Perhaps our seer is not a little extravagant in the use of language, and by "Omnipotent power" he means merely a very great, but yet finite and limited power.

If so, we have only to reply, that his "great positive mind," in that case, is a being finite and imperfect like ourselves, and is not the deity to whom the intellectual and moral nature of universal mind is fundamentally and immutably correlated. A Deity of absolute infinity and perfection is the only "great positive mind" that responds to the nature of universal finite mind. According to this theology, the final ultimate of matter, rational mind, is fundamentally correlated to the unreal instead of the real, as far as God is concerned. The theology of our seer therefore breaks the harmony of nature, instead of filling out and perfecting it.

3. We now advance to the consideration of a difficulty fundamentally involved in our seer's theory of creation, a difficulty which demonstrably renders the validity of that theory an absolute impossibility. According to this theory, creation, or the formation of worlds, had a beginning, in time. This fact is distinctly affirmed by the author himself. The time was, he tells us, when the great central, primal mass was "one world," when it "contained the power of progression, but had not progressed." He not only represents the process of creation as having had a beginning in time, but as not being yet completed, — the sixth circle of suns and worlds being now in a process of unconsummated completion, the other five having had their origin, and having attained to their completion in time. According to our seer, also, the process of creation is *progressive*, and progressive in one direction exclusively, *from the less to the more perfect.* "Array no arguments, therefore," he says, "against the truthful and magnificent doctrine of progressive development." Now "progressive development," that is progress from the less in the direction of the more perfect, the doctrine every-

where proclaimed by our seer, implies a beginning in time; otherwise creation would now, the progress having been eternal, and consequently infinite, have already attained to infinity and perfection. It has not thus attained, even according to our seer himself. It therefore had a beginning in time. This will be universally admitted. From eternity up to a given period, this now central mass, this "ocean of liquid fire," pervaded by the "great positive mind," existed alone, not having evaporated or radiated any substances adapted to the formation of worlds. Had this evaporation been from eternity, so also must have been the formation of worlds, or, by the laws of matter, that formation never could have occurred at all. As by the law of necessity, which is fundamental in the philosophy of our author, what did not occur could not possibly have occurred, this mass, this "ocean of liquid fire," pervaded by the "great positive mind," had existed from eternity to the period named, without the possibility of producing any evaporations whatever suitable to the formation of suns and worlds. How shall we account for the *commencement* of evaporation from this "expanse of liquid substance," at the moment referred to? Would not the same reasons which rendered it impossible for this cause to produce this result from eternity to the moment referred to, have rendered it impossible for the same identical cause to produce that result to eternity? From eternity to the period named, according to this theory, this mass could, by no possibility, produce these evaporations. From that moment onward, it could not possibly but produce them. Yet the mass itself, with all the laws and causes, external and internal, operating upon it, remained all the while immutably the same. If a theory involving such contradictions can be true, then it is possible for the same thing, at the same time, to exist and not to exist. Evaporation, at the time, and from the cause assigned in this theory, is nothing else than an event without a cause.

From the immutable laws of matter also, evaporation can take place but upon one condition, the *impregnation of portions of matter with degrees of heat which they did not before possess*, and thus changing them from a solid to a vaporous state. No such change could have occurred, at the moment referred to, in any portion of this "mass of liquid substance." The heat must have been equally diffused through all parts of it alike, and that from eternity. No new causes existed to generate new degrees of heat, in any portion of the mass, or in all combined. The evaporations then from which, according to our seer, the universe was formed, must have been an event without a cause, and by no possibility could have been any thing else. His theory is fundamentally self-contradictory and absurd, and its validity an absolute impossibility.

4. Another difficulty, equally fundamental, is found in our seer's "nebulous zones," formed around the central mass, as the material for the institution of his six circles of suns and worlds. If from a mass of liquid substance existing in empty space, evaporations should occur, they would be in all directions equally, and could not possibly be otherwise. If from these evaporations, nebulous formations should be constituted at any distance from the surface of the central mass, they would of necessity assume the form of hollow spheres, and not of zones, as our seer affirms, that is, worlds would be formed in all directions alike and equally around this mass, and not in circles, as asserted by our seer. The formation of such zones in the circumstances supposed,

is an absolute impossibility, and that from the known immutable laws of matter. Consequently, if systems of suns and worlds were constituted from these nebulous formations, they would be in the form of converging spheres, and not of circles. Here, then, the theory of our seer falls to pieces upon another self-evident principle of science.

5. But let us grant the formation of the nebulous zones referred to. The formation of systems of suns and worlds from them, would be an absolute impossibility. The central mass of liquid substance may be conceived of as surrounded or not surrounded with an atmosphere. In the latter case, all evaporations would be collected immediately around the central mass, and no nebulous zones or spheres could be formed. Should any portions of the matter thus evaporated become consolidated, they would thereby become heavier than the other portions of the evaporations around them, and would, by the laws of gravitation, fall back into the central mass from which they had been separated. If the mass referred to were surrounded with an atmosphere, the theory of our seer, the matter evaporated would be borne upward till its specific gravity, and that of the atmosphere sustaining it, became equal. There such matter would remain in the form of clouds, till portions of the same should become consolidated. Such portions, by that means, becoming heavier than the atmosphere which had previously sustained them, would then, as in the case above stated, fall back again into the central mass, and not remain as systems of suns and worlds. From the immutable laws of matter no other results could follow. This is demonstrably evident. The universe cannot have been constituted in accordance with the theory of our author, unless there has

not only been an event without a cause, but in opposition to the immutable laws and constitution of universal nature.

So much for our seer's theory pertaining to the "institution" of the system of suns and worlds now existing in the immensity of space; a theory which any schoolboy can perceive, on a moment's reflection, can by no possibility be true. We might specify additional contradictions and absurdities in this theory to the burdening of our readers. The above are sufficient, however, to accomplish what we intended, when we took up our pen, — the demonstration of the fact, that its validity is an absolute impossibility. As a philosopher, our seer evinces the profoundest ignorance of the most palpable and generally known laws of matter, the only real substance, according to his "divine revelations." As a theorizer, he is a very poor copyist of Lamarck, and the author of the development theory — a theory which any man of real science would now be ashamed to avow, which science has long since exploded, which has not a single decisive fact in the wide universe to sustain it, or render its truth even probable, and which is most absolutely contradicted by all the facts of geology and other sciences bearing upon the subject.

Having shown, by a reference to his central principles, that as a teacher of science, he is nothing but a false light, we shall follow him no further in this department of inquiry, but will now advance to a consideration of his *reliability as a narrator of facts*, facts about which we have certain knowledge. We shall give but a few examples. These, however, will be of such a decisive and fundamental character as to enable our readers to form an unerring judgment upon our revelator's real merits.

In his revelations pertaining to the book of Nehemiah, page 449, we find the following sentence. "For a truthful understanding of the contents of some of the previous books, *this* [the book of Nehemiah] and *following* ones, I would refer the reader to the theological writings of Swedenborg, the enlightened philosopher — especially to the valuable work entitled 'Summaria Expositio Sensus Prophetici.'" In regard to the important statements referred to as in these works, we have the authority of Prof. Bush for saying, — 1. That in none of his writings has Swedenborg given any account or explanation of the book of Nehemiah. 2. That he has never written any work whatever under the title above named. 3. That the exclusive design of the only work which he did write in respect to the prophets, was to show, that the prophetic writings have a meaning which our seer affirms attaches to no parts of the Bible whatever. How safe to follow our author implicitly in professed revelations pertaining to the invisible, when we find him such a safe guide in respect to the visible!

The next statement to which we refer is found on page 507, and is regarded by our seer as of very great importance, his design being nothing less than to do away with the evidence in favor of the divine origin and authority of Christianity, derived from miracles. "It is said," he remarks, "that Christ had a *divine commission*, to prove and establish which, he performed many incomprehensible miracles. How such an opinion can be derived from the literal teachings of the New Testament, it is impossible to conceive; for although Matthew and the apostles seriously believed in miracles, they have not, in all their writings, intimated that these are designed as a confirmation of Christ's mission, nor do they represent him as ever making any such declaration." A more false and reckless statement, we think, can hardly be found in any author, ancient or modern; a statement indicating the grossest ignorance of what children ought to understand, or a very singular presumption in respect to the ignorance of his readers. In Matt. 9: 6, Christ is affirmed to have performed a miracle for the express and avowed purpose of confirming his divine mission. "That ye may know, that the Son of man hath power on earth to forgive sins," then having made this appeal, it is affirmed that he performed this miracle, the healing of the sick of the palsy. In Matt. 11: 4–6, Christ is recorded as having appealed to his own miracles in proof of the fact that he was the Messiah. In John 11: 15, Christ is recorded as affirming, that one object of the miracle which he was about to perform, the raising of Lazarus, was the confirmation of the faith of his disciples in his divine mission; "to the intent that ye may believe." At the grave, prior to the performance of this miracle, he makes a direct appeal to God, affirming that that appeal was made, not on his own account, but on that of the people around him, to induce them to believe in his divine mission. "Because of the people which stand by, I said it, that they may believe that thou hast sent me." To the same purpose are the words of Christ, as recorded John 10: 37, 38, "If I do not the works of my Father, believe me not. But if I do, though ye believe not me, believe the works; that ye may know and believe that the Father is in me, and I in him." In John 15: 2, Christ also is recorded as saying, that, but for his miracles, no guilt would attach to the Jews for not believing in him; and that because of the same, they were without excuse. We need not multiply quotations and references, on a point so clear.

One visible existence our seer reveals, most incorrectly reveals, and that is the Scriptures of truth.

On page 497, we find the following statement, affirming a fact which is entirely new to us. "Luke represents Jesus as being about thirty years of age when he began to preach, and that at *that* time, [the time when he began to preach,] Herod sought his life, while Matthew relates that Herod died before he returned from Egypt." Now every commonly taught Sabbath school child knows, that Luke nowhere affirms that any man bearing the name of Herod, at any time, sought the life of Christ, much less at "*that* time," the time when Christ began to preach. In chapter 13 : 31, Luke affirms that certain Pharisees, after Christ had been for some years preaching the gospel, told him that if he remained in the place where he then was, that Herod would kill him. Christ gave them full leave to inform Herod of his whereabouts, at the same time asserting that no danger was to be apprehended from that quarter. Nor does Matthew anywhere affirm that *this* Herod had died before Christ left Egypt.

We shall adduce but one other example of our seer's safety as a guide in history. We refer to various statements which he has put forth, in regard to the sacred canon, the New Testament especially. On pages 497, 498, he affirms of the books of Matthew and Luke, that "these manuscripts were uncollected and uncompiled for more than three hundred years after the birth and life of Christ." On pages 547, 548, we have the following: "Also remember, reader, that when you read the encyclopædia of religious knowledge called the *Bible*, you are merely reading a book pronounced the word of God by three hundred exasperated bishops, and sealed by their

Emperor Constantine. Moreover, reflect that nearly as many manuscripts as are now embodied in the Old Testament, suffered *martyrdom.* And why, or how, or by whose imperative command, shall we believe that those which *are saved* are the word of God, any more than those which were destroyed?"

On page 644, he tells us, that the books of James and Jude, and the Revelation of John, "were not received into the New Testament as pure and canonical until nearly three hundred years after the Council of Nice." This council met in the year 325, at the command of the Emperor Constantine, and was, according to our seer, originally constituted of two thousand and forty-eight bishops, who were, as he further attests, assembled to settle the sacred canon. The following is his, (our seer's,) account of this council. On account of their violent and vociferous conduct, "Constantine," he says, "was obliged to disqualify seventeen hundred and thirty from having a voice in deciding which books were, and which were not the word of God; and only three hundred and eighteen were left. These decided that the books which composed the Bible, as subsequently known, were the word of God. Several books, however, have since that time, been rejected, but of fifty gospels then extant, they decided that those only of Matthew, Mark, Luke, and John, were worthy of being preserved; while they *rejected entirely* the books of James, Jude, and the Apocalypse. After this decision, Constantine solemnly declared that the same should be considered as sanctioned by the divine will, and that the books thus fixed upon should thereafter be implicitly believed as the word of God. Those manuscripts that were rejected, (among which were three well-written gospels,) were committed to the flames." Our seer has said much more to the same purpose. But this must suffice.

Now what are the real facts of the case, relative to the above sweeping statements? Aside from the fact that the council referred to did assemble at the time designated, and at the call of the individual named, we think that we are quite safe in the affirmation that there is not, in the above extracts, a solitary statement that is true, that is not, in all respects, the total opposite of what is true. We will specify a few examples.

1. Two thousand and forty-eight bishops never assembled as members of this council. Nor were seventeen hundred and thirty, nor any other number, forcibly excluded by Constantine. All but the three hundred and eighteen which did sit as members of the council were there as mere spectators, on account of the intense interest which was universally felt in the question of doctrine then to be acted upon, and this is a well-known fact in history.

2. The canon of Scripture was not, in any form, agitated, or voted upon in this council. Nor was there any disagreement among the different and opposite parties in the council on this subject. The object for which the council was called was altogether another and different affair, namely, the settlement of the Arian controversy, the Orthodox and Arians being as perfectly agreed in respect to the canon of Scripture, as the Orthodox and Unitarians now are. In the sentence passed upon Arius, in the letter sent forth by the council to the churches, in the famous creed then formed, and in the canons passed, there is not a solitary allusion to what, according to our seer, was the main subject of dispute in the council. Our seer might, with the same propriety, have made the same assertions pertaining to the

sacred canon, in reference to any other council of the church, ancient or modern, as in regard to this.

3. No books whatever, claimed to be a part of the sacred canon, were directed to be committed to the flames by this council. The only books which suffered martyrdom, by its order, if any did, were the works of Arius, works which were perfectly at one with the Orthodox portion of the council on the subject of the sacred canon.

4. Instead of deciding, as our seer affirms they did, "that of fifty gospels then extant, only those of Matthew, Mark, Luke, and John were worthy of being preserved," they passed no resolutions on the subject, one way or the other.

5. Instead of "rejecting James, Jude, and the Apocalypse," they and all the other books of the New Testament were assumed as belonging to the sacred canon, just as much, and for precisely the same reasons, that they are thus assumed in all assemblies of the saints which are held in modern times. The question of the reception or rejection of these or any other books claimed to belong to the sacred canon was not moved or acted upon in the council in any form whatever.

6. This council had nothing to do with questions pertaining to the sacred canon, for the obvious reason that such questions had long previously been settled. In the writings of the Christian fathers prior to this council, we find formal catalogues perfectly agreeing with our own. We also find commentaries on the same. Origen, about a century previous, wrote a threefold commentary on the New Testament, and gave a catalogue of the books embraced in it, comprising all now contained in it, and none others. These books were, as they now are, most extensively quoted as of divine au-

thority, and none others were ever thus quoted. Several years prior to this council, Athanasius the great leader of the Orthodox party, and Eusebius, one of the most influential members of the Arian, gave forth formal catalogues of the books of the New Testament. That of the former perfectly agrees with ours, and that of the latter with this exception. Eusebius affirms that all these books but James, Jude, 2 and 3 of John, and Revelation, had, from the first, been universally regarded, by the church, as of divine authority, and that these had been thus received by the majority. While the books now constituting the New Testament, were thus received by the church, none but these were received, as of divine authority, none others were included in the catalogues given by the Christian writers of the sacred books. None, as such, were made the subjects of commentary, or were thus cited in their writings. These are the simple facts of the case, facts as well known in history as any others can be. It is in the presence of such well-known and undeniable facts, that the broad, sweeping, bold, and impious assertions of our seer, pertaining to the sacred canon, are put forth.

7. Our seer affirms, that the gospels of Matthew and Luke were "uncollected and uncompiled for more than three hundred years after the birth and life of Jesus." At least, one hundred years prior to the period here named, one Christian writer published a harmony of these and the other two gospels; another attempted to reconcile the genealogies given in them, and another still, wrote commentaries upon them, and numbered them expressly among the books universally received in the churches, as belonging to the sacred canon. More than a century previous to the same period, another Christian writer, Irenæus, a disciple of Polycarp, who

was a disciple of John, names the authors of the four Gospels, states the circumstances in which these books were written, and then affirms that no other gospels but these were received as of divine authority in the churches. Many other references equally to our purpose might be made. These, however, are sufficient.

Such is the credibility of our divine revelator in the narration of facts of history. We have made our selections almost at random, and we leave the examples adduced to speak for themselves. Any one who would receive with confidence the professed revelations of a person in respect to things invisible, who has been convicted of such errors, misstatements, and falsehoods in regard to "things seen," would heed no remarks of ours upon the subject. In our judgment, our seer has hardly a parallel, as far as recklessness in statements pertaining to matters-of-fact is concerned.

Before leaving this department of our subject, however, the relations of our seer to the visible, we will present a single example of his revelations in respect to things to us invisible. Of the inhabitants of Mars, we have the following description: —

"Sentiments arising upon their minds become instantly impressed upon their countenances;" [they have no hypocrites there who "steal the livery of heaven to serve the devil in;"] "and they use their mouth and tongue for their specific offices, and not as agents of conversation. But that glowing radiation which illumes their face while conversing, is to us inconceivable. Their eyes are blue and of a soft expression," ["variety is *not* the spice of life" there,] "are very full and expressive, and are their most powerful agents in conversation. Where one conceives a thought and desires to express it, he casts his beaming eyes upon the eyes of another, and his sentiments instantly become known."

On reading the above, we were powerfully "impressed" with a fact or two which occurred when we were crossing the ocean. On board the same vessel was a young man of respectable appearance, who had one very singular peculiarity. He would become almost distracted if he wanted any thing, and it was not instantly brought to him. One day he and ourself were sitting in opposite corners of "the smoke room," while the other passengers were taking their dinner, we being unable to partake from that form of sickness so common under such circumstances. While we were thus seated, one of the waiters passed by the door, at the corner of the room the most distant from the place where the young man was seated. As soon as the waiter appeared, the young man leaped up, and rushing forward, cried out at the top of his voice, and with a perfect wail of anguish, "Waiter! waiter! waiter!" We have seldom heard a louder cry, or one uttered with greater apparent anguish. "What do you want?" replied the waiter. "*I want some rice pudding*," was the deeply sorrowful reply. If we had only been inhabitants of the planet Mars then, the distracted young man would have just "cast his beaming eyes upon the eyes" of the waiter, and the latter would have instantly perceived the exact object desired, namely, "*some rice pudding*." During that voyage, we had also, at a particular period, a somewhat to us, singular experience. For several days previous we had hardly been able to partake of a particle of food, and it *seemed* to us that we should never desire to taste it again. At length one specific object which had never before been a favorite article with us, became, to the total exclusion of all others, an object of most intense desire, that of a cold boiled turnip. We finally, in the midst of our sufferings, forced our way to the kitchen, and asked the waiter if he could not furnish us with that one object. What was our suffering, when he told us, that there was no such article in readiness. O, had we been crossing one of the oceans of Mars, at that time, all that we should need to have done, would have been to "cast our beaming [blue] eyes upon the eyes" of one of the waiters as he appeared, and he would instantly have perceived, with absolute distinctness and accuracy, the great thought that lay with such weight upon our heart, and the wish, too, that was the father of that thought, the idea of a cold boiled turnip. Such is the blissful condition of the inhabitants of Mars according the "divine revelations" of "Andrew Jackson Davis, the Poughkeepsie Seer," and "he is a heretic dog that but adds Betty Martyn" to what that divine seer has written. His other revelations in regard to things unseen, are just as credible as the above.

We now advance to a consideration of the last topic of remark in this article, namely, the real moral character of this professedly divine revelator. There are but two points of light in which *we* can regard him — as a self-deceived enthusiast who honestly supposes himself uttering "truth eternalized," while he is giving expression to the merest errors, contradictions, and absurdities conceivable, — or, like the founder of Mormonism, a deliberate impostor. It is in the latter character exclusively that we are compelled to regard this individual, and we will give our reasons for thus regarding him.

We have long been taught to estimate no man's moral character as being better than his deliberately formed and entertained moral principles; and we hold the truth of such a maxim to be self-evident. We believe that no man is practically honest who entertains and propagates a system of belief, that in all respects gives the lie to the immutable dictates of his own moral nature. If there is any thing that is an immutable dictate of that nature, it is that there is an eternal and immutable distinction between actions as morally right or morally wrong; that the most sacred and inviolable *obligation* rests upon us to do the one and avoid the other; and that the *desert* of good or ill necessarily attaches to us, as we comply or refuse to comply with the behest of the law of duty. When an individual denies these distinctions, and cherishes the opposite sentiment, the bottom has dropped out of his moral character, and no foundation is left upon which to build a character for integrity, purity, and virtue.

Now what are the principles of our seer on this subject? — principles to the propagation of which he has consecrated his life? He has one merit here, that of self-consistency. He is an openly avowed materialist, and, as such, is throughout a consistent necessitarian. All the actions of all beings, man not excepted, he teaches, are subject to one immutable law. In the circumstances of their occurrence, they cannot be otherwise than they are. Man, therefore, cannot be under obligation to do differently from what he does, or incur, by any actions he may perform, the desert of moral good or ill. Moral obligation has no place in his system, and he does not profess to give it a place there. "Sin indeed," he says, "in the common acceptation of the term, does not really exist; but what is called sin is merely a *misdirection* of man's physical or spiritual powers which generates unhappy consequences." All effects, human conduct not excepted, are, according to our author, a necessary result of the immutable laws of nature, and cannot, by any possibility, be otherwise than they are. How, then, can such results be a *misdirection* of such powers?

It is with the moral principles of our seer, however, that we now have to do. In another place he tells us, that, "The nature of the mental and physical constitution of mankind is divine, perfect, and harmonious. This will never deceive. It is perfectly good, and represents the divineness of its origin and cause. Deception, however, exists in the world, and all description of dissimulation. But these do not flow from the interior of man's nature, but arise merely as a consequence of his unholy, imperfect, and vitiated situation in reference to his fellow beings. Unholy situations produce unholy effects. But the interior principle which is of *divine* origin, cannot be made evil, nor can it be contaminated. And all evil is of external and superficial origin, and is felt by all as external; and hence, in order to banish all evil from the earth, a change must occur in the social condition of the whole world." Again he says: "The innate divineness of the spirit of man prohibits the possibility of spiritual wickedness, or unrighteousness." In other words, the external actions may be wrong, in consequence of the wrong situation of man physically, but the existence of real moral depravity or wrong is an absolute impossibility. Man can no more sin, according to the proper signification of that term, that is, perform an act really and strictly morally wrong, than a steam-engine!

Such are the sentiments which our seer glories in propagating. Now we say that no man can hold and teach such sentiments, and yet retain his moral integrity and purity, any more than individuals can deliberately perpetrate acts of piracy, murder, arson, seduction, robbery, theft, and not perpetrate acts morally wrong. The moral sentiments can be corrupted only by internal moral depravity and corruption.

We will not judge him, however, merely by his principles, but by his acts,— at least by one of them, which, in our judgment, is sufficiently decisive to mark his real character, indelibly. The past fall and winter, nearly one year ago, our seer performed a mission in some of the western States. When in the city of Cleveland, (we were there at the time,) and while delivering a public lecture, he suddenly stopped, and for some minutes seemed to be in one of his favorite states of abstraction, or spiritual revery. On coming to himself, he remarked that he was deeply, painfully impressed with woman's rights. "Will Horace Mann," he exclaimed, "lecture in this city, this winter? He will. Will his subject be Woman? It will." Our seer then requested that portion of the audience who should hear Mr. Mann, to compare what he should now utter with what Mr. M. should utter on his arrival, and carefully mark the correspondence between them. He then delivered a very spirit-stirring paragraph, in which the audience was intensely interested. He professed to the audience that, during the revery referred to, he had had a *vision* of Mr. M.'s manuscript, and thus obtained the extract delivered. When our seer was through, a gentleman in the audience arose, and remarked that he also *was impressed* to say, that what the speaker had just uttered, as obtained through a vision of an unprinted manuscript, could be found, word for word, in a certain number of the *New York Tribune;* and that, if desired, he would produce the paper and read the paragraph to the audience. Our seer, of course, was taken all aback by such an announcement, and remarking that he did not read the newspapers, went on with his lecture.

We state facts as they were published in the daily papers of that city, while our seer was there; and to our knowledge they have never been contradicted or explained by him or his friends. An individual who boarded at the same house with our seer, while he was in that city, remarked to us that Mr. Davis was, while there, to his personal knowledge, a very diligent reader of the papers. On his arrival in that city, Mr. Mann remarked to us, that up to that time, he had regarded Mr. Davis as a sincere but self-deceived enthusiast; but that now he was compelled to regard him as a deliberate impostor; and that for the reason that not a single sentence contained in the extract could be found in his manuscript; that the former was a very condensed report of a lecture which he had previously delivered in the city of New York. Such a fact, in our judgment, speaks volumes, and it "tells us no lies," but places our seer in the same position as the Mormon prophet.

Our remarks upon these "divine revelations," have been very concise, and were designed to be. Enough has been written, however, to characterize the whole work and its author. If the philosophy on which these revelations are based is intrinsically absurd and contradictory; if, in the statement of known facts of history, he is proved to be a gross deceiver; and if his moral principles are fundamentally subversive of all morality; his character as a "divine revelator" is a fixed fact, and no further examination of his orgies is demanded. We have said enough, we think, to establish, incontrovertibly, all these propositions. Aside from the design of exposing the character of these revelations, we have had two ulterior designs in the preparation of this article.

We have designed, in the first place, to indicate the fundamental objections which lie against the doctrine of materialism, in all the possible forms in which it may be developed. If the theory of our seer cannot be true, and we think we have shown that it cannot, then no form of materialism can be true; for precisely similar objections lie against every other form of that system as against this. The objection that lies against every form of the system that can be devised, may be thus stated: If materialism, in any form, is true, then creation cannot have had a beginning in time, but must have been from eternity. Creation had a beginning in time: therefore that system, in all its forms, must be false.

This article was also designed as preparatory to another, an article on the character of modern "spirit revelations." In giving our readers some principles by which they could judge of the character of these revelations, we deemed it advisable to begin with the founder of this new religion, and especially to reveal the character of "the harmonial philosophy," which "the spirits" seem almost if not quite universally to have adopted. If "the spirits" are fundamentally wrong in their philosophy, and we think we have already shown them to be, they are most assuredly not worthy to be trusted in any of their revelations.

PART II.

THE MISSION OF "THE SPIRITS," OR THE PHENOMENA OF SPIRITUALISM EXPLAINED, AND EXPOSED.

The tendency of human depravity, in all ages, has been to supplant the worship of "the incorruptible God" by that of "corruptible man, and birds, and four-footed beasts, and creeping things." "In these last days," this same principle is being carried out, by attempting to substitute for the revelations of the spirit of this "incorruptible God," those of pretended spirits of corruptible men. No revelations which descend to us from this professed mission of "the spirits," lay claim to any higher origin. A revelation coming from the bosom and heart of infinity and perfection, absolutely adapted, in all respects, to meet perfectly the spiritual necessities of universal humanity, and revealing in its own nature and intrinsic adaptations, as well as in its external evidences, the clearest possible indications of its origin from no other cause than the spirit of God, is, if the mission of "the spirits" attains its end, to be supplanted by pretended revelations of the spirits of men, revelations as discordant in themselves as the jargon of Babel, having no adaptations to the necessities of humanity, in any form, physical, intellectual, or moral, and which are totally wanting, as we expect to show, in any positive claims to any connection whatever with any real spirits in "the spirit land," much less with those whose honest intention is to reveal nothing but the truth.

We may be permitted, in the outset of our remarks, to recur to a fact noticed, in our first article, on the general subject under consideration, a fact which throws a most "disastrous twilight" of worse than uncertainty over this mission of "the spirits;" the fact that, in almost no one point, do they so unanimously agree, as in affirming the truth of the "harmonial philosophy,"—a philosophy which, as we have already shown, can no more be true, than the proposition, that things equal to the same things are *not* equal to one another. Among the standard works issued from "the spirit press," we have, for example, a professed revelation from the spirit of Thomas Paine, pertaining to the original condition of matter, and the origin, progress, and consummation of the work of creation. In this production, which was commended to our high regard by a very intelligent man in most respects, a graduate of Yale College, as solving most completely the great mystery under consideration, the fact of matter as the only substance, its original condition, a condition in which up to a certain period it had remained inoperative for any creative effects, from eternity, as a mass of liquid fire, and the origin and cause of creation from the spontaneous activity of this mass at that moment, are given precisely as set forth in "the divine revelations" of our Poughkeepsie seer. Here the two revelations diverge a little. According to the latter, all systems of suns and worlds were "instituted" from clouds of vapor spontaneously thrown off from the central mass. According to the former, from this same mass there was, at the moment referred to, spontaneously, from a law inherent in matter, thrown off masses of matter which passed away into the depths of space, and then stopping in their flight at the proper points, took their places as suns and worlds, each spontaneously revolving around its own axis, worlds beginning, in the same manner, to move in proper orbits around their central suns, and satellites around their respective centres, and all together constituting one harmonious universe. The individual that would for a moment credit such an account of creation, that does not instantly perceive it to be as absurd, self-contradictory, and its truth as impossible, as the supposition, that creative power resides in empty space, is prepared to believe any thing but truth, — truth revealed in all her internal harmony and self-consistency, and attended with all possible external evidence of its reality. Truth is too insubstantial a substance to find a lodgement in such a mind. Yet such is the philosophy of the spirits in regard to creation, of which they profess a perfect knowledge. Whatever else they know, they are certainly very poor philosophers. Of the real laws of mind they know almost nothing; of those of matter quite as little, and of neither do they know any thing correctly.

Equally absurd is their theory pertaining to the condition of the spirits in the invisible world, — their existence, we mean, in seven concentric circles or spheres. We have the authority of "the spirits" themselves, for discrediting any revelations even from them which do not accord with the great principles of matter and spirit already revealed to us, by experience and observation. Now what is there in the analogy of human experience, or in the laws of our physical, mental, or moral nature, to indicate a future existence in such kind of spheres? Absolutely nothing. Besides, if the law of human progression, which is to continue forever, demands seven such spheres, it would, for the same reason, demand seventy thousand — indeed an infinite number. "The spirits" are now, they affirm, distributed along through these different circles or spheres, from the first to the seventh, according to intellectual and moral attainments. Among those in the first six circles, there is a continuous advance towards the seventh, where they all finally meet, and to all eternity remain together upon one common level. Now, if the progress of those in the sixth circle, for example, demands an ultimate admission to the seventh, why should not the advancement of those in this last demand an admission to one still higher, and so on to all eternity? On what principle of classification, also, are "the spirits" all arranged into seven, with no intermediate circles? The same principles which would demand this number, would require just as many circles or spheres as there are individual spirits; for there are no two precisely alike. Besides, such a separation as the system under consideration presents, is the most unfavorable conceivable to the great ends for which the arrangement itself is made, to wit, universal intellectual and spiritual progression. The most wise and the most pure are separated at the greatest remove from those who most need the influence of their instruction and example. Jesus Christ, we are informed in the work connected with the name of Judge Edmonds, is so far advanced, that such spirits as those of Swedenborg and Bacon, though they have been one or two centuries in the spirit land, have never yet got even a sight of him. For ourselves, we think this must be true of the spirits lubricating in that work. But think of the idea of the state even of the virtuous dead, as shadowed forth in such an arrangement of spiritual existences, an arrangement in which those who most need the highest forms of illumination are placed at an unapproachable remove from it! Then the particular account given of these circles or spheres has but one characteristic which commends it to our regard, a perfect adaptation to secure the faith of credulous minds, namely, its perfect absurdity. That given by the spirit of Thomas Paine, we will notice as an illustration.

All the circles or spheres for the inhabitants of this world, have the earth for their common centre. The first encircles the earth at about five thousand miles from its surface, if we rightly remember. A pretty solid pavement "the spirits" must have to walk upon there. What wonderful scenery they must have there in the presence of which "the spirits" may realize the great idea of endless progression; scenery consisting of luxurious prairies in endless perspective, "hills peeping o'er hills," and mountains, rivers, lakes, oceans of corresponding sublimity, orchards, vineyards, fields of waving grain, all beaming with immortal luxuriance, imperishable habitations, towns and cities with their alabaster foundations, gates of pearl, and streets of gold, looming up into untold magnificence, through their "cloud-capped towers, gorgeous palaces, and solemn temples." We have the most positive revelation from "the spirits," that the soul on escaping its clayey tenement does not escape the curse of labor. The first thing it is called to do, on entering the spirit land, is to erect its own habitation, and make provisions for its own sustenance, by a careful cultivation of the soil there. We think the soil is rather light up there in empty space, five thousand miles from the surface of the earth.

The next sphere, with a scenery of still greater beauty and sublimity, is located at a still greater distance from the earth's surface, and so unto the seventh,

4

which encircles the universe. To what depths must human credulity have descended, when it can resort to sources from which such revelations as these proceed, for reliable information pertaining to the soul's immortal destiny!

We will now descend from the sphere of philosophy to a direct consideration of the claims of spiritualism to the high regard of which its advocates deem it so worthy. We wish to handle these pretended substantialities, "the spirits," and see if there is any thing really substantial about them.

In discussing the subject before us, three, and only three, questions will occupy the attention of the reader, namely, whether we have any valid evidence that spirits out of the body have any agency in the production of these so called spirit manifestations? what is the *tendency* of this spirit movement? and, certain topics of a miscellaneous character, bearing upon the general subject before us.

CHAPTER I.

HAVE WE VALID EVIDENCE THAT DISEMBODIED SPIRITS HAVE ANY AGENCY IN THESE MANIFESTATIONS?

At the outset of our investigations, in respect to this question, it will be necessary to any thing like a scientific procedure, to lay down definitely, certain fundamental principles, which we may apply, as decisive *tests* of truth, in reference to any conclusions which have been, or may be deduced from the facts which lie in our way, — and then to specify the character of the *facts* on which spiritualists rely, as proof of the truth of their theory. As fundamental test principles which should guide our investigations, and determine our conclusions on this subject, we specify the following —

TEST PRINCIPLES.

1. No facts occurring in the world around us, are to be referred to any supernatural, or *ab extra* spirit causes whatever, which facts can be adequately accounted for, by a reference to causes known to exist in this mundane sphere.

2. No facts are to be referred to any *particular* supernatural, or *ab extra* spirit cause, unless they are of such a nature, that they can be accounted for, upon no other supposition.

3. When particular causes are known to exist, all effects within and around us are to be attributed to such causes, effects *resembling* and *analogous* to those known to proceed from such causes, effects especially which occur in circumstances where such causes may be reasonably supposed to be present.

4. Even those facts for the occurrence of which no mundane causes, at present known, can be assigned, are not to be attributed to any *ab extra* causes whatever, or to the agency of disembodied spirits, when such facts are similar and analogous, in their essential characteristics, to other facts which once appeared equally mysterious and unaccountable on any mundane hypothesis, but for which science subsequently discovered actual mundane causes. Such facts manifestly lie in the track of scientific discovery, and we must suppose them to be the result of mundane causes, which are yet to be discovered, though at present unknown to us.

5. To establish the claims of spiritualism, its advocates must show, (1.) that the facts which they adduce are wholly dissimilar and unanalogous, in their essential characteristics, to any facts resulting from any mundane causes, and (2.) that the occurrence and characteristics of these facts can be accounted for, but upon one exclusive hypothesis, the agency of disembodied spirits. If similar and analogous facts do arise from purely mundane causes, it is a violation of all the laws and principles of science and common sense, to attribute these phenomena to any *ab extra* cause whatever.

The validity of these principles will be universally recognized as self-evident. Their applicability, as fundamental tests of truth, to our present inquiries, is equally manifest and undeniable. Their validity has been universally acknowledged by Christians, in reference to all miraculous attestations of the claims of Christianity to a divine origin and authority.

FACTS ADDUCED TO SUSTAIN THE CLAIMS OF SPIRITUALISM.

The *facts* on which the reality of the agency of spirits out of the body, in the production of these manifestations, is affirmed, are all, without exception, comprehended in the following classes, namely: —

1. Facts of a purely physical character, such as the moving of tables, chairs, etc., movements which sometimes accord with the thoughts and suggestions of inquirers.

2. *Intelligent* communications, by means of rapping sounds, speaking, and writing, phenomena which, in many instances, to say the least, occur wholly independently of the direct conscious agency of the mediums, or any other persons present, on the occasion.

3. Communications pertaining to subjects of which the *mediums* are profoundly ignorant, and yet found to be correct.

4. Correct communications pertaining to facts believed to be known only to the inquirer himself, and the particular spirit with whom he is professedly communicating.

5. Similar communications containing correct responses to purely *mental questions.*

6. Communications conveying, in some instances, correct information, in respect to *facts unknown to the inquirer, or any other person present.* Facts falling under one or the other of the classes above named, are continuously occurring, it is claimed, in all parts of Christendom, and can be accounted for but upon one supposition, namely, that these communications proceed from disembodied spirits.

Such is the argument of spiritualists, as stated by themselves, and stated as strongly as ever, to our knowledge, given forth by any writer or speaker, who advocates the spirit theory. Either of the following positions may be taken by those who deny this theory. 1. They may *deny the facts* put forward by spiritualists, and then meet the evidence adduced by them in favor of the actual occurrence of such facts. 2. Or they *may admit the facts*, and then meet the arguments based upon them. 3. Or, finally, they may *deny both the facts and the conclusions* based upon them, that is, they may take the ground, that the facts claimed by spiritualists are impositions, on the one hand, and that, if admitted as real, they do not sustain the claims of spiritualism, on the other. In each and every case alike, the burden of proof rests wholly upon the advocates of this new theory. All that its opponents have to do, unless they choose to proceed further, is to meet the facts and arguments adduced by its advocates to sustain its claims For ourselves, in conducting the argument, in the present treatise, we shall admit the facts claimed by spiritualists, and join issue with them simply and exclusively in regard to the conclusions which they deduce from them. We admit the facts for the all adequate reason, that after careful inquiry, we have been led to conclude that they are real. We think that no candid inquirer, who carefully investigates the subject, can come to any other conclusion. While we honestly believe, that there is more imposition connected with this movement, than with almost any other that can be named, yet we as fully believe, that a denial of the facts claimed by spiritualists, as comprehended under the classes above named, has its exclusive basis either in ignorance, or a state of prejudice which is blind to valid evidence. We have ourselves witnessed physical manifestations which, in our judgment, can be accounted for, by no reference to mere muscular action.

A lady, for example, places her fingers gently upon a table or stand. Soon the object moves after her around the room, while yet no other person is in contact with the object, or in many feet of it, and her own fingers so lightly touch the smooth surface, or top of it, that the parts touching it are not perceptibly flattened in the least, on the one hand, nor the blood at all driven from under the finger nails, on the other. Who does not perceive, that the movements of such objects, under such circumstances, can be accounted for by no muscular pressure and action whatever? Yet we feel quite safe in vouching for the reality of just such facts, facts which are produced by individuals utterly repudiating spiritualism, in all its forms, facts utterly fatal, as we shall hereafter see, to its claims, as far as physical manifestations are concerned. That *intelligent* communications are obtained in the spirit circles, communications undeniably indicating their origin from some intelligent cause, is now doubted by none, and admitted by all. Equally undeniable is the fact, that correct responses are often obtained to questions pertaining to subjects of which it is honestly believed, and no reasons exist for an opposite conclusion, that all present are profoundly ignorant, but the inquirer and the spirit with whom he is professedly communicating. A stranger, for example, from the most distant part of this, or from any foreign country, in passing through a place which he never visited before, and in consequence of an unexpected delay, goes immediately and unattended from the cars into some spirit circle, where no one could have expected him, and where he meets not a solitary countenance or form of which he has the most distant recollection. To all present, therefore, he has the best possible evidence that he is an utter stranger, whose visit no one anticipated. This individual, under these identical circumstances, may call for the spirit of some departed friend, and, on inquiry, obtain correct answers pertaining to the name of that spirit, his age at the time of his death, etc., the only condition required being, that the inquirer shall himself know what answers should be given, and, at the time, have those answers distinctly before his mind. That facts of this character have occurred, we have the most valid evidence, and any one can verify them, in his own experience, who will take the pains to do it. In the same circumstances, and on the same condition, individuals can obtain, in some instances, to say the least, correct answers to purely *mental questions.* A gentleman of our acquaintance, for example, called upon the Misses Fish and the Foxes, when they were in Cleveland, Ohio, and to the supposed spirit of a departed sister, put mentally, and in succession, twelve questions, and to each received a perfectly correct answer, he knowing, in each instance, what the answer should be, and having his attention, at the time, definitely fixed upon it. This, and cases of a similar kind, which might, without number, be adduced, establish the reality of the class of facts under consideration. The gentleman above referred to, however, wrote out these same questions upon twelve blank cards, and putting them together, the sides containing the questions from him, and having shuffled them so that he could not know what question he might put down, in any instance, put each one successively upon the table, the question downward, and requested the same spirit to give an answer to the question laid down, while he should write that answer upon the blank side. Twelve answers were, accordingly, obtained, but one of which was, in any form, correct; the answers, in most instances, having no relations whatever to the question put. Such facts, which are continually occurring in spirit circles the world over, throw, in the judgment of all reflecting minds, more than suspicion over the truth of the whole spirit theory. The spirit of that sister, or any other truthful, or even lying spirit, a lying spirit who did not wish to bring this theory into universal discredit, would never attempt to answer questions under such circumstances; but would, at once, disavow ability to do it. There can be no doubt on this subject. Truthful spirits, we know certainly, would not give such responses; and lying ones would not, upon any laws of mind known to us, unless they desired, a case not credible, to shut themselves and all other spirits wholly out from all communication with minds in the body.

As an example of facts coming under the class last named, we will state one which recently came to our knowledge, and for the occurrence of which we feel quite safe in vouching. A friend of ours who had been, since the summer of 1850, till September last, in Europe, and who, on his return, left two daughters there, one in London, and the other in France, Calais, if we rightly remember, called, not long after his return, upon a venerable Quaker family, in the State of Rhode Island. As the conversation, during the evening, turned upon the merits of spiritualism, the lady of the house proposed to call in, which was done, a friend of hers who was a medium, but never acted as such for remuneration. This medium, our friend had never before seen, and the character of the family precluded the idea of any form of imposition. When the required preparation was consummated, our friend inquired if any spirit was present who would communicate with him, and if so who? Elizabeth B——, was immediately rapped out. He had had a mother, sister, and wife, all now dead, of that same name. After specifying the two former, and receiving a negative answer, he was told that it was the spirit of the latter. To all questions pertaining to their family, such as names, ages, etc., correct answers were given. He then inquired about the *present* location of their daughters, and was told that each of them was in London. The eldest he supposed to be there, and the other in France. To every inquiry pertaining to the whereabouts of the latter, however, the answer was, London. The next steamer brought a letter from that daughter dated London, to which city she had come six days prior to the time when that professedly spirit communication was received. The unbelief of our friend in spiritualism was very strongly shaken. In a subsequent interview with that spirit, after receiving all the evidence of identity which he had ever done, he asked the question, Where did you die, and where was your body buried? The reply was, Durham. After asking whether the place named was located in Ohio, Michigan, New York, or Massachusetts, and receiving to each inquiry a negative answer, the spirit was asked to name the State herself. Pennsylvania was rapped out. The wife of our friend died in Buffalo, N. Y., and her body was there interred. It is thus, that all reflecting minds who are inclined to place confidence in "the spirits," find their faith continually running upon snags by which it is, in a short period, utterly submerged. We leave such facts, for the present, to speak for themselves. Their full, and, as we hope, perfectly satisfactory explanation will be given hereafter. We might multiply authentic cases, in which correct statements are made relatively to facts unknown to all within the circles where such statements are given forth. One, however, when the reality of the facts is admitted, and all agree, in regard to the class to which they belong, is sufficient. That we may not be misunderstood, in our admissions, we would remark, that while we admit the actual occurrence of the class of facts last named, we also believe, from the best information which we have been able to obtain, that to inquiries pertaining to such subjects, excepting in cases where only a positive or negative answer is required, and one must be true, hardly one answer in a hundred is correct. We have a friend in Europe, for example; we ask the question of "the spirits," Is he dead or alive? Here we are, at any rate, as likely to obtain a right as wrong answer. But suppose we ask, is he alive, and if so, where he is, and what is he *now* employed about? we having no means of forming even a probable conjecture of what is true on such subjects. In such cases correct answers are not, in our judgment, obtained in one case in a hundred, if in a thousand. Yet a sufficient number of such cases do occur to constitute the class above named, cases which need to be accounted for. We would further remark, that according to the best information that we have been able to obtain, incorrect answers are continuously, as in the case cited above, given forth to inquiries pertaining to subjects fully known both to the inquirers and the spirits professedly communicating, answers of such a character as to destroy all rational confidence in the claims of spiritualism.

ISSUE STATED.

Such, as we understand the subject, are the facts before us, and such are the principles which should guide us in their investigation. To sustain the claims of spiritualism, it must be shown, that *similar* and *analogous facts are produced by no mundane causes whatever, on the one hand, and that they can be produced by no other agencies than disembodied spirits, on the other.* In opposition to the claims of this new system, we propose to show:

1. That from known mundane causes, precisely similar and analogous facts do arise.

2. That these so called spirit manifestations actually occur, in circumstances in which such causes are known to exist and to act, and that by a reference to such causes, all these manifestations can be accounted for.

3. That from such causes, and not from the agency of disembodied spirits, these manifestations do proceed. When we shall have proved the first two propositions, we shall have totally annihilated the claims of spiritualism, and when we shall have established the third, we shall have proved that theory false. We shall attempt the accomplishment of both these objects. We will take up the first two propositions together, and having established their truth, will then proceed to argue the last.

FIRST TWO PROPOSITIONS ESTABLISHED.

Spiritualists, as well as their opponents, admit, that if spirits do produce these manifestations, they do it by controlling a certain force preëxisting in nature. No one supposes that they make rapping sounds, guide the hands or tongues of mediums, or move tables, by themselves striking against physical objects, taking hold of the hands or tongues of mediums, or of tables and other objects, and thus controlling their motions. All is done through the medium, or instrumentality of some natural force or power. To proceed intelligently in our investigations, we must, first of all, determine the properties and laws of this mysterious power in nature.

SECTION I.

ELECTRICITY, MAGNETISM, AND ANIMAL MAGNETISM DISTINGUISHED

In accomplishing the object immediately before us, we would remark, that philosophers have unitedly affirmed, and the public generally are now fully aware of the truth of that affirmation, the existence and action of the three following distinct powers or forces in nature, namely, *Electricity*, *Magnetism*, and *Animal Magnetism*. While they all have many characteristics in common, each is distinguished from the others by properties altogether special and peculiar. They all have in common *polarity*, and with it the power of strongly attracting and repelling certain bodies. The points of agreement and distinction between electricity and magnetism are thus set forth by Prof. Olmsted: "Electricity and magnetism agree in the following particulars. 1. Each consists of two species, the vitreous and resinous electricities, and the austral and boreal magnetisms. 2. In both cases, those of the same name repel, and those of opposite names attract each other. 3. The laws of induction in both are very analogous. 4. The force, in each, varies inversely as the square of the distance. 5. The power, in both cases, resides at the surface of bodies, and is independent of their mass.

" But electricity and magnetism are as remarkably unlike in the following particulars. 1. Electricity is capable of being excited in all bodies, and of being imparted to all: magnetism resides almost exclusively in iron in its different forms, and with a few exceptions, cannot be excited in any but ferruginous bodies. 2. Electricity may be *transferred* from one body to another; magnetism is incapable of such transference; magnets communicate their properties merely by *induction*, a process in which no portion of fluid is withdrawn from the magnetizing body. 3. When a body of an elongated figure is electrified by induction, on being divided in the middle, the two parts possess respectively the kind of electricity only which each had before the separation; but when a bar of steel or a needle magnetized by induction is broken into any number of parts, each part has both polarities, and becomes a perfect magnet. 4. The directive properties and the various consequences that result from it, the declination, annual and diurnal variations, the dip, the different intensities in different parts of the earth, are all peculiar to the magnet, and do not appertain to electrified bodies."

Animal magnetism has, in common with the two forces above named, as we have said, *polarity*, and consequently the property of attraction and repulsion. This statement is verified by an experiment with which all who have seen persons in a magnetic or mesmeric sleep are familiar. When the ends of the fingers of the magnetizer, for example, are brought near those of the magnetized, the latter being perfectly blindfolded, so as not at all to be aware of what is being done, the hand of the person magnetized will instantly be attracted towards that of the magnetizer, and will follow it in any direction, just as the loadstone, and evidently for the same reason, draws after itself the needle, or any object in respect to which it has attractive power. Here stands revealed the *polarity*, and consequently the attractive force of this mysterious power in nature. Its essential dissimilarity from electricity, is equally manifest in the fact, that *living* bodies can be charged with the former in circumstances in which they cannot be with the latter, that is, in the presence of electric conductors. The human body, for example, can be charged with the electric fluid, only by being placed upon glass, or some other non-conductor. In direct and immediate contact with such non-conductors, the same body may be most fully charged with animal magnetism. From magnetism it is distinguished with equal manifestness, by the fact, that it may be excited, in all its force, in *animal* bodies, while the former is developed, in force, only in *iron* and kindred substances. We might refer to other characteristics, in which this substance, or force in nature, is distinguished from electricity on the one hand, and from magnetism on the other. The above, however, are sufficient for our present purpose. It remains to specify some of the peculiar characteristics of this power, as developed in animal bodies, the human body, we now refer to. Among these we would specify the following to which very special attention is invited, as they will hereafter be seen to have a fundamental bearing upon our present inquiries.

EFFECTS OF ANIMAL MAGNETISM UPON THE HUMAN SYSTEM.

1. It operates with immense power upon the muscular system, imparting to the limbs a rigidity and inflexibility which render any motion at the joints almost as impossible as at any other parts. We will give a single fact in illustration, a fact which occurred some years since in the city of Cleveland. The subject was a young woman who labored as a domestic in the family where the fact occurred. After putting the individual into a magnetic sleep, and while she was sitting in a chair, the magnetizer extended her right arm in a horizontal direction, and having made a few passes of his hand from the shoulder to the hand of the subject, he requested the pastor of the First Presbyterian Church of that city, who was present by invitation, to bring that arm down from the position referred to. Taking hold of the hand and wrist of the subject, and pressing downwards with much weight, he expressed the fear that he should break the arm, should he add to the pressure. On being assured by the magnetizer, that he had no reason for apprehension on that subject, Dr. Aikin affirms,

that he laid out all the strength he could command, without being able to move the limb downward. It seemed to possess the inflexibility of a rod of steel. The above fact comes from a source which will command universal belief, and is but one among numberless others of a similar nature that might be cited. With what astonishing power must this force act upon the muscular system to produce such results!

2. Such also is the effect of this substance, or force, upon the physical system generally, that the mind is thereby, in many instances, wholly insulated from any communication with the external world, through any of the senses, and, in instances not a few, rendered equally insensible to any effects produced upon the physical organization itself. A limb may be amputated, for example, and the subject experience no pain, nor any conscious sensation whatever, from the operation. The senses also are all locked up from any communications with the world around but through those with whom, and in respect to objects with which, they are in mesmeric communication. Facts falling under this class are too well authenticated to be denied, and too well known to need illustration, or explanation by the citation of particular examples.

3. In some instances, under the influence of this same substance, the perceptive faculties are greatly quickened, so that the mind perceives objects which lie wholly beyond, and at a great remove from, the reach of the ordinary senses, when the mental and physical powers are in a normal state. That perceptions of this character are to be numbered among real facts of clairvoyance there can rest upon no candid mind, which has made adequate investigations, any doubt whatever. "However astonishing," says Sir W. Hamilton, "it is now

proved beyond all rational doubt, that in certain abnormal states of the nervous organism, perceptions are passible through other than the ordinary channels of the senses." "It has been, I believe," says Dr. Wayland, "proved beyond dispute, that persons under this influence have submitted to the most distressing operations without consciousness of pain; that other persons have cognized events at a great distance, and have related them correctly at the time; and that persons totally blind, when in a state of mesmeric consciousness, have enjoyed for the time the power of perceiving external objects." As we wish to have very special attention directed to this class of facts, on account of their bearings upon our subsequent inquiries, we will confirm the truth of the above statement of Dr. Wayland, by the following extract from a letter addressed to him by J. M. Brook, Esq. of the United States Navy, and contained in the work from which the above is taken, namely, "Wayland's Intellectual Philosophy."

WASHINGTON, Oct. 27, 1851.

"SIR, — It affords me pleasure to comply with your request, made through my brother William, relative to some experiments performed on board the United States steamer Princeton, in the latter part of the year 1847; she being then on a cruise in the Mediterranean. Nathaniel Bishop, the subject of the experiments, was a mulatto, about twenty-six years of age, in good health, but of an excitable disposition. The first experiment was of the magnetic or mesmeric sleep, which overpowered him in thirty minutes from the commencement of the passes made in the ordinary way, accompanied with a steadfast gaze and effort of will that he should sleep.

In this state he was insensible to all voices but mine, unless I directed or willed him to hear others; he was also insensible to such amount of pain as one might inflict without injury, that is, what would have been pain to another. He would obey my directions to whistle, dance, or sing. When aroused from this sleep he had no recollection of what occurred while in it. That such an influence could be exerted, I was already aware, having previously witnessed satisfactory experiments. Of clairvoyance I had never been convinced; indeed, considered it nothing but a sort of dreaming produced by the will of the operator. I became aware of its truth rather through accident than design.

"It happened, one day, that some of my brother officers asked a question which the others could not answer. Bishop, who had been a few moments before in a mesmeric sleep, gave the desired information, speaking with confidence and apparent accuracy. As the information related to something which it seemed almost impossible to know without seeing, we were very much surprised. It struck me that he might be clairvoyant; and I at once asked him to tell me the time by a watch kept in the binnacle, on the spar or upper deck, we being on the berth or lower deck. He answered correctly, as I found upon looking at the watch, allowing eight or nine seconds for time occupied in getting on deck. I then asked him many questions with regard to objects at a distance, which he answered, and, as far as I could ascertain, correctly.

"For example, one evening, while at anchor in the port of Genoa, the captain was on shore. I asked Bishop, in the presence of several officers, where the captain then was. He replied, 'At the opera with Mr. Lester, the consul.' 'What does he say?' I inquired.

Bishop appeared to listen, and in a moment replied, 'The captain tells Mr. Lester, that he was much pleased with the port of Xavia; that the authorities treated him with much consideration.' Upon this, one of the officers laughed, and said that when the captain returned he would ask him. He did so; saying, 'Captain, we have been listening to your conversation while on shore.' 'Very well,' remarked the captain, 'What did I say?' expecting some jest. Then the officer repeated what the captain had said of Xavia and its authorities. 'Ah,' said the captain, 'who was at the opera? I did not see any of the officers there.' The lieutenant then explained the matter. The captain confirmed its truth, and seemed much surprised, as there had been no other communication with the shore during the evening. I may remark that we touched at several ports between Xavia and Genoa.

"On another occasion, an officer being on shore, I directed Bishop to examine his pockets; he made several motions with his hands, as if actually drawing something from the officer's pockets, saying, 'Here is a handkerchief and a box; what a curious thing! full of little white sticks with blue ends. What are they, Mr. Brooks?' I replied, 'Perhaps they are matches.' 'So they are!' he exclaimed. My companion, expecting the officer mentioned, went on deck, and meeting him at the gangway, asked, 'What have you in your pockets?' 'Nothing,' he replied. 'But have you not a box of matches?' 'Oh! yes!' said he, 'How did you know it? I bought them just before I came on board. The matches are peculiar, made of white wax with blue ends.'

"The surgeons of the Princeton ridiculed these experiments, upon which I requested one of them (Farquharson), to test for himself, which he consented to do. With some care he placed Bishop and myself in one corner of the apartment, and then took a position some ten feet distant, concealing between his hands a watch, the long hand of which traversed the dial. He first asked for a description of the watch. To which Bishop replied, ''Tis a funny watch, the second hand jumps.'

"The doctor then asked him to tell the minute and second, which he did; directly afterwards exclaiming, 'The second hand has stopped!' which was the case; Dr. Farquharson having stopped it. 'Well,' said the doctor, 'to what second does it point, and to what hour, and what minute is it now?' Bishop answered correctly, adding, ''T is going again.' He then told twice in succession the minute and second.

"The doctor was convinced, saying, that it was contrary to reason, but he must believe. I then proposed that the doctor should mark; and directed Bishop to look in his mother's house, in Lancaster, Pa., (where he had never been,) for a clock; he said there was one, and told the time by it; one of the officers calculated the difference in time for the longitudes of Lancaster and Genoa, and the clock was found to agree within five minutes of the watch time."

4. The relations existing between the magnetized, when in the magnetic state, and the magnetizer or other persons in mesmeric communication with the person magnetized, next claims our special attention. Among these relations the following may be specified as having a special bearing upon our present investigations. (1.) Any *sensations* induced by any cause in the magnetizer are instantly reproduced in the individual magnetized, and that when it is impossible to induce

any such feelings by any effects directly produced upon the physical organization of the latter. If the magnetizer tastes, smells, or touches any particular object, the person magnetized instantly experiences the same sensations. Any sensations *unexpectedly* induced in the former, by secretly twitching his hair, pinching his body, or pricking it with a needle or pin, and when this is done in a manner and form which preclude the possibility of any knowledge of what is done, on the part of the latter, any sensations, we say, even thus induced in the magnetizer, will be instantly reproduced in the person magnetized, each individual, in almost all instances being affected in the same part of the physical system. A gentleman of our acquaintance, to remove all doubt from his own mind in regard to the question of collusion, called a magnetizer aside, and while speaking to him, put a vial of hartshorn to his nose, the vial having just before been sent for from a distance: "Do take that from my nose," instantly exclaimed the subject who was in a magnetic state. The world is full of facts of a precisely similar nature wherever the mesmeric phenomena have been witnessed.

The *law* which obtains in these circumstances seems to be this. This mysterious power acts with such force upon the sensitivity of the individual under its influence, (the person magnetized,) that it can, for the time, be affected but through this one power. Any feeling or sensation induced in the magnetizer acts upon this power, and through it upon the sensitivity of the person magnetized, reproducing there the same feelings which had previously been induced in the magnetizer.

(2.) In a similar manner, the *thoughts* of the magnetizer are reproduced in the mind of the individual magnetized, especially when the former wills it. This holds true not only in regard to common conceptions, but equally of all acts of the imagination. A very intelligent and pious lady, a member of the Baptist church in Poughkeepsie, N. Y., while upon her death-bed, made the following statement to her pastor, from whom we received the same. When you come to investigate the facts of mesmerism, she remarked, you will find this to be true, that the clairvoyant when in mesmeric communication with you, *can speak your thoughts.* I was once present when A. J. Davis, then a lad, was in this state, and was requested to touch his forehead with my own. I did so, and found that he would instantly speak out any thought that came into my mind. A scientific gentleman from the interior of New England, while in the city of New York, some years ago, called upon, and was put into mesmeric communication with a clairvoyant whom he had never seen before. The latter mentally accompanied the former to his (the inquirer's) father's residence, describing the facts of the journey, the external and internal appearance of the house and the surrounding scenery just in accordance with his recollections and conceptions at the time. He then *imagined* a meeting-house standing before the front door of that residence, (no such object existing,) and asked the clairvoyant, "what do you see now?" "A meeting-house," was the answer. The object was then described in exact accordance with the image preëxisting in the inquirer's mind, both in regard to location, form, size, color, etc. The fact of the transfer of thought in the mesmeric relations is too well known and undeniable to require any further confirmation or elucidation.

Many curious inquiries are often raised pertaining to the question, *How* are such effects produced? On this subject we will venture the expression of an opinion.

How is it, that by *vocal* utterance we reproduce our own thoughts in the minds of others? The action of our vocal organs induces a vibratory motion of the atmosphere, the ultimate result of which (not to specify particulars) is the production, in the mind of the hearer, of certain *sensations* with which those thoughts are associated. Through those sensations, thus induced, the thoughts referred to are reproduced in the mind of the hearer. Suppose that when a thought exists in the mind of the magnetizer, the feelings thereby induced in him act upon this force so as to induce, in the magnetized subject, the same or similar feelings or sensations that would be induced by the vocal utterance of that thought, when each was mentally and physically in a normal condition. That thought would be reproduced in one instance for the same reason precisely, and upon the same principle, that it is in the other, there being a difference merely in regard to the immediate cause of the sensation with which the idea is associated. This we believe to be the real relation between the individuals under consideration, and this the reason why the thoughts of the one are reproduced in the mind of the other. We have already shown that *sensations* are reproduced upon this one principle. Why should we not conclude, that upon the same principle thoughts are reproduced? The fact of the transfer of thought in the mesmeric relation will not be doubted, however, whatever may be thought of the above explanation.

(3.) A control equally perfect can the magnetizer exercise over the *muscular* system of the individual in a magnetic state. By simply willing it, with no external motions whatever, the latter can render the whole body, or any given member of the same perfectly stiff and motionless, and hold it in any given position for any given length of time. This power often continues for a period subsequent to the time when the subject has come out of a mesmeric state. Take as an illustration and confirmation of this statement, the following additional extract from the letter of J. M. Brooke, Esq.: "The power which I acquired by putting him to sleep remained after he woke, and was increased by its exercise. If not exerted for several days, it decreased, sometimes rendering it necessary to repeat the passes, and again put him to sleep. While awake, and under my influence, I made many experiments, such as arresting his arm when raising food to his mouth, or fixing him motionless in the attitude of drinking. On one occasion I willed that he should continue pouring tea into a cup already filled, which he did, notwithstanding the exclamations of those who were scalded in the operation. These influences were exerted without a word, or change of position on my part."

(4.) Hence I remark, in the last place, that the entire mental and physical activity of the magnetized, is, in many instances, under the complete control of the magnetizer, while the mesmeric relation between them continues, a relation which, as we have seen, often continues for a period longer or shorter, after the subject has come out of a mesmeric sleep. The wildest imaginings of the latter are thus reproduced in the mind of the former, the objects of those imaginings appearing as objects of real external perception. The magnetizer puts his handkerchief, for example, into the hands of his magnetic subject, and it becomes, to that subject, a flower of surpassing beauty, a kitten, lap-dog, an infant, or a serpent, just as the magnetizer secretly wills. Mr. Brook says still further of his subject: "He remembered or forgot what he saw when clairvoyant, as I willed, of which I satisfied myself by experiment. All his senses were under control, so completely indeed, that had I willed him to stop breathing I believe that he would." A magnetizer agreed with a friend of ours, a gentleman of the most unquestionable veracity, to induce his magnetic subject to sing, she being a beautiful singer, and to stop the singing the instant our friend should raise his finger. As the singing proceeded, and while the singer was uttering a long note, our friend raised his finger, and the voice instantly ceased, with that note half finished. The magnetizer willed the singing to proceed again, and that note, a thing impossible to a person in a normal condition, was finished, and with it the remainder of the stanza. This was done, while the subject was deeply blindfolded, and the magnetizer stood several feet from her, with his eyes fixed intently upon our friend, waiting for the raising of his finger. No collusion therefore was possible. The following facts we adduce, with leave, on the authority of Mr. Covert, formerly president of Central College, Ohio, and now of the Female College on College Hill, near Cincinnati. The facts occurred in Columbus, in the presence of a select company of witnesses. After fully satisfying himself, by experiments about which there could be no mistake, that any sensations induced in the magnetizer were instantly reproduced in the magnetic subject, the latter uniformly experiencing the corresponding sensation in the very part of the body in which it was induced in the former, and after witnessing wonderful exhibitions of the absolute control which the magnetizer had, at will, over the magnetized individual, President Covert called the former into a separate room, the door being closed between them and the subject of the magnetic influence, and requested him, in a tone of voice that could be heard by no one but themselves, to will that his subject should leave her seat, come into the room where they were, and seat herself in a particular chair which was designated, many others being in the room at the time. The magnetizer did as directed, and that without moving at all any part of his body. Immediately the magnetic subject opened the door, entered the room, and passing to the other side of it, sat down in the very chair referred to, her eyes all the while being perfectly closed, and the magnetizer, we repeat, giving not the least indication by word, look, or gesture, of what he willed her to do. He then, at President Covert's subsequent request, so uttered that none but the individual spoken to could have heard, willed her to leave that seat, and seating herself at the piano, entertain them with music and singing. This she did accordingly. Thus it is, that the magnetizer, at will, completely controls the mental and physical activity of his magnetic subject. Facts of the most authentic character, and bearing with equal force upon the same conclusion, might be multiplied to any extent. These, however, are abundantly sufficient. From all the facts above adduced, pertaining to the action of this mysterious power in nature, the following conclusions are undeniable : —

1. There is in nature a medium of communication between mind and mind, other than that by which communications are had, through the ordinary channels of the senses.

2. Through this same force, one mind may, when the proper conditions are fulfilled, control the action of the mental and physical powers of another mind.

3. The action of this force upon the physical system, and through it upon the mind of the magnetized, is as the feelings, thoughts, and purposes of the magnetizer.

4. Through this same power, the mind of the person magnetized, when he happens to be in mesmeric communication (rapport) with any object however distant, and however removed from the reach of the senses, will have a direct and immediate cognition of the same.

5. The action of this force, when certain conditions are fulfilled, is determined, in many important particulars, by mental states and acts, and accords with the same, and here its nature and relations to mind stand revealed, a fact of fundamental importance, but which seems not hitherto, to have been distinctly and generally recognized by philosophers. Mesmeric facts have demonstrated the existence of this power in nature, and thereby laid the foundation for the explanation of many facts around us which have, to this time, appeared to be totally inexplicable.

SECTION II.

THE ODYLIC FORCE.

To prepare the way still further for the full and distinct elucidation of the subject before us, we will now advance to a consideration of a peculiar force in nature, a force the existence, properties, and laws of which philosophers had developed and verified, by the most careful and decisive experiments, years prior to the appearance of these so called spirit manifestations, and which they had denominated the Odylic Force. This force, which indeed pervades all bodies in nature, has many properties in common with electricity and magnetism, *polarity*, and with it, the property of *attracting* and *repelling* other bodies, for example. At the same time, it differs from these forces in particulars equally fundamental, being, for example, undeniably transmissible through magnetic and electric non-conductors. The physical organisms of individuals of peculiar physical temperaments, become, in some instances, in certain localities, permanently and very strongly charged with this force. The following may be enumerated, as among the more important phenomena which characterize its developments under such circumstances.

1. It acts upon other objects, and is reacted upon by them, as a very strong *attractive* and *repulsive* power; objects, in many instances, even without visible contact, being drawn towards or driven from such individuals, and in other particulars acted upon in a very singular and unaccountable manner.

2. Upon the walls, floor, and ceiling of rooms occupied by such individuals, rapping sounds, very much like those produced by striking against such objects with the knuckles, or with a mallet, are not unfrequently heard; such phenomena being also occasionally attended with a sensible jarring of surrounding objects, and sometimes with rumbling sounds, resembling the roaring of distant thunder.

3. The physical systems of such individuals are very powerfully affected, so powerfully as, in many instances, to derange totally the action of the mental powers.

4. In the mental developments thus induced, we have, without exception, all the mesmeric and clairvoyant phenomena, as above presented.

5. This force, when developed in the human organism, has generally a special location in some of the *nerve centres.* When such centre is not immediately connected with the brain, then the action of this force, like that of magnetism, is simply that of a repulsive and attractive power, without the characteristics of intelli-

gence. When that centre is the brain, then the *direction* of the action of this power bears, in many important particulars, the characteristics of intelligence, the action of the force, in such cases, being not only in accordance with, but evidently directed by, mental states.

In illustration of the above statements, and in verification of the same, we will now present a few well authenticated facts. We cite only such facts as have a direct and immediate bearing upon our present inquiries. Those who would understand the science of the Odylic Force, are referred to the fundamental works upon the subject which are now before the public.

With facts which really and truly indicate the existence and action of such a force in nature, so far especially as its attractive and repulsive properties are concerned, almost every one is, no doubt, familiar, though these facts, as generally witnessed, having nothing of a startling character about them, have, for the most part, escaped any special notice. Who has not witnessed, for example, in passing his hand over the head of another, the evidence of an attraction between the hand and the hair upon the head of such individual, an attraction sufficient to disarrange the hair, and cause the ends of it to rise from the head? Such facts clearly indicate the existence of the attractive force of which we are speaking. Some months since, as we called upon an aged clergyman who was just recovering from sickness, he related to us a somewhat interesting fact which had just occurred in his own experience. While engaged, a day or two previous, in adjusting some papers for the purpose of putting them on file, on withdrawing his hand from the paper which he had placed upon the top of others, that object followed his hand, being evidently attracted by it. After repeated attempts, he found it impossible to adjust that paper, because it would follow his hand when he would withdraw it. His attention being thus attracted, he was led to make some special experiments. On placing the ends of his fingers upon the paper, and raising them up, the object adhered to them, and remained, for some time, suspended, just as a needle and other objects are raised and suspended by the magnet. On trial, he found that no such attraction existed, at the time, between his hand and any other paper before him for the obvious reason, that this attractive force, the presence of which is here undeniably evinced, was not thus relatively developed between his hand and any other paper, as between it and this one. We have only to suppose this same force developed between the organism of this individual and some heavy object, such as the table, and developed to a certain degree of strength and intensity, and for the same reason that this paper was attracted by his hand so as to be raised from the table, the table itself would be drawn after him all around the room, or thus driven from him, if the polarity of this force, as developed in his organism and the object were different or opposite from what we have supposed it to be. The table itself, also, attracted by the hand of the individual just as the paper referred to was, might, like that object, be lifted from the floor and for the same reason. Suppose further, that this force should happen to be developed at the same time, and in the same form, in the table and the floor beneath it. In that case, on the known principle, that, with all forces having polarity, opposite poles attract, while the same ones repel each other, the table would be spontaneously lifted from the floor, and, for a time, held, as by an invisible power, suspended in the atmosphere. If the same force was developed at the time, in some object near, but with opposite polarity, then the table would be drawn towards such object, whirled over and thrown, it might be, with much violence upon the floor. Thus alternately attracted by some objects, and repelled by others, it would now be driven forcibly against some individuals, and fly from others with seeming terror, and tumbled strangely about the room, till all present were convinced that it must be bewitched, while all these terrifying phenomena are the exclusive result of the natural and necessary action of a peculiar force existing in nature all around us, a force which, like electricity in a thunderstorm, happens, at this time, to be developed with special power, in this particular locality, and in connection with the objects referred to, and when these *now* strange and unaccountable phenomena lose all their power to astonish and to terrify, as soon as the existence and properties of the force from which they result come to be recognized and understood.

A lady attempts to spread out upon a table a silk dress, for the purpose of ironing it. The article adheres to her hand, winding all around it, so that she finds it very difficult or impossible to adjust the article so as to accomplish her object. We state a case which actually occurred in our own family, some months since. Another individual adjusts the same article without any difficulty, no such attraction appearing between her hands and the object referred to. In the case of the first individual, this force happened to be, at the time, developed in such relations between her hands and the object, the dress, as to occasion the singular phenomena under consideration. Such facts which are of almost every-day occurrence in the world around us, render manifest the existence, in the human organism, and in external nature, of the force of which we are speaking, and when wisely considered, prepare us to look with scientific scrutiny, and with less wonder, incredulity, and scepticism upon authentic cases in which this same power is developed in the organism of individuals to such a degree, as produce the phenomena which astonish mankind. To a few of these cases, all of which, we believe, have all the marks of credibility that we can, with any show of reason, demand, very special attention is now invited.

The first case that we adduce is that of Angelique Cottin, of which we have two well authenticated accounts, one of which is given by Catharine Crowe, in the "Night-side of Nature," and the other in the "Courier des Etats Unis," of Paris. Both of these accounts are combined in the following extract from "Roger's Philosophy of Mysterious Rappings," to which we are indebted for other important facts hereafter to be cited.

"Angelique Cottin was a native of La Perriere, aged fourteen, when, on the 15th of January, 1846, at eight o'clock in the evening, while weaving silk gloves at an oaken frame, in company with other girls, the frame began to jerk, and they could not by any efforts keep it steady. It seemed as if it were alive; and, becoming alarmed, they called in the neighbors, who would not believe them, but desired them to sit down and go on with their work. Being timid, they went one by one, and the frame remained still till Angelique approached, when it recommenced its movements, while she was also attracted by the frame; thinking she was bewitched or possessed, her parents took her to the presbytery, that the spirit might be exorcised. The curate, however, being a sensible man, refused to do it, but set himself, on the contrary, to observe the phenomenon; and, being perfectly satisfied of the fact, he bade them take her to a physician.

"Meanwhile, the intensity of the influence, whatever it was, augmented; not only articles made of oak, but all sorts of things, were acted upon by it, and reacted upon her; while persons who were near her, even without contact, frequently felt electric (?) shocks. The effects, which were diminished when she was on a carpet or a waxed cloth, were most remarkable when she was on the bare earth. They sometimes entirely ceased for three days, and then recommenced. Metals were not affected. Any thing touching her apron or dress would fly off, although a person held it; and Monsieur Herbert, while seated on a heavy tub or trough, was raised up with it. In short, the only place she could repose on was a stone covered with cork; they also kept her still by isolating her. When she was fatigued, the effects diminished. A needle, suspended horizontally, oscillated rapidly with the motion of her arm, without contact; or remained fixed while deviating from the magnetic direction. Great numbers of enlightened medical and scientific men witnessed these phenomena, and investigated them with every precaution to prevent imposition. She was often hurt by the violent involuntary movements she was thrown into, and was evidently afflicted by chorea,"* or St. Vitus' dance.

The French paper mentions the circumstance that, while Angelique was at work in the factory, "the cylinder which was turning was suddenly thrown at a considerable distance without any visible cause; that this was repeated several times; that all the young girls in the factory, terrified, fled from the factory, ran to the curate to have him exorcise the young girl, believing she had a devil." After the priest had consigned her to the physi-

* See Night-side of Nature, p. 380.

cian's care, the *Courier des Etats Unis* goes on to say: "The physician, with the father and mother, brought Angelique to Paris. M. Arago received her, and took her to the observatory, and in the presence of MM. Laugier and Goujon made the following observations, which were reported to the Paris Academy of Sciences.

"1. It is the left side of the body which appears to acquire this sometimes attractive, but more frequently repulsive property. A sheet of paper, a pen, or any other light body, being placed upon a table, if the young girl approaches her left hand, even before she touches it, the object is driven to a distance, as by a gust of wind. The table itself is thrown the moment it is touched by her hand, or even by a thread which she may hold in it.

"2. This causes instantaneously a strong commotion in her side, which draws her toward the table; but it is in the region of the pelvis that this singular repulsive force appears to concentrate itself.

"3. As had been observed the first day, if she attempted to sit, the seat was thrown far from her, with such force that any person occupying it was carried away with it.

"4. One day a chest, upon which three men were seated, was moved in the same manner. Another day, although the chair was held by two very strong men, it was broken between their hands.

"5. These phenomena are not produced in a continued manner. They manifest themselves in a greater or less degree, and from time to time during the day; but they show themselves in their intensity in the evening, from seven to nine o'clock.

"6. Then the girl is obliged to continue standing, and is in great agitation.

"7. She can touch no object without breaking it or throwing it upon the ground.

"8. All the articles of furniture which her garments touch are displaced and overthrown.

"9. At that moment many persons have felt, by coming in contact with her, a true electrical shock.

"10. During the entire duration of the paroxysms, the left side of the body is warmer than the right side.

"11. It is affected by jerks, unusual movements, and a kind of trembling, which seems to communicate itself to the hand which touches it.

"12. This young person presents, moreover, a peculiar sensibility to the action of the magnet.

"When she approaches the north pole of the magnet she feels a violent shock, while the south pole produces no effect; so that if the experimenter changes the poles, but without her knowledge, she always discovers it by the difference of sensations which she experiences.

"13. M. Arago wished to see if the approach of this young girl would cause a deviation of the needle of the compass. The deviation which had been foretold was not produced. The general health of Angelique Cottin is very good. The extraordinary movements, however, and the paroxysms observed every evening, resemble what one observes in some nervous maladies.

"The great fact demonstrated in this case, is,

"That, under *peculiar conditions*, the human organism gives forth a physical power which, *without visible instruments*, lifts heavy bodies, attracts or repels them, according to a law of polarity, — overturns them, and produces the phenomena of sound."

For the following quite striking case, we are indebted to the *Spiritual Telegraph*, of New York city, a case which is given in that paper from another paper published in that city, and dated March 10, 1789.

"Sir: — Were I to relate the many extraordinary,

though not less true accounts I have heard concerning that unfortunate girl at New Hackensack, your belief might, perhaps, be staggered, and patience tired. I shall, therefore, only inform you what I have been eye-witness to. Last Sunday afternoon my wife and myself went to Dr. Thorn's, and, after sitting for some time, we heard a knocking under the feet of a young woman that lives in the family. I asked the doctor what occasioned the noise; he could not tell, but replied that he, together with several others, had examined the house, but was unable to discover the cause. I then took a candle and went with the girl into the cellar; there the knocking also continued; but, as we were ascending the stairs to return, I heard a prodigious rapping on each side, which alarmed me very much. I stood still some time, looking around with amazement, when I beheld some lumber which lay at the head of the stairs shake considerably. About eight or ten days after, we visited the girl again. The knocking still continued, but was much louder. Our curiosity induced us to pay the third visit, when the phenomena were still more alarming. I then saw the chairs move; a large dining-table was thrown against me, and a small stand, on which stood a candle, was tossed up and thrown in my wife's lap; after which we left the house, much surprised at what we had seen."

The case which we next cite is so well authenticated, as to remove all reasonable doubt, to say the least, of its actual occurrence. The facts occurred in the family of Mr. Joseph Barron, of Woodbridge, New Jersey, in the year 1834. We give the account as published, at the time, in the *Newark Daily Advertiser*.

"The first sounds were those of a loud thumping, apparently against the side of the house, which commenced one evening when the family had retired, and continued at short intervals until daylight, when it ceased.

"The next evening it commenced at nightfall, when it was ascertained to be mysteriously connected with the movements of a servant girl in the family, — a white girl, about fourteen years of age. While passing a window on the stairs, for example, a sudden jar, accompanied with an explosive sound, broke a pane of glass, the girl at the same time being seized with a violent spasm. This, of course, very much alarmed her; and the physician, Dr. Drake, was sent for; came, and bled her. The bleeding, however, produced no apparent effect. The noise still continued, as before, at intervals, wherever the girl went, each sound producing more or less of a spasm; and the physician, with all the family, remained up during the night. At daylight the thumping ceased again. In the evening the same thing was repeated, commencing a little earlier than before; and so every evening since, continuing each night until morning, and commencing each night a little earlier than before, until yesterday, when the thumping began about twelve o'clock at noon. The circumstances were soon generally spread through the neighborhood, and have produced so much excitement that the house has been filled and surrounded from sunrise to sunset for nearly a week. Every imaginable means have been resorted to, in order to unravel the phenomenon. At one time the girl would be removed from one apartment to another, but without effect. Wherever she was placed, at certain intervals the thumping noise would be heard in the room. She was taken to a neighboring house. The same result followed. When carried out of doors, however, no noise is heard. Dr. Drake, who has been constant in his attendance during the whole period, occasionally aided by other scientific observers, was with us last evening for two hours, when we were politely allowed a variety of experiments with the girl, in addition to those heretofore tried, to satisfy ourselves that there is no imposition in the case, and, if possible, to discover the secret agent of the mystery. The girl was in an upper room, with a part of the family, when we reached the house. The noise then resembled that which would be produced by a person violently thumping the upper floor with the head of an axe, five or six times in succession, jarring the house, ceasing a few minutes and then resuming as before. We were soon introduced into the apartment, and permitted to observe for ourselves. The girl appeared to be in perfect health, cheerful and free from the spasms felt at first, and entirely relieved from every thing like the fear or apprehension which she manifested for some days. The invisible noise, however, continued to occur as before, though somewhat diminished in frequency, while we were in the room. In order to ascertain more satisfactorily that she did not produce it voluntarily, among other experiments we placed her on a chair on a blanket in the centre of the room, bandaged the chair with a cloth, fastening her feet on the front round, and confining her hands together on her lap. No change, however, was produced. The thumping continued as before, except that it was not quite so loud; the noise resembling that which would be produced by stamping on the floor with a heavy heel, yet she did not move a limb or muscle, that we could discover. She remained in this position long enough to satisfy all in the room that the girl exercised, voluntarily, no sort of agency in producing the noise. It was observed that the noise became greater, the further she was removed from any other person. We placed her in the doorway of a closet in the room, the door being ajar to allow her to stand in the passage. In less than one minute the door flew open as if violently struck with a mallet, accompanied by precisely such a noise as such a thump would produce. This was repeated several times, with the same effect. In short, in whatever position she was placed, whether in or out of the room, similar results, varied a little perhaps by circumstances, were produced. There is certainly no deception in the case. . . . The noise was heard at least one hundred yards from the house."

In this case also, as well as in those previously cited, there is no ground for the least suspicion of the action of any other than an exclusively physical cause.

The following somewhat lengthy extract from "Roger's Philosophy of Mysterious Rappings," presents two additional cases, of much interest and importance, in their bearings upon our present inquiries. The author will pardon us, for making, for the sake of science, such a free use of his facts and remarks.

"The wonderful occurrences at Stockwell,* in England, in January, 1772, are of the same character as the above. We can barely give the most important parts of the phenomena here, and leave the reader to consult the work referred to in the note. No intelligence was manifest in this case.

"On Monday, January 6th, 1772, about ten o'clock in the forenoon, as Mrs. Golding (the hostess) was in the parlor, she heard the china and glasses in the back kitchen tumble down and break; her maid came to her, and told her the stone plates were falling from the shelf; Mrs. Golding went into the kitchen, and saw

* See Catherine Crowe's Night-side of Nature, page 370.

them broken. Presently after, a row of plates from the next shelf fell down likewise, while she was there, and nobody near them; this astonished her much, and while she was thinking about it, other things, in different places, began to tumble about, some of them breaking, attended with violent noises all over the house; a clock tumbled down, and the case broke. The destruction increased with the wonder and terror of Mrs. Golding. Wherever she went, accompanied by the servant girl, this dreadful waste of property followed.

"Mrs. G., in her terror, fled to a neighbor's where she immediately fainted. A surgeon was called, and she was bled. The blood, which had hardly congealed, was seen all at once to spring out of the basin upon the floor, and presently after the basin burst to pieces, and a bottle of rum that stood by it broke at the same time.

"Mrs. G. went to a second neighbor's, as the valuables that were conveyed to the first were being destroyed. And while the maid remained at the first (Mr. Greshem's) the former was not disturbed, but while the latter was 'putting up what few things remained unbroken of her mistress', in a back apartment, a jar of pickles that stood upon a table turned upside down;' and other things 'were broken to pieces.'"

"Meantime the disturbances had ceased at Mrs. Golding's house, and but little occurred at the neighbors while Mrs. G. and her servant remained apart. But as soon as they came into each other's company the disturbance would begin again.

"'At all these periods of action,' says the detail, 'Mrs. Golding's servant was walking backward and forward, in either the kitchen or parlor, or wherever some of the family happened to be. Nor could they get her to sit down five minutes together, except at one time, for about half an hour toward the morning, when the family were at prayers in the parlor; then all was quiet; but, in the midst of the greatest confusion, she was as much composed as at any other time, and, with uncommon coolness of temper, advised her mistress not to be alarmed or uneasy, as she said these things could not be helped. Thus she argued as if they were common occurrences, which must happen in every family.'

"' About five o'clock on Tuesday morning, Mrs. Golding went to the chamber of her niece, and desired her to get up, as the noises and destruction were so great she could continue in the house no longer; at this time all the tables, chairs, drawers, etc., were tumbling about.' In consequence of this resolution, Mrs. Golding and maid went over the way, to Richard Fowler's. The latter left her mistress, and returned to Mrs. Pain's, to help this lady dress her children. ' At this time all was quiet. They then went to Fowler's, and then began the same scene as had happened at the other places. It must be remarked, all was quiet here, as elsewhere, till the maid returned.'

" When they reached Mr. Fowler's, he began to light a fire in his back room. When done, he put the candlestick upon a table in the fore room. (*This apartment Mrs. Golding and her maid had just passed through.*) This candlestick, and another with a tin lamp in it, that stood by it, were dashed together, and fell to the ground. A lantern, with which Mrs. Golding was lighted across the road, sprung from a hook to the ground. The last thing was, the basket of coals tumbled over, the coals rolling about the room.

" Mrs. G. and her servant now returned home, when

the same scene was repeated. Mr. Pain then desired Mrs. Golding to send her maid for his wife to come to them. When she was gone, all was quiet. Upon her return, she was immediately discharged, and no disturbances happened afterward. This was between six and seven o'clock on Tuesday morning.

"The whole account contains the following important particulars:

"1. The phenomena commenced at ten o'clock, A. M.

"2. They always depended upon the presence of the servant-maid.

"3. They occurred always with the greatest energy when the mistress was in the company of the maid.

"4. When the maid passed *through* a room alone there would be little or no disturbance of its contents; but, if she was soon after followed by Mrs. Golding, various articles would begin to play the most singular pranks, as if Puck himself had come again.

"5. Very often one article would be attracted by another, or they would fly towards each other, and, striking together, fall upon the floor, as if both had been charged with some physical agent which made them act like opposite poles. Then, also, one would fly from another, as by repulsive forces.

"6. The phenomena were accompanied with violent concussive sounds about the house.

"7. Every thing which Mrs. Golding had touched seems to have been in some way affected, so that afterward, on the approach of the maid, it would be frequently broken to atoms, sometimes without even her touch. Even the blood of Mrs. G. was highly susceptible under the same circumstances, and the bowl in which it was contained, and the glass ware standing by it, burst to pieces.

"In the year 1835, a suit was brought before the sheriff of Edinburgh, Scotland, for the recovery of damages suffered in a certain house owned by Mr. Webster. Captain Molesworth was the defendant at the trial.* The following facts were developed: Mr. Molesworth had seriously damaged the house, both as to substance and reputation,

"1. By sundry holes which he cut in the walls, tearing up of the floors, etc., to discover the cause of certain noises which tormented himself and family.

"2. By the bad name he had given the house, stating that it was haunted. Witnesses for the defendant were sheriff's officers, justices of the peace, and officers of the regiment quartered near by; all of whom had been at the said house sundry times to aid Captain M. detect the invisible cause of so much disturbance.

"The important facts bearing upon our subject were the following: —

"1. The disturbance consisted in certain noises, such as knockings, pounding, scratching sounds, rustlings in different parts of a particular room, — sometimes, however, in other parts of the house.

"2. Certain boards of the floor would seem to be at times most infected with the noises. Then certain points in the walls (at which Mr. M. would discharge his gun, or cut into with an axe, all to no purpose, however).

"3. The bed whereon a young girl, aged thirteen years, had been confined by disease, would very often be raised above the floor, as if a sudden force was applied beneath it; which would greatly alarm her and the whole family, and cause the greatest perplexity.

* See Night-side of Nature, page 400.

"4. This force was soon discovered to be in some strange way connected with this invalid.

"5. The concussions which it often produced on the walls would cause them visibly to tremble.

"6. Wherever the young invalid was moved, this force accompanied her."

How perfectly similar the above occurrences are to those which happened in the family of Rev. Dr. Phelps, of Stamford, Ct., occurrences which consisted of rapping sounds, moving of tables, etc., and which commenced March 10, 1850. Of these singular events the Dr. makes, among many others, the following statements.

"The phenomena consisted in the moving of articles of furniture in a manner that could not be accounted for. Knives, forks, spoons, nails, blocks of wood, etc., were thrown in different directions about the house. They were seen to move from places and in directions which made it certain that no visible power existed by which the motion could be produced. For days and weeks together, I watched these strange movements, with all the care, and caution, and close attention, which I could bestow. I witnessed them hundreds and hundreds of times, and I know that in hundreds of instances they took place when there was no visible power by which the motion could have been produced. Scores of persons, of the first standing in the community, whose education, general intelligence, candor, veracity, and sound judgment, none will question, were requested to witness the phenomena, and, if possible, help us to a solution of the mystery. But as yet no solution has been obtained. The idea that the whole was a 'trick of the children,'—an idea which some of the papers have endeavored, with great zeal, to promulgate,—is to every one who is acquainted with the facts as stupid as it is false and injurious. The statement, too, which some of the papers have reiterated so often, that 'the mystery was found out,' is, I regret to say, untrue. With the most thorough investigation which I have been able to bestow upon it, aided by gentlemen of the best talents, intelligence, and sound judgment, in this and in many neighboring towns, the cause of these strange phenomena remains yet undiscovered."

A writer in the *New Haven Journal and Courier* relates the following facts, of which he was an eye-witness.

"While we were there," says he, "the contents of the pantry were emptied into the kitchen, and bags of salt, tin ware, and heavier culinary articles, were thrown in a promiscuous heap upon the floor, with a loud and startling noise. Loaves of delicious cake were scattered about the house. The large knocker of the outside door would thunder its fearful tones through the loud-resounding hall, unmindful of the vain but rigid scrutiny to which it was subjected by incredulous and curious men. Chairs would deliberately move across the room, unimpelled by any visible agency. Heavy marble-top tables would poise themselves upon two legs, and then fall with their contents to the floor, no human being within six feet of them."

According to the statements of Dr. Phelps, the following are some of the circumstances attending these manifestations. "1. They were most violent when the whole family were together," "less frequent and feebler when but one of the two children (belonging to Mrs. Phelps, she being the doctor's second wife,) were in the house," and "more frequent in connection with a lad (one of the above children) of about eleven" years of age. "2. These children had been frequently mesmerized into the trance and clairvoyant state by their father," and one was subject to "spontaneous trance, and was found, at one time, in the barn, in a cataleptic state." 3. "When these children, with their mother, removed to Pennsylvania, the phenomena did not follow them." No facts can more clearly indicate the presence and action of an invisible, but purely physical cause, a cause connected with the organism of particular individuals, than these.

The following letter, which has been kindly furnished us by Rev. E. N. Kirk, will be read with interest, and the facts stated will not be doubted by our readers.

Rev. A. Mahan:—

Dear Brother, — By your request, I commit to paper the following narrative:—

In the course of my residence in Albany, as pastor of the Fourth Presbyterian Church, somewhere about the year 1834, (I have no means at present of recalling the precise year,) I was witness to phenomena, at that time totally beyond the sphere of all former experience; and, by me, utterly inexplicable.

I had been preaching three times on a Sunday, and was lying on the sofa in my house, at about 10 o'clock, when a gentleman entered the parlor in a highly excited state of mind. He spoke very hurriedly, saying, "a young woman is possessed of the devil, and wishes you to come and pray with her." Without waiting for further explanations, I hastened to follow him. On entering the house I saw a girl of about twenty years of age, lying quietly on a large bed, surrounded by a few persons. They described her as seeing frightful spirits, who threatened to carry her off. And their approaches to her were always indicated to the spectators by a convulsive action of her whole frame; an earnest entreaty to be saved from them; and a peculiarly sudden, sharp knocking. I at once suspected some collusion, and made as thorough an examination of the premises as I could; but nothing appeared which could furnish any explanation of the sounds they described. I then treated her as I would any other person in sickness calling for the counsel and prayers of a clergyman. At about midnight I concluded that my presence was no longer needed, and that my curiosity was not to be gratified by witnessing any thing marvellous. I accordingly went to the bed and leaned upon the high footboard, (the bedstead being of the French pattern;) as I looked earnestly into her face, she suddenly started from her reclining posture, screaming and staring wildly; and, at the same instant, three distinct, sharp raps, as if made with the knuckles of the fist, upon the very board on which I was leaning, startled me. I examined if her feet were touching the board; or if any visible connection existed between the board and the floor, except that of the bedposts. Nothing of the kind was visible. I then requested her friends to lay the bed on the floor on the opposite side of the room, and furnish me a lamp, that I might go into the room beneath, and watch the floor, (for the room was directly over the cellar). After watching there for half an hour, the rappings were repeated, but with no visible cause. I then left the house. On the next day, as I was informed, President Nott of Union College went to see the girl; but no knockings occurred after I saw her.

When this case occurred, I remember a gentleman stating that something similar had been witnessed in Poughkeepsie, many years ago, of which I now speak, only to put you on the track of inquiry, if you wish to accumulate evidence of these phenomena having occurred long before the present day.

Wishing you divine guidance, and great success in rescuing our fellow men from hurtful delusions,

I remain, cordially yours,

EDW. N. KIRK.

BOSTON, June 26, 1855.

In the above cases which might be multiplied to any extent, we have all the physical phenomena connected with "the spirit manifestations," with the exception of those which present the characteristics of intelligence. We will now adduce a case belonging to this latter class. We give this case, also, as cited by Mr. Rogers in the valuable work above referred to. The facts are so well authenticated, that nothing but their strangeness can induce any one to discredit them. We must learn, however, the important lesson, that we cannot tell what powers exist in nature but through their manifestations, and that we cannot determine *a priori* what those manifestations shall be. The facts which we are about to present were recorded at the time of their occurrence, were then attested by multitudes of the most intelligent and credible witnesses, and an uninterrupted tradition, from that time to the present, has preserved among the people of the place and the surrounding country, an undoubted conviction of their occurrence. Such is the evidence. Without further remarks, we give the facts as condensed by the author referred to.

"The singular case of the Drummer of Tedworth, in England, will throw still further light upon this mysterious subject. It seems that Mr. John Mompesson,* of Tedworth, in the county of Wilts, about the middle of

* See *Sadducismus Triumphus*, by J. Glanvil. London, 1726, p. 270.

March, in the year 1661, being in a neighboring town, and hearing a drum beat, inquired of the bailiff of the town, at whose house he was stopping, what it meant. The bailiff answered that they had for some days been troubled with an idle drummer, who demanded money of the constable by virtue of a pretended pass, which he thought was counterfeit. Upon this, Mr. Mompesson sent for the fellow, and asked him by what authority he went up and down the country in that manner with his drum. The drummer answered that he had good authority, and produced his pass, with a warrant under the hands of Sir William Cawley, and Colonel Ayliff, of Greatenham. The pass and warrant were both found, on examination, to be counterfeit. He was therefore conveyed by a constable to a justice of the peace, for trial. Whereupon he confessed, and begged earnestly to have his drum, which was promised him in case he was, as he had asserted himself to be, Colonel A.'s drummer. The drum was therefore left with the bailiff, and the drummer was released.

"In April the bailiff sent the drum to Mr. Mompesson's house, just as the latter was about leaving on a journey to London. Soon after leaving home, Mr. M.'s family began to be very much disturbed by sundry strange sounds about the house, as of persons trying to break in. This continued at intervals, until Mr. M. returned. 'And he had not been home above three nights, when the same noise was heard. It consisted of poundings on his door, and on the sides of the house. Pistols in hand, he went about the house. Instantly, on going to one door, the sounds would be made at another. On going outside, nothing could be seen, but still the sounds would be heard. On returning to bed, it commenced on the top of the house, and resembled a species of *quick-pace drumming*. After this, the sounds became very frequent, usually five nights together, and then they would intermit three.

"'The noise constantly came *as they were going to sleep, whether early or late.* And, after a month's disturbance on the outside, *it came into the room where the drum lay*, four or five nights in seven, within half an hour after they were in bed, continuing almost two hours, beating on the drum and on the doors,' etc. The sign of it, just before it came, was, they heard a hurling, as if in the air, over the house; and, at its going off, there was *the beating of a drum, like that at the breaking up of a guard.* It continued in this room for the space of two months, which time Mr. Mompesson himself lay there to observe it. In the fore part of the night it used to be very troublesome, but after two hours all would be quiet.

"At one time there was a cessation for three weeks. After this, it returned in a ruder manner than before, and followed and vexed the young children, beating their bedsteads with that violence that all present expected when they would fall in pieces. In laying hands on them [the bedsteads] no *blows* would be felt, but they would be felt to shake exceedingly. For hours together there would be drummed out the *tat-too, cuckolds, round-heads, and several other* points of war, as well as any drummer could execute. Then there would be scratching sounds under the children's beds. The children would be lifted up in their beds. If they were taken into other rooms, the sounds would follow them there, and, for a while, haunted none particularly but them. A board in their room was moved backwards and forwards and up and down towards a servant, who requested it to move thus, which was observed by a whole room full of people, and during the daytime. At night the minister and many neighbors came to the house; and then, in sight of the company, the chairs walked about the room of themselves. The children's shoes also flew about, and every loose thing moved about the chamber. A 'bed-staff,' for instance, moved towards the minister, as if attracted, and there rested quiet, without moving further.

"Mr. M., perceiving that it so much persecuted the children, lodged them out at a neighbor's house, taking his eldest daughter, ten years old, into his own chamber, where the sounds had not been for a month before. As soon as she was in bed, the disturbances commenced here again, continuing three weeks, — *drumming* and other sounds.

"It was observed that it would *exactly answer, in drumming, any thing that was beaten* by persons present, or any tune *called* for.

"Mr. M.'s servant was next seized with the infection. He was a stout fellow, and of a sober conversation. He had remained free until now, when all at once his bedclothes would unaccountably creep off the bed, and it required considerable skill to keep them on. His limbs would become paralyzed, or seized with rigid spasms; *but if he could get hold of his sword, this spasm would leave him.*

"A little after this, the son of a gentleman for whom the drummer had worked came and told Mr. Mompesson what the drummer had said to him in the prison, which was the following: The drummer asked of several who came to see him, from Mr. M.'s neighborhood, 'What news in Wilts?' To which they replied they knew none. 'No?' says the drummer; 'did you not hear of a gentleman's house that was troubled with the beating of drums?' They told him again, if that were news, they heard enough of that. 'Ay,' says the drummer, 'it was because he took my drum from me; if he had not taken away my drum, that trouble had never befallen him; and he shall never have his quiet again, till I have my drum, or satisfaction from him.'* These words were not well taken by Mr. M., and as soon as they were in bed, the drum was beat upon very violently and loudly, giving the drummer's tunes.

"Strange singing was also heard. And one night, about this time, lights were seen in the house. One of them came into Mr. Mompesson's chamber, which seemed *blue* and *glimmering* (see Reichenbach), and caused great stiffness in the eyes of those that saw it. The light was seen also four or five times in the children's chamber. The doors also were opened and shut without the contact of any mortal present.

"During the time of the knocking, when many were present, a gentleman of the company said, 'Satan, if the drummer set thee to work, give three knocks and no more;' *which it did very distinctly, and stopped.* Then the gentleman knocked, to see if it would answer him, as it was wont; but it did not. For further trial, he bid it for confirmation, *if it were the drummer*, to give five knocks and no more that night; *which it did*, and left *the house quiet all the night after.* This was done in the presence of Sir Thomas Chamberlain, of Oxfordshire, and divers others. At another time, it played four or five several tunes on one of the doors, and then seemingly went off in the air. At another time, when a blacksmith was stopping over night, they heard the *imitations of a smith shoeing a horse.*

* See Mr. Mompesson's Letter to Mr. Collins. Preface to Second Part of *Sadducismus Triumphatus*, page 221.

"Mr. Glenvil, who gives this case, visited the house, and by his own careful observations confirms what others had observed. He noticed one remarkable phenomenon, which many others had also witnessed,—that of a panting sound in the room where the children lay. 'The motion caused by it was so strong,' says he, 'that it shook the room and windows very sensibly.'

"A little child, newly taken from the nurse, was now seized with spasms and fright; and the other children were also affected so that they had to be removed again. There was a purring sound in their bed, like a cat. The clothes were raised up, and 'six men could not keep them down.' The children were affected with spasms in their legs, which were irresistibly beaten upon the bed-posts. Thus we have not only the epidemic character of this disorder, which is also represented in our present mania, but the same characteristic symptoms are exhibited in both.

"The drummer, on account of saying what we have already mentioned, was tried as a witch, and condemned to transportation. By some means he escaped and returned. And it is observable, says our author, *that during all the time of his restraint and absence the house was quiet, but as soon as ever he came back at liberty the disturbances returned.** So we have known it in our rappings."

In the above and the cases previously cited, all the physical facts attending the spirit manifestations are perfectly paralleled. In addition to these, we notice also the accordance of those strange phenomena with the *mental states* of spectators who come into *rapport*

* Ibid. p. 280. Baxter confirms the above story, having seen a number of the witnesses who were living in his days. See his Certainty of the World of Spirits, p. 19.

with the mysterious power by which those phenomena were produced. The "drum would exactly answer, in drumming, any thing that was beaten by persons present, or any tune called for." So of the rapping sounds about the house. At one time three knocks, and at another five, were called for, and precisely these numbers were given and no more. A request was made, that after a certain number of these sounds were given, they should cease for the night, and that request was complied with. The singular accordance of these strange facts with the phenomena of the spirit manifestations on their first appearance in the family of Mr. Fox in Arcadia near Rochester, N. Y., will hereafter be noticed. This accordance will be seen to throw much light upon the question of the origin and cause of these manifestations, especially as far as the characteristics of intelligence are concerned.

We now adduce the case of Mrs. Frederica Hauffe of Provost, a small village located in the mountainous districts of Germany. The facts of the case are given by Dr. Kerner, her attendant physician, and given as recorded at the time of their occurrence. The facts, moreover, were witnessed by multitudes of scientific men, and others, of Germany, many of whom are now living. In these regions, as we are informed by her biographer, "a sort of St. Vitus's dance becomes epidemic, so that all the children of the place are seized with it at the same time," who, "like persons in a magnetic state, are aware of the precise moment that a fit will seize them." "If they are in the fields when the paroxysm is approaching, they hasten home, and immediately fall into convulsions, when they soon rise upon their feet, and move for an hour or more with the most surprising regularity, keeping measure like an accomplished dancer.

They then "awake as out of a magnetic sleep, without any recollection of what has happened."

It was in such a locality that the individual above named became subject to a peculiar magnetic disease which finally terminated, in the year 1822, in a magnetic sleep which continued about seven years with occasional interruptions. The following may be enumerated as among the important facts of this case. We adduce only such as have a bearing upon our present inquiries.

1. The early developments of the disorder were characterized by "knockings on the walls, noises in the air, and other sounds which were heard by many different people," in her father's house. Many efforts were made to discover the cause of these noises, but all in vain. "However suddenly a person flew to the place to try to detect whence the noise proceeded, they could see nothing." "If they went outside, the knocking was immediately heard inside, and *vice versa*." Her father became so alarmed that he declared he could stay in the house no longer, the noises being "not only audible to everybody in it, but to passengers in the street, who stopped to listen to them as they passed." Whenever any one would sing or play on the piano, these sounds would commence on the walls. Articles of furniture, crockery, etc., were also moved about, when no cause for such movements were visible.

2. The *progress* of the disease was marked by great physical suffering and convulsions, so that when placed under the care of Dr. Kerner, "on the 25th of November, 1826," she appeared, "a picture of death — wasted to a skeleton, and unable to rise or lie down without assistance."

3. While under Dr. Kerner's care, it was found, that these rapping sounds not only continued in the room

and house where she was, but that she could regulate them at will, and even produce any number she chose in the neighboring houses of individuals who had previously been with her, and had thus come into *rapport* with the mysterious force with which her system was charged. The following is the statement of Dr. Kerner on this subject.

"As I had been told by her parents, a year before her father's death, that at the period of her early *magnetic state* she was able to make herself heard by her friends, as they lay in bed at night, in the same village, but in other houses, by a knocking — as is said of the dead — I asked her, in her sleep, whether she was able to do so now, and at what distance. She answered that she would sometimes do it. Some time after this, as we were going to bed — my children and servants being already asleep — we heard a knocking, as if in the air over our heads. There were six knocks, at intervals of half a minute. It was a hollow yet clear sound, soft but distinct. We were certain there was no one near us, nor over us, from whom it could proceed; and our house stands by itself. On the following evening, when she was asleep — when we had mentioned the knocking to nobody whatever — *she asked me whether she should soon knock to us again;* which, as she said it was *hurtful* to her, I declined."

Other individuals had precisely similar experiences in their own habitations. She not only was enabled to produce these sounds, under such circumstances, but to cause her voice to be heard by such individuals, even when at a distance from her.

4. At times her perceptive powers were so quickened that she could perceive distant objects, objects located entirely beyond the reach of the senses.

5. At other times her intellectual faculties were elevated, so that she would discourse on high themes in language of corresponding excellence. In some instances, for days in succession, all her thoughts were uttered in verse.

6. She could discern and repeat the *thoughts*, and tell the *physical states* of those who came into magnetic communication with her, precisely as mesmeric subjects can do in respect to those with whom they are in mesmeric communication. All the facts of mesmerism and clairvoyance, in their entireness, presented themselves in this case.

7. As in the case of Angelique Cottin, surrounding objects were attracted towards, or repelled from her. Sometimes objects, without any visible cause, would advance towards, or recede from her. At one time Dr. Kerner, on placing the ends of his fingers near those of hers, found that there was so powerful an attraction between them that, on raising his hand upward, her body was lifted entirely from the ground, and suspended in the air, just as the magnet suspends a piece of iron. This experiment was subsequently, at sundry times, repeated by himself and others, with the same results. We have here a perfect demonstration of the existence of a polar force, analogous, in all these respects, to magnetism.

The case which we next adduce is cited from the work of Mr. Rogers, from which we have taken so many extracts, and we give it as cited by him.

"Another singular case is that of Mademoiselle Elizabeth de Ranfaing,* of Lorraine, who, it was supposed, became possessed with the devil, about the year 1620.

* See Calmet on the "History and Philosophy of Spirits," etc., chap. xxvi. p. 123.

The facts were published, at Nancy, in the year 1622, by M. Pichard, a doctor of medicine, and physician-in-ordinary to their highnesses of Lorraine. This lady had been a very virtuous person, and had established a kind of order of Nuns *of the Refuge*, the principal object of which was to withdraw from profligacy the girls or women who had fallen into libertinism.

Mademoiselle Ranfaing, having become a widow in 1617, was sought in marriage by a physician named Poviot.

"As she would not listen to his addresses, he first of all *gave her philters to make her love him, which occasioned strange derangement in her health.* At last he gave her some *magical medicaments.* The physicians could not relieve her, and were quite at fault with her extraordinary maladies.

"After having tried all sorts of remedies, they were obliged to have recourse to exorcisms. This treatment commenced 2d September, 1619, in the town of Remiremont, whence she was transferred to Nancy; there she was visited and interrogated by several *clever* physicians, who, as a final decision, 'declared that the casualties they had remarked in her, *had no relation at all with the ordinary course of known maladies*, and could only be the rusult of *diabolical possession.*' [These were as wise doctors as some we have now.] The Bishop of Toul then ordered the nomination, for exorcists, of M. Viardin, a doctor of divinity, counsellor of State of the Duke of Lorraine, a Jesuit and Capuchin. A host of monks, and many of the highest dignitaries of both church and State, were present at the exorcisms, together with a large body of learned men.

"The physical phenomena presented in this case were spasms and involuntary motions. Calmet, however, has not seen fit to say much about this class of symptoms; but he implies the fact of her being subject to them, in what he has given with regard to the devil throwing the woman upon the ground, etc. M. Pichard, however, has given them, in his account. The phenomena from cerebral irritation are very wonderful.

"When she was exorcised in either Hebrew, Greek, or Latin, she always replied pertinently to them,—she who could hardly read Latin. M. Nichols de Harley, very well skilled in Hebrew, exorcised her in this language, and he found her capable of answering him correctly merely from the *movement* of his *lips*, without his pronouncing a word. This was proof, to him, that she was really possessed of a devil.

"The questions and commands were therefore addressed, not to the woman, but to the supposed devil. All the replies, made involuntarily by the woman, were therefore taken for granted to be the replies of the demon.

"The Rev. Father Abbert, Capuchin, having observed that the demon (that is, the woman) wished to overturn the *bénitier*, or basin of holy water, which was there, he ordered him (the woman) to take the holy water and not spill it, and he (she) obeyed. The Father commanded him (her) to give marks of possession; he (she) answered, 'The possession is sufficiently known.' The Father added, in *Greek*, 'I command thee to carry some holy water to the governor of the town.' The woman replied: 'It is not customary to exorcise in that tongue.' The Father answered, in *Latin*, 'It is not for thee to impose laws on us, but the church has power to command thee in whatever language she may think proper.' Then the woman took the basin of holy water, and carried it to the keeper of the Capuchins, to the Duke Eric of Lorraine, and to other lords.

"He discovered secret thoughts, and heard words that were said in the ear of *some* persons which he was not possibly near enough to overhear, and declared that he had heard the mental prayer a good priest had made before the holy sacrament.

"They proposed to him very difficult questions concerning the Trinity, the incarnation, the holy sacrament of the altar, the grace of God, freewill, the manner in which angels and demons knew the thoughts of men, etc., and he replied with much clearness and precision. She discovered things unknown to everybody; and revealed to certain persons, but secretly and in private, some sins of which they had been guilty.

"The demon (the woman) did not obey the voice only of the exorcists; he obeyed even when they simply moved their lips, or held their hand, or a handkerchief, or a book, upon the mouth. A Calvinist having one day mingled secretly in the crowd, the exorcist, who was warned of it, commanded the demon (the woman) to go and kiss his feet; he (she) went immediately, rushing through the crowd.

"An Englishman having come from curiosity to the exorcist, the woman told him several particulars relating to his country and religion. He was a Puritan; and the Englishman owned that every thing she had said was true. The same Englishman said to her, in his language, 'As a proof of thy possession, tell me the name of my master who formerly taught me embroidery.' She replied, 'William.' They commanded her to recite the *Ave Maria*. She said to a Huguenot gentleman who was present, 'Do you say it, if you know it; for they don't say it amongst your people.' M. Pichard relates several unknown and hidden things which the woman revealed, and that she performed several feats which it is not possible for any person, however agile and supple he may be, to achieve by natural strength or power."

On the above case the following remarks are deemed of special importance. 1. The cause of these singular phenomena is too manifest to admit of a doubt in regard to its nature, and that cause was exclusively mundane and physical. 2. The entire mental and physical activity of this individual was controlled by those who came into magnetic *rapport* with her, precisely as those who are mesmerized are by their mesmerizers. The individual supposed herself possessed of the devil, simply and exclusively, because her self-assumed and self-deceived exorcists supposed her thus possessed, just as the mesmeric subjects would suppose themselves subjects of similar possessions, did the mesmerizers entertain this opinion of them. Answers and communications were received *as* from the devil, just as they would come as from him from mesmeric subjects, if the same conditions were fulfilled. 3. We have, in this case, the same transference of thought, as in the mesmeric relations. Hence the singular revelations of secret thoughts, and secret acts, and answers to questions pertaining to subjects of which all were profoundly ignorant but the inquirers themselves, and all this in whatever language the individual was addressed.

Similar facts occurred in the family of Cotton Mather, in the case of some children whom he had taken under his care, in consequence of their being supposed to have been bewitched. These children would repeat the secret thoughts of those who came into communication with them. Even when passages from the Hebrew or Greek scriptures were read to them, they would give the correct interpretation, that is, the meaning which the *reader* attached to said passages. Where passages were read in the Indian language, however, a language of course not understood by the reader, the interpretation could not be given. Any thought in the inquirer's mind was instantly reproduced in that of the child, precisely in accordance with what occurs in the mesmeric relations. Cases of this kind were commonly accompanied with physical manifestations in accordance with those which we have above noticed. Our fathers were as familiar with the rapping sounds, the movement of articles of furniture, etc., as we are. They, in their ignorance, attributed these manifestations to satanic agency. We, in our wisdom, have attributed them to the interposition of departed spirits. However mysterious the facts above cited may appear, the following conclusions pertaining to them are too manifest to be denied, to wit: 1. The *cause* of these strange phenomena is exclusively mundane and physical. Nothing can be more unphilosophical than to attribute such phenomena to the interposition of disembodied spirits. 2. This power when developed in the human system, in connection with the brain, as its nerve centre, accords in its action, in certain respects, with the mental states of such individuals, and is determined in its action by such states. 3. When other individuals come into certain relations to such persons, the mental states of the former arc, in many instances, by means of this force, reproduced in the minds of the latter, and this precisely in accordance with what occurs in the mesmeric relations. 4. Individuals, under the influence of this same force, often present all the peculiar perceptions and other phenomena which characterize what is called independent clairvoyance. They have perceptions by other means than the organs of sense, and of objects located totally beyond the reach of the senses. 5. With the terrible mental and physical effects induced in such individuals by this force, it operates in their physical systems as a very strong polar force, attracting and repelling other bodies, in accordance with the peculiar phenomena of Electricity and Magnetism. 6. Other bodies in contact with such persons, or in their immediate vicinity, often become charged with the same force, so as to be strongly attracted towards, or repelled from each other. The force which produces these effects is denominated the Odylic Force. Its properties have been most carefully investigated by such philosophers as Richenbach, Metteucci, Thelorier, Lafontaine, and Ashburner, in Europe, and the validity of their experiments has been indorsed by the highest scientific authority of both continents.

THE ODYLIC FORCE IDENTICAL WITH THAT WHICH IS THE IMMEDIATE CAUSE OF THE SPIRIT MANIFESTATIONS.

We now enter upon a very important department of our investigations. Spiritualists themselves admit, as we have already said, that spirits do not cause these manifestations directly, but *mediately*, that is, through the instrumentality of a certain force of some kind pre-existing in nature, a force which they have learned to control. The agency of the spirits is manifest, if at all, not in the existence, or properties of this force, but in the *direction* of its action. The mere fact that sounds are heard, and objects moved in these circles, no one has the folly to adduce, as proof of an *ab extra* spirit interposition of any kind. Such interposition, on the other hand, is inferred from the accordance of these phenomena with intelligence, and other considerations of a kindred nature. This force, also, spiritualists, as well as others, admit to be exclusively *physical* in its nature. So far, no difference of opinion, as far as our knowledge extends, exists between them and their opponents. The question which here arises, and to which a specific answer is here demanded, is, what is the nature of this mundane, physical force, which is the immediate cause of these so called spirit manifestations? We answer, *it is identical with the Odylic Force* which we have above developed. This we argue from the following considerations: —

1. The relation of these causes to certain specific localities, is a very decisive proof, in connection with other facts, of their absolute identity. In Boston, for example, the centre of the phenomena of witchcraft, and where the odylic phenomena have ever manifested themselves, mediums were developed as soon as the circles were constituted. In Philadelphia, on the other hand, where the odylic phenomena had hardly, if ever appeared, months elapsed before any of the so called spirit manifestations appeared, though the most careful and persevering efforts were made to induce them. It is also known, and published by spiritualists themselves, that individuals who were good mediums in one locality, have utterly lost the power, by simple change of locality. The origin of "the Rochester Rappings" should not be overlooked in this connection. All agree that these phenomena first made their appearance in a certain house occupied by Mr. Michael Weekman, of the village of Hydesville, in the town of Arcadia, Wayne county, New York. Of the facts which occurred when he was a resident of the house, we have the following account.

"Mr. W. resided in this house for about eighteen

months, and left sometime in the year 1847.* Mr. Weekman makes the statement in substance as follows: That one evening, about the time of retiring, he heard a rapping on the outside door, and, what was rather unusual for him, instead of familiarly bidding them 'come in,' stepped to the door and opened it. He had no doubt of finding some one who wished to come in, but, to his surprise, found no one there. He went back and proceeded to undress, when, just before getting into bed, he heard another rap at the door, loud and distinct. He stepped to the door quickly and opened it, but, as before, found no one there. He stepped out and looked around, supposing that some one was imposing upon him. He could discover no one, and went back into the house. After a short time he heard the rapping again, and he stepped (it being often repeated) and held on to the latch, so that he might ascertain if any one had taken that means to annoy him. The rapping was repeated, the door opened instantly, but no one was to be seen! He states that he could feel the jar of the door very plainly when the rapping was heard. As he opened the door, he sprung out and went around the house, but no one was in sight. His family were fearful to have him go out, lest some one intended to harm him. It always remained a mystery to him, and finally, as the rapping did not at that time continue, passed from his mind, except when something of the same nature occurred to revive it."

The Weekman family, at length, left the house, and in December, 1847, the Fox family entered it. In the following March, the mysterious sounds were heard again.

* See History of the Mysterious Communications with Spirits, by Capron and Barron, p. 10.

"It seemed," they say, "to be in one of the bedrooms, and sounded to them as though some one was knocking on the floor, moving chairs, etc. Four or five members of the family were at home; and they all got up to ascertain the cause of the noise. Every part of the house was searched, yet nothing could be discovered. A perceptible jar was felt by putting the hand on the bedsteads and chairs; a jar was also experienced while standing on the floor. The noise was continued that night as long as any one was awake in the house. The following evening they were heard as before, and on the evening of the 31st of March the neighbors were called in for the first time."

The following is Mrs. Fox's statement of these strange occurrences: —

"On Friday night we concluded to go to bed early, and not let it disturb us; if it came, we thought we would not mind it, but try and get a good night's rest. My husband was here on all these occasions, heard the noise, and helped search. It was very early when we went to bed on this night, — hardly dark. We went to bed early, because we had been broken so much of our rest that I was almost sick.

"My husband had not gone to bed when we first heard the noise on this evening. I had just lain down. It commenced as usual. I knew it from all other noises I had ever heard in the house. The girls, who slept in the other bed in the room, heard the noise, and tried to make a similar noise by snapping their fingers. The youngest girl is about twelve years old; she is the one who made her hand go. As fast as she made the noise with her hands or fingers, the sound was followed up in the room. It did not sound any different at that time, only it made the same number of noises that the girl did. When she stopped, the sound itself stopped for a short time.

"The other girl, who is in her fifteenth year, then spoke in sport, and said, 'Now do just as I do. Count one, two, three, four,' etc., striking one hand in the other at the same time. The blows which she made were repeated as before. It appeared to answer her by repeating every blow that she made. She only did so once. She then began to be startled; and then I spoke, and said to the noise, 'Count ten,' and it made ten strokes or noises. Then I asked the ages of my different children successively, and it gave a number of raps corresponding to the ages of my children.

"I then asked if it was a human being that was making the noise; and, if it was, to manifest it by the same noise. There was no noise. I then asked if it was a spirit; and, if it was, to manifest it by two sounds. I heard two sounds as soon as the words were spoken." *

"These 'manifestations' caused great excitement in the village, and many persons called at the house of Mr. Fox to hear the noises. Many questions were asked and answered by *raps* correctly. Sounds were only made when an affirmative answer was the correct one to a question, or when numbers were to be designated. When the alphabet was called over, there was rapping at particular letters.† Soon the experiment was carried still further, and, by request, entire names and sentences of considerable length were spelled out. A signal for the alphabet was soon understood to be five raps in quick succession.

* See Account by D. M. Dewey, Rochester, N. Y. Also, History of the same by Capron and Barron, p. 14.

† See Account by E. E. Lewis, Canandaigua, N. Y.

"In a few months after the manifestations were first heard by the Fox family, several of the members removed from Hydesville to Rochester, and resided with a married sister, Mrs. Fish. The sounds were here heard in the presence of Margaretta Fox and Mrs. Fish. They were talked about, and elicited general attention, — got into the newspapers, and were immediately speculated upon in all parts of the Union. The third town in which the *raps* were heard was Auburn, N. Y. Catharine, the youngest daughter of Mr. Fox, visited this place, and the sounds were made at the houses she visited. In Rochester the *raps* have not been confined to the Fox family. Since the 'manifestations' in Auburn, they have been communicated with in Greece, Monroe county, N. Y., in Sennett, Cayuga county, N. Y., in New York city, on Long Island, at Troy, N. Y., at Boston and Springfield, Mass., and a number of other towns and cities."

Who can doubt, that the immediate cause of these phenomena was a physical one, a cause developed in the physical organisms of those individuals, in consequence of a residence in that particular locality? Equally manifest is the fact, that that cause is identical with the Odylic Force, as developed in the cases above cited. How perfectly do the facts above given correspond with those connected with Frederica Hauffe and others, and how manifest is the identity of causation in these cases.

2. The absolute identity of the physical phenomena of these two forces, as physical causes, presents, in their action upon surrounding objects, the most decisive proof of their identity. In both cases the rapping sounds have the same relations to the organism of individuals. The rapping and other sounds are precisely similar in

their nature, and are frequently attended with the same jarring of surrounding objects, and each alike is occasionally attended with the same rumbling noises, as of the rolling of distant thunder. The same manifestations of an attractive and repulsive power between the physical organism and surrounding objects, appear in both cases. What facts can reveal an identity of causation, if these do not? We might, with the same propriety, affirm that each clap of thunder is occasioned by a new and before undeveloped force in nature, and that such phenomenon is proof of the fact, as to refer the two classes of phenomena under consideration to different and opposite causes.

3. A similar identity of *effects upon the physical organism* on the one hand, and upon the *mental powers*, on the other, argues, with equal absoluteness, the perfect identity of these two causes. "Catalepsy, trance, clairvoyance, and various involuntary muscular, nervous, and mental activity in mediums," are among the effects enumerated by Mr. Ballou, as accompanying the action of this force in connection with the so called spirit manifestations. Precisely similar phenomena mark the action of the Odylic Force, in all cases like those which we have enumerated. Every mental and physical phenomenon which characterizes the manifestations of the one power, is equally characteristic of those of the other. Is "speaking, writing, preaching, lecturing, philosophyzing, prophesying, etc.," attendant on the action of this force, in one instance? They are equally so in the other. The same holds equally true in all other instances. We have no right to reason at all, from phenomena to the nature of the substances to which they pertain, or to attempt to identify causes, by arguing their nature from their peculiar effects, if we may not infer the identity of the causes under consideration, from the phenomena which they everywhere exhibit.

4. There is a peculiar effect which individuals often experience, on approaching mediums, on the one hand, and those who are under the influence of the Odylic Force, on the other, an effect which renders the identity of the two forces under consideration undeniable. Those who approached Angelique Cottin, for example, were often affected with what they denominated an electric shock. Spiritualists themselves, in their own writings, often speak of having experienced in themselves precisely similar effects, when approaching mediums, similar phenomena, also, occurring in the presence of those who are in a mesmeric state. It would be a violation of all the laws of science not to admit an identity of cause, in the presence of effects bearing such undeniable characteristics of absolute similarity.

On this point we need not enlarge, as the proposition under consideration, we may safely assume, will not be disputed by intelligent spiritualists anywhere, it being, as far as our knowledge extends, admitted by them, that spirits produce these manifestations, if at all, by controlling this very force.

THE IMMEDIATE CAUSE OF THESE MANIFESTATIONS IDENTICAL WITH THAT FROM WHICH RESULT ALL THE PHENOMENA OF MESMERISM AND CLAIRVOYANCE.

We now advance to another very important proposition. It is this: *The immediate cause of these manifestations is identical, not only with the Odylic Force, on the one hand, but with that from which the phenomena of mesmerism and clairvoyance result, on the other.* The truth of this proposition is rendered undeniably evident from the following facts and considerations, the most if not all of which are proclaimed by spiritualists themselves, in their own writings.

1. Mesmeric subjects, and those who had become clairvoyants through mesmeric influence, have, to a very great extent, become mediums, and of all other persons, most readily become such. This is a fact which no one will deny.

2. Mesmerizing and pathetizing are among the common means proclaimed by spiritualists, of developing mediums. When individuals desire to render some persons in their circles mediums, persons who have been accustomed to be pathetized are first put into a mesmeric state, and then, as the persons thus affected sit with others around the table, they become mediums, thus showing that the two states are the results of the same force developed in different degrees.

3. But a fact still more decisive of this question, is this: in these circles, as spiritualists themselves affirm, some individuals become mediums, while others, under precisely the same influence, not unfrequently become clairvoyant. Under the same cause, and in the same circumstances, the mesmeric phenomena on the one hand, and the so called spirit manifestations on the other, appear, thus indicating that the immediate cause of these two classes of phenomena are, in all instances, one and the same.

4. Individuals who have had experience of the mesmeric force, recognize themselves at once as subject to the action of the same cause, when sitting in the "spirit" circles, the effects which they experience in both cases being so perfectly identical, that they feel that they cannot be mistaken in regard to the nature of the causes themselves.

5. In approaching mesmeric subjects on the one hand,

and mediums on the other, the same electric shocks are, as before observed, not unfrequently experienced, indicating that the two classes of individuals are charged with the same force.

6. The perfect identity of the conditions of entering these two states, and of the disturbing causes common to both, present a very strong evidence of the perfect identity of the immediate causes of the two classes of phenomena. To enter the mesmeric state, on the one hand, and to become mediums, on the other, one and the same condition is requisite in both instances, namely, a state of *mental passivity.* It is a fact also equally well known, that no mesmerizer can pathetize his subject, when a strong mesmerizer is by, who internally resolves that that effect shall not be induced. It is a fact equally notorious and undeniable, that the same class of individuals, when sitting in the spirit circles, can, by internally and strongly willing it, and that when no one is aware of their mental states, render it impossible for the circles to obtain any responses whatever. Who can doubt, in the presence of such facts, the absolute identity of the immediate causes of these two classes of phenomena? A very strong mesmerizer, for example, was once sitting in a spirit circle, by the side of an invalid, who was there for the purpose of being operated upon by the spirits, for the restoration of her health. None of the usual effects produced upon her appeared, till this gentleman took hold of her hand, when the desired results appeared, and appeared with much greater power, the spiritualists present remarked, than they had ever witnessed before. The gentleman left the circle, and all the supposed spirit phenomena instantly disappeared. The cause of the effects which then appeared cannot be doubted. They differed, however, only

in degree from what had been witnessed on previous occasions, showing that the same cause had been operating in all instances alike.

SECTION III.

PRINCIPLES AND FACTS APPLIED TO THE ELUCIDATION OF THE SO CALLED SPIRIT PHENOMENA.

We shall assume it, then, as an established and admitted fact, that the *immediate cause* of the so called spirit manifestations is identical with that which produces the phenomena of mesmerism and clairvoyance, and that this cause is none other than the Odylic Force. We believe that we are authorized to make this assumption, by evidence the validity of which will not be denied. We are now prepared to apply our facts and deductions to the elucidation of the mysterious phenomena, denominated the Spirit Manifestations. There are, among others that might be named, three conditions in which the Odylic Force is developed in the human organism, so as to induce certain abnormal physical and mental phenomena, — a residence for certain periods, on the part of individuals of a peculiar physical temperament, in certain localities, — by manipulations and the various forms of pathetizing, — and finally by circles of individuals sitting together around tables or similar objects. In the phenomena resulting from the action of this force in the first two relations, we have no evidence whatever of their occurrence through the interposition of disembodied spirits. On the other hand, we have the highest evidence, that these phenomena are the exclusive result of purely mundane physical causes. It is true that clairvoyants sometimes imagine themselves to see and converse with spirits, and thereby to obtain revelations from them. We are not now discussing the question what clairvoyants see, but what is the *cause* of their perceptions? Undeniably the spirits do not cause the perceptions of which they are themselves the objects. Such a supposition would be presuming too far upon our credulity. We deny, that such individuals do see spirits at all, and shall speak on this topic in full, in its proper place. We are not now speaking, however, of what the clairvoyant *sees*, but of the *cause* of the peculiar phenomena connected with the action of the Odylic Force, in the circumstances named. There is not, and no well informed and candid mind will assert the contrary, the least evidence, we repeat, that any of these phenomena, physical or mental, are caused by the interposition of disembodied spirits. On the other hand, we have all the evidence that we can have, in any case whatever, that these phenomena are the exclusive result of purely mundane causes and of nothing else. What shall we conclude of the phenomena attending the action of this force, in the circumstances last named? Do we here find unmistakable evidence, that these manifestations are determined, in their essential characteristics, by the interpositions of disembodied spirits? If so, it must be, because the facts occurring in those circumstances, are, in all their fundamental characteristics, totally dissimilar and unanalogous to those connected with the action of the same force, in the other relations, and of such a nature, that they can be accounted for, but by a reference to one specific cause, the interposition of disembodied spirits.

Are Spiritualists prepared to meet the issue here raised? Are they prepared to show, that the facts which they adduce, are wholly dissimilar and unanalogous, in all their essential characteristics, to any facts which are the exclusive results of mundane causes, and of this one cause in the two classes of circumstances above named? We think not. As far as our knowledge extends, they have never looked at the subject in this, the only truly scientific, point of light. We affirm, without the fear of successful contradiction, that the entire circle of facts which they do adduce, or can in truth adduce, to sustain their theory, are, in all respects what we might suppose beforehand, from a careful induction of facts pertaining to the action of the Odylic Force, in circumstances where no *ab extra* spirit agency is supposable, they would be, if no such agency were concerned in their production. There is not a single valid fact which they do adduce which a philosopher, who had carefully investigated the properties of this force, might not have predicted, as resulting from it, in the spirit circles, were he informed, which is the fact, that, in those circles, this force should be strongly developed. If these very phenomena should not appear in these circles, supposing that no disembodied spirits at all do exist, their non-appearance would be an anomaly for which no account could be given. Develop this force where you will, in connection with the human organism, and these very phenomena must appear, and they must appear *as* coming from spirits, among all those who hold the spirit theory, just as the responses obtained through Mademoiselle Elizabeth de Ranfaing came *as* from the devil, while those whose thoughts were reproduced in her, *thought* her the subject of diabolical possessions. We may take all the so called spirit phenomena physical and mental, intelligent and unintelligent, and take them one by one, and we can present, in the first place, facts precisely similar resulting from the action of this force, when undeniably and totally unconnected with any *ab extra* spirit agency whatever, and then show that this one fact, instead of being anomalous, or unaccountable in its nature, is just what might have been anticipated in these very circumstances, from the known and immutable properties of the cause itself. We will now proceed to elucidate and verify the above statements, by a reference to the so called physical spirit manifestations on the one hand, and to the intellectual on the other.

PHYSICAL MANIFESTATIONS.

As an example of the physical manifestations, we will adduce the following case, which is so well attested as to remove from all candid minds all rational doubt in regard to its actual occurrence. Among the signers of this document which originally appeared in the *Springfield Republican*, we have the names of such men as Prof. Wells of the Cambridge Laboratory, and other individuals of such character for intelligence and integrity, as to demand the credence of the public. The document is entitled, " *The modern wonder — a manifesto.*"

" The undersigned, from a sense of justice to the parties referred to, very cordially bear testimony to the occurrence of the following facts, which we severally witnessed at the house of Rufus Elmer, in Springfield, on the evening of the fifth of April: —

"1. The table was moved in every possible direction, and with great force, when we could not perceive any cause of motion.

"2. It (the table) was forced against each one of us so powerfully as to remove us from our positions, together with the chairs we occupied, — in all, several feet.

"3. Mr. Wells and Mr. Edwards took hold of the table in such a manner as to exert their strength to the best advantage; but found the invisible power, exercised in the opposite direction, to be quite equal to their utmost efforts.

"4. In two instances, at least, while the hands of all the members of the circle were placed on the top of the table, and while no visible power was employed to raise the table, or otherwise move it from its position, *it was seen to rise clear of the floor, and to float in the atmosphere for several seconds*, as if sustained by a denser medium than the air.

"5. Mr. Wells seated himself on the table, which was rocked to and fro with great violence; and at length it poised itself on two legs, and remained in this position for some thirty seconds, *when no other person was in contact with the table.*

"6. Three persons, Messrs. Wells, Bliss, and Edwards, assumed positions on the table at the same time, and while thus seated the table was moved in various directions.

"7. Occasionally we were made conscious of the occurrence of a powerful shock, which produced a vibratory motion of the floor of the apartment. It seemed like the motion occasioned by distant thunder, or the firing of ordnance far away, — causing the tables, chairs, and other inanimate objects, and all of us, to tremble in such a manner that the effect was both seen and felt.

"8. In the whole exhibition, which was far more diversified than the foregoing specification would indicate, we were constrained to admit that there was an almost constant manifestation of some intelligence which seemed, at least, to be independent of the circle.

"9. In conclusion, we may observe that D. D. Hume, the medium, frequently urged us to hold his hands and feet. During these occurrences the room was well lighted, the lamp was frequently placed on and under the table, and every possible opportunity was afforded us for the closest inspection, and we submit this one emphatic declaration: *We know that we are not imposed upon nor deceived.*

DAVID A. WELLS, WM. BRYANT,
B. K. BLISS, WM. EDWARDS."

To present the whole subject at one view, we now adduce the following extract from "Rogers' Philosophy of the Mysterious Rappings." The authority by which the occurrence of the facts stated is verified, is of such a character as to place those facts out of the circle of rational doubt.

"The following, also, were developed at the house of Rev. Dr. Griswold, New York. Among the persons present were Mr. J. F. Cooper, George Bancroft, Rev. Dr. Haws, Dr. J. W. Francis, Dr. Marcy, Mr. N. P. Willis, William Bryant, Mr. Bigelow of the *Evening Post*, Mr. R. B. Kimball, Mr. H. Tuckerman, and General Lyman.

"The mediums present were the members of the Fox family.

"Only Mr. Cooper, Dr. Francis, and Mr. Tuckerman, seemed to come into close rapport with the psychological and nerve-centres of the mediums. The others, according to the account, could develop few or no intelligent characteristics, and could obtain a development of the physical force alone. Thus giving us a plain hint of the distinction we are to observe between the physical phenomena and the psychological characteristics which frequently accompany them.

"The physical force stands alone *as* a physical force. It bears no characteristics in its action but that of itself, unless some other is made to impress its characteristics upon it, as the intelligent will do in the movement of the arm. But the physical force may move the arm without intelligence, as in spasms, etc.

"The following peculiar physical phenomena were developed during the evening: —

"'One little peculiarity, hitherto unremarked,* came to our notice. The questioner's seat (to give him access to paper and pencil) was on one side of the table; and, chancing to occupy the place between him and the ladies (mediums), we [Mr. Willis] had accidentally thrown our arm over the back of his chair. Whenever the knockings occurred, we observed that his chair was shaken, though our own intermediate chair and the two standing immediately behind were unmoved. We called attention to it, and it was corroborated by the other gentlemen.

"'With such heavy weight in the chair as Mr. Cooper's or Dr. Francis', it would have taken a blow with a heavy hammer to have produced so much vibration.' The table was not moved, though requested.

"An experiment was tried as to what would be the effect with one of the ladies alone, or with two without the third, or with a gentleman and one or two of the ladies. 'The strongest knockings were on the floor beneath, when the widow and her two sisters stood anywhere together. With two of them the knockings were fainter. We placed ourself between the widow and one

* Taken from Willis' *Home Journal.*

of the young ladies,' says Mr. Willis, 'and *no* sounds were produced as a consequence. With *one* of the mediums alone, there were no phenomena.'

"These peculiar characteristics of the conditions are worthy of careful consideration. We have found several cases where no decided physical phenomena could be evolved without the presence of two persons, both in a palpable abnormal state, and we shall give one case, in a future chapter, where three clairvoyants were required.

"All such conditions clearly indicate the physical agency to belong to the physical organism. These characteristics will be considered in a more fitting place. We would simply direct attention to them here. The most important phenomena of this character, however, have not been sufficiently observed to develop their laws.

"But to return. An experiment was tried of another kind, in this circle at Dr. Griswold's. Three gentlemen placed themselves on the outside of the door, and three on the inside, and watched it closely, when suddenly it was knocked with great violence, without any visible instrument. 'We witnessed this,' says Mr. Willis, 'with one hand upon the panels; and what can it be but the exercise of a power beyond any thing of which we have hitherto known the laws? That it is subject to human control,' he continues, 'seems probable, for it acts at present in a certain obedience to human orders [not of the medium, however], and is most obedient to those who have used it longest.'

"Mr. Ripley, of the *Tribune*, in speaking of the same sitting says: 'The ladies were at such a distance from the door as to lend no countenance to the idea that the sounds were produced by any direct communication with them.'—'Other sounds were made which caused sensible vibrations of the sofa, and apparently coming from a thick hearth-rug before the fireplace, as well as from other quarters of the room.'"

Rev. H. Snow, in his work entitled "Spirit Intercourse," gives an apparently well-authenticated case, in which a medium was himself "raised entirely from the floor, and held in a suspended position by the same kind of invisible power." For ourselves, we have no disposition to question such a statement, knowing as we do, that cases perfectly similar and analogous are attested by evidence which we are compelled to regard as valid.

That musical instruments have given forth musical sounds, in these circles, when no persons were touching such instruments, we also freely admit, and admit for the reason, that the facts of the case are affirmed by authority which we cannot, with the consciousness of moral integrity, call in question. A very intelligent Christian lady, an utter disbeliever in spiritualism, for example, told us, that in her presence, a guitar was once placed in the middle of the room, that when no one was within several feet of it, musical sounds proceeded from it; that when she extended her hand toward it, it was instantly raised up and attracted to her hand, just as the appropriate objects are drawn towards the magnet, when it is placed near them, and that when she laid hold of the instrument, it was, by a force which she could not control, wrested from her hand, just as objects charged with electricity are wrested from our hands when we grasp them. Facts affirmed by such testimony, we regard ourselves as bound to admit.

Such are the valid, physical facts which lie at the basis of spiritualism, and sustain its claims to our high regard. On these facts, we remark:—

1. That we have the highest conceivable evidence, that the immediate cause of these phenomena, to say the least, is exclusively physical and mundane. This is undeniable, and will not, we are quite confident, be denied.

2. There is not among all these phenomena a single fact, or characteristic of such fact, which demands, as the condition of its explanation, the supposition of the interposition of disembodied spirits, or presents the least positive evidence of such interposition. The reason is obvious. The identical force from which all these phenomena result, undeniably produces precisely the same phenomena, when not controlled by spirits at all. Are physical objects "moved" in the spirit circles "in every possible direction, and sometimes thrown against individuals so powerfully as to move them from their positions?" The same phenomena attend the action of this same power, when undeniably uncontrolled by disembodied spirits. Are objects in the former relations raised from the floor, and suspended "in the atmosphere for several seconds, as if sustained by a denser medium than the air?" So they are in the latter. Are individuals, in these circles, "made conscious of the occurrence of a powerful shock, which produces a vibratory motion of the floor, and of the apartment," a vibratory motion like that "occasioned by distant thunder, and the firing of ordnance far away?" Precisely similar phenomena, as we have seen, attend the action of this same power in circumstances where it would be infinitely absurd to suppose, that the agency of disembodied spirits is at all concerned in their production. Do the facts which occur in these circles, the peculiar motions of bodies, the playing of tunes on musical instruments, when no person is touching them, etc., indicate the controlling influence of

"some intelligence which seems, at least, to be independent of the circles?" The same holds equally true of the action of this very force, in relations where no disembodied spirits can, with any show of reason, be supposed to control such action. So undeniably in all other instances. How astonishing that even educated minds should infer the interposition of spirits from the mere fact that mediums, as well as other objects, are sometimes, from no visible cause, lifted from the floor in these circles, when it is well known that by the same power, uncontrolled by spirits, individuals have been raised up in a similar manner, together with the beds on which they were reposing. Nothing conceivable can be more unphilosophical and absurd than the reference, as the only condition of their explanation, of the physical phenomena occurring in their circles to the interposition of disembodied spirits.

3. In view of a careful induction and classification of all the phenomena resulting from the action of this force, in the two relations first named, the non-occurrence of the entire mass of valid facts reported by spiritualists, as occurring in the spirit circles, would be a matter of far greater wonder, than their actual occurrence, supposing no disembodied spirit had ever entered one of them. It would be far more necessary to suppose the agency of spirits to account for the *absence*, than for the *presence* of these facts in these circles. Wherever this force is strongly excited in connection with the human organism, and that in the presence of the mental states of those who constitute and visit these circles, it would be a miracle, if these or similar physical manifestations did not occur in them. A careful examination of the phenomena attending the action of this force in other circumstances, necessitates this conclusion.

4. The wonderful things performed by mediums, are also performed by individuals who utterly repudiate the spirit theory, and are performed for the purpose of disproving that theory. Suppose that we put our hands upon a table, and call upon some spirit, or upon the spirits in general, to move the object, and it is moved accordingly. We call upon the spirits to give to the object a specific motion, and this, also, is performed. We again place our hands upon the same object, and without invoking the spirits, simply will that precisely the same effects shall follow, and they do follow, as before. We then place our hands upon the table a third time, and having willed the occurrence of the same results, we defy all the spirits who have been supposed to produce said results, to prevent their occurrence, and yet they occur, as before. These experiments are repeated any number of times, with exactly the same results. How infinitely foolish and absurd would it be in us to argue from such facts, that they are the result of the agency of disembodied spirits. Yet precisely such facts as these are occurring continuously in this country. What is performed in the spirit circles, is performed in other circles in which the whole doctrine of Spiritualism is utterly repudiated. Such circles exist in the city of Cleveland, and as we are credibly informed, elsewhere. We ourselves have witnessed the phenomena of table moving in such circles. Among these unbelievers, "movements (of tables and other objects) occur as a response to a calling of the alphabet, for the purpose of spelling out messages from some invisible presence," the very case cited by spiritualists as the highest proof of their theory, and such messages are spelled out, and from their character, the absence of spirit agency, in their production, is inferred. We

know whereof we affirm, when we make these statements. We met, for example, but a few days since, a clergyman of the Episcopal church, resident in this city, (not a pastor,) an individual whose intelligence or veracity will not be impeached, who informed us, that just such facts as those above stated had, for a long period, been occurring in his family, that he himself, in connection with members of his family, could now produce them, and had produced them for the interest and entertainment of others, and that from the most careful observation and experiment, and that contrary to his original expectation, he had come to the full conviction that spirits have nothing whatever to do with these manifestations, that what of intelligence appears in them, is the exclusive result of the unconscious control exercised over this mysterious force, by the minds in the circle, and not by spirits out of it. Such undeniably is the state of facts on this subject. Nothing can be more contrary to all the laws of correct reasoning than to argue from such facts the truth of spiritualism. It has not in them the shadow of a foundation.

A few weeks since, we met with a clergyman of the Methodist denomination, a clergyman stationed over one of the churches in Cleveland, who informed us, that having, a short time previous, occasion to spend an evening with a circle of friends, he found them, on his entrance, conversing upon the theory of spirit manifestations which we had just before presented to that community, and each was giving facts in illustration and confirmation of it. He then stated to the company, that if they all, with one voice, repudiated wholly the doctrine of Spiritualism, and adopted that under consideration, and wished, as a mere matter of science, to witness, with him, a practical illustration of the truth of the theory they had all adopted, he would sit with them around a table, and they would see what manifestations could be obtained, without the presence of the spirits, unless they should intrude themselves unasked, and exert their power for the destruction of Spiritualism itself. The circle was formed accordingly, and shortly the table, one of considerable weight, began to move. It was soon found, that the direction of its motions was under the complete control of one or two individuals, who were manifestly more affected by the power developed than the rest. If they willed it to turn round, it would do so with great rapidity. At their bidding, it would stop, turn round in the opposite direction, stand upon one or two legs, and tip out, by the alphabet, intelligent answers to any questions put to it, the answers corresponding to the thoughts of individuals present. It was asked to give the age of this clergyman. A certain number of motions up and down were made, and then they ceased. On inquiry, before the individual had answered the question, whether a right answer had been given, it was found, that the number designated was the precise number previously fixed upon, by one or more of the controlling minds present, though it was wrong by some eight or ten years. Such were the manifestations obtained for the very purpose of proving Spiritualism false. Who can believe that spirits would produce movements thus to disprove their own favorite system? We might adduce many other cases of a precisely similar character. We should be guilty of infinite folly, then, did we attribute such facts to the agency of disembodied spirits.

5. We remark, finally, that no additional light

whatever is thrown upon these mysterious occurrences, by referring them to the agency of spirits out of the body. The occurrence of these events is, in no sense, made more intelligible than it was before, by such reference. If the force by which these phenomena are produced has polarity, and consequently the power of attraction and repulsion, all the movements of tables, chairs, etc. — movements not indicating, by their direction, intelligent control — are accounted for, together with all the antics and strange motions which they exhibit. If this force has not this quality, spirits cannot impart said quality to it, and their assumed presence and agency throw no light whatever upon these facts. As far as these movements accord with intelligence, if spirits control the action of this force, so as to produce these intelligent movements, they must do it by their *thoughts*, *feelings*, or *acts of will*. It is just as reasonable, and far more so, to suppose that this power is thus controlled by the thoughts, feelings, and determinations of the minds in the organisms in which it is developed and energizing, as by the mental states of disembodied spirits who may happen to be present, and who sustain no relations known to us to any powers in nature around us. When, for example, one of the Fox girls said to the mysterious power which was rapping on the walls of the room where the family was assembled, "Now do just as I do. Count one, two, three, four, etc., striking one hand into the other at the same time," and that power "appeared to answer her by repeating every blow she made," it is far more reasonable to suppose that her thoughts and mental acts determined the action of that power, in that case, than to suppose that the thoughts and mental acts of some disembodied spirit did it. That this force was then developed in the organism of that individual, is undeniable, from the fact, that its presence was manifested, in connection with that organism, when she went abroad. It is a known property, as we have already seen, of this power, when in certain relations to mind, to be governed, in the direction of its activity, by the acts and states of that mind. How much more reasonable, then, to suppose, that the mental states of the individuals in whose organism this force is known to be developed, control and determine its action, when that action accords with intelligence, than to suppose that the same phenomena are produced by the mental states of spirits of whose locality we know nothing, and who, if present, sustain no relations, known to us, to this or any other power in nature around us. This power, if controlled by spirits, must possess the following characteristics: It must possess a very strong attractive and repulsive force, on the one hand,—and from its nature, such must be its relations to mind, on the other, that it is, when certain conditions are fulfilled, controlled in the direction of its activity, by mental states. Now, if this is the nature of this force, and for ourselves we believe that it is, then of all theories for accounting for mysterious facts, the so called spirit theory is the most unreasonable; it being infinitely more reasonable to suppose, that the mental states of the spirits *in* the organism in which this force is developed, control the direction of its activity, than that those of spirits out of those organisms do it.

All the *physical* manifestations adduced by spiritualists to establish their theory, are undeniably accounted for, by a reference to known mandane causes. All their facts are paralleled by perfectly similar and analogous facts resulting from such causes. From the very power in nature, also, by which all their facts are, as they will admit, immediately produced, effects do in fact result, effects in all respects similar to those adduced by them, and that when that power is manifestly uncontrolled, in its action, by spirits out of the body. So far, then, spiritualism fails utterly to be sustained by the least shadow of positive valid evidence.

Before leaving this department of our investigations, we will allude to what appears to us, as a very strange want of strictly logical and scientific deduction, in the reasonings of the most intelligent spiritualists, from their facts to their conclusions. To us, nothing is more manifest than the total want of logical consecutiveness, or connection in such cases. We will take as an illustration, a single fact adduced by Rev. H. Snow in the work to which we have already alluded: "The most remarkable instance of this kind," he says, "within the limits of my own experience, was the following. With myself sitting in a common chair, my feet being entirely off the floor, a large-sized light stand in front of me, with the medium's hands resting lightly on the top, — the invisible power exerted was sufficient to shove me along some five or six feet, on a *carpeted* floor. This took place at the house of a friend, in the presence of several witnesses, among whom was a teacher of long established and excellent repute, who had never seen any thing of the kind before, and who expressed his astonishment in words like these, "Do you call that simple electricity? you might as well say, that a mouse bores the Hoosac tunnel!" Suppose we do not call it "simple electricity," or give it any particular name. In the name of reason and logic both, may we not ask, what evidence is there here of the presence and agency of disembodied spirits? Had our friend familiarized himself with the authentic facts recorded of Angelique Cottin and others, he would have known, that there is in nature a purely mandane cause from which, when undeniably not controlled by spirits, precisely similar and far more startling facts do arise. Yet, by just such facts, spiritualists expect to convince the world of the truth of their theory, and are astonished that all the world are not already convinced. For ourselves, till far different and higher evidence is adduced, we shall remain among the stubborn unbelievers in that theory. Till other than purely mundane facts are adduced, we shall maintain our scientific and logical consistency, by denying the evidence of the presence and action of extra mundane causes.

INTELLIGENT COMMUNICATIONS.

We are now prepared for a consideration of those so called spirit manifestations on which, of course, the strongest reliance is placed, to establish the claims of spiritualism, to wit, intelligent communications, *as* from spirits, by means of rapping sounds, writing, speaking, etc. Before we can legitimately argue from such facts, the reality of which we freely grant, the truth of the spirit theory, or adduce them as presenting any form or degree of evidence even of its truth, it must be shown, as we have already said, and as none will deny, that such communications can, in fact, be obtained from no exclusively mundane causes, and from no other source but the specific one assigned, to wit, revelations from disembodied spirits. If precisely the same or similar communications can be obtained from minds in the body, and uncontrolled by spirits, then these same revelations can never, without a flagrant violation of all the principles of rational and scientific deduction, be adduced, as having any decisive bearing whatever in favor of this theory.

THE THREE CLASSES OF MEDIUMS.

Before proceeding to argue this question, a few remarks are deemed requisite, pertaining to the manner in which these manifestations are produced, through the action of the force under consideration, as developed in different classes of mediums. In three important particulars, there is a perfect agreement between us and spiritualists, as we suppose, on this subject, namely, that these manifestations are produced, directly and immediately, through the instrumentality of this, or some kindred force existing in nature around us; that this force is directed, in the production of the class of phenomena under consideration, by some *intelligent* cause; and finally, that this controlling cause is the minds constituting the circles, or disembodied spirits out of the circles. So far, and that for the most obvious and conclusive reasons, no difference of opinion obtains. But how, it may be asked, can the thoughts, feelings, and mental determinations of the minds constituting these circles, unconsciously, as must be the case in most instances, control this force, so as to produce these manifestations, and that through rapping sounds, writing, and speaking? The mystery, it should be borne in mind, and here lies the grand mistake of spiritualists, is not at all removed, by supposing, that the same force is controlled, in the production of the same phenomena, by the thoughts, feelings, and mental determinations of disembodied spirits out of these circles, this being the only way in which such spirits ever control the action of this power, if they do it at all. Suppose that a given thought exists in a mind in a circle, and in that of a disembodied spirit out of it. That thought becomes embodied in one of these so called spirit communications. We affirm that it is much more reasonable to suppose, that the thought lying in the mind in the organism in which this force is developed, guided its action, in the production of this phenomenon, than to suppose that the same idea existing in the mind of a disembodied spirit out of the circle, and sustaining no known relations to any mundane cause whatever, guided the action of the same force, in the production of the same phenomenon. This statement we hold to be self-evidently true.

Still a mystery hangs around the question pertaining to the *manner* in which mental states, whether pertaining to minds in the body or out of it, act upon this force, in the production of these phenomena. In regard to this subject we would observe, that there are three distinct classes of mediums, through whom such communications are obtained—the rapping, writing, and speaking mediums. In the last two classes the action of this force is attended with convulsions, and very great agitation of the physical system. In the first, such phenomena very seldom, we believe, appear. The reason is obvious. In the first class, this force, owing to peculiarities of physical condition in the subject, passes off, when excited to a certain degree, to some odylic conductor, causing, when striking the object to which it passes, the rapping sounds under consideration. In the former cases, it remains in the physical organism as a disturbing force, and thus causes the convulsions referred to. As the direction of the action of this force, in the organisms of such persons, and that from its nature and relations to mind, accords with, and is controlled by, the mental states of minds in odylic rapport with such mediums, the direction of their hands, or vocal organs, will be determined by such states, just as the mental states of the mesmerizer are reproduced in the minds of mesmeric subjects. So far the facts themselves, and their manner of occurrence, perfectly accord with those which occur in the mesmeric relations, and no *ab extra* spirit agency is even apparently demanded, to account for the embodiment of any thought preexisting in these circles, in communications thus given forth. So obvious is this accordance, that to us it has been a matter of surprise, that such phenomena have been referred to spirits out of these circles.

The case of rapping mediums is not so obvious, at first thought, to say the least. A moment's reflection, however, will show that this class of phenomena are equally explicable with the others. The physical systems of the individuals in these circles, may be compared to a galvanic battery which is continuously, but more especially on occasions of the least extra excitement, developing this force. As soon as it is developed to a certain degree, in the organism of the rapping medium, it passes off to some object near, a chair, table, the ceiling, or floor, as the case may be, and produces, in passing into the object, the raps which have astonished the world so much. The presence of a particular thought, in any mind, the putting of a question, any such occurrence is sufficient to occasion the excitement necessary to develop this force to the degree requisite to produce the raps, in the manner explained. An inquirer, for example, asks if a spirit is present that will communicate with him? The putting of the question excites him, and through him the medium, sufficiently to develop the force to that degree that occasions the number of raps understood as implying an affirmative answer. He now asks the name of the spirit, his own mind being fixed upon some individual. As the letters of the alphabet are called, the moment the first letter of the name of that person is pronounced, the mind of the inquirer is sufficiently excited to occasion, in the manner described, a rap. So also as each subsequent letter of that name is pronounced, till the whole is given. On principles precisely similar, answers to questions proposed may be obtained. Suppose, on the other hand, that the inquirer has no particular name in his mind. When the first letter of the name of a certain individual is pronounced, the law of unconscious association may produce the excitement requisite to occasion the rap, and thus the name may be given. These suggestions, together with the fact most abundantly established, that this power acts in many important particulars in accordance with mental states, and is determined in the direction of its activity by the same, will, we think, satisfy the reader, as far as any inquiries may arise in his mind, in regard to the *manner* in which these rapping sounds are produced.

We will now proceed to argue the question, whether we have evidence that disembodied spirits have any agency in the production of these intelligent communications. On this subject, we would invite very special attention to the following considerations: —

1. The identical communications which are obtained in these circles, can, without exception, be obtained in circumstances and relations in which there is the highest evidence of the total absence of all *ab extra* spirit interposition. We enter a spirit circle in which we are total strangers, and where our visit was wholly un-

expected. We put our questions pertaining to every subject on which spirits are ever questioned there, and receive every form of answer which is ever reported, as coming from spirits. We then go into the presence of an individual rendered clairvoyant by mesmeric influences, an individual to whom we sustain the precise relations above specified. We here put the identical questions we did before, and receive in return, the identical communications which we then and there obtained. We then repeat the same experiment, with precisely the same results, in the presence of other individuals similarly related to us,—individuals rendered more permanently clairvoyant, by the influence of drugs, or a residence in certain localities, as in the case of Frederica Hauffe, or Mademoiselle Ranfaing. In the two instances last named, our communications are undeniably obtained in the total absence of the agency of disembodied spirits. If any individuals, to save the doctrine of spiritualism, should assert the contrary, he would not only be guilty of denying what the world know to be true, and he himself has hitherto admitted as self-evident, but would betray a degree of ignorance and moral obtuseness which would render him unworthy of being reasoned with at all. We may as reasonably affirm, that all our mental perceptions of every kind, are from spirits, and are caused exclusively by their interposition, as to affirm, that the mental perceptions of clairvoyants are thus induced. Yet we obtain, through these individuals, all the responses, with all their peculiar characteristics, which are obtained, or can be obtained, through spirit mediums. Do we obtain *intelligent* communications through the latter? So we do through the former. Do we obtain, through the latter, correct responses to questions pertaining to subjects of which they are profoundly ignorant? So we do through the former. Do we obtain, through the latter, responses to purely mental questions? So we do through the former. De we, in some instances, through the latter, obtain correct responses to inquiries pertaining to subjects of which ourselves, and all present, are ignorant? So we do through the former. Do our communications, through the latter, come *as* from spirits? So, by simply willing it, the same communications may come to us, through the former, *as* from spirits, the same spirits, too, invoked through the latter. There is not a single communication, or characteristic of any communication, which is obtained, or can be obtained, through the mediums, which are not, and may not be obtained, through clairvoyants, when under the exclusive influence of purely mundane causes, the identical causes by which all these so called spirit communications are immediately originated. How can the claims of spiritualism to be sustained, by an appeal to such communications, communications perfectly identical with those which proceed from exclusively mundane causes? The system falls to pieces upon its own fundamental facts. It has adduced, and can adduce not a solitary fact, physical or mental, whose occurrence and total characteristics may not be, and are not accounted for, by a reference to exclusively mundane causes. None but purely mundane facts are adduced. How can we argue from these, the presence and interposition of *ab extra* mundane causes? Nothing can be more illogical than any such deductions.

2. As we said of the physical manifestations, so we now affirm of those under consideration, nothing but precisely these or similar communications could have been anticipated, from a careful induction and classi-

fication of all the facts pertaining to the action of this force in relations and circumstances, where no spirit agency is to be supposed, the very force through which these manifestations are immediately induced. We have, in these circles, the same power operating, and operating upon and through individuals, in precisely similar relations to each other, as in clairvoyance. The circles are to the mediums, what the magnetizers and others in magnetic communication with the magnetized, are to such individuals. If similar phenomena were not developed in the spirit circles to what now appear, supposing no disembodied spirits were ever present in them, such a fact would be an anomaly in the history of the action of this force, when developed in the human organism; a fact just as wonderful and unaccountable on any other supposition than some *ab extra* mundane agency to prevent their occurrence, as their occurrence now appears to those who are ignorant of the peculiar properties of this mysterious force in nature. Their non-occurrence in these circles would be a much higher proof of the presence and interposition of spirits, than is their actual occurrence.

3. The admissions of the most intelligent and influential spiritualists, indeed of the whole sect, as far as our knowledge extends, next claim our attention, and claim it too, as having a fundamental bearing upon our present investigations, the admissions, that *all* these communications are more or less determined, in their characteristics, by the mediums themselves, — and that many of them are *wholly* caused, not at all by disembodied spirits, but by the mediums or by individuals in the spirit circles. "The medium," says Mr. Ballou, and we have yet to hear of the first spiritualist who dissents from this view, "is a sort of amanuensis, a

translator or interpreter of the spirit's leading ideas. In this character media will exhibit, in various degrees, the defects of their own respective rhetoric." Again, he says, "It is amazing to see the unreasonableness and pertinacity of our opponents. They have taken the ground that *none* of these manifestations, *none* of these communications are from departed spirits. We have taken the position that *some* of them *are* from departed spirits, and others *not*." The italics are our author's. In another place still, we have the following very important statements: —

"I am now to treat of cases under Class Second; i. e. 'those in which some of the important demonstrations were probably caused or greatly affected, by *un*departed spirits.' I mean by *un*departed spirits, persons in the flesh who by their *will* or psychological power, control the agency which gives forth sounds, motions, etc. I refer not to *impostors*, playing off *counterfeits*. I am treating of phenomena caused by mental power alone, coacting with the mysterious agency under consideration.

"I have cases such as the following: —

"1. In which the bias, prejudice, predilection, or will of the medium evidently governed and characterized the *demonstrations*. In these cases the answers given to questions, the doctrines taught, and the peculiar leanings of communications spelled out, were so obviously fashioned by the medium's own mind, as to leave no doubt of the fact.

"In absolute confirmation of this, questions have been written out and presented to the medium, with a request that the answers should, if possible, be given *thus* and *so*. And they were given by *raps* accordingly. I myself gave questions in this way to a certain medium, and found that answers could be obtained in the affirmative or negative, or in flat contradiction to previous answers, if the medium would but agree to *will* it. At the same time, I made myself certain that this medium could not procure the *rapping* agency at will. It *came*, *stayed*, and *went* as it would; and in *that* respect was uncontrollable. But when it chanced to be *present*, it could be overruled, biased, and perverted more or less by the medium.

"2. In other cases there has been an overruling psychological influence exerted by some powerful mind or minds present in the room with the medium. In such cases this powerful influence, *with* or without the consciousness of the medium, has elicited answers just such as had been wished or willed by the managing mind. And these answers have alternately contradicted each other in the plainest manner, during the same half hour's demonstration.

"In one instance a strong-willed man resolved to reverse certain disagreeable predictions frequently repeated through two *tipping* media who often sat in conjunction. The result was, he could overrule *one* of them sitting *alone*, and get a response to suit himself. But both of them together overmatched his psychological powers. I might give names, places, and dates and details in this connection; but it is unnecessary. There can be no reasonable doubt of the facts just stated. It may be set down as *certain* that there are cases wherein some of the important demonstrations are caused or greatly affected by *un*departed spirits. How far influences of this sort extend and characterize spirit manifestations, remains to be ascertained. We can positively identify them in many cases.

"In some, they are known to the parties concerned and

acknowledged to have been consciously and intentionally exerted. In others they may be justly suspected, where no consciousness of them is felt by the medium, or by any dominant mind."

"I do not, of course, mean," says Rev. H. Snow, "that I believe in *all* the claims that have been advanced, of this character; on the contrary, I am of opinion that much which purports to come from unseen beings does in reality come, either partly or wholly, from minds in the body."

If the validity of the above admissions and statements were denied, undeniable facts affirming their validity are so multitudinous, and decisive in their bearing, as to induce the most unwavering conviction in all candid minds. So conscious do mediums become of the control which they can exercise over the action of this force, when developed, that they no doubt often direct its action for the purpose of deceiving the circles in which they are holding forth. We will give, in illustration, a fact which occurred some years since, when a medium was entertaining circles in Cleveland, at the house of the distinguished spiritualist, Joel Tiffany, Esq. We do not hold him responsible at all for the acts of the medium. The case was this. A gentleman, a member of the bar in that city, on his first introduction to the spirit circles, was strongly inclined, to say the least, to embrace, in full, the doctrine of Spiritualism, so inexplicable, on any other theory, did the undeniable facts presented appear. Subsequently, however, he became fully convinced, that while the rappings were a reality, and no imposition, the force which produced them was, sometimes consciously, but more generally unconsciously, controlled by spirits in and not out of the body. He, accordingly, having gained the confidence of the medium, one of the best that ever appeared among us, united with her in deceiving temporarily, for his own amusement, some of his friends, who visited these circles. On one occasion, he remarked to those present, that none of the tests which they had applied were, or ought to be, fully satisfactory; because that, in all instances, they had to depend upon the testimony of individuals, in regard to the question, whether their inquiries were or were not correctly answered. He would propose a test about which there could be no mistake, and of the character of which they could all alike judge for themselves. He would retire from the circle, and write down seven questions, and having returned, he would put them in succession mentally, no one, as they could all testify, seeing the paper but himself. The answers, as rapped out, they should take down, and when completed, he would read each question in order, and they should read the answer, and see for themselves how they corresponded, each to each. Seven questions were accordingly written out, and put as suggested, and seven answers were rapped out. When compared it was found, that each question had been specifically and correctly answered. We will give three of them as examples of the rest, namely, the first two, and the last." Question. How many days are there in a week? Ans. Seven. Ques. Who performs these wonders? (This was put in Latin.) Ans. The spirits. Ques. What do the spirits think of any in this circle who are not now convinced? Ans. If an angel from heaven should speak to them, they would not believe." All who understood not the facts as they were, were astounded and convinced, of course. The gentleman subsequently informed his wondering friends, that he had, prior to that meeting, put all those answers in writing into the hands of the medium, informing her, that corresponding questions would be put in the form stated, and that she must prepare herself accordingly. The answers, as he affirms, were given, word for word, as he wrote them. The *spelling*, however, was hers, she being a poor speller. Yet the rappings, he further adds, were no imposition, and remain to this day, to his mind, a deep mystery. The deception lay exclusively, in persuading the persons present, that spirits out of the circle, and not the minds in it, controlled the action of the force by which the answers were given forth.

In this case, no one can doubt, that the cause of the manifestations, was exclusively mundane. The fact, then, that many of these communications are wholly from the minds in the circles, and in no form from spirits out of them, is not only admitted by spiritualists, but is too manifest to be doubted or denied, for a single moment. Now these facts and admissions are far more sweeping in their necessary consequences, than spiritualists appear to have ever imagined. All evidence of the truth of their theory, derived from all their several classes of facts but the last, the fact, that events are sometimes correctly reported in these circles, events of which all present were previously ignorant, is utterly annihilated. If *one* thought existing in these circles may become embodied in these communications, without the agency of disembodied spirits, any other and all others may be. If one question, whether put verbally or mentally, pertaining to any subject of which the inquirer, or any one present is informed, may be correctly answered, without the interposition of spirits, any other such question may be thus answered, and all evidence of the truth of Spiritualism, derived from such communications, is utterly annihilated. Yet upon precisely such facts, the claims of this theory have hitherto been mainly based. We obtain, in these circles, it is argued, *intelligent* communications, thus evincing the fact, that they originate from an intelligent cause. Responses are obtained to questions pertaining to subjects about which the mediums and all present, but the inquirers, were profoundly ignorant. Purely mental questions, also, are thus answered. All this is freely granted. We must bear in mind, however, that answers to precisely such questions, every class of them, are obtained, in the total absence of any control or agency of disembodied spirits; a fact so undeniable, that even spiritualists universally admit it. How can the truth of that theory, then, be argued from such communications? The entire evidence of its truth derived from any one of these classes of facts, or from all of them together, is utterly annihilated. All its claims, all the hopes of its abettors to sustain it, hang exclusively upon one solitary class, the simple fact, that in some instances, correct responses are obtained to inquiries, where the true answer was not previously known to any persons in the circles, at the time when the meeting commenced. When we shall have accounted satisfactorily for this one class of facts, we shall utterly have annihilated *all* the evidence of every friend of the truth of spiritualism. To a careful consideration of this class, we will now advance. All that we have to do, to gain our point, is to prove that there are existing and operating in these circles, purely mundane causes from which, without the interposition of disembodied spirits, this new information may have been brought into the circles, and thus have been embodied in the responses referred to. On this point, we have occasion to call attention merely to the following decisive considerations.

1. There are known to be present, and in active exercise, in these circles, three forms of mental activity, which are abundantly sufficient to account for this entire class of facts, on the supposition that disembodied spirits have no connection with them whatever, namely, the Imagination, the principle of Conjecture or Guessing, and Clairvoyance. A question is proposed in one of these circles. The attention of every one is consequently fixed upon it, with the curiosity of all intensely excited. Each individual, of course, forms in his own mind, through the action of the imagination, some conception of what the answer should be, and among the many possible answers which should be given, he will almost of necessity conjecture or guess that some specific one is true. This act of the imagination on the one hand, or the conjecture on the other, becomes embodied in the response rapped, written, or spoken out through the medium. In some instances, of course, and the case could not be otherwise, when the guessing principle and the imagination are continuously, in myriads of circles, occasioning responses of this kind, the answer given forth will be right, and the perfect coincidence between it and the state of facts a matter of surprise. Now suppose, which is true and notoriously so among spiritualists the world over, that all wrong answers are set aside as of no account, while every response which happens to be true is set down as certain proof of this theory. We should, in that case, find in the works with which the community is being flooded from the spirit presses the same wonderful facts adduced in favor of the claims of spiritualism that we now have. Now we record it as our solemn conviction, and we speak advisedly in what we utter, that there is not one in a hundred of the well authenticated cases of this

kind that has ever occurred in these circles that cannot be accounted for on the principles under consideration, and that would not be just what it is, supposing spirits to have no connection whatever with these communications. Then to account for the very few facts which perhaps should not be referred to these principles, we need only refer to what is known and affirmed by spiritualists themselves to be true, the occasional occurrence of states of clairvoyance in these circles. Suppose that when a question is put, the medium, or some other individual, is in a state clairvoyance, and happens, at the instant, to come into rapport with the real facts inquired after. The perceptions thus obtained would, of course, be embodied in the response given forth, and thus, without the interposition of spirits, we should have the wonderful revelations which are now being spread before the world as coming from spirits, and as proof of their presence and interposition. All this might occur, and the clairvoyant not be distinctly conscious of what had happened, just as individuals, as spiritualists themselves admit, often produce responses when honestly supposing that spirits do it. Now, on the supposition that no disembodied spirit was ever present in any of these circles, we could not fail to have, from the action of the three causes under consideration, all the wonderful revelations, just as they occur, which spiritualists are holding before the public mind as proof of their theory. We have no occasion to refer to an *ab extra* spirit agency to account for any real revelation that has ever been given forth in any circle in the wide world, and consequently nothing can be more absurd than such reference. Facts which could not but occur, with all their peculiarities as they are, if no disembodied spirits were present, cannot, without a flagrant violation of all the laws of scientific and common sense procedure, be adduced as proof of their presence and agency. No other facts ever have been or can be adduced in favor of the claims of spiritualism.

2. These revelations bear all possible characteristics of an origination from the very causes to which we have referred them, and none which they would bear, did they come from spirits, and especially from *the* spirits to whom they are referred. Did they originate from these three causes exclusively, then the responses pertaining to subjects of which all in the circles were ignorant, would be, in instances very "few and far between," right, and strikingly so, and in all others, wrong. Now this undeniably is the precise character of all these professed spirit revelations pertaining to such subjects. If, on the other hand, they came from intelligent spirits, good or bad, who did not wish to stand revealed to the world as superlative liars and deceivers, we should find, what we do not now find, that these responses are generally, to say the least, correct, and only in instances "few and far between," wrong. Spirits of common prudence, such as is possessed by men in the flesh, and not utterly reckless of their character for truth and veracity, would be exceedingly careful about the answers which they should give forth to such inquiries. On no other principle could they distinguish their responses from those originating from the causes above named, and thus give evidence of their own agency in these revelations. Yet these so called, par excellence, spirit revelations have none of the characteristics which they certainly would have, did they come from spirits, and all and none others, that they would have, did they originate from the causes to which we have assigned them. The validity of these statements cannot be shaken, and spiritualists, we think, will

not attempt to do it. Yet here lies an immovable rock, namely, facts which cannot be denied, upon which this system must fall to pieces. Their facts, the only facts on which they can rely, are just such as would not come from spirits good or bad, and just such as could not but originate from the very mundane causes to which we have assigned them.

3. The very principle on which the entire claims of spiritualism rest, would, if its validity were admitted, affirm with equal absoluteness, the most false and absurd claims of the grossest impostors that ever existed. A devoted spiritualist, for example, made an inquiry in a spirit circle, in reference to a subject of which he was ignorant, and wished to be informed, and accompanied the inquiry with this statement: "If the answer obtained turns out to be wrong, it will not shake my confidence in spiritualism itself, in the least." A very influential and devoted spiritualist, in conversation with us, some months since, referred to certain startling predictions which "the spirits" had just uttered in regard to the affairs of Europe, predictions which were to be fulfilled by the middle of February last, predictions not one of which has been verified, but all proved false. The reference was accompanied with this remark: If these predictions turn out to be true, very well, if not, they go for nothing. This is the precise principle everywhere assumed by spiritualists, in arguing for the truth of their theory, and in doing so, they sell themselves to be deceived. Take a case in illustration. A friend of ours, a clergyman, when on the way to visit a family belonging to his congregation, some time since, forecast in his own mind whom of the family, and whom of the neighbors, he should find in the parlor, on his arrival, and where each should be seated, etc. On his arrival, he

found that these foreimaginings were, in almost every particular, correct. Suppose, now, that he had wished to impose himself upon his people as a divinely inspired prophet; that for this end, he should begin to give public utterance to numberless foreshadowings of a similar kind, one in a hundred or a thousand of which could not, of course, fail to be true; that he had also occasional revelations by means of clairvoyance, and that these should be mingled with the other professed revelations; and that his people should receive every prediction and utterance which happened to be fulfilled as a proof of his assumed claims, while, by universal consent, they should pass by all false ones as having no bearings, one way or the other, upon the subject. Who does not see, that such an individual, through such a principle, would soon stand revealed to the people as a divinely inspired and authorized prophet, with as high claims as Isaiah or Elijah, and with an authority as absolute as Jesus Christ, though he were one of the darkest impostors that ever existed? No other result could arise from such a principle of judging, and upon this very principle exclusively, the entire claims of spiritualism are based. Predictions and communications which happen to be true, are trumpeted through the world as demonstrating its claims, while the hundred or thousand false ones, to one that turns out to be true, are dropped, as having no bearing either way. Were they to present to the world a true record of the false responses continuously given forth, in their own circles, with the true ones standing here and there in their midst, solitary and alone, the world would turn in utter disgust from the spectacle, and spiritualists themselves would blush with shame, to intimate a spirit origin for such monstrosities.

4. The information *not* communicated, as contrasted

with what is, in these professed revelations, presents another undoubted indication of the non-spirit origin of these communications. According to the fundamental teachings of "the spirits," if such are the intelligences responding to our inquiries, in these communications, we are all continuously surrounded with guardian spirits, who deeply sympathize with us in our joys and sorrows, our pleasures and sufferings mental and physical, and who are able to communicate to us, as they choose, through these mediums, any information which they may possess, and which might alleviate our sorrows or increase our joys, by being communicated to us. Now, if these communications do proceed from this source, such, we may safely conclude would be their character, and we should find, by experience, that here is an *available* and *reliable* source of information, on such subjects. Now, this is the precise kind of information which cannot be obtained through "the spirits." As a source of information, it is not an available one, on the one hand, nor a reliable one, on the other. Hundreds of thousands of families and individuals in England and France, for example, had their husbands, sons, brothers, and endeared relations in the Crimea, and were under the most agonizing apprehensions, of course, in regard to their condition, and that while all individual communications were for long periods suspended. In the greatest agony of apprehension, wives, parents, brothers, sisters, and "nearer and dearer ones," have rushed to the spirit circles, and entreated "the spirits" to relieve that agony, by giving the information desired. What an opportunity was here presented, in which "the spirits," in the presence of the world, could, by manifesting their sympathy with human suffering, and revealing themselves as reliable informants on subjects of vital importance, have established the claims of spiritualism immovably in the high regard of mankind. What an opportunity, also, to reveal themselves to the heart of grateful nations, as being really and truly what their apostles affirm them to be, *the guardian spirits* of humanity. But no. To all appeals made to their compassion by agonizing sufferers, they stood revealed, exclusively, as "dumb dogs," from whom no responses could be obtained. This ominous silence indicates a total ignorance of what *guardian* spirits ought to have known, or a most barbarous, if not fiendish indifference and callousness to human suffering. All the world are aware of the living death which Lady Franklin has been enduring these many years, and how deeply the great heart of England and of Christendom has sympathized with her mental agony. Why have not her guardian spirits sped to those northern regions and brought back the intelligence which would relieve that mind from that heart-sickness which arises from "hope deferred?" Why has not the spirit of the lost one, if *alma lux*, the light of life, has departed, winged his way to the sufferer at home, and revealed his fate to her? Why, to say the least, did not some of his, or of his associates' guardian spirits fly to her with the information which she so much desired? It would seem, that they must have got fast frozen up in some of those ice mountains, or that they must carry hearts of ice in their bosoms. Where was the spirit, or guardian spirits of Emma Moore, or those of her agonized friends, that from none of them were tidings brought to those friends during the interval between the time of her disappearance and the discovery of her body, of her untimely end? When the fell seducer, as a stealthy boa constrictor, is following the footsteps of unsuspecting innocence, why do not these guardian spirits who can read even the secret thoughts and purposes of men, reveal to the intended victim the terrible perils which encircle her? Why have they not rendered themselves a "terror to evil-doers," by unmasking their dark designs, when they have had such myriads of avenues to the public mind? — avenues through which such information would be most gladly communicated? "The spirits" appear to have no hearts for such forms of well-doing as these. As informants of facts to us unknown, their revelations bear very different and opposite characteristics. Let us consider a few of them.

An individual who has a husband in California, who has learned, by experience, that it is not only not good for *man*, but for woman also "to be alone," and who, in her loneliness, has come so far within the attractive influence of one who is not her husband, as to make "a local habitation and a name" with him an object of strong desire, enters a spirit circle, and is there accosted, very unexpectedly, it is affirmed, by the spirit of her husband, from whom she had failed to obtain information at the time expected. With the tenderest expressions of affection, he informs her that he is no longer in the body, but an inhabitant of the "spirit land." There was one thing, and only one, requisite to the completion of his happiness there — her *immediate* union, in marriage, with the individual above referred to. The ceremony must be performed the very next evening — we think that was the time — at such an hour, and in such a room, which was to be darkened, where he would be present, and himself as a rapping revelator, preside over and conduct the exercises. Of course the mourning widow was not "disobedient to the heavenly vision," and the desired union was consummated accordingly. After the lapse of a few weeks, however, a letter arrived from the California husband, bearing date some days subsequent to the ceremony in the dark room. So strong was the sympathy of "the spirits" for human woe, in this instance, that they were willing to become reckless liars for its relief. New but false information was here conveyed. Such are some of the credibly reported doings and new revelations of the spirits in the State of Ohio.

In another instance, a husband went to California under the belief, as his friends affirm, of infidelity to him, on the part of his wife, who subsequently, in appearance, as they further affirm, drawn by a new attachment, was making efforts to obtain a divorce from "her liege lord." But while the law was "dragging its slow length along," behind the "hot haste" of human desire, the spirit of that husband addressed the wife, through a medium, in a spirit circle, and informed her, that she was now "loosed from the law of her husband," "and would not be an adulteress, though she should be married to another man." Subsequent intelligence confirmed, in this case, the revelation of the spirits, though there are yet among his friends doubters of the fact of the death of the individual referred to. This is one among the cases on which the claims of spiritualism are based.

The spirit of a certain lad is affirmed to have told, some time after his death, where a pen-knife which he had lost, while living, might be found, and it was found accordingly. In two public debates held at Cleveland, at an interval of several years from each other, that fact was adduced by the same speaker, one of the leading spiritualists in the country, and introduced in both instances as one of the main pillars of his "high argument."

The following wondrous facts, we take from the *Spiritual Telegraph*, the leading organ of the sect in the city of New York. We give the statements as quoted from that paper, in the *Evening Post*, with the introductory remarks of the editor of the latter paper.

"The believers in rappings and communications from the 'land of spirits' are increasing in this city. Private families, in circles of from six to a dozen persons, nightly indulge in the 'grave amusement.' A regular organization meets every Sunday at Dodworth's Hall, in Broadway, next to Grace Church, where any one is allowed to give his views on the subject.

"Conferences are also held during the day and evening each week at the head-quarters of the spiritualists in Broadway, near Prince street. At the assemblies many 'tough yarns' are told. The *Spiritual Telegraph*, the organ of the 'faith' in this city, gives us some samples of recent occurrence. It says: —

"'A gentleman from New Haven related the following: A Mr. Fairfield, a medium, was some weeks ago sent from Springfield, Mass., to the house of a Mr. Barnes, another medium, in Fairhaven, (a village near New Haven,) Conn. He knew not the purpose of his mission, and when he got to the house of Mr. Barnes, found he had not money enough left in his purse to pay his fare home. On the evening of the same day he and Mr. Barnes were both simultaneously entranced, when they put on their overcoats and went out. Our informant, who was present, followed them. They went up the road some distance and stopped, when Mr. Barnes began to scratch in the snow, which was about three inches deep, as if in search for something.

"'Presently he grasped something in his hand, and they both returned to the house, where, on opening his hand to the light, it was found to contain two quarter eagles, which, in obedience to the spiritual impulse, were divided equally between the two mediums. They went out again, our informant following them as before; and when they came directly in front of a certain church, they began to grope in the snow again, and digging out a board which had been covered up, they threw it aside. They then commenced a search where the board had lain; as the hand of one of them was passing to a particular spot, the narrator distinctly saw a small object lying there, which on being picked up proved to be a silver coin — a quarter of a dollar, if we remember.

"'They then went and scratched in the snow and dirt on the steps of the Odd Fellows' hall, and found another coin.'"

There is a medium in the State of Ohio, of whom it is affirmed, in illustration of the *new* things revealed by "the spirits," that at times, when under their inspiration, he will walk for miles with his eyes shut, passing, in the mean time, over fences and through forests, till he arrives at a particular place, when he will order, in the name of "the spirits," those who have accompanied him to dig down at a certain spot which he designates. They do so, and find at length, some dry bones, an Indian hatchet, and other pieces of old iron of equal value. A very intelligent spiritualist told us, that he had been present, and witnessed these very wonders.

Such are "the spirits," as informants of facts which we do not know. We do not affirm, that no higher facts are ever revealed in these communications. These, however, are fair examples of what we do obtain, spiritualists themselves giving the record. If these revelations are from disembodied spirits, judging from what they do and what they do not reveal, we affirm, without fear of contradiction, that they are, almost without exception, beings of the most debased morality, and demented intelligence, and that to regard such communications as coming from the inhabitants of the immortal spheres, tends to produce nothing in us, but corresponding debasement and dementation.

5. Before closing our remarks on the class of facts now under consideration, we should make the following undeniable statement in regard to them, a statement which has a very important and decisive bearing upon the question of their origin. The statement is this. Most of the cases of this kind reported to the public have, and are found, on careful inquiry, to have either no foundation in fact, or to be characterized by very great exaggerations, while the well authenticated cases are very few, much fewer than we should expect from the myriads of sources from which these manifestations proceed, even supposing them not to be given forth by disembodied spirits at all. In listening to the popular lecturers on spiritualism, we find, as they approach this class of facts, that they uniformly begin, by telling their hearers that they could spend the whole night in relating cases which they themselves have witnessed personally, and then out will come the old pen knife story, and other hackneyed facts of a similar character. How few are the cases related by Mr. Ballou, and other great defenders of this new faith, and how far do they have to travel to collect even these. To us, after having investigated the nature of the power by which these manifestations are produced, there is but one matter of surprise, namely, that this class of manifestations are not,

in the spirit circles, of more frequent occurrence than they are.

SECTION IV.

THIRD PROPOSITION ESTABLISHED, NAMELY, THAT WE HAVE POSITIVE AND CONCLUSIVE EVIDENCE THAT THESE MANIFESTATIONS ARE THE EXCLUSIVE RESULT OF MUNDANE CAUSES, AND NOT OF THE AGENCY OF DISEMBODIED SPIRITS.

We believe that we have now fully established our first two propositions, namely, that there are, in the world around us, purely mundane causes, from which phenomena, in all respects similar and analogous to those adduced by spiritualists, do arise, — and that these so called spirit manifestations occur in circumstances in which these very causes are known to be present and in efficient action, and that consequently we have no occasion to go beyond these causes to account for these manifestations, in their entireness. We have thus utterly annihilated all positive evidence that from developments hitherto made, any thing can be adduced in favor of spiritualism As far as any claims to an *ab extra* spirit origin are concerned, it stands before us, as an "airy nothing," without a "local habitation or a name." Our third proposition yet remains to be established, namely, that *from these exclusively mundane causes, and not from the agency of disembodied spirits, these manifestations do in fact proceed.* When we shall have established this proposition, we shall have proved spiritualism to be exclusively, as far as its claims to a spirit origin are concerned, a system of error and delusion. This we now propose to do. It may be important in this connection to remind the reader of the precise points of agreement and difference between ourselves and spiritualists, on this subject. On all hands it is agreed, 1. That the *immediate* cause of these manifestations is some force, by whatever name it may be called, a force existing in the world around us; 2. That this force is controlled, in the production of these phenomena, by some intelligent cause or causes; and 3. That this controlling cause is the minds in the circles, or disembodied spirits out of the same. A difference of opinion obtains only in regard to the *location* of this controlling cause. We maintain that this force, in the production of these communications, is controlled either consciously or unconsciously, for the most part, without doubt, unconsciously, by the minds constituting these circles. Spiritualists, on the other hand, maintain that it is controlled by disembodied spirits out of these circles. Here only do we differ, as far as the question at issue, in this department of our inquiries, is concerned. We will now proceed to adduce the evidence in favor of the former hypothesis and against the latter. The facts and arguments which we have to present, may be ranged together under the following classes: —

1. All the laws of scientific deduction require us, in view of the propositions already established, to regard as true the hypothesis which we maintain, and the opposite one as false. Whenever any portion of a given class of facts are shown and admitted to result from a given cause, it is always assumed as positive proof, that the facts remaining are produced by the same cause, unless the most absolute evidence to the contrary is adduced. Especially is this the case, when it has been shown that by a reference to this one cause, all the facts alike can be readily and adequately accounted for.

In our preceding discussions, it has been proved, (1.) That *some* of these manifestations are produced exclusively by the minds in the circles, and not by spirits out of them, and (2.) that this one cause, in the circumstances supposed, is all that is requisite to account for *all* these manifestations. It would, therefore, be a violation of all the laws of scientific deduction, to attribute any of these phenomena to any other cause. This conclusion is undeniable.

2. The great fact that we next adduce is, in our judgment, of the most absolutely decisive character conceivable, the undeniable fact, that no *new truths* or *principles* are found in these communications.* They come to us as affirmed revelations from the highest minds, among others, in the immortal spheres. Yet they are, in fact, no revelations at all. They are, on the other hand, a mere chaos of truth and error, with which the world was familiar before. We hazard nothing in affirming, that amid all these manifestations there is not a solitary new truth, or new fundamental principle pertaining to the universe of matter or spirit, although "the spirits" present themselves as most benevolent, self-sacrificing, and indispensably needed guides in reference to both. They come to free men from error, and to "guide them into all truth," and then they simply reaffirm all forms of mere *human* opinions in reference to this world and the next, and that without revealing to us a solitary new truth, or presenting us with a solitary new principle by which we can distinguish truth from error. They come to enlarge the sphere of human science and discovery, and then, as far as they assert

* We here distinguish, of course, between mere information pertaining to matters-of-fact, and important truths and principles. It is to the latter that we now refer.

any thing that is true, simply follow *iniquis pacibus*, in the track of human research and discovery. If there is any thing that we can know *a priori* of such minds as Francis Bacon, if they should, after dwelling for centuries amid the illuminations of eternity, descend to earth, as our guides and teachers, it is this, that they would not only impart to us new truths, but higher and more perfect forms of thinking than those with which all the world are perfectly familiar. Especially may we affirm, with absolute certainty, that such minds, instead of giving utterance to such truths and such thoughts, would not retail, as forms of the highest wisdom, the senseless gossip of every-day thinking among men. How self-evident is the truth of the saying of the forerunner of Christ: "he that is of the earth is earthly, and speaketh of the earth: he that cometh from heaven is above all." Now we have, in the spirit manifestations, the professed teachings of the very class of heaven descended minds referred to; and what have we in these revelations? All possible characteristics of an origin purely and exclusively earthly and nothing else. We should, therefore, be guilty of the highest folly should we attribute them to any higher origin. Since the mission of "the spirits" commenced, great advance has been made in scientific research and discovery, in respect to very important principles and facts pertaining to the earth and the heavens, and that in reference to realities about which "the spirits" have largely discoursed, and about which it is absurd to suppose those who are affirmed to have come from heaven to teach us, were ignorant. Yet they never have anticipated the advance of human research and discovery, but have very tamely followed it. The Poughkeepsie Seer, after being reminded of the fact, that many new planets had been discovered, since his "divine revelations" were given forth, revelations in which he affirmed himself about to reveal every "visible and invisible existence," was asked why it was that he had not anticipated the march of human discovery, by announcing beforehand the existence and location of these planets? The prophet was silent of course. We put the same question in reference to "the spirits." If they are from heaven, why have they not anticipated the march of scientific research and discovery, which they professedly come to perfect and hasten? The reason and the only reason is, that these revelations are mere human thoughts unconsciously reaffirmed by spirits in the body, and not what they are by some thought to be, revelations from spirits out of the body. The great and undeniable fact before us admits of no other explanation.

It remains with spiritualists to deny the statements above made, and to prove them false, by adducing the truths and principles whose reality is denied, or to account for the facts affirmed and in that case admitted, consistently with the claims of their theory. The former we are quite sure they will not attempt to do; the latter we know absolutely is an impossibility. Whatever inexplicable facts may be connected with these manifestations, the total absence of any new truths or principles, and the undeniable presence in them of mere preëxisting human opinions only, renders demonstrably evident their exclusively mundane origin. It is the height of folly to refer mere mundane facts to extramundane causes. A greater absurdity cannot be conceived of than to suppose that the great minds from the upper spheres have descended to earth, here to retail as new and eternal verities, old and hackneyed thoughts with which mankind have been familiar for ages.

3. Another fact equally decisive of the question of the origin of these manifestations, is this. The opinions and sentiments revealed in them, uniformly take *form from, and correspond with, those peculiar to the particular circles* in which they originate. In China, "the spirits" — for they have spirit circles there — are all followers of Confucius. In Siam, they are equally devoted Buddhists. In Hindostan, they are worshippers of Juggernaut. In Christendom, they are Catholic or Protestant, Christian or Infidel, Churchmen or Dissenters, Orthodox and Heterodox, of all opinions and no opinions, just according to the peculiar complexion of the circles in which they appear. This is true, not only of different classes of spirits, but equally of the same identical spirits. Take any spirit that can be named, and introduce him into each circle on earth in succession, and he will affirm, as only true, the peculiarities of opinion existing in each circle, and as positively deny every opposite opinion, though he has, for thousands of times, asserted its truth before. This he will do, with the most unblushing effrontery, boldly denying, in every circle, that he has ever, since he entered the spirit land, changed his opinions, or at any time, or in any place, contradicted his present teachings. There is not a solitary form or shade of human belief, the denial of the existence of spirits excepted — a form of belief held by Christian, Turk, or Infidel — which has not been absolutely affirmed and denied by the same authority. "The spirits," and the same individuals among them too, take all sides of every question, just as occasion requires, advocating, in succession, the peculiar doctrines of each circle that chances or chooses to call upon them. We have our orthodox circles, in which all the peculiarities of the evangelical

faith are solemnly affirmed, without contradiction, by every spirit that appears among them. There is one such circle, at the present time, in the city of Cleveland, and in this circle, we have all the physical and mental manifestations that can be obtained anywhere else. In the town of Madison, Geauga county, Ohio, during the progress of a revival of religion, the minister became a spiritualist. He found a medium of the same faith with himself. A perfectly orthodox circle was thus formed, into which the oldest and strongest Universalists and Infidels were introduced, and *as* from their own children, relatives, and friends, were assured, that their sentiments were all wrong, and that under their influence they were descending, with infallible certainty, to the gulf of eternal death. The spirit of a Deacon Branch, who, for many years, had lived in the place, and had died there in the esteem and confidence of all, appeared in the circle. Between him and these unbelievers, the most solemn communications, to the following import, passed: — Tell us, Deacon Branch, is what is affirmed in the Bible and by Christians, of heaven and hell, true? It is. Is hell as terrible a place as it is represented to be? Far more so. What must we do to escape it? You must "repent and believe on the Lord Jesus Christ." In that circle, "the spirits" affirmed absolutely, that all communications of an opposite character, which had ever been given forth in any spirit circles, were exclusively from "the father of lies" and his agents, and were given forth for the fell purpose of deceiving men to their eternal ruin. Yet in no circle in the wide world, has there ever been given more conclusive evidence of the presence and teachings of disembodied spirits. A friend of ours, for example, entered that circle in company with his wife. They had buried two children, in different towns, in another State, and were perfectly certain, that none present but themselves knew any thing of those children. Yet their names, one or both having double names, the places of their birth and burial, their ages, even to the specific number of years, months, weeks, and days, etc., were given forth with perfect correctness. At length "the spirits" found, in this place, another medium of different and opposite sentiments, and round her formed a circle of corresponding character. In this circle, they unitedly affirmed, the spirit of Deacon Branch among the rest, that no spirits at all had, at any time, made any communications whatever in the orthodox circle. Deacon Branch, however, immediately reappeared in the circle last named, and solemnly affirmed, in a communication to his own son, in whose house the sceptical circle was meeting at the time referred to, that he had had no connection at all with the communication which had thus been sent forth from the latter circle, as from him. Such is the state of facts the world over. In the infidel and kindred circles, the spirits of orthodox ministers appear, and with expressions of the deepest regret, abjure their earthly teachings and ministrations. In the few orthodox circles, and we could multiply them by thousands and tens of thousands, yes, we could fill the world with spirit voices if we chose, — Infidels and Universalists of every grade, as from the world of despair, affirm every article of the orthodox faith, and abjure their own earthly opinions, as being nothing else than "the doctrines of devils." Now what evidence can be conceived of more conclusive of the truth of any proposition, than is here presented of the exclusive mundane origin of these communications, in the two undeniable facts before us, namely, that in these communications none but mundane opinions appear, and that the former vary as the latter vary? No questions pertaining to this world or the next can be settled, by any evidence whatever, if this question is not settled by the evidence before us.

4. We now present, as confirmatory of the views which we hold on this subject, a class of *apparent* exceptions to the facts above adduced. It is true, that the answers obtained do not *always* correspond with the sentiments of those who make inquiry, nor with those of the majority of the persons present, on any given occasion, though this is generally the case. An individual, as stated in an extract given above from the work of Mr. Ballou, wished to have certain disagreeable communications which he had obtained, when two mediums were present, reversed. He could have his wish, when one of them was absent, but not when both were present. "He could," in the language of the author, "overrule *one* of them, sitting *alone*, and get a response to suit himself. But both of them *together* overmatched his psychological powers." As is the *prevailing* psychological power, for the moment, such will be the character of the responses obtained; and this power, at times, may be with the mass in the circle, in opposition to that exerted by individuals, as in the orthodox circle above referred to where sceptics were making inquiries; and in some occasional instances, owing to peculiar coincidences, it may be with individuals, in opposition to the sentiments of the majority. A medium, for example, on one occasion was, in a circle in Leroy, N. Y., — a circle which had met to obtain communications through her, and which was constituted almost, if not quite, exclusively of sceptics. As the so called spirit

influence came upon her, this solemn affirmation came out, as from the spirits, "Ye must be born again." All were astounded, and none more so than the medium. Yet during the entire evening, nothing could be obtained from "the spirits," whatever questions were asked, and many were, but this one sentence, "Ye must be born again." How shall this fact be accounted for? The answer is plain. The medium was of orthodox sentiments, and had just come from another meeting, in which this and kindred truths had been very deeply fixed in her thoughts. This would account for the expression of that truth, in the first instance. Then its sudden and unexpected appearance in the circle would fix all minds most intently upon it, so intently, that no other thought could find an expression during that sitting. Just such facts as these would occasionally occur in these circles, if our theory were true, and would not occur, if that of Spiritualism was true. Such exceptions therefore confirm instead of contradicting the conclusion deduced from the important facts included in the last two classes above presented.

5. There is still another characteristic of many of these revelations which renders demonstrably evident the fact, that they cannot come from the spirits to whom they are referred; and if they do not come from these, we are bound to suppose that they do not come from any spirits at all, and thus discredit the whole theory of spirit manifestations. We have professed revelations from minds such as Bacon, who have been progressing for centuries in light and knowledge, amid the revelations of eternity. We have also the recorded ideas of the same minds upon the same themes, while they were in the body. We have then here a fair opportunity to compare their present and past mental condition and

capacities. What is the conclusion to which any intelligent and candid mind must come, as the result of such careful comparison? It is this and no other — that if it is really and truly the author of the great Organon who is speaking in the work given forth as from him and other kindred spirits, by Judge Edmonds and his associates, that mind cannot but be in a state of absolute and hopeless idiocy, before it has been among "the spirits" for two centuries longer. We made this remark some time since to a very intelligent lawyer who had publicly defended, and that with great ability, the doctrine of the spirit manifestations, and who had read with much interest the work referred to. "I must admit," his reply was, "that you are right there;" and no intelligent man who is acquainted with the writings of Bacon, can come to any other conclusion. The posterity of that man, if any exist, ought to be able to obtain heavy damages in a suit for slander against these individuals, for attributing such thoughts to their great ancestor. We hazard little in affirming, that it is about as reasonable to suppose, that Michael the archangel is the author of the celebrated work entitled, "The house that Jack built," and that this is the highest production that he could originate, as to suppose that it is the spirit of the immortal Bacon that is communicating in the senseless production referred to. So, in other instances, we have seen essays from the spirit of the great Franklin, on electricity, essays given forth through the best of mediums, and which have all the evidence that he is their author, that any of these revelations do that they come from any spirits at all; essays commencing very much like the composition of a certain tyro on perseverance, namely, "Perseverance is the best thing that ever happened to man," and bearing throughout marks of corresponding perfection of thought and style. One thing is undeniable to an intelligent and unprejudiced mind, in regard to these manifestations, that "the spirits" are not speaking in them at all, or that their progression is altogether towards idiocy, and nowhere else. For ourselves, we do not believe that this is the direction of progress with them. We therefore draw the only possible conclusion consistent with that belief, namely, that it is the spirits of the living and not of the dead that are here in reality speaking to us.

6. The general character of these communications, considered in a mere *intellectual* point of view, in comparison with the productions of minds in the body, precludes wholly the supposition, that they are from disembodied spirits. Communications coming from the high spheres above, we cannot but know, as we have already observed, would move upon a level altogether above the highest forms of thinking among men in the flesh. We cannot but be mentally and morally degraded ourselves, to entertain any other ideas of a future state. Suppose that we have masses and floods of communications professedly descending to us from those high spheres, communications which, while they contain nothing new, not only never rise above the higher forms of mundane thinking, but almost, if not quite, invariably fall incomparably below them, very seldom, indeed, rising above mere commonplace, and more frequently embodying the most senseless puerilities conceivable. What higher evidence can we have of an exclusively mundane origin, than is thus presented? When we will consent to receive such forms of thinking as from spirits, spirits, too, from the higher celestial spheres, as these are generally affirmed to come, we consent to our own mental and moral deg-

radation, and voluntarily subject ourselves to influences of all others most efficient to produce that result. We will cite a few passages, as examples of "spirit wisdom." Our citations are exclusively from books advertised in the *Spiritual Telegraph* of New York, as among the standard spiritual productions which are kept for sale at that office, books embraced in the catalogue, to all of which the "reader's attention is particularly invited." In a communication of upwards of forty pages from George Washington, a communication contained in a book entitled, "Love and Wisdom from the Spirit World," we find the following important announcement. "If men were governed by love, truth, wisdom, and harmony, then they would be under one grand, universal government of peace and harmony." No one can fail, we think, to understand the important principle here affirmed by the father of our country, and it is certainly just as true as the momentous proposition, that an oyster is an oyster. Further on we are told, that in order that mankind may "become acquainted with the natural and spiritual laws which govern their own being," knowledge requisite to "enjoy peace, harmony, and happiness," "it is necessary that they obtain light on these important subjects." The meaning of the last part of the following sentence is not to us quite so plain as the foregoing. "These glorious realities," the blessings of one universal brotherhood among men, "cannot be enjoyed until there is a general reformation in all governments, laws, institutions, and modes of teaching the generation together with the present." At the head of the address, presenting throughout corresponding perfection of thought and style, we have a likeness of the author, a likeness at the bottom of which we find a scrap of poetry made by Washington himself, as we are given to understand, for the express purpose of accompanying that likeness. The poetry reads as follaws: —

"When the likeness of this portrait you see,
Remember that it is to represent the likeness of me,
But the spirit in its brightness you cannot see,
For that is far above the likeness of thee.
G. WASHINGTON."

The likeness of Franklin, which stands, in the book above named, at the head of a long essay from him on "Progression of the mineral, vegetable, animal, and spiritual kingdoms," is also accompanied by the following lines, composed by that great mind, in his "angel's home."

"The likeness of this portrait is to represent
The likeness of man when he dwelt here below,
But the likeness of the spirit you would like to know,
And this would be no more than I would like to show;
But the mind is not prepared the likeness for to see
Of the spirit in his angel's home as bright as we.
B. FRANKLIN."

"The elevated spirits" communicating in this book, affirm, we are told, that they "impressed every word and sentence" found in it upon the medium's mind before it was written. We have then here, it would seem, an infallible criterion by which we can judge of the progression of these minds in "love and wisdom" during their residence in the celestial spheres. From another work, entitled "Light from the Spirit World," we take the following specimens of spirit thinking and composition. An essay on Wisdom commences thus: —

"Wisdom is what is wise, and what is wise is wisdom. Wisdom is not folly, and folly is not wisdom.

Wisdom is not selfishness, and selfishness is not wisdom. Wisdom is not evil, and evil is not wisdom." Again, "Wisdom is wisdom. All is not wisdom. All is not folly." Further on we are told that if we would get wisdom, those of us who have it not, we must "get it where it is to be found." For ourselves, much as we value this priceless treasure, we feel very little inclined to resort to "the spirits" to get it, though we can obtain from them the great truth that, "Men are what they are," together with the momentous information that, "Change is alteration," and although they assure us, that they come to us, "in wisdom which is from heaven," "with glad tidings on their tongues, with the rainbow of promise over their heads, with the cup of salvation in their hands, with the wine of consolation to the mourner, and the balm of healing to the sorrow-stricken and the despondent." We must give one additional quotation. The essay "On Works" thus commences: "Works are the doings of a worker. Indolence is not work. Industry is work. Industry, accompanied with wisdom, works a wise work. Wisdom works wisely, and the works of wisdom are not works of vanity." The medium through whom these great thoughts are communicated to us, assures us, that "the spirits" express themselves, after reviewing what they have here communicated, well satisfied with their work. In a work entitled, "Discourses from the Spirit World, dictated by Steven Olin, through Rev. R. P. Wilson, writing medium," we have the following somewhat original definition of the phrase, "the kingdom of God:"—

"By the phrase, 'kingdom of God,' is meant, 1. The most internal essence, or the love, wisdom, and will principles. 2. The subordinate principles of expansion, attraction, and circulation. 3. The agencies of heat, light, and electricity. These principles and agencies constitute the realm of this kingdom, with reference to its internal nature and relations." So much for the theological lore of "the spirits," for their wondrous insight into the secrets of spiritual wisdom and knowledge.

We shall not multiply quotations further. We contend, that what we have presented is not an unfair representation of the real wisdom of "the spirits." For ourselves, we have searched in vain among these communications, and we have examined the works commended to our regard, by the best informed spiritualists in the country, as among the fundamental and standard spirit productions; we have searched in vain, we say, among all these productions, for a *new* or a *great* thought. We have found, almost without exception, forms of thinking far below those which appear in the ordinary productions of men in the flesh, and which shock all our hallowed sentiments, and debase all our conceptions, in regard to immortality, when received as from spirits inhabiting the celestial spheres. A friend of ours, Hon. George Bradburn, as he has affirmed before the public, has read upwards of six thousand pages of these productions, and has turned from them with the identical impressions above stated. They have absolutely none of the characteristics which we cannot but know they would have, did they come to us from spirits standing amid the high revelations of eternity. On the other hand, they have all the marks, and none others, of an origin purely and exclusively mundane. For example: 1. None but *mundane thoughts* are here embodied, thoughts which vary in their forms with the opinions of the circles in which they originate. 2. These communications present the precise *kinds* of thinking which we know would proceed from the surface of minds in the very passive and unthinking state in which mediums affirm themselves to be, when they suppose themselves under the inspiration of the spirits, and which can proceed from no other source. We find just such thoughts as these in these communications, and little else. 3. All the peculiarities of style, and manner, which characterize the mediums, and those who are around them, when communicating, are embodied in these communications. No spirit, from any sphere, can spell correctly, speak grammatically, or utter any thing but senseless puerilities, when communicating through certain mediums. 4. We find all the peculiarities of sentiment, forms of expression, and mere ignorance of the mediums and spirit circles reflected in these productions. We find, for example, in a communication given forth as from the spirits, through Mrs. Fish, when in Cleveland, such expressions as the following: "Go, sit under the teachings of that orthodox D. D., who says that all these rappings and other physical manifestations are humbugs," etc. Again: "This conclusion that all these spiritual manifestations are a humbug, because spirit cannot have power to make such manifestations, strikes their own pretended faith flat in the face." There is one fact which has struck our minds with peculiar interest, in reading these works. Whenever the inquirer asks questions of the spirits, pertaining to subjects which real spirits must be acquainted with, but of which he is ignorant, and about which he is perplexed, we always find, that the spirits here responding not only do not know any thing more than he does, but that his ignorance and perplexity are reflected in the responses which he obtains; thus indicating most decisively, that the inquirer, and he only, is answering his own questions. The following we give, as examples, from Rev. H. Snow's work, entitled, "Spirit Intercourse."

"Can you give any idea of the manner in which spirits converse?

"You had better not attempt to penetrate so deeply into our affairs, for it can be of no use to you. There is, however, with us a common and universal method of holding intercourse, but of which you can form no just idea until you are permitted to make use of it.

"Are there any evil-disposed or mischievous spirits that have it in their power to approach and communicate with us?

"You cannot fully understand what you wish to know upon this subject either. It is not in our power to enlighten you much in this respect.

"Can it be explained, without implying deception on the part of spirits, how great men are said to be present, and to communicate, when what is communicated shows plainly that the great men are not present?

"You must not think that we can give you all the satisfaction you wish on this point. It may be said, however, that it is not *necessary* to suppose deception, as there are other ways of accounting for such facts. You cannot understand the matter fully," etc.

Thus it is, that every peculiarity in the state of the inquirer's mind, is perfectly reflected back upon him, in the responses which he obtains. If he understands, is ignorant of, or perplexed about the subject about which he inquires, his own knowledge, ignorance, or perplexity, and nothing else, will be presented in the answer obtained. 5. Finally, how great soever the number, and diverse the character and relations of spirits which communicate through one and the same medium, the style of each will be one and the same, with that of all the others, thus showing that they are the product of one, and not of many minds. What perfect identity of style, for example, characterizes the various productions of different minds, professedly communicating their thoughts to the world, in the two volumes published by Judge Edmonds. We must repudiate all the laws of criticism, and ignore the entire dictates of common sense, before we can admit that different minds are here communicating. So, in regard to all of these works. The same spirits, communicating through different mediums, are wholly unlike themselves, in style and manner, and forms of thinking. All minds, on the other hand, communicating through the same channel, present a perfect unity, in these respects.

There is an apparent exception to the above statements, an exception which, instead of contradicting, really and truly confirms the principle which we have assumed. When the medium, or some one present, knows the style of the individual whose spirit is professedly communicating, such style will sometimes be in some degree copied, though almost without exception, very imperfectly. So also when an imaginary character is communicating, such as a news-boy, forms of expression which that class of persons are known to use, will sometimes be embodied in the communications obtained. In all other cases, we believe, and we think we cannot be mistaken, the principle under consideration fully obtains. No one spirit has any thing like a fixed style by which he can be identified, as he appears in different circles and communicates through different mediums. All spirits, on the other hand, with the exceptions above named, when communicating in the same circles, and through the same mediums, have a perfect identity of style; a style, too, which varies as the character of the circles and mediums varies. We noticed, for example, some weeks since, several communications purporting to have come from the spirits of Messrs. Webster, Calhoun, Clay, and others, communications obtained through one of the Miss Foxes in the city of New York, and in a circle constituted of such men as the Hon. J. R. Giddings. Mr. Calhoun is affirmed to have announced his own presence in an elliptical style peculiar to himself, namely, "I'm with you," and this was assumed as proof positive of his actual presence. It was forgotten that some persons present knew well what were his peculiarities in such forms of expression. As soon as he and the others began to make formal communications, however, all peculiarities of their earthly style and manner disappeared at once, and all adopted one and the same style, a style too utterly unlike, and infinitely beneath what was so peculiar to each when in the body. Now, if such facts as these do not prove the exclusively mundane origin of these communications, we may well ask, what can be established by evidence? We cannot have higher evidence, when standing before a mirror, that it is our own image that we see reflected there, and that our presence is the cause of that reflection, than we have, in such facts as these, that these communications are nothing but the reflections of the thoughts of the mediums, and of the persons constituting these circles, and are caused by those thoughts, and not by those of spirits out of the circles. The time is not distant when the only sentiment of mystery connected with these manifestations will be, that in this country, in the middle of the nineteenth century, the belief could have obtained among any intelligent portion of the community, that such productions, such forms of thought, could have descended to us, from spirits inhabiting the celestial spheres. If this is a true vision of immortality, we say, in all sincerity, give us annihilation.

7. We now refer to an important class of facts which have been developed by inquiries put by individuals for the specific purpose of satisfying their own minds on the question, whether spirits have, as a matter of fact, any connection with these mysterious phenomena. The inquiries to which we now refer have generally been made by individuals who had formed no particular theory upon the subject, and made simply for the purpose named. They have assumed, and for the best of reasons, that if spirits are really and truly responding here, individuals will, of course, get no answers, if they call for those who cannot be present, and that if they can get the same answers from such spirits that can be obtained from any others, and in all respects the same evidence of spirit presence and agency, then Spiritualism, whatever else may be true of these facts, must be false. These experiments have established undeniably the fact, that in all respects the same answers can be elicited, and the same evidence of an actual presence as the authors and cause of these communications, can be obtained from the following classes of spirits, as from any others that ever have been or can be evoked, namely, from the departed spirits of devils; from the departed spirits of individuals yet alive, or who never existed; from the departed spirits of the lowest orders of brute beasts, insects, and reptiles; and finally, from the departed spirits of shrubs and stones. All tests of identity, all indications of intelligence, of a knowledge of our secret thoughts, all forms of information, all kinds of manifestations, physical and mental,

that can be obtained from any spirits whatever, can be obtained from each and every class above named. "I do n't understand these mysterious occurrences," said the father of a certain medium, an honest and intelligent farmer; "but there is one thing that I do know about them, and that is, that we can obtain just as intelligent answers from the spirits of beasts, shrubs, and stones, as from any spirits that can be called upon. This I know absolutely; for I have made the experiment myself, till I am perfectly satisfied upon the subject." Mr. Ballou admits that facts of this kind do occur, and attributes their occurrence to a low order of spirits who are ready to appear in any characters that men desire. "This," he also says, "is the explanation given by truthful spirits." This explanation, however, is self-contradictory and absurd; for this low order of spirits exhibit all the intelligence that any others do. They have the same power to respond to our secret thoughts, to answer test questions, and to convey information of facts unknown to us. They will discourse as profoundly upon all subjects that can be named as any others whatever. Now what more decisive evidence can we have of any truth than is here presented, that these responses do not come from spirits. The facts of the case could not be as they are, if invisible intelligent beings were really and truly communicating with us in these manifestations. They could not, on the other hand, but be as they are, if the spirits constituting the circles were unconsciously producing the answers which they obtain to their own inquiries. In this case, and in this alone, any spirit named, whether existing or not existing, would give the same responses as any other.

The spiritualist, we know, has an answer ready for such facts. The individual putting such questions, he says, is in a dishonest state of mind, and therefore by the law of spiritual communications, draws lying spirits to himself, and from these he obtains his answers. This answer, if admitted as valid, proves far more than the spiritualist intends. It renders demonstrably evident one fundamental fact pertaining to all these communications, the absolute impossibility of *identifying* at all any spirits which are communicating with us, if any are. If lying spirits can answer as correctly as any others, all test questions given to identify the spirits who are communicating with us, it is absolutely impossible for us, to determine whether the spirit communicating with us, on any given occasion, is not a lying spirit instead of the one we suppose. All ground of confidence, therefore, in the validity of any of these communications is taken away. It cannot be denied that all evidence of the *reality* or *validity* of all such communications is utterly annihilated by the facts before us, facts which cannot be denied.

But the assumption that the putting of such inquiries implies dishonesty in the inquirer, is wholly unauthorized. The questions are put for the single and honest purpose of determining the fact, whether these responses do proceed from disembodied spirits or not. They are perfectly adapted to secure that result, and consequently may be, and no doubt often are, put with the most perfect integrity; a state of mind which, if the law of spirit communication referred to is real, would repel and not draw to itself lying spirits. Truth-telling spirits, and they only, would be drawn into communication with the inquirer to solve his honest doubts.

The relation of the responses obtained under such circumstances to the state of the inquirer's mind, should not be overlooked in this connection. They are always in the fixed relation of *consequence* to that state, as *antecedent.* As is the state, so are the responses. As the former changes and varies, so do the latter. This is the fixed law of their occurrence. Now if this fact does not reveal the state referred to as the cause, and the responses as the effects of the action of that cause, and therefore exclude the supposition of *ab extra* spirit interposition, what relations of antecedence and consequence can reveal that of cause and effect? None but those who are determined to be deceived can, as it seems to us, avoid the conclusion which we draw from these facts.

8. There is a class of facts which should not be overlooked in this connection, a class against which no objection, like that above alluded to, can be raised. We refer to responses which individuals obtain, when they, with the most honest desire for true information, call for the spirits of friends whom they sincerely *suppose to be dead, but who are yet alive.* In all such cases, all the evidence of actual presence and identity is obtained that is ever obtained in any instances whatever, and inquirers are just as certain to get responses, when they call for the spirits of such persons, as in any other cases. We have two friends, for example, one of whom is alive, and the other dead, both of whom, however, we, with equal honesty, suppose to be in the spirit world. We are just as sure to get an answer, when we call for one of these spirits, as for the other, and we can obtain, in all respects, the same evidence of actual presence and identity in one case, that we can in the other. The facts cannot be denied. They would be as these are, if the responses originated within the circle. Could they be so, if they came from spirits out of those circles? But one answer can be given to such a question.

A child, for example, in an intelligent Christian family which we have known for nearly twenty years, recently became a table-moving, writing, and rapping medium. We have ourselves seen phenomena of the first class, and heard the raps connected with that child, and have fully satisfied ourselves that there is no intentional deception in the case. The evening after the child announced the fact that he was a medium, the family formed a circle by themselves, and when the rappings commenced, took the alphabet, and called for the name of the spirit present, if any was present, and was producing these mysterious sounds. The name of a young man, who had been, for a considerable period, a member of the family, and had left for New Orleans in the spring of 1854, and from whom, though he had promised to write, they had never heard since, was given. In answer to subsequent inquiries, the following statements were all rapped out, namely, that on the 24th of May, 1854, he had died in New Orleans, of the yellow fever. Since that occurrence, that young man has reappeared among us, and thereby established the fact, that he is not dead. In this case, every question was put with the utmost sincerity, and there was nothing whatever to draw responses from lying spirits. Of this, however, the entire family are perfectly aware, that the answers obtained represented their own previous convictions of facts, and to those convictions they have sense enough to attribute the communication which they did obtain.

A somewhat remarkable case of this kind recently occurred in Cleveland. A young man, some seven or eight months ago, went from that city to Chicago. From the latter city he wrote to his friends, that he was to leave that place for St. Louis. For upwards of five months subsequent to the reception of this letter, no intelligence whatever was received of him, and it was supposed that he was dead. His mother, having accompanied a female friend, a devoted spiritualist, to the residence of a medium, and while listening to the communications which others were then receiving, felt something like a human hand grasp her own, as if for the purpose of an affectionate salutation. She asked the medium what that meant, and was told that it was an indication to her, that a spirit was present who desired to speak to her. To her inquiry, who the spirit was, the name of her son was given. She was then informed, as from him, that on his way down the Mississippi, the boat took fire, and he, in his fright, leaped overboard and was drowned. "You know, mother," said the spirit, "that while alive, I ridiculed spiritualism. I am exceedingly glad to find it true, as I can now communicate with you." The mother was then requested to call again, at a time named, when he would have other important communications to make to her. The medium in this case was a speaking one, and the mother, though she had never met the medium before, nor had ever heard of her, recognized a perfect likeness to her son's voice and manner. She called as directed and received other communications. She then called upon two other mediums, both total strangers to her, and through them also received substantially, as from her son, the same messages as before. To the question, how can I know that it is really and truly my son that is communicating with me, she was told in reply, that he would accompany her home, and remain with her there, till all doubts were removed from her mind. The disconsolate mother returned home with the most absolute conviction, that her son was dead, and that she had communed with his spirit. On her arrival, however, she was met by that very son who had returned during her absence. He had written home, but none of his letters had arrived, and this was the cause of the apprehension that he was dead.

Now this case, which we ourselves obtained directly from the family itself, this case, we say, and others of the same character, to any number desired, might be adduced, establishes most unquestionably the following facts. (1.) There was here the most perfect honesty and sincerity in the mind of the inquirer, and the consequent absence of all causes which, according to the principles of spiritualism, would draw lying spirits into rapport with her mind. (2.) All conceivable evidence, physical and mental, of the presence of the particular spirit supposed to be present was given, that is or can be given, in any other case. (3.) Nothing is requisite to obtain all the evidence of the actual presence of the disembodied spirits of individuals who are yet alive, that can be obtained in reference to that of any person who is dead, but an honest conviction, on the part of the inquirer, that the living individual, whose spirit is called for, is actually dead. (4.) To suppose that lying spirits can thus personate other minds, and none others, if any do, can respond, in such cases, is to annihilate all evidence, that any one can have, that he has ever communicated with any particular spirit, on any occasion whatever, on the one hand, and that all these communications, if from spirits at all, are not from "the father of lies," or his agents on the other. (5.) We need suppose no other cause for such responses, but the state of the inquirer's mind, in the circumstances actually existing, to account for all the facts which here present themselves. The recollection of her son would, of course, be very vivid in the mother's mind, and this would give form to the words, voice, and manner of the medium. (6.) It would be the height of absurdity, consequently, to refer such communications to any *ab extra* or spirit cause. There is to our minds no escaping these conclusions. (7.) If such cases are not, and no one will pretend that they are, to be referred to the agency of spirits, it would be the height of absurdity to refer any other of these communications to such agency. (8.) No tactual impressions, no likeness in these communications to the voice, style, or manner of persons living or dead, can be any real proof of the truth of spiritualism. This, we think, is undeniable.

9. We now adduce a class of facts perfectly similar to those above named, and which occur under circumstances that entirely free them from all the objections that can be raised, even by spiritualists, against the conclusions undeniably deducible from them. We refer to responses obtained in these circles by devoted spiritualists themselves, answers purporting to come from individuals *supposed* and *honestly supposed* to be dead, but who are yet alive, or never existed at all. Here, of course, there is the most perfect integrity in the inquirer's state of mind, and the consequent total absence of all causes to induce the presence and action of lying spirits. In precisely such circumstances, just the same kind of communications are obtained, and all test questions put to identify "the spirits" communicating are answered with the same correctness, as in any other instances. A very striking case of this kind came under our own observation. A friend of ours was believed by herself, her physicians, and by all around her, to be in the very last stages of consumption, within one or two weeks, at the utmost, of death. At

this time she was visited by a number of relatives, who were most devoted spiritualists, and who took very great pains, but without success, to interest her in the subject. She was feasting on more substantial realities than "the spirits" revealed to her. These individuals took their final leave of our friend, and returned to their distant homes with the most undoubted conviction, that in a very few days she would be in eternity. A few weeks subsequent, the husband of our friend received from those individuals a letter containing a special and affectionate communication from the spirit of his departed wife, — a communication obtained from that identical spirit and none other, in the spirit circle which these individuals attended. In that circle they inquired if the spirit of that supposed to have been dying, and consequently then dead friend, was present. The answer was, yes. After all proofs of identity were given that are ever required, and all the circumstances of our friend's departure and her then happy state were given, a wish was expressed by her to send a communication of consolation, etc. to the bereaved husband that was left behind. This communication was then given and forwarded, as stated above. It so happened that that very disembodied spirit thus identified, and thus communicating with the living, was then with her husband in the body, and to the wonder of all around, is yet alive, with a prospect of seeing years to come.

A very notable case of a similar character appeared in the public prints recently, as connected with Judge Edmonds and others. In a certain paper in the interests of Spiritualism, and published in California, a paper called *The Pioneer*, a professedly spirit communication appeared, as from the spirit of a Mr. Lane. This communication was subsequently indorsed by "the spirits" in a spirit circle as a genuine spirit production. It was then forwarded to Judge Edmonds, who forwarded to *The Pioneer* a communication which he had obtained, in the city of New York, from the spirit of this same Mr. Lane. On the appearance of this last communication, an editor of another California paper published the fact that he was well informed about Mr. Lane and his communications, that no such person ever had existed, and that the communication which first appeared in *The Pioneer* was of an exclusively mundane origin. Yet this very spirit appeared to Judge Edmonds, with all the evidence of an actual presence and identity, that he ever had of that of Bacon or any other spirit.

We recently met with a very intelligent Christian lady who utterly repudiates the claims of Spiritualism, a lady who was left a widow by the celebrated William Leggett of New York, and whose present husband is a devoted spiritualist. While a circle was being held in her own parlor, her husband being a member of it, and she sitting in another part of the room, and no one in the circle could obtain any communication at all, the question was asked, whether there was any spirit present that wished to communicate with Mrs. —— Instantly a number of very loud raps were heard upon the top of the table. She was earnestly requested to enter the circle and receive communications. On her refusal to comply, individuals in the circle put questions themselves, and received ready answers to all their inquiries. The spirit responding purported to be that of a brother of Mrs. ——, a brother who had sailed some twenty years ago as the commandant of a vessel, from the port of New York, and had never since been heard from, the vessel and all on board having, no doubt, been lost. All particulars of the loss of the vessel, and the subsequent death of all on board, the brother having languished for thirty-six days on a raft, before he died, were given to her, as she affirmed, with a disgusting and even shocking minuteness. She had another brother, Stephen, from whom no tidings had been received for upwards of two years. The elder brother, on being questioned on the subject, affirmed that Stephen was with him in the spirit land; that he had died on a steamboat, at a particular place and time named, on the Mississippi river; that he had six thousand five hundred dollars with him when he died; that this treasure was taken possession of by three individuals, one a female, who had since died, and with the greatest agony of mind, had confessed the wrong to the spirit of the brother named above, etc. Soon after she received a letter from a sister in New York, saying, "I have just received a letter from brother Stephen, and he will be with us in two or three weeks." The statements pertaining to the elder brother could not, of course, be tested. Those pertaining to the other, however, statements equally specific and worthy of credit, she happily had the means of informing herself about. But one explanation can be given of the communications obtained in this instance. The husband of this lady knew about the brothers, honestly supposed them both alike to have been dead, and hence the responses obtained.

The fact is undeniable, that whenever there is an honest belief that an individual is dead, whether he is alive or never existed at all, even spiritualists can obtain all the evidence of the presence, identity, and agency of his spirit, that can be obtained in any other case whatever. Any persons, that in the presence of such facts will attribute these manifestations to spirits, and especially to particular ones, hold their minds open to any delusions that may be sent to them from any source whatever.

10. We now invite very special attention to a class of facts of the most absolute and decisive bearing upon our present inquiries. We refer to certain observations and experiments which individuals have made, with this one specific purpose in view, namely, to determine the *location* of the cause of these manifestations, whether that cause pertains to the minds in the circles, or to disembodied spirits out of them. As the facts now to be adduced are perfectly fundamental in their bearing, we shall make a quite extensive selection from the great mass that lies around us, and which might be adduced, did our limits permit.

We will begin with a fact connected with clairvoyance, and then parallel it with another connected with these manifestations. Some years since, Rev. J. H. S., then pastor of the Baptist church in Poughkeepsie, N. Y., met, on a certain occasion, several individuals at the house of a friend. Among the individuals present was a Mr. L., who first mesmerized A. J. Davis. Mr. L. expressed to Mr. S. much surprise that the latter should hold the doctrine of future retribution, when such palpable evidence to the contrary could be presented. Here, he says, is a young man now present whom I will introduce into a clairvoyant state, in which he will have a direct vision of the condition of the spirits of the dead. Let us see what report he will bring back of that state. This was done. As the young man was subjected to the actions of the odylic [mesmeric] force, his head, he being seated in a chair, was drawn between his knees, till his hair touched the floor. In this state he remained for about two hours, without apparent injury or wearisomeness. During this time many very wonderful facts were developed which we have not space to detail. At length Mr. L. introduced his subject among the spirits of the dead, that is, willed, that he should have such visions, and asked him what he saw. With the greatest delight conceivable, he testified that all, *all* were happy, very, very happy. What do you think of that, Mr. S., says the mesmerizer? How can you resist such evidence? Put me in communication with the young man, says Mr. S., and let us see what will then appear. This was done. Mr. S., without speaking at all, fixed his attention upon one of the most depraved characters that ever appeared in this country, an individual who had been executed in that place, a short time previous, for murder, and who died as he had lived. Soon the clairvoyant began to scream, with the greatest anguish and entreaty conceivable. "Do let me off! Do let me off! I can't endure it," he exclaimed. Mr. S. asked him what he saw. The individual referred to, and to whom no allusion had before been made, was named. Where is he? asked Mr. S. "In hell," was the reply. "I can't endure the sight of him," exclaimed the young man. "Do let me off." What do you think now, Mr. L.? said Mr. S. No one can doubt the cause of these diverse and opposite visions in this case. They simply represented the ideas of those in mesmeric communication with the clairvoyant. That is all. Had he been put in communication with individuals holding every variety of sentiment that exists on earth in reference to a future state, his visions would, in succession, have represented them all, just as they did those of the individuals referred to, and that for the same identical reason.

We will now attend to a case of perfectly similar characteristics, connected with these manifestations. A gentleman of our acquaintance, now a member of the bar in Cleveland, held a discussion on this subject, some years since, in North Adams, Mass. That he might be prepared for the discussion, he called, in company with the leading physician of the place, upon a neighbor whose daughter was a medium, and requested the privilege of witnessing some of "the spirit" phenomena. The first evening was spent in witnessing physical manifestations. With these they were perfectly astonished and even confounded. The medium placing simply the ends of her fingers upon the top of a large table standing in the centre of the room, called upon the spirit of an individual who had previously died in the place to move the object referred to. It was moved accordingly. Our friend got under the table and attempted to hold it still. Yet the object, and himself with it, was drawn over the floor, his utmost efforts to the contrary notwithstanding. The physician placed a sheet of paper under the fingers of the medium, and drew it out while the table was being moved, and that without any sensible indications of pressure upon it. They consequently left, with the impression that they should be compelled to confess before the audience to the truth of Spiritualism.

On the next day they agreed with three individuals, leading members of the three denominations of the place, one a Congregationalist, one a Baptist, and the other a Universalist, to meet them the evening following at the house referred to, neither being informed at all of the object to be obtained, nor of the fact that either of the others was to be there. When the circle was formed, the Congregationalist was introduced.

The same spirit was present that moved the table the evening before. In answer to inquiries put by the individual last referred to, the evangelical view of heaven, hell, and eternal retribution, was absolutely affirmed as immutably true. To the question what mode of baptism is correct, *sprinkling* was rapped out. With a pledge of secrecy, he was then dismissed, and the Baptist called in. In answer to inquiries made by the latter, the same view of eternity as before was given. To the question, what mode of baptism is right, *immersion* was rapped out. He being dismissed, the Universalist was introduced. The same spirit which had given the responses above stated, now denied the doctrine of retribution altogether, stoutly asserting the doctrine of universal salvation, and manifested a total indifference to the question of baptism, in any form. When the audience had assembled to listen to the discussion, these individuals were called upon to testify to the spirit communications which they had received, and did so with a result which we need not specify. In a similar manner, every sentiment held by every people or sect on earth, might have been absolutely affirmed and denied, by the spirit which responded in that circle, or by any other spirit which appeared there, or ever appeared in any other circle on earth, and that for the identical reason, that precisely similar answers can be obtained from the mesmeric subject. Who, in the presence of such facts, and this is the immutable character of these manifestations the world over, can doubt their origin? It would be an impeachment of the common sense of our readers, to argue the question.

The above case, while it bears with the most decisive weight upon the question of the location of the real controlling cause of these manifestations, clearly evinces the reality of an important fact, the honesty and sincerity of some mediums, of one, to say the least. Any person who was voluntarily, and by known but occult and deceptive means, producing these rapping sounds, would never, at the same sitting, rap out such contradictory communications. Many other facts, equally palpable and undeniable, evince to our minds most indubitable evidence, that many other mediums are not intentionally deceiving the public, but honestly suppose themselves organs of communication between the inhabitants of this and the spirit land.

Let us now consider another case of a similar character to the one just adduced. A gentleman who was then at the head of one of the literary institutions of the State of Ohio, entered one of these circles, and inquired if the spirit of a dear friend, his mother, we believe, was present, and received an affirmative answer. Being perfectly assured that that spirit, if present, and no one in the circle but himself, did know his age, for the exclusive purpose of identification, he asked the spirit to reveal his age. To his surprise, precisely the right number was rapped out, namely, thirty or thirty-one years. To satisfy himself in respect to the *cause* of the answer, he fixed his attention distinctly upon another and different number, twenty-five, and asked the same spirit to give his age once more. The identical number upon which his attention was then fixed was given, and not the correct one given before. He asked if the doctrine of eternal retribution is true? He received an absolute affirmation that it is. He induced a voluntary doubt in his mind of the truth of that doctrine, and assumed that of the opposite one. To his questions now, his own mother stood revealed as an uncompromising Universalist. He asked, which denomination of Christians is most nearly correct in doctrine and discipline, at the same time fixing his attention upon his own. That one sect was named. He fixed his attention upon another denomination, internally *assuming* that it was most nearly conformed to the Scriptures, and repeated the question just answered. This one sect was now designated. He thus went through the entire circle of denominations that occurred to his recollection, so putting his questions that the medium's mind was not disturbed, and found his own mother a Presbyterian, Methodist, Baptist, Episcopalian, Universalist, Christian, Unitarian, and any thing, and every thing, just according to his own mere internal assumptions. He knew absolutely that such was not her character, and that upon no known or reasonably imagined laws of mind, could he account for such responses, as proceeding from any intelligent spirits, good or bad. On the other hand, he saw clearly, that just such communications would be obtained, if these manifestations are caused by the mental states of the individuals constituting the circles. He consequently left the circle, as any reasonable man would, with the undoubted conviction that the cause of these communications was within the circle, and not from disembodied spirits out of it. Just such answers may be obtained, and are obtained, in all these circles everywhere, in all cases where the inquirer acts with corresponding deliberation, and where the responses are not controlled by the influence of other minds present. Precisely similar and analogous experiments were made by Miss Catharine Beecher, with precisely similar results, experiments made in the most decisive forms, and so varied and repeated, that a mistake is hardly conceivable, and by no means supposable. With the same identical results, a gentleman made very extensive experiments in the various circles in Great Britain. At one time, for example, he *imagined* that a great fortune had just fallen to him by legacy, in a certain city. He immediately received from "the spirits" an important communication, corresponding, in all respects, to his own imaginings, and having no other foundation in fact. What higher evidence can we have that any facts are exclusively mundane in their origin, than is here presented in respect to the facts under consideration?

Two gentlemen, partners in business in Cleveland, have given us the privilege of making use of the following facts of which they were both witnesses. On one occasion they witnessed the following facts in mesmerism. We here repeat, on account of present bearings, a fact stated in another connection, adding some circumstances not then stated. The mesmerizer agreed to induce the subject, a lady who was perfectly blindfolded, to sing, and to stop the singing, the instant Mr. A. should raise his finger. When the singing commenced, the mesmerizer was standing some two or three feet from the subject, with his eyes fixed intently upon Mr. A. who was standing in a distant part of the room. When the singer had partly finished a very long note, Mr. A. raised his finger. The voice instantly stopped, with the note half finished. As the mesmerizer willed it, the singing was resumed, and that note, and the rest of the stanza were finished. After the lady was brought out of the magnetic state, Mr. A. saw her engaged in conversation with a friend, with the fingers of her hands interlocked together. Without uttering a word, or making a motion, he fixed his attention upon her hands, and willed that they should adhere together so firmly, that she should be unable to separate them. When the conversation was finished, she, to her perfect surprise, found it impossible to draw her hands apart, till Mr. A., by an act of will, permitted it. These facts occurred in the presence of other most credible witnesses, who testify to their occurrence as here related.

On a subsequent occasion, these gentlemen visited, in company, a spirit circle formed in this city by Mrs. Fish and the Fox girls. Mr. A., when it came his turn to inquire, fixed his thoughts distinctly upon his father who was then living, and with the same distinctness framed in his own mind the communications he should receive. Instantly the departed spirit of that father appeared, his name being rapped out in answer to the question, what spirit will communicate with me? that spirit, we say, appeared and took from his son's mind the thoughts preëxisting there, just as the printed page is taken from the stereotype plate. He dismissed his father from his mind, and fixed his thoughts as distinctly as possible, upon five or six other individuals. Immediately a corresponding number of raps were heard upon the top of the table. "Five or six spirits now respond to you," says Mrs. Fish. Such was the correspondence between the thoughts of the inquirer, and the answers obtained, a correspondence which always obtains, when there is the same deliberation and distinctness of thought on the part of the inquirer, and when the action of the invisible force is not disturbed by the mental states of others in the circle. Myriads of undeniable facts confirm this statement. Mr. L., the other partner, now communicated with "the spirits." Every question, whether put to the departed spirits of individuals living or dead, and he communicated with each class, was answered in exact correspondence with his own preformed conceptions. At length, having put a question, he instantly, by an act of will, confused his own mind, so that there was no thought in it to be represented. In a moment, the rappings stopped, just as the singing was interrupted in the instance above adduced. Thus he found that the action of this mysterious force, was under his absolute control. He could induce, suspend, and direct its action at will, just as he could that of his own hand or arm. The same holds true, in all cases, when the same conditions are fulfilled. Every one who has tried the experiment has found, that correct answers can be obtained, when the inquirer knows what the answer should be, and keeps his mind distinctly fixed upon it, and that every thing is confused, or that no answers at all can be obtained, when he asks a question, and then either confuses his thoughts, or turns them upon other subjects. If such facts do not reveal the relation of cause and effect between the mental states of individuals in these circles, and the communications there obtained, no such relation can, by any possibility, be established between any causes and facts in the universe around us.

The case which we next cite is, if possible, more fundamental and decisive in its bearings than any others that we have yet adduced. A gentleman of the city of Cleveland made very extensive and careful experiments and observations, for the purpose of satisfying his own mind in regard to the origin of these manifestations. He entered upon the inquiry with the earnest hope of finding valid evidence, that these manifestations come from disembodied spirits. He was equally dissatisfied with the doctrine of eternal retributions, on the one hand, and with that of Universalism, on the other. The general teachings of the spirits appeared to affirm an intermediate view, which corresponded with what, to say the least, he wished to find reliable evidence for believing. He accordingly put, and received answers to, upwards of one hundred questions, in the circles of Mrs. Fish and the Foxes, in this city. A large portion of these questions, probably more than one half, as he says, were asked mentally. The following are the most important facts developed.

(1.) In every instance, without exception, the answer referred to the *subject-matter* inquired about. Here he found the immutable relation of antecedence and consequence, cause and effect. (2.) In every instance in which he knew what the answer should be, a perfectly correct one was obtained. (3.) When he was in doubt what the answer should be, those doubts were reflected, and nothing positive asserted. For example, a sister of his had died of a lingering disease, of the nature of which there was doubt among the physicians, and in his own mind, some five or six different diseases having been assigned, and none fixed upon with certainty. He inquired of the spirit of that sister, what was the disease of which she did die? All the diseases which he had heard suggested as the cause, and none others, were named, each designated with very feeble raps, and neither positively affirmed as the real cause. So in all other similar cases. (4.) When he was mistaken in regard to the facts about which he inquired, and when the spirits of whom he was inquiring did know, and could not have forgotten, the answers invariably corresponded with his mistaken apprehensions, and not with the real facts, as he subsequently became informed, and as they were known to the spirits professedly answering. For example, he inquired of the spirit of his own sister her age at the time of her death, he supposing, at the moment, that twenty-eight was the true answer, and that number was rapped out. On a subsequent reference to the family records, he found that she was really aged at the time upwards of thirty years. A friend of his had lost his life in California, by drowning, and that, as he had been informed, in a certain river, by accidentally slipping through a raft of logs. All the facts of the occurrence were given, professedly by the spirit of that friend, as he had supposed them to be. From four individuals present when the event occurred, he subsequently learned that his friend actually came to his end in another part of the State, in another river, and by a totally different accident. The answer corresponded with the supposed, and not with the real facts as known to the spirit professedly communicating. He put a question to another spirit, pertaining to a transaction about which, as he well knew, that spirit was perfectly informed, and he, as he subsequently learned, himself had been misinformed. The answer corresponded with his misinformation, and not with the real facts, as known to the spirit professedly responding. (5.) To every question, without exception, pertaining to subjects of which he was ignorant, a wrong answer was obtained. As the result of his experience, he drew the following inferences.

(1.) That disembodied spirits can have no connection with these communications, and we envy not the candor or logical consistency of the individual who draws from such facts a different conclusion. (2.) That no information is ever communicated, in these circles, beyond what is previously known to the inquirer. We suppose that not one person in a thousand would draw any different conclusion from similar investigations in these circles, investigations conducted upon similar principles. The only exceptions that do occur are, as we suppose, some solitary revelations through clairvoyance, revelations which no one has reason to expect, when he resorts to these circles, and certain answers corresponding to and evidently occasioned by acts of imagination and conjecture.

Let us now look at another very important case. A gentleman in Boston, a devoted spiritualist, while sitting in a spirit circle, was struck with the revelation to his mind of the fact, that the responses to the questions propounded by inquirers, so frequently corresponded with the conceptions previously formed in his own imagination. This led to more careful reflection and observation, and finally to important experiments in which he found, that he could determine beforehand what answers should be given to any questions propounded by any persons present, and that he had, in a similar manner, been unconsciously directing the action of this mysterious force, and that while he had been supposing that spirits out of the circles had been doing it. A totally new theory pertaining to these so called spirit manifestations now stood revealed to his mind. He saw that mere reflections of the thoughts of individuals, in the circles, had been mistaken for the voices of spirits out of the circles.

A gentleman of very strong mesmeric power in the State of New York also found, after the most extensive experiments, that he could enter any circle whatever, and by simply willing it, could utterly silence "the spirits" so that no communications whatever could be obtained from them, that he could, in a similar manner, utterly confuse their responses, or determine beforehand, the answers which should be given to any questions proposed by any persons present. The bearing of such facts cannot be mistaken. Any person that in their presence will attribute these manifestations to disembodied spirits, must be a spiritualist by mere dint of will, and because he is determined to be deceived.

A professor of the Ohio Medical College, at the earnest solicitation of friends, visited on one occasion the spirit circle of Mrs. Fish and the Foxes in the city of Cleveland. All his questions, the first excepted, his mind not being in a collected state at the moment, were answered with perfect correctness, though they pertained to subjects with which he alone, of the members of the circle, was acquainted; all his questions, we say, were correctly answered, till the spirit communicating, that of a sister, was requested to specify the given name of their father. The moment he put the question, his thought recurred to his brother concerning whom he had just before been inquiring. The name of the brother instead of the father was immediately rapped out. The occurrence, he remarked, threw a flood of light upon his mind in regard to the origin and cause of these manifestations. The spirit professedly communicating understood the names of each of the individuals referred to as well as the professor himself, and would have corrected the mistake, had it been that person that was communicating. No such correction, however, was made. He concluded, therefore, that his own thought caused the answer, and not that of a spirit out of the circle. Who can doubt the correctness of his conclusion? Had it been an intelligent mind out of the circle, especially the mind professedly answering, it could have made no difference whatever to what subject the thoughts of the inquirer should turn, after asking his question. If, on the other hand, the action of this power in the production of the answer, was controlled by the mental states of the inquirer himself, then the accidental diversion of attention, in this instance, would occasion the identical answer that was received. On no other principle can its occurrence be accounted for.

This case also reveals the principle on which so many wrong answers are obtained in these circles to questions pertaining to subjects in respect to which both the inquirers and the spirits professedly answering are perfectly informed, and when such answers are not only unintentionally but unexpectedly obtained. It is by the accidental diversion of attention from the subject inquired about to some other subject. We shall have occasion to recur to this class of facts again, as they will be seen to have a very important bearing upon the question before us. All that is now required is to suggest the principle in accordance with which they occur.

This case also suggests a class of facts of very conclusive and decisive bearing upon our present inquiries. It has been found, by careful observation and experiment, that the following relations, among others, exist between the mental states of the inquirer, and the answers obtained, when such responses are not disturbed and modified by the undeniable psychological influence of other minds. (1.) If the inquirer fully commands his thoughts, and keeps his attention fixed upon the subject inquired about, the responses, whether right or wrong, will invariably relate to that one subject. (2.) If he knows what the answers should be, they will be almost if not quite, invariably right, and if he does not know, and the spirit professedly communicating most manifestly does, the answer, excepting when a mere yes or no is required, and where, and on the principle of mere guessing, there is as much likelihood that the answer shall be right as wrong, the answer, we say, will be nearly as invariably wrong. (3.) When the inquirer is misinformed, and the true answer is known to the spirit professedly communicating, the answer will uniformly embody the misinformation of the inquirer, instead of the truth as known to the spirit, all the apparent exceptions admitting of a ready explanation, without supposing the interposition of spirits. (4.) When the true answer is known both to the inquirer and to the professedly answering spirit, if the attention of the former is either intentionally or accidentally diverted and fixed definitely upon something else, this new thought, and not the answer referred to, will be embodied in the response obtained. (5.) If, either by accident or design, the mind of the inquirer becomes so confused, that there is in it, no thought at all to be represented, no answer whatever will be obtained. (6.) If the inquirer is not able, or does not think, to command his attention, so as to prevent his thoughts becoming confused and wandering, the answers will perfectly accord with his mental states at the time, the answers being sometimes relevant and at others strikingly irrelevant, and sometimes right, and at others wrong, and that when the true answer, in every instance, is perfectly known both to the inquirer and the spirit professedly communicating with him. (7.) Let an individual write out a series of questions, the true answers to all of which are perfectly known to him, and to the spirit of a deceased friend, let the former put those questions into the hands of an individual who knows nothing about the facts to which the questions pertain, and let this individual put these questions to that spirit, and the following will be the invariable result. If this individual puts the questions without forming in his own mind any imaginary answers, or fixing attention upon the subject at all, there will be either no responses at all, or they will all have the undeniable characteristics of mere imaginings, on the part of individuals who know nothing about the subjects referred to. If, on the other hand, he frames in his own mind, a distinct and definite imaginary answer to each question, and keeps his thoughts distinctly fixed upon that answer when he puts the question, the response obtained will accord with his imaginings and not with the facts, as known to the individual who wrote the questions, and to the spirit professedly responding to them. Experiments of this kind have been tried in so many instances, and in such a diversity of forms, as to establish the truth of the above principle. If any still doubt, they can verify that principle, by making the experiments themselves. (8.) Any inquirer who can command his own thoughts, and think with entire deliberation under such circumstances, especially if he has considerable mesmeric power, can, at will, make any spirit that shall professedly answer his call,—and such individuals can call up any spirits they choose,— give any answer he pleases to any question he may choose to put. He can make such spirit affirm and deny successively any sentiment that can be named, and contradict himself any number of times he pleases, provided always, that the process is so conducted, as not to disturb the medium, or break the odylic harmony of the circle. Most of the above statements have been most fully verified by the facts already stated. Others will be in those which we are about to present, and all could be still further, by numberless undeniable additional facts which we might present. We affirm, without fear of contradiction, that these facts can be accounted for but upon the truth of the hypothesis which we maintain, namely, that these communications originate exclusively from the minds in these circles, and not from disembodied spirits out of the same. If such were their origin, they could not but have these identical characteristics, and they could not have these characteristics, if they did originate from intelligent minds, good or bad, out of these circles, minds governed by any mental laws known to us. We have made the above statements to prepare the way for the presentation of the following very interesting and important facts which we have obtained, since our visit to Boston, and while the preceding portions of this treatise were going through the press. Our convictions of the truth of our hypothesis have been greatly strengthened, by the perfect accordance which we have found to exist in the character and bearings of the fundamental facts developed by careful observers in this city, and those which we had previously collected and arranged by means of our own observations and inquiries. The individuals whose names and facts will now be presented, will please to accept of our grateful acknowledgments for their kindness in furnishing us with facts so important, and especially for permitting us to use their names in connection with these facts.

FACTS WHICH OCCURRED AT THE HOUSE OF REV. STARR KING.

The facts which we first adduce occurred at the house of Rev. Starr King, pastor of the Hollis Street Church, Boston. The circle was a select one, and the individual through whom the communications were obtained was the celebrated medium, Mrs. Hayden. The main questioner was an individual of great self-command, and of corresponding power of intellectual concentration. The circumstances then were as favorable, in all respects, as we can well conceive, for eliciting important and decisive facts. The first object of the questioner was to ascertain distinctly and conclusively, whether the name of an individual of which he was thinking, and when no one present could have the least suspicion of what name he was thinking, could be spelled out, through the medium, by raps, and that when the medium could, by no possibility, have any knowledge of the movements of his hand when he should point at the requisite letters. He accordingly placed himself where the medium could not see him at all, nor any other person who could report his motions to her. The right name was thus given, and also the place where the individual bearing that name had died, namely, the Tremont House. He was, therefore, as he ought to have been, most fully satisfied, that there was present a power through which his most secret thoughts could be externally expressed, and this too, when he had given not the least indication to any one what those thoughts were. He then wished to know whether his own mind controlled the action of that power, in the production of such communications, or that of some spirit out of the circle, no other hypothesis being supposable in this case. To solve this one problem was the object of the questions subsequently put. He accordingly asked the spirit professedly communicating, how long a time it was since he died? "Twelve days," was the answer rapped out. You are wrong there, replied the questioner, addressing the spirit; it is only ten days since you died. I know absolutely that this is the fact, and you must be aware of it too. Please answer that question again. "Twelve days" were again given. Again and again he reasoned with the spirit on the subject, affirming absolutely to him, that ten days was the only right answer. Again and again the same number as before was given. He then asked the spirit to designate the day of the week on which he died. Saturday was given. You are wrong again, says the inquirer, and you must be aware of the fact. You died on Monday. Please correct the mistake. Saturday was given, as before. Again and again the spirit was told that Monday was the true answer, and was expostulated with for not giving it. Again and again, when requested to correct his mistake, Saturday was given. The man did die on Monday, and had been just ten days dead. How were these singular answers obtained? When the inquirer asked the spirit to tell the time which had elapsed since, or the day of the week on which he died, the inquirer would internally, and wholly unknown to any one but himself, fix his thoughts and hold them fixed, upon the number twelve, or Saturday, as the case might be. When he had reminded the spirit of his mistake, and asked him to correct it, he would then, while the response was being rapped out, fix his attention upon the wrong number or the wrong day, and the answer, in every instance, corresponded to that number or day, and not to the right one, as absolutely known both to the inquirer and the spirit professedly responding. Between the thought in his mind at the moment, and the answer obtained, there was, even in this case, the fixed and immutable relation of antecedence and consequence, a relation so immutable and fixed as to demonstrate the existence between them of that of cause and effect.

The individual then called up other spirits, and went through precisely similar processes with them, and that with the same invariable results. A friend of his, for example, had died in the city of New York. After obtaining the same evidence of presence and identity as before, the inquirer, secretly fixing his own attention upon Salem, then asked the spirit of that friend to name the place where he died. Salem was rapped out. He solemnly assured the spirit that he was wrong, affirming that New York was the right answer, and asked him to correct his error, the inquirer fixing his own attention, as soon as the request was made, upon Salem. This last name was given as before. So with many other spirits, with precisely similar results, no one present having the least suspicion of what the inquirer was doing, until he himself disclosed the fact, after he had finished questioning the spirits. In every experiment, he found it absolutely impossible to induce any spirit he could call up, — and he could, we repeat, call up any one he chose, — to give the true answer to any question he might propose, however absolutely that answer was known to himself and the spirit too, if his attention at the moment was only fixed upon some other answer, an answer known to himself and the spirit too, to be false, and when the spirit was entreated not to give that answer, but the true one. He always obtained a correct response when he would allow his attention to be fixed upon it, and a wrong one, when his attention, for the moment, was directed towards that, and in all instances, the answers perfectly accorded with the secret movements of his own mind. No person, we are free to say, will have the effrontery to assign any other controlling cause for these communications, than the mental states of this individual. From these most decisive facts, the following conclusions in regard to these communications are rendered undeniably evident: (1.) There is in nature a force, whose action, when certain conditions are fulfilled, corresponds with our mental states; and is determined by the same,—a force through which our own thoughts may be reflected back upon us, as if they came from other minds, minds, to us invisible, and apparently from the spirit land,—a very important truth, unquestionably. (2.) There is also in this so called spirit movement a power by which, without any external motions or signs whatever on our part, our most secret thoughts may be revealed and expressed. (3.) This may be done in the total absence of all *ab extra* spirit agency, none being supposable in the facts before us. (4.) No such revelations can be adduced as presenting any evidence whatever of an *ab extra* spirit origin. (5.) We have no occasion to go beyond the force developed in these circles, and the mental states of the individuals constituting them, to account for any revelations embodied in these communications, those pertaining to secret thoughts being, of all others, in themselves the most wonderful and unaccountable, far more so than those which pertain to mere physical objects, however distant. (6.) We have the highest positive evidence of the exclusively subjective origin of these so called spirit manifestations. Any persons that, in the presence of such facts, can draw any other conclusion, is, in our honest judgment, far removed, in his reasonings from facts to conclusions, off from the true line of scientific or common sense deduction.

The communications received by Mr. King himself, though not, in all respects, so decisive in their bearings, were yet very interesting and important. Being informed, by the appropriate raps, that a spirit was present who would communicate with him, he asked, first, for the initials of his (the spirit's) name, Mr. K. at the time fixing his attention upon a certain individual who had died some time before, an individual whom no one present but himself was likely to think of. The initials of the very name that rose in his mind were given. He then called for the name in full, and it was given accordingly. Many important test questions were then asked, and all, without exception, which came within the recollection of Mr. K. himself, were answered with the most perfect accuracy. The spirit was asked to give the title of the work which he prepared for the press just before his death, Mr. K. knowing what it was. The entire title was given accordingly. " Now give," says Mr. K., " the first sentence of that work," the work being present, but Mr. K. having no recollection whatever what that sentence was. Several most abortive efforts were made to form a sentence; but nothing was expressed which at all corresponded to any part of the sentence referred to. Such facts leave no reasonable doubt upon the question of the origin of these manifestations.

IMPORTANT FACTS FURNISHED BY DR. BELL.

We now invite very special attention to some interest ing and important facts which have been kindly furnished us by Luther V. Bell, M. D., who is at the head of the McLean Lunatic Asylum of Somerville, near Boston. For the past two years, as Dr. B. informs us, he has, as far as his official duties permitted, carefully observed and studied the spirit phenomena, physical and intellectual, and that for two reasons — the interest which attaches to the phenomena themselves — but more especially from the fact, that not a few of the inmates of that institution were there through the influence of this one cause. The following may be stated, as among the more important results of his investigations. We make our citations from " two dissertations on what is termed the Spiritual Phenomena, read at the meetings of the Association of Medical Superintendents of American Insane Hospitals at Washington and Boston, in 1854 and 1855," dissertations, the manuscripts of which he has very kindly put into our hands, with the permission to make such extracts from them, as, in our judgment, the interests of science might seem to require. The following are the results of his observations, which were most carefully made through upwards of twenty sessions in the spirit circles.

1. They most fully sustain the claims of Spiritualism, as far as the mere fact of *physical manifestations* are concerned, namely, the movement of heavy bodies, both with and without physical contact, their movement, too, in accordance with intelligence. We will give a single case in illustration, a case related in the following extract from Dissertation II.

"The following is the minute of one of the physical manifestations. Went to the house of Jonathan Brown, Jr., Esq., cashier of the Market Bank, with Mr. Homer Goodhue, just returned from the South. Mr. Goodhue for twenty years was the supervisor of our male department, and well known in character, at least, to many members of this association. He is a gentleman of orthodox faith, and not free from the prejudices of that denomination against this new thing as a religious element. He never before had been present, or seen any manifestations. In fact, he had never seen a 'medium,' or attended a 'circle.' Mrs. Brown and a young woman, Mr. Brown's niece, made up the list of the five persons present. This 'medium' is exceedingly small, not weighing more than eighty to ninety pounds, and yet her gifts appear to be very great in effecting infractions of gravitation, but not certain or strong in the other classes of powers. We sat in the double parlors joined with folding doors, or rather, doors sliding on trucks along an iron rod projecting one half to three quarters inch above the level of the carpet. We began the operations by opening the family dining-table, and inserting two or three leaves, elongating it from about six to perhaps nine or more feet. I state this, as it allowed an eye to be kept, as to wires, etc. It had six legs, and was of such a weight, that when the castors were all in a right line for motion, I could with both my hands, and as strong a pull as my strength of fingers would allow, just put it in motion.

"After an evening's performance of all the usual responses, motions of the table with hands upon it, with the fingers' ends just touched, etc., which were satisfactory it was proposed, especially as the motions were unusually facile and free *with* contact, to make the trial *without* touch. I was master of ceremonies, and directed things to suit my own views. We stood on the sides of the table, three and two, and back from it from twelve to eighteen inches. Our hands were raised above it about the same distance. As the table was rather low and my height is unusual, I was able to see between the bodies of all present and the table. We spoke as if we were addressing persons in reality, and once in a while we received remarks from the 'spirits' as is assumed, the medium being 'impressed,' and writing on paper before her.

"The table commenced its journey down the room, keeping midway, reached the iron crossing at the sliding doors, surmounted it and passed on. One of us ran and pushed away a centre-table in the middle of the other parlor, intending to allow as long a journey as possible. It moved on, sometimes slowly, then with a rapid slide, a foot or two at once. At length it reached the end of the second parlor, as near as the mirror made it safe to go. I expressed my thanks to the 'spirits' for the completeness of the manifestation, and begged that they would gratify us by returning the table back to the point of beginning. It reversed its course. At a momentary halt, I suggested to the company that we should all gradually remove from it our bodies and hands, to see how far the 'influence' would extend. It was found that when we withdrew more than about eighteen or twenty inches, the motion ceased. And indeed on returning, the capacity of motion seemed to be lost for three or four minutes afterwards, as if a certain accumulation of power were in progress. When the fore legs of the table reached the iron bar, it came to a dead stand. We waited, and the table heaved and trembled and creaked, but could not rise above the obstacle. Presently the medium was impressed, and wrote, that if we would lift those two legs over the iron, they, that is 'the spirits,' thought they could bring the other four along. We did not hesitate to afford the suggested aid. Whereupon the spirits succeeded in moving the whole on, without interruption, until the table was as high up in the room from which it started as it was at commencing, but about four feet over from the central line at one side. I expressed my gratification at their success, but said, 'there is one thing more I wish you to do — move the table at right angles, so that these chairs will be right to sit in, as they were at first.' The table immediately moved at right angles as desired, into the precise position designated. This evening's performance now closed, no person of us having the remotest doubt as to the fact of this considerable motion having taken place with no human power. The entire space passed over was about fifty feet."

On this case we deem it important to make the following observations:—

(1.) Every circumstance which surrounds this case combines with every other, to remove it from the most distant suspicion of trick or fraud.

(2.) The fact of the movement of heavy bodies without visible contact is most fully established, and will not be questioned by any who have not fully made up their minds to blindly follow the maxim practically, at least, adopted by David Hume, that the occurrence of no strange event can be established by testimony.

(3.) Equally manifest is the fact, that this movement was immediately caused by an attractive and repulsive physical force developed in the organisms of the individuals present, and the object before them. We bring an object called the magnet within a certain distance of another object, a piece of iron, for example, and the latter object is drawn towards and after the former. We remove the object to a somewhat greater distance, and the phenomena of attraction disappear. It is thus that the existence of magnetism, as a force in nature, is demonstrated. How was it in the case before us? The table moved, when and only when the hands of the individuals referred to were within a certain distance of it, and ceased to move, when they were removed to a greater distance. We have, then, in these movements, the same evidence of the presence and action of an attractive and repulsive physical force, that we have, or can have, of the existence of magnetism, as such a force.

(4.) This force differs fundamentally from magnetism and electricity, and all other mere physical forces in nature, in this, that the *direction* of its action accords with acts of intelligence and will, and is determined by the same. How perfectly were all those movements conformed to the mental states of the individuals constituting that circle, and how perfectly manifest is it, that these movements were determined by the thoughts and wills of some minds within that circle, or without it. We can have but little, if any more, evidence, that our physical organisms act in accordance with our own mental states, and are directed, in many important particulars, by the same, than we have that these movements were directed and controlled by the mental states and acts of some intelligences located somewhere, either in the circle or out of it.

(5.) We have only to suppose the presence of a power having the very attractive, repulsive, and mentally directive qualities which we see that this must have, together with the known mental states of the individuals constituting this circle, to account most fully and satisfactorily for every fact that occurred there, and this without the supposition of any *ab extra* controlling cause whatever. When Dr. Bell said, let the spirits move the table so and so, the thoughts of every mind present were fixed intensely upon that one movement, and the unconscious, but really united and strong fiat of every will was, let that movement be made. Instead of its being a cause of wonder that the phenomena did appear under those circumstances, it would have been a miracle if they had not occurred. We have no more occasion to go out of the circle, and suppose the interposition of spirits to account for these facts, than we have to go out of our bodies, and suppose the interposition of spirits, to account for the movements of our own physical organisms.

(6.) Not a solitary ray of light is thrown upon any of

these facts, by referring them to the agency of disembodied spirits. If spirits did do it, it must have been, by simply willing the motions which the individuals constituting the circles wished to have made. Why should we suppose, that such power attaches to the mental states of the former, and not to those of the latter? If the mental states of spirits out of the circle have such power, much more must we suppose, that those of minds in the organisms in which this force is developed, would have the same efficiency. The supposition of the interposition of spirits, therefore, is the most uncalled for hypothesis conceivable, to account for these facts, an hypothesis which throws not a solitary ray of light upon one of them.

(7.) Hence we remark, finally, that there is not in these facts, and if not in these, in none of the physical facts of Spiritualism, the least conceivable evidence of the controlling interposition and agency of spirits. The fact that the spirits were requested to move the table, and that it did move accordingly, as if in answer to such request, presents no such evidence at all; for the two following reasons, that, as we have seen in other cases, the same movements would have occurred, had the object been commanded to move, and no reference at all made to spirits, or if the same command had been given and the spirits challenged to prevent the movement. No such interposition is demanded to account for any of the facts, and they are, in all respects, what we know they could not but be, from the nature of the force developed, and from the relations of the minds present to the same.

2. The facts developed by Dr. Bell fully sustain the claims of Spiritualism as far as concerns any questions pertaining to the real existence of a power to obtain,

through mediums, a revelation of our most secret thoughts, and to obtain also, as from spirits, correct answers to any questions pertaining to any subjects known to the inquirer and to the spirits professedly communicating with him, however remote such knowledge may be from the cognizance of the mediums, or of any other persons present. No candid person, we feel quite safe in making the affirmation, can read these dissertations, without having every doubt removed from his mind, on this subject. We will give two examples. The first is contained in the following extract from the first dissertation: —

"I asked, 'Is any spirit friend of mine present?' Answer, '*Yes.*' 'Who is it?' Answer, '*Any one you may choose to question.*' I certainly felt that this was a sufficiently broad latitude, and my mind instantly elected, as the object of my converse, a deceased brother, the late Dr. John Bell of New York city, because he was entirely unknown to anybody in the section where I resided, having been dead nearly five and twenty years, and never having been a resident of Massachusetts. In fact, he left New England about 1820. A gentleman at my elbow said to me, 'You need not speak the name of any friend you may call upon. Put your question mentally.' I did so, and then said, 'Is the spirit I have just thought of present?' Answer, '*Yes.*' 'Give me some proof by indicating the year of your decease.' I passed the pencil secretly over the numerals, and the figures 1–8–3–0 were successively indicated (1830). *This was the year.* I then remarked aloud, '*Coincidences are not proofs*, — Confirm the fact of your presence by stating the place at which you were, at your decease.' There was then rapped out on the alphabet the letters, t-h-i-b-a-u-d-e-a-u.

When it had proceeded thus far, the medium and all the others acquainted with the processes, exclaimed,— 'That is no word; it is a mere jumble of letters: Go back and recommence.' 'No,' said I, 'let him go on, and see what he will make of it.' The rapping continued,—v-i-l-l-e,—forming the word Thibaudeauville, a small town in Louisiana, near which my brother lived on a plantation, and at which he received and sent his letters. The fact of his death at or near that place, could not have been known, probably, to any other person in Massachusetts except myself, and years had passed by since it had passed through my mind. The medium was an uneducated young girl, living in the city of Boston, unknown to me; and the other parties present were three eminent clergymen, and the two gentlemen I have before referred to."

The next is taken from the second dissertation, and must stand for many other cases recorded, of equal pertinency.

"Recurring again to my own experience, I entered upon a series of six weekly examinations with the same medium and associates, whose names would be recognized as among the distinguished in literature and theology of this vicinity. Having already received evidence as I felt, (as detailed last year,) that I had obtained correct replies to mental questions, and that many things not possibly within the knowledge of any person present had been correctly given to me, I arranged my plans, 1st. To verify this in full, and ascertain whether there was any thing known to me and a deceased person *alone* which could be reproduced. 2d. Whether a correct reply could be got to any thing known, *ex necessitate rei*, to the spirit invoked, but not known to the questioner, as subsequent inquiry should demonstrate. I had, as I thought, a very complete test, to understand which I must go into a brief domestic narration. I had a brother, Dr. John Bell, (alluded to in my last year's experience,) who died in Louisiana in 1830. He was settled in New York city as a medical practitioner. He was seized with Hæmoptysis in 1824, and as the celebrated Laennec, whose pupil he was, had some years previously diagnosed pulmonary disease, his case was regarded as highly critical. Abandoning at once the brightest prospects of professional success, he decided to go to the South on horseback. Mounting his animal, he first made a farewell visit to his friends in New England. I was at the time of his visit here, attending lectures at a country college, but learning that he would be in Boston about a certain date, I proceeded to that city. Arriving late at night, I could make no attempts to find him, but early the next morning, I set out to visit the various hotels, which were much crowded at that season, to meet with him. I succeeded in finding his name at what was known as the 'City Hotel.' On inquiring, I found that he had just settled his bill, and probably would be found about starting. I passed into the shed connecting the hotel and its stables, and there found him arranging his horse's stirrups, etc., preparatory to mounting to take his departure. I there had what I, and probably he, felt to be our last interview, and which in fact so proved, although his health was partially recovered, and he lived several years afterwards. This interview had always been very clearly recollected, and as I never had communicated it to any person, I had often remarked to my 'spiritual' friends, that if any medium could reproduce that occasion in its essentials, I would admit that the spirit of my brother was present; indeed I must do so, because I could see no alternative. I may as well remark here, that I was too hasty in my logic, in proffering such admissions. At the first or second of the series of investigations, I was informed that the spirit of my brother would communicate. I took occasion to question him pretty thoroughly on such points as I thought none could know except myself or other immediate friends. I think the nature of the questions will leave no room for the suspicion that the medium, who was an entire stranger to us, and born since the events referred to, could have been 'crammed' into an ability to answer correctly. I will give the questions and answers, observing that every one except the last, [given in another connection,] was perfectly correct and true.

" *Q.* When you went to Paris, as a medical student, who was your fellow passenger? *A. Wells.* N. B. I had previously requested, as the communications were to be in the tedious alphabetical process, that he should reply in the briefest terms. A gentleman asked his Christian name. *A. John D.* *Q.* The name of the vessel? *A. Brig Caravan.* *Q.* On that voyage to France, where did you land? *A. In Holland.* N. B. At that date (1821) there was no direct French trade, and passengers were obliged to take circuitous passages. *Q.* You once obtained a medical prize: what was the subject? *A. Smallpox.* *Q.* Where was our last interview in life? *A. In Boston.* *Q.* Where in Boston? *A. City Hotel.* *Q.* What were you doing? *A. Preparing to mount my horse for a journey.* *Q.* A journey! where? *A. To the South.* *Q.* What part of the South? *A. Natchez.* *Q.* Who went with you? *A. James Dinsmore and Stephen Minor.*

" This Stephen Minor was a young gentleman of Natchez who had been sent north for an education, had become insane, and had been a resident for some years at the late Dr. Chaplin's private insane retreat at Cambridgeport. His friends took the opportunity of their going to Natchez to procure his return home. Mr. Dinsmore was a cousin of my brother's who remained with him at the South as long as he lived. I might observe that I am not conscious of this young man, Stephen Minor, having been in my memory for five and twenty years!"

We leave these cases to speak for themselves. Any persons, that in their presence, would deny the existence of the power under consideration, would not be convinced by any facts or arguments bearing upon this subject.

3. The facts adduced by Dr. Bell, while they most fully sustain his and our conclusion, that no valid evidence exists of a connection between the extraordinary facts of this new science and another world, or with departed spirits, the same facts as fully sustain the truth of our present proposition, the exclusively subjective and mundane origin of these manifestations. Two hypotheses are before us pertaining to the origin and controlling cause of these manifestations — the supposition that the action of this force is controlled, in their production, by the mental states of the minds in these circles — and that it is controlled by those of spirits out of the same. Suppose that we find these communications bounded wholly by the range and limits of the former, and not by those of the latter, being generally correct where the former is, erring where they err, even when the spirits cannot but know the truth; blundering where they blunder, varying as they vary, moving when and as they move, and stopping where and when they stop. In this case, all the laws and principles of science and

common sense require us to affirm the truth of the first hypothesis. If, on the other hand, we find these communications uniformly harmonizing with facts as they are when they are mutually known to the inquirer and the spirits professedly answering; that when he errs, they accord with the facts as known to the spirits, and that when he is wholly ignorant, and the spirits are known to be well informed, the real facts, and not incorrect answers, are uniformly given, then we should be bound to adopt the latter hypothesis. We have already shown, that the phenomena of Spiritualism are just what they would be, were the former hypothesis true, and just what they could not be, if the latter was true. This conclusion is most fully sustained by the facts adduced by Dr. Bell.

He affirms, in the first place, that during all his observations and experiments, neither himself, nor any individuals associated with him, were able to obtain, in a single instance, correct answers to any questions pertaining to subjects lying beyond the circle of their knowledge, and this when the questions pertained to facts of which the spirits manifestly answering, if any were, must have been fully informed, and could not have forgotten, or to subjects of which they might or might not, but positively affirmed themselves to have been well informed, and that in connection with cases where the most surprising accuracy was preserved in statements, where the truth was known to the inquirer. Take the following as an example. The spirit of an only sister of the Dr., who "had died and was buried in St. Augustine, East Florida, in 1830, and was a total stranger in this vicinity," responded on one occasion, and after having stated the place of her decease and burial, the following facts occurred.

"I then asked, 'with whom did you board when at St. Augustine?' *Mr. Wallen.* True. 'What physician attended you?' Dr. *Samuel Anderson.* The fact was, his name was Andrew. 'Who performed your funeral services?' *Mr. Nott.* 'What was his other name?' *Handel.* Now the fact was, that among the many visitors for health at that city, was a New England clergyman of that name, who actually performed these services. These facts could be known to no other person but myself. I thought of them at the time, as the questions were put. I may remark, however, that I knew Dr. Anderson's Christian name, *as well as I did my own.* These were but a few of the many questions of a domestic nature which I put, and which were all answered correctly, the responses being *all* known to me.

"I also made a series of inquiries, predicated on a previous arrangement with the family at home, by which every quarter of an hour they were to do some act, and I was simultaneously to ask what was doing. In every case, the spirit declared it saw distinctly what was doing, and gave a ready response. What was done, and what was said to be done, were acts of the same general nature, that is, putting the match in the bed, upsetting furniture, etc., but in no example was there any near coincidence."

In cases also where a mistake existed in his mind, and the real facts were known to the spirit professedly answering, the answers, as in cases which we have already adduced, corresponded with the mistake of the inquirer, and not with the knowledge of the spirit. At the same time, while a spirit would be wholly unable to answer, while the facts remained unknown to the inquirer, a right answer would be given at once, as soon as he became informed. The following extract, the first part of which contains the remainder of the long communication which Dr. B. held as with the spirit of his brother, and the other part other important facts developed in subsequent interviews, presents a full verification of each of the above statements.

" *Q.* Who was with you at the time of your death? *A.* Dinsmoor, Sears, Whitney.

" Now I knew the true replies to every one of these questions, except the last, and they were all truly given. I had, of course, some anxiety, as all the others had been answered truly, to ascertain how the unknown one would prove. Fortunately Mr. D. was still alive in Kentucky, and I wrote him. He replied that he was *not* present at the death, as I had always *supposed* he was, and mentioned the persons who were. Neither of them was of those named!

" At another time, with another medium, this same brother appeared. As usual, he replied to all common questions I could frame, by any ingenuity, the replies of which were within my mind. After a while I said, 'my brother, I have brought here two letters which, on leaving home, I slipped out of a file of old date, and put in my pocket without looking at them. Now as you have answered certain things here (alluding to a selection of certain rolled up pieces of paper) which show that if you really are present, you are capable of *seeing* clearly, I will unfold these letters behind me, and you will rap out alphabetically the names of the writers.' He replied that he could not do it.

" I made trial again of this important test some weeks after, by holding letters open behind me, which I had drawn from my file unlooked at. I first asked the spirit if he saw me 'clearly and distinctly,' as we saw each other, face to face. He replied that he did. I then said, 'of course you can see and read this letter, or its signature, which I hold open behind me.' Some reply was made, a mere subterfuge, not *ad rem;* something about things being afterwards clear to me. I then cast my eye upon the signature, and saw who wrote the letter, and then remarked that I was now sure that we should get the name correctly, *because it was in my own mind.* The result proved the truth of my surmise."

On a particular occasion, — we now relate what was given to us verbally, — the spirit of a son of Dr. B., a son who had died some time before while a student in college, responded to a young man, a former associate and friend of the son. A very marked accuracy of memory, as far as related to things known to the inquirer, characterized the entire answers coming from this spirit, so much so, that the young man supposed that a mistake in regard to real presence and identity was hardly possible, and so presented the subject to Dr. B. The father then wrote out twelve questions pertaining to facts well known to himself and son, but wholly unknown to the young man, and requested the latter to take the questions with him to the circle, and when the spirit of the son should appear again, ask him to answer the same. This was done, and a prompt and unqualified response was given to each question. Not one of these answers was found to be correct, while the form of each was such as to render it certain, that it was a mere guess suggested by the question itself, thus evincing the truth of the principle above stated, that in all such cases, the answers will not only uniformly, if not invariably be wrong, but will accord with the imaginings and guesses of the person putting them, and not with the facts as known to the author of them, and to the spirit professedly responding.

Such are the principles which control these manifestations, the world over. The individuals who, in their presence, will still hold on to the belief, that their controlling cause is the mental states of spirits out of the circles, instead of the minds constituting them, we must "leave them alone in their glory."

THE STATEMENTS OF DR. BELL CONFIRMED BY KINDRED ONES FROM N. I. BOWDITCH, ESQ.

In the manuscript volume containing the above-named dissertations, is a letter from N. I. Bowditch, Esq., addressed to Dr. Bell, on the subject discussed in those dissertations. From this letter we take, with leave, the following extract, containing very conclusive corroborations of the general and particular statements of Dr. B. The character and standing of Mr. Bowditch, together with his well-known relations to spiritualism, will add much interest and weight to his facts and statements.

"I have found my most successful sessions to be those where I was alone with the medium, or attended only by one friend. During the whole two hours I have had often entirely accurate answers to a series of mental questions, some of them such that the answer could not be known to any other human being than myself. For instance, I wrote certain lines as from a young girl, lately dead, to her father, describing her reunion with her deceased mother, the love they both bore him, etc. The answers gave the character of the paper, the number of its lines, and, at my request, accurately repeated the last lines of the last stanza, namely, —

'And while thy years of life shall last,
Life's noblest ends still keep in view,
By each dear memory of the past,
To us, thyself, thy God, be true'"

"I am satisfied, as you are, that the answers are according to our *thought* or *belief*, even if erroneous. On two different occasions, once when I was in communication, a spirit gave its *own* name as William instead of Thomas, *because I thought it was William.* And, at another time, when a *friend* was in communication, a wife made the same mistake in her *husband's* name. My friend announced the mistake, as a gross failure. I suggested this disturbing influence, and shut up my eyes, while he tried the question again, and got the true name, Thomas.

"A strong and determined *will* can also get answers known to be *false.* Dr. H. T. Bigelow went with me to Mrs. Heyden (while we used pencils). The letters touched by him would be negatived, (by single raps,) some of them five or six different times; but after knocking at a particular letter over and over again, *three* raps would at last come. Having once come, Dr. B. would say, Are you sure that this is the right letter? — *three raps, or yes.* In this way he *compelled* the spirit to say that its name was 'Miserable Humbug' — that spirits lived on 'Pork and Beans,' etc., through a series of absurdities. Had I never been present at any other session, I should unhesitatingly have arrived at his conclusion; namely, that the medium knew (by his loud and emphatic pointing and striking at particular letters) where the raps were wanted, and *made them accordingly;* and that it was all a delusion.

"Like you I have failed, in a single case, to *verify* as true a fact stated which at the time *was not in my own mind.* On the contrary, time and time again, answers have been made, without any words of doubt or hesitation, which have proved to be *false.* Some-

19*

times, however, there has been a candid statement of *inability to answer*. I had asked mentally the number of my watch. It was given correctly, 5,763. Mr. S. G. Ward was present, and said aloud, 'Can you give the number of my watch?' Neither of us knew it. I repeated the question, and got, No. I said, 'Why?' The alphabet spelt out, '*I cannot do it.*' I said, 'If W. shows it to me, can you then repeat it?' 'Yes.' Mr. W. opened his watch under the table and showed me the number, and I at once got the true answer. *Excuses* are sometimes made for palpable blunders. Thus the same young friend (dead only ten days before) gave Nathaniel Bowditch Mason instead of Alfred Mason, as the name of a young cousin who had died a few years before. *The true name was known to me.* I asked, 'How could you make such a mistake of name?' It was a mental question. The answer was, 'The fact is, I am so much absorbed in my new and beautiful home that *I have almost forgotten my own name.*'"

We make but two remarks upon the important facts and statements here presented: —

(1.) The particular conclusion which the friend of Mr. B. drew from the ludicrous facts which he witnessed, was occasioned by the assumption, on his part, that those responses were produced by spirits, or by imposition on the part of the medium. Had the third hypothesis been in his mind, he would undoubtedly, if well informed in regard to facts, have drawn the far more evident conclusion, that the action of this force was, in this case, governed by his own mental states, the supposition that such answers could come from spirits, good or bad, being out of the question.

(2.) The fact that such men as Dr. Bell and Esq Bowditch, in all the widely extended investigations which they have made, have never "been able, in a single case, to verify as true a fact stated, which was not in their mind at the time," goes very far to justify the very common opinion, that no such revelations are ever obtained in these circles. For ourselves, we have yet, to our best recollections, to meet with the first individual, not a spiritualist, who has himself obtained any such communication, or witnessed its occurrence, on the part of others. We still think, however, that such communications have, in instances exceedingly rare, been obtained, and that for the following reasons: —

(a.) The evidence presented in such facts as are now before us, only render the non-occurrence of such communications probable, and not certain.

(b.) We think that adequate evidence of their real occurrence, in the form stated, is before the public.

(c.) From the analogy of facts attending the action of this force, in other relations, there *ought* to occur just such facts as are authentically reported to occur, in these circles, supposing no agency of spirits is ever exerted in them, and they ought to have the identical characteristics, and none others, that they do possess. For ourselves, we are rather embarrassed in the development of our theory, with the infrequency of such occurrences, than with the real facts themselves, or with any of their characteristics.

Mr. B. says, "I have found my most successful sessions to be those when I was alone with the medium, or attended only by one friend." The reason is obvious. There were, in such cases, no other minds present, minds whose mental states would disturb the action of the odylic force, and whose thoughts would be, consequently, unconsciously intermingled with those of the inquirer. This fact strikingly corroborates the theory which we maintain. If spirits out of the body controlled the action of this force, it would make no difference how many living persons were in the circle.

IMPORTANT FACTS FURNISHED BY A NEW ENGLAND CONGREGATIONAL CLERGYMAN.

The last case which we cite was furnished us by a New England Congregational clergyman of unquestionable integrity and intelligence, (names are withheld by special request,) and presents so many interesting features bearing fundamentally upon our present inquiries, that we would invite very special attention to it. It presents a number of facts which he witnessed in a circle of which, by mere accident, he became a member, he having in the course of a walk for a totally different object, called at the house of a friend whose daughter was one of his former pupils in an academy of which he had been for several years the principal, and was, as he learned, after he entered the house, a medium. A spirit circle was accordingly formed, consisting of the teacher, the father, mother, and daughter, the gentlemen sitting on one side of the table, and the ladies on the other. The following are the prominent facts developed during this sitting which continued upwards of four hours: —

(1.) The same evidence of presence and identity, the same ability to read correctly our secret thoughts, to reveal names, and ages, and any events of the past as they one and all stood in the mind of the inquirer, was manifested by the spirit of brutes, and even of inanimate objects, as are, in any instances, manifested by the spirits of men. It was found, also, that the great central wonder of Spiritualism, one spirit going after an absent one and returning with him at a specified time agreed upon, could be perfectly paralleled by the spirit of the brute. The spirit of a certain animal, for example, was asked, if he could go and bring that of another that was named? and answered, yes. He was told to do it, and be back again in just one and a half minutes by the watch. The instant the hand of the watch came over the right second, there was a rap to indicate the arrival of the spirit sent for. After affirming his actual presence, he was asked, as proof of his identity, to give his age. The precise number, nineteen, existing in the mind of the inquirer, was promptly given by raps. It was subsequently found, that there was a mistake of several years in the answer given, thus most fully evincing the fact, that the spirit of the brute fails precisely where and as that of man does.

(2.) This clergyman, by observations and experiments about which there could be no mistake, found that he could exercise an absolute control over the action of this power in the medium. When, for example, she would attempt to write, she being a writing as well as rapping medium, he could, by simply willing it, while no one had the least suspicion of what he was doing, stop her hand entirely, cause it to move up and down, so that the pencil should make nothing but dots on the paper, and then cause her to go on with the writing as before.

(3.) He also obtained the most palpable and conclusive evidence, that the medium was in a mesmeric state, that the other persons present sustained the precise relations to her, that the mesmerizer does to the person mesmerized. For example, having occasion to reach his hand across the table to a letter of the alphabet, as his hand came near that of the medium, hers was instantly forcibly attracted towards his, so that the end of the pencil in her hand struck his with such violence as to leave a mark there, and to occasion some pain at the time. Recollecting that this was the first rude act that he had ever witnessed in her, he was led to look into her eyes and immediately discovered, from her appearance, that she was in a magnetic state. To verify that thought, he said to her, "your hand is fastened to the top of the table, and you can't take it off." The medium made every possible effort to withdraw her hand, but found it impossible to move it. "Now," says the minister, "your left hand must come up and be fastened by the side of the other." The medium declared, with the intensest excitement, that it should not be so. The hand, however, gradually came up, and when it came over the top of the table, descended upon it, as if suddenly drawn down by a resistless attractive force. By no effort could she move either hand, till, by an act of will, he released her. By subsequent experiments, he found that her entire powers, mental and physical, were under his absolute control. Without any external sign whatever, for example, he simply willed, that she should turn round, and fix her eyes upon a picture that hung upon the wall of the room. Instantly she turned round and fixed her eyes upon the object referred to. He then willed, that she should look steadfastly at an object in the hands of her mother, and her eyes were instantly fixed in that direction. When asked why she looked at those objects, her answer was, that, at that time, she wanted to do it. He then merely willed that she should leave her chair and seat herself upon the sofa, and she did so. At one time, he made her weep at the thought that she had disobeyed her mother, nothing of the kind having occurred, and at another, made her think, that her own father was a rude and vulgar boy which she had before seen. As a last experiment, he wished to know, whether he could induce in her a mental perception of an object of which he had a remembrance, but which was unlike any thing of which she had any knowledge. He recollected having seen, in Virginia, years before, a cedar tree about twenty feet high, a tree the boughs of which were in a conical form, from near the ground to the top. The body of the tree was encircled by a trumpet vine, the blossoms of which, then in full bloom, completely covered it in all directions, just standing out in the midst of its foliage. All together it was the most beautiful object that he had ever seen in the vegetable kingdom before. He consequently stopped for some time to look at and admire it. The medium, as he well knew, had never in her life seen a cedar tree of that species, nor such a vine, and especially the two combined as in this instance. Nor had she ever heard of his having seen such an object. He wished to know whether he could induce in her, and that without uttering a syllable himself about the object in his own mind, a mental perception of that object. He accordingly put a book into her hand, requesting her to look into that mirror, and tell him what she saw. The book immediately became a mirror to her, and after looking into it a few moments, she exclaimed with the intensest delight; "I never saw so beautiful an object in my life. It is a tree; I never saw such a tree. It looks somewhat like a hemlock, and it is covered all over with beautiful flowers. They are shaped like a trumpet, and they are of an orange color. I never saw so beautiful an object in my life." Thus, he said, she described that before to her totally unknown and unheard of object, as distinctly as he could have done himself, so perfectly was his own purely mental conception reproduced in her mind, and that without a motion on his part to afford the remotest indication of the particular object of which he was thinking.*

The reader will not be surprised to learn, that through these important and fundamental facts, the mysteries of Spiritualism stood distinctly revealed to the mind of this individual, and that from that time onward, he has had the most unwavering conviction, that the medium after all, is none other than a magnetic subject in whom the thoughts of those in the circles are, upon principles and laws purely natural, unconsciously reproduced, and for that reason, received as responses from spirits out of the circles. There is not a solitary phenomenon of Spiritualism which does not fall in with this view, and when rightly apprehended, does not affirm its truth. On the same principle, that the medium's hand was so powerfully attracted towards that of her teacher, the table itself, or any other object between which and her organism, the same force was developed in the same manner, would have followed her all round the room. Or, if it was developed between them, in different polarity, then it would have fled from her in apparent terror, running violently against certain objects, and from others. If the same force, as in some instances, was developed in still greater power, then there would have been a sensible jarring of surrounding objects, and rumbling sounds, as of distant thunder, or the far-off firing of ordnance. The medium was undeniably, at the same time that she was a writing and rapping medium, in a clairvoyant state. Suppose, that like the mesmeric

* Since writing the above, we have read the same to the individual from whom the facts were derived, and he indorses the whole as unqualifiedly correct.

subject of J. M. Brook, Esq., she had also, as might have been the case, possessed the power of *independent clairvoyance* which that subject possessed. Then, while the thoughts of those who were present were reproduced in her, and embodied, as spirit voices in her communications, there would have been mingled with these the revelation of certain facts perceived by her, on purely natural principles, at the moment, facts unknown to any present, and all together presented, as from spirits. Thus we have the *new information* which is sometimes obtained in these circles,—revelations none of which present the least indication of the presence and agency of spirits, but all of which are perfectly explicable upon purely natural principles.

A passing remark is deemed requisite, in this connection, upon a fact noticed by Dr. Bell and others, as peculiarizing these revelations, the fact, that the *thought*, and not the *language* of the inquirer is commonly embodied in them. In general it is, as in the mental perception of the tree above presented, the thought only that is reproduced in the medium's mind. Sometimes, but not generally, both the thought and language are reproduced. This accords with the statements of spiritualists themselves. They affirm, that as a general thing, it is only the thought of the spirit which is uttered, (they supposing the revelation to be from spirits), the language in which it is clothed being that of the medium.

11. We now call attention to a certain class of *false answers* which are continuously given forth in these circles. Of the false answers in general here obtained, we will speak in another place. We now refer to a particular class only, a class to which we have already alluded, namely, the continuous occurrence of false

answers to questions pertaining to subjects well known both to inquirers and to the spirits professedly communicating, and in respect to which a failure of memory, or inadvertent mistake on the part of spirits, is not supposable. The following statement of Dr. Bell, is but the embodiment of the constant experience and observation of every one, as far as our knowledge extends, who has had any considerable personal experience in the spirit circles: —

"The 'spirits' of your friends, while they announce to you many most extraordinary facts and truths, even in reply to unspoken questions, fail in many others, where you cannot yield them the charity of having forgotten, or being in ignorance. I do not now allude to the silly tests which many very sagacious persons have put, such as complex questions in mathematics, or in far-off dialects, as if spirits were presumed to be omniscient, or in relation to future events, as if they had the gift of foreknowledge! I mean that when you test your deceased relatives, while they are most free in expressing advice, etc., to you, — with such simple questions as involve a recognition of the most marked events of your mutual knowledge, they constantly fail."

Now we affirm that such facts cannot be accounted for, in accordance with any laws of mind known to us, on the supposition that these communications proceed from intelligent beings, good or bad, who are holding intelligent communication with us, and who know whereof they affirm. Much less can they be accounted for, on the supposition, that they come from the particular class of departed spirits from whom they professedly proceed. No such facts characterize any forms of intercourse between any class of minds in the body. We know very well, that the worst liars on earth do not thus falsify. Much less did our venerated parents, when with us in the flesh, as their assumed spirits now do, continuously falsify in regard to subjects well known to us and to them, and when they well knew that the falsehood must be at once detected. Never did such answers come to us from them, when they were with us. How then can we suppose, that such answers proceed from their spirits, when they come to visit and communicate with us, from their "angel's home?" It is impossible to account for such communications, even on the supposition that these communications generally are from fallen spirits. Devils even would not thus falsify.

On the other hand, if these communications are the unconscious echoes of our own thoughts, they could not but have these very characteristics. We ask a question, for example, and then before the answer is given, turn our thoughts in some other direction. If the responses follow the current of our thinking at the moment, and are determined by the same, then a wrong answer will be obtained of course, and just the kind of answer that is obtained.

It is upon this one supposition, only, that we can, by any possibility, account for the facts before us. A brother, as we have stated in another connection, asks the spirit of a sister to give the name of their father, which is John, for example, and before the answer comes, his thoughts happen, by the laws of association, to be turned upon that of their brother, which is Thomas. If the answer is determined by the thought in the inquirer's mind, at the moment, then Thomas, the name of the brother, and not John, that of the father, will be given, of course. This is the precise character of the false answers continuously given forth as by the spirits in these circles. We say that such facts cannot be accounted for, but upon the supposition, that these communications proceed not from spirits, but that they are the unconscious product of the wandering thoughts of the inquirers themselves. We are perfectly certain, that spiritualists will never account for the facts before us, in accordance with their theory.

12. We now refer to a class of experiments which individuals have made for the purpose of determining, not only the location of this cause, but of ascertaining the *kind* and *extent* of control they could exercise over it. It is well known that no spirits, good or bad, will voluntarily render themselves the objects of the contempt and ridicule of those over whom they desire to retain a controlling influence, as the spirits undeniably do over the minds of men in this world. Yet we find, among these communications, numberless responses obtained for the express purpose of determining, in the first instance, how far they can be controlled, and, in the next, of rendering the whole subject ridiculous. If spirits also respond to inquiries drawing forth such responses, they must do it with a perfect knowledge of the designs of the inquirers, and of the tendency of the answers given to their questions. By no laws of mind can we account for responses given to questions which are put for such a purpose, and when the answers must be known to be adapted, most perfectly so, to secure the intended result and none other. Let us consider a few facts of this class, examples of which are everywhere occurring in these circles. The case of the gentleman in Boston, to whom the spirit communicating revealed himself under the name, Miserable Humbug, and affirmed that spirits in the celestial spheres live on pork and beans, and all this in accordance with a previous determination in the inquirer's

mind, is already before our readers, and is a case now in point. Let us consider another case of a similar character. When Mrs. Fish was in the State of Ohio, she visited the village of Hamilton for the purpose of multiplying disciples, not to hint a pecuniary motive. Her success, for a time, was wonderful, all who entered the circles being convinced. At length, some ten individuals agreed together to determine, by an experiment, what answers could be obtained from the spirits. They accordingly framed their questions and answers beforehand, and agreed upon a mode of questioning, which would not awaken the suspicions of the medium. The departed spirit which responded to the first inquirer, gave his name as "the devil," affirmed himself to have been dead for two years, and to sustain to the inquirer the relation of uncle. The departed spirit which responded to the next inquirer, was that of our informant, who was then in the circle. This spirit had been dead for six months, and died of hydrophobia. By this time, some of the circle found it impossible to restrain their laughter, when Mrs. Fish remarked, that the spirits were probably lying to the inquirers. On being informed of what had transpired, the circle was broken up; and the next morning she left the place. Who can believe, that if intelligent minds stood behind this power, and directed its action, they would suffer themselves to be thus trifled with, and would lend their own voluntary agency to render themselves the objects of deserved contempt and ridicule? Yet "the spirits," in any circle on earth, will as readily respond to such questions as to any others, and will become, when the inquirer wills it, and has presence of mind and self-command sufficient to carry out his purposes, the agents of their own infamy or contempt. No limits can be set to the extent to which this power can be used for such purposes. Now, we say, that depravity itself never assumes such forms, and by no laws of mind can we account for such communications coming from disembodied spirits, either good or bad. If, on the other hand, our theory is true, nothing else could be expected. Just such phenomena, in that case, would appear, and in the very form in which they now present themselves, and upon no other hypothesis can such facts which, in legion forms, everywhere present themselves in these circles, be explained.

Since the child, in the family to which we have referred, became a medium, and since the communication from the spirit of a living person, supposed by them at the time to be dead, was obtained, the members of the family have been accustomed to amuse themselves by seeing what absurd communications they can obtain, as illustrations of the absolute control which they can exert over this mysterious power. The following may be stated as the results of their experiments and observations, and we have had an opportunity to converse with the family every week, since these phenomena appeared, which was at or near the commencement of the present year. (1.) Any spirits will answer that they choose to call up. (2.) Any answers can be obtained from any spirits, that they will mentally conceive of, and choose to have rapped or written out. (3.) They now obtain, as a general fact, absurd and ridiculous answers, answers indorsed by odd names, because they choose to have such and no others, the answers and names always according with their previous choice. (4.) Nothing is, or can be more manifest to their minds, than the fact, that they themselves, and not spirits out of the body, control this force, in all the answers which they obtain.

(5.) That control has remained just as absolute, since they came to this conviction, as before; since they have utterly repudiated the doctrine of Spiritualism, as when they were sincerely inquiring whether it was true or not. A daughter of ours, when present on one occasion, without having said any thing at all, while the force was being developed, willed secretly, for the very purpose of illustrating to her own mind the fact, that persons in the circles and not spirits out of it, are the real causes of these manifestations, that her own name should be written out by the medium. Her name came out accordingly, the moment his hand was moved. We repeat, that it is wholly unaccountable that spirits either good or bad should lend their own agency, not only to render themselves ridiculous, but to disprove their own agency, in phenomena which, if Spiritualism is true, they wish to have all the world understand, they alone can produce.

13. We now invite very special attention to the testimony and experience of intelligent persons who have themselves been mediums. Facts derived from this source must be regarded as most decisive in their bearings, because such persons have had the best opportunities for examination; and when they have come to the full conclusion, that phenomena presented through them, are produced by exclusively mundane causes, their opinions and statements must be deserving of the greatest consideration. Among the cases falling under this class, we notice the following:—

We are well acquainted with a very intelligent gentleman, for example, through whom, when the proper conditions are fulfilled, all the phenomena of the spirit rappings can at any time be obtained. He says that he has no conception, that these phenomena are connected at all with any *ab extra* spirit agency, and that for this reason, that when it is known what answer should be given to any question proposed, the true answer will uniformly be given, and when this is not known, the answer will be right or wrong, just as it happens. These are the uniform characteristics of these communications everywhere. If the inquirer or medium knows what the answer should be, it will be generally right. In all other cases, it has the characteristics of the most uncertain guessing. What facts can with certainty identify any communications as being wholly earthly, and not at all *ab extra* spiritual in their origin, if these do not?

We met recently a very intelligent lady who had been a medium, and who had presented such communications as to convince an aged atheist among others, of the reality of spiritual existences. To us she remarked, that when she first became subject to these influences, she had no doubt whatever of their *ab extra* spiritual origin, so unconscious was she of any agency of her own in their production. But when she narrowly watched her own mental operations, and marked the perfect and regular correspondence between these phenomena and her own prior mental states, she was led to doubt the whole system of Spiritualism altogether. If all mediums were thus self-reflective, and thus honest, they would all, we venture to affirm, come to the same conclusion.

A scientific physician in the State of Michigan, who has, for a long period, been a writing medium, has, after similar observations and experiments, come to the same conclusion. There is a mystery about the subject, as he stated to our informant, President Fairfield of the Freewill Baptist College in that State, which he has never been able to explain. Yet the facts taken together, precluded wholly the idea of their spirit origin. They are too puerile, too self-contradictory, and lawless in their character to admit of any such supposition.

The following case we cite from Rogers's Philosophy of Mysterious Rappings. On many accounts it possesses much interest: —

"Now take the following case, the like of which we have seen in several other instances: Jane A. D., daughter of a physician, had become a 'writing and tipping medium,' and could obtain slight responses by the sounds. She believed herself to be a 'medium' for communications from a deceased cousin, who, with herself, had been passionately fond of poetry. Jane carried on these communications by herself for some time, for her own satisfaction, but mostly as a writing medium. She had not, after some few of the first communications, the slightest doubt of the reality of all this being the work of a pure spirit, until the following circumstance took place. A communication was made of a beautiful stanza of poetry, from what purported to be the spirit of her young friend, and was declared as original. Jane was so much delighted with the remarkable circumstance, and with the perfect sweetness of the lines, that she took them to her father and related the circumstances. He saw that the style of handwriting was that of his daughter's late friend, and was greatly amazed at the mystery. The fact of the identity of the handwriting was not, indeed, to be questioned; and since he knew his daughter to be truthful every way, he determined to examine into the wonderful phenomena. The following evening was, therefore, spent in experiments and conversation upon the subject. Every thing was, however, to be kept profoundly secret in the family, as there was so much said in derision of the 'rappers.' 'That night,' says Jane, 'while I was dwelling on those beautiful lines, and my heart was swelling with joy, that my own dear parents had become interested in the phenomena, it flashed across my mind that I had either heard or read the same lines before, *somewhere*. But I did not wish to think so, and yet I desired to know the truth. It, at last, appeared to me, fresh in my memory, the very place where and when, I had read it. It was while alone and lonely, just after the setting of a beautiful September sun, and the lines were from that sweet poem of Longfellow, 'The Footsteps of Angels.'

'Uttered not, yet comprehended,
Is the spirit's voiceless prayer,
Soft rebuke, in blessings ended,
Breathing from her lips of air.'"

No one can wonder, that the confidence of this medium and that of her friends, in the doctrine of Spiritualism, was utterly shaken by such an occurrence. This communication was, undeniably, exclusively mundane in its origin, and yet it bore upon its face, all the evidence of an exclusively spirit origin that any other does, or can do. It came *as* from a spirit. It was positively affirmed by that spirit whose integrity could not be doubted, to have been original, and it was given in the *handwriting*, not of the medium, but of the individual whose spirit professedly originated it, and directed the hand that wrote it. The medium, too, had no consciousness, at the time, that any thought preexisting in her own mind, had any thing to do with the subject. This single case, therefore, utterly annihilates the highest evidence ever adduced by spiritualists in proof of the spirit origin of these manifestations; for it embodies the most fundamental facts which they ever do adduce for this end. At the same time, it presents the most conclusive proof of the truth of the opposite theory, that which we maintain as the only true one.

A few weeks since, we met with an intelligent clergyman, one to whom we have already referred in another connection, of the Episcopal Church, who has, for some years, had the phenomena of table-moving and other spirit manifestations in his own family, himself, wife, and daughter, together being mediums. When these phenomena first appeared in his family, he sincerely believed in their real spirit origin, and supposed that they could be reduced to scientific principles. After the most careful and extensive experiments and observations, however, he had come to precisely the opposite conclusion. In questioning any spirit, for example, some responses appear to indicate his actual presence. Others which arise in the same connection, however, utterly preclude such a supposition, the supposition, too, that they do or can come from any intelligent minds out of the body, the communications, from whatever minds apparently proceeding, being often so utterly puerile, self-contradictory, and lawless in their character. If there is in nature, he remarked, a nerve fluid whose action accords with our mental states, and commonly with the ordinary random thoughts which run off from the surface of the mind, and these manifestations are the result of such action, they would, in that case, be just what I have found them to be. Now we affirm, without fear of contradiction, that a more striking and accurate description of the character of these manifestations, can, by no possibility, be given, and this is most manifestly their real cause. The facts preclude any other supposition.

Of a precisely similar character and bearing is the following fact, which we find in the North American Review. "We are confirmed in our belief of the subjective character of these phenomena by a conversation with a highly respectable clergyman, who a few years ago, to his own surprise found himself a writing medium, and was, for many months, in the frequent habit of writing under this singular influence, without premeditation, often without knowing what he was inditing, or whose name he was going to sign. He at first fell into the popular notion, but became gradually convinced, by the incongruity and absurdity of much he wrote, and by the dreamlike character of the whole, that he had been putting upon paper, not the behests of unseen spirits, but the results of some unexplained mode of his own consciousness."

We adduce but one additional fact connected with the class under consideration. A venerable lady, Mrs. C., of the Society of Friends, in Rhode Island, herself a medium, and who had, for a long time, been a most devoted spiritualist, requested Hon. Mr. B., a member of Congress, whose wife, the sister of Mrs. C., had died some time before, to sit with her at a table, and receive communications from the spirit of their departed friend and endeared relation. Mr. B., though an unbeliever in Spiritualism, of course, complied with the request, and for an hour or two, held a very interesting conversation apparently with the spirit referred to. At length Mr. B. asked the following question: "What did you do with those letters which passed between us before our marriage, letters which I committed to your care some eight or ten years ago, and you promised to preserve? I have searched for those letters in every place where I can even imagine them to be, and have not been able to find them. What did you do with them?" "I burned them," was the reply received. "Why did you do that?" "I thought that no good would come from preserving them," was the reply, "and therefore burned them. And now, as I assure you, that I love you as truly and ardently as I did, when with you in the body, you will not regret that I burned those letters." Subsequently those letters were found carefully preserved, as promised. The faith of Mrs. C. in Spiritualism itself was of course terribly shocked, when this fact was made known. The conversation referred to presented all the evidence of real spirit intercourse, that can be presented in any case whatever, and no spirit could be identified, if that of her sister was not, on that occasion. Yet the known character of her sister utterly precluded the supposition that such a reckless falsehood could proceed from her spirit. On the other hand, if the thoughts of the husband really determined the answer obtained, its character was accounted for, and this was the only explanation which the facts of the case admitted. How any individual, in the presence of such facts, can remain a spiritualist, is to us a greater mystery, than is involved in any of the so called spirit manifestations of which we have ever heard.

14. There are forms of disagreement and contradiction among these communications, which are utterly incompatible with the idea of their *spirit*, and equally demonstrative of their exclusively *mundane* origin. Differences of opinion do, on certain subjects, as we well know, obtain among men in the flesh, and, for aught that we know, may obtain among disembodied spirits. There are certain subjects, however, on which minds in the same locality never differ. There is no dispute in this country, for example, in regard to any such question as this,

Whether Boston or New York is located on the Atlantic or Pacific coast. It is upon precisely similar questions pertaining to the spirit world, that an irreconcilable difference of opinion does obtain among "the spirits." In regard to the *location* of the spirit circles, for example, the *mode* of living and intercourse among spirits, their relations to other worlds, the *character* of spirits, whether all are good or not, whether evil spirits return to virtue, or eternally progress in sin and misery, — in regard to all such subjects, about which spirits can no more differ than living men can differ about the question, whether grain harvests, in these northern latitudes, come in summer or winter, the most contradictory and irreconcilable accounts are given by "the spirits," and by spirits, too, of the highest orders that ever speak to us in these communications. In a spirit circle, in the city of Cleveland, for example, the spirit of Dr. Channing affirmed absolutely, Mrs. Fish being the medium, that there are no evil spirits at all in eternity, and that there is no unhappiness there, that when "the body dies, propensity to evil dies with it, and that *all* of man progresses in happiness." In the same circles another spirit equally reliable, affirmed, with equal absoluteness, that while the good, in eternity, "eternally progress in goodness," "the evil eternally progress in evil." A similar difference and contradiction obtain on all subjects whatever about which the spirits communicate. Let any one read the accounts given by the spirits of Paine and others, and in the publications of Judge Edmonds, about the spirit circles, and he will perceive at once that here are contradictions which could not obtain among minds speaking from personal knowledge, — the subjects being of such a nature that there can be no motive to deceive, and no essential difference of opinion in regard to them, among minds speaking from such knowledge. Just such a diversity, however, could not fail to obtain, did these communications contain nothing but the reflections of human opinions on these subjects, and were they caused by the same.

15. The last class of facts which we adduce, are the numberless false communications which are continuously received in these circles, communications pertaining to subjects of which we cannot suppose "the spirits" to be ignorant, and in respect to which it is the height of absurdity to suppose they would intentionally convey false information, or to subjects about which they would not make positive affirmation if not well informed. Even men in the flesh do not falsify without a motive, and especially when they cannot but know that their falsehoods will soon be revealed. Now "the spirits" have not the common prudence of deceivers among men, in the particulars under consideration. They often, as is well known, give false information in respect to subjects of which it is absurd to suppose them ignorant, and where the error, as real spirits must be aware, will not fail, in a very short time, to come to light. We cannot but know that truthful spirits will not make such communications. They will not profess a knowledge of that of which they are ignorant. They will not assert as true what they know to be false, nor make positive assertions, when they cannot but know that they should profess nothing but uncertain guessing. Nor will lying spirits do the same, when they cannot but be aware that their attempted deceptions will soon be detected, and confidence in their communications will thereby be annihilated. Precisely such communications as these are

continuously given forth in these circles. A friend of ours, for example, once requested a medium who was then under the immediate control of "the spirits," as much so as any medium ever is, or professes to be, to ask "the spirits" how many gas-burners were then burning in the room where they were at the time. "I do not know," said our friend, "and keep your own head down, so that you will remain ignorant of the real number." On being asked by the medium, "the spirits" gave the number as four. After being requested to decide with perfect deliberation, they adhered to the number first given. The true number was found to have been *five*. The medium, who had been a professed Christian, had just before said, that he had given up faith in the Scriptures, to follow the higher light of Spiritualism. There, said our friend to him, you have rejected that blessed book which has been the light and consolation of the good, in all ages, to follow spirits who, when put to the test, cannot count five.

One of the test experiments made by the gentleman in Cleveland, the gentleman to whom we referred in another connection, was the following: While a circle was being held in an upper room, an individual present was requested to go below, and collect in a particular place named, any number of individuals, from those known to be in the lower part of the house, that he should choose. When he had been gone a sufficient time, the spirits were requested to give the number of individuals and their names, who were in the place agreed upon. Five names were rapped out. On inquiry, it was ascertained, that but two individuals were there. Such questions, the spirits are everywhere and always ready to respond to, and for the most part, in doing so, are equally successful, in betraying their ignorance and folly. Now, we affirm, from the known laws of universal mind, that no spirits good or bad would ever give forth such responses as these. They would, in such cases, not answer at all, or give only correct answers. Yet precisely such communications would, without fail, be obtained, if our theory were correct.

In some cases, "the spirits" betray a degree of ignorance, or forgetfulness, which indicates progression in any direction, rather than towards higher and higher intelligence. Some years ago, for example, the whole realm of spirits seemed to have concentrated their efforts upon converting to the faith one of our leading editors. He was overwhelmed with spirit communications, urging and entreating him to embrace the new doctrine. The spirits compelled the medium to write, and would then give her no rest, till their communications through her were forwarded. At length a series of communications were sent him, each signed, "Your uncle." As he could call to mind no such relative who had died, he requested the medium to ask his uncle to give him his name in the communication next presented. The spirit, however, had forgotten his own name.

We will give but one additional illustration. Some years ago, while the people of this country were in painful suspense in regard to the fate of an ocean steamer, the Atlantic, and when "hope deferred had made the heart sick" upon the subject, an individual who was desirous of crossing the ocean, and who shrank from doing it, while in doubt of the fate of that vessel, entered a spirit circle to obtain the desired information upon the subject. He was a most confirmed believer in "the spirits," and is, as we are informed, to this day. He inquired of "the spirits" if they could inform him of the state of that vessel. They positively affirmed that they could, and then stated absolutely that, after being destroyed by a terrible conflagration, it had gone to the bottom of the ocean with all on board, with two or three exceptions. These had escaped in a boat, and would probably survive to tell the tale of the terrible disaster. We have all the evidence that this communication came really and truly from "the spirits" that we have that any do. It was obtained in the same circumstances, through the same instrumentality. That it did not come from truth-telling ones is self-evident. That it came not from lying spirits is almost equally manifest from the principles stated above. This last supposition also totally annihilates all confidence in any spirit communications whatever. The inquirer was in a perfectly honest state of mind. He wished to know the truth on the subject, whatever it was, and nothing else. If one honest inquiry may be answered by a lying spirit, all may be, and all these revelations may be nothing but "doctrines of devils." The supposition is altogether inadmissible, therefore, that real disembodied spirits of any character had any thing at all to do with such a communication. This supposition, however, destroys all evidence that any of these phenomena whatever proceed from "the spirits," for this has all the evidence of such an origin that any of them have. Apply this principle to the positive affirmations which are continuously made by "the spirits" in these circles, and the supposition of their *ab extra* spiritual origin is rendered demonstrably false. They are affirmations which truthful spirits cannot, and lying spirits would not, make. On the other hand, they are precisely such affirmations as we should suppose would be made in these very circumstances, were they unconsciously produced by the individuals constituting the circles, and not by spirits out of them. They pertain to subjects about which the inquirers desire to be, and suppose that "the spirits" are informed, and the answers accord with the mental states, the hopes, fears, opinions, or guesses of those who inquire of them. We must, we repeat, reject the supposition that this class of affirmations has an *ab extra* spirit origin. Yet the same conclusion which thus forces itself upon us, destroys wholly all evidence that any of these so called spirit revelations have such an origin, for all are given forth in the same circumstances and are attended with the same identical evidence of an *ab extra* spiritual origin. How any intelligent persons can sit in these circles and witness the numberless positive affirmations which are there made, affirmations so many of which are known at the time by persons present, and if not then known, soon after ascertained to be false, and yet suppose that real *ab extra* spirits have any thing to do with these communications, is to us a mystery more inexplicable far than is involved in any question pertaining to the origin of these phenomena. A moment's reflection will convince any one that truthful spirits would not, and could not, give such false answers. They would not, we repeat, profess knowledge when they were ignorant, nor make positive affirmations when they were only guessing, and not very prudently at that. Nor would lying spirits make the same affirmations, unless, a case not supposable, their object was to unmask their character as superlative liars, and thus destroy all confidence in their own communications. Yet these very communications or none others must be received as coming from "the spirits;" for all transpire in the same circumstances, and are attended with precisely the same evidence of an *ab extra* spiritual origin.

We here draw our argument, on this point, to a close. To our mind, the facts which we have adduced, facts the reality of which cannot be disproved, and will not, we judge, be denied, clearly and unmistakably locate the cause of these phenomena, however mysterious in themselves, within this mundane sphere, and as clearly and unmistakably exclude the supposition, that that cause is any *ab extra* spiritual agency. We leave the subject with the reader, with the calm assurance, that our facts will not be denied, nor our arguments invalidated, nor our conclusions rejected.

CHAPTER II.

TENDENCY OF SPIRITUALISM.

In discussing the question next in order, *the tendency of Spiritualism*, we assume, 1st, that we have shown incontestably, that all the so called spirit manifestations may be satisfactorily accounted for, by a reference to exclusively mundane causes, and that to refer the same to any *ab extra* spirit cause or causes, is consequently a violation of all the principles of science and common sense bearing upon the subject; and, 2d, that by arguments equally incontestable, we have proven, that these manifestations are, in fact, produced by mundane and not *ab extra* spirit causes. The question of *origin* being thus disposed of, we now advance to a consideration of that of *tendency*. This spirit movement is, no doubt, progressive, and progression is the great theme of its advocates. The question before us is, the *direction* of this movement. Progression may be in the direction of evil as well as good, — of darkness, ignorance, superstition, and even of idiocy, as well as upward and onward towards higher light, and more perfect forms of thinking and action. The question, *whence* a thought originates, is not so important as this: what is its character? The tendency of Christianity depends more fundamentally upon what is intrinsic in the truths which it reveals, than upon the mere fact of their origin; though mental harmony with the truth, and faith in its divine origin, are indispensable to its highest efficiency. Suppose that in "the spirit land," as well as, in this world, there are myriads of idiotic minds, liars, and villains, and that they have found out a mode of communicating with mankind. Is the mere fact, that *spirits* are communicating with us, any reason why we should heed their communications, and frame our systems of belief, in regard to time, or eternity either, in accordance with their teachings? We are not to believe every spirit out of the body, any more than every spirit in the body. All spirits alike are to be tried by the same tests. The remarks which we have to make on the topic now before us, will be comprehended under three general divisions, the tendency of Spiritualism to the benefit or injury of mankind, *physically*, *intellectually*, and *morally*.

SECTION I.

TENDENCY OF SPIRITUALISM TO THE GOOD OR ILL OF MANKIND PHYSICALLY.

To show that Spiritualism benefits mankind physically, it must be proved, that, in these circles, the health, not of the sick, but of those in a normal physical state, is benefited, and that, by visiting these circles, and subjecting ourselves to the influences there generated, the most perfect forms of physical development may be secured. That which is medicine to the sick, is poison to persons in health. If diseased persons are medicinally benefited, by visiting these circles, that is a sufficient reason why individuals in health should avoid those places. We may safely assume, that no intelligent individuals of this latter class, ever visit these circles, with the expectation of thereby lengthening life, or of securing to themselves or posterity, more perfect forms of physical development. Suppose, on the other hand, that the tendency of the action of the force there generated, is to derange the physical system, and to derange it to such a degree, as to disturb fatally the normal action of the mind itself. Then, as the masses of persons visiting these circles are in a normal state, mentally and physically, we should be bound to regard the tendency of Spiritualism, physically considered, as evil, and almost exclusively so, and that in a very aggravated degree.

"Catalepsy," one of the most terrible of all physical disorders, — "trance, clairvoyance, and various involuntary muscular, nervous, and mental activity," are among the effects attributed by Mr. Ballou to this force, as it acts "in mediums." The reports of our lunatic asylums everywhere disclose the appalling effects of the action of this terrible force in such persons. We once saw a speaking medium, when "the spirits" were in him. We have no wish to have the vision renewed. We seriously doubt, whether "the seven devils" in Mary Magdalen produced in her more revolting physical and mental manifestations than we then witnessed. Those terrible contortions, and convulsions of the whole physical system, together with the wild and incoherent utterances, — we have often wished to banish the remembrance of them from our mind. What terrible thirst is often induced in such persons, under such circumstances. A single medium has been known to drink more than a dozen tumblers of water, during a single evening. In other instances, the senses are utterly disordered. A tumbler of ginger water, for example, was handed to a medium in the presence of a friend of ours. She affirmed that it tasted like licorice. A tumbler of pure water was then handed to her. It was to her as bitter as wormwood, and so nauseating that she could not retain any portion of it in her mouth. Another medium, a strong man, when on his way to attend his spirit circle, one of the coldest days of the past winter, found himself under the influence of this terrible force. He was utterly unable to stand upon his feet, and when subjected to the freezing cold, with his outer garments thrown off, the perspiration ran from him, as from a laboring man under a vertical July sun. No wonder that early graves, and our lunatic asylums, are peopled, to such an alarming extent, from this class of individuals. We believe this force to be one of the life forces, as ordinarily developed in the human system, and for that reason, a death force, when developed unduly, as it is, and from the circumstances of the case, must be, in such persons.

Precisely similar effects in kind, though but in few instances in degree, must be produced in those who frequent these circles. A gentleman of our acquaintance, a very influential and devoted spiritualist, told us, some months since, that he received a special message from "the spirits," urging him to devote his time and influence to the promotion of this great cause, he having leisure and means, and a liberal education. He accordingly introduced a medium into his own house, for the purpose of carrying out the plan proposed. The effect of frequent subjection to "the spirit" influence, however, was such upon his health, that the spirit of his own father told him that he must send the medium from his house and dismiss the subject from his mind, or his health would erelong be hopelessly prostrated. We state this fact merely in illustration of the physical effects produced by the action of this terrible power upon the human organism; for such we honestly believe to be its unvarying tendency. Upon many the effect of sitting in these circles is such, that it cannot be endured. A friend of ours, after sitting but a short time under such influences, had to be carried from the room, and more than two hours elapsed before she was able to return to her place of residence. A medium whom another friend accidentally met, some time ago, put one hand into one of hers, and placed the other upon the top of her head. Instantly our friend felt a very strong mesmeric force coming over her, she having frequently been subject to it before. We allude to this fact as another illustration of the identity of the mesmeric force and that from which these manifestations immediately result. On the subsequent evening, after she had been seated but a few minutes in a spirit circle, by the side of the medium referred to, she found her eyes immovably closed, and herself unable to stir or to speak. Her limbs became stiff and rigid, and her breathing very difficult, while the pulsation of the heart became perfectly unnatural; the feeling induced in her brain was as if a heavy mass of cold iron or lead had been laid upon it. At length, by the greatest effort, she was enabled to utter a scream sufficiently loud to indicate her condition to those present. She was accordingly taken from the circle, and after a time, was restored to her natural state. Such is the effect of this power upon susceptible temperaments. Yet the tendency, in all other instances, is precisely the same, unless (cases of very rare occurrence) they happen to be affected with peculiar forms of disease upon which this force acts medicinally. For ourselves, we should deem it as criminal in us to subject ourselves to its frequent influence, as it would be to habituate our physical system to the continued action of small quantities of arsenic.

A power which acts with such terrible effects upon the physical, and especially upon the nervous system, cannot fail to disorder, to a greater or less degree, if not fatally, the normal action of the mind. When the physical systems of individuals are so disordered, for example, that they cannot distinguish ginger water from licorice, or pure water from wormwood, which of their senses can we trust on any subject? What court of justice would receive the testimony of such persons in regard to any facts, which they may affirm themselves to have witnessed, when in such a state? To such individuals the most discordant sounds may possess an angelic melody, and the wildest vagaries of thought all the characteristics of the highest wisdom. These remarks apply not only to mediums, but to individuals constituting these circles, and apply to the full extent to which they have become subject to the action of this force. When we read the communications there obtained, and find that sensible and even educated persons present, regard them as embodying angelic thoughts, we affirm, that but one account can be given of such facts, namely, that the minds of such individuals have become so disordered, that they cannot distinguish the really beautiful, true, and good, from their respective opposites. The individual, for example, who could not distinguish ginger water from licorice, or pure water from wormwood, supposed herself speaking and acting under the immediate inspiration of the apostle Peter. As thus inspired, her communications were received by her auditors. Yet when questioned, this apostle thus speaking and thus received, had forgotten the particular feast at which Christ was crucified, the names of the mountains on which Jerusalem was built, and all facts of a kindred character. The audience, however, which attended upon her ministrations, and which was gathered from one of the most intelligent and educated communities in northern Ohio, and was constituted of persons, numbers of whom, to say the least, were by no means void of intelligence, were not at all shaken in their faith in the reality of the Petrine inspiration of the medium, by such manifestations of ignorance. Her incoherent ravings, too, were received as the very height and perfection of inspired wisdom. To us such facts are far more mysterious than any others connected with Spiritualism, and can be accounted for but upon the supposition, that mediums and the members of the circles around them, are subject to a common mental disorder.

For these reasons we receive, with great caution, and with many and large subtractions, the accounts of very wonderful events, as having occurred in these circles. Such events invariably almost occur, when spiritualists, with few or any exceptions are present, and when the so called spirit power is operating with very great force. All these minds are under the influence of one common physically and mentally disordering force, a force which unifies the perceptions and thoughts of those upon whom it acts. A very ordinary event may *appear* to such minds as possessed of even miraculous characteristics. A single sound from some musical instrument is raised in the circle, or a combination of sounds, which, to an car in a normal state, would grate harsh discord. To minds in the circle it may seem as super-angelic music. A single sound produced on such instrument, by some one in the circle, may subsequently reverberate in those minds as the highest melody proceeding from the object referred to, when its chords are swept by invisible hands. The mesmerizer throws his handkerchief into the lap of his magnetic subject. To the latter it is a beautiful infant, a bouquet, a golden fringed mantle, a fur boa, or a terrible serpent, just according to the arbitrary imaginings of the former. So, to minds under the influence of the same disordering force, in these circles, some quite common event may successively assume a corresponding diversity of forms, all of which will appear to all these minds, not only absolute, but distinct and separate realities, which they unitedly and honestly suppose themselves to have witnessed. A member of Congress, for example, told us, that while in Washington, he once had occasion to step into the room of another member, who is a devoted spiritualist, and steady attendant on the spirit circles, a man of high worth, and much political eminence. In the window of that room lay a very beautiful paper-weight of such a form, that the rays of the sun shining through it, were deflected so as to form a bright spot upon the wall. The occupant of the room, discovering the luminous spot, said, with much excitement, "I do wish I knew the cause of that light upon that wall. I do *wish* I knew what caused that light." Our friend, who had taken his seat by the window, passed his hand over the object referred to, and the light disappeared. "There," exclaimed the excited spiritualist, "it is gone. I do wish I knew the cause of that light." The hand was removed, and the exciting vision reappeared. "There, it has come again. I do wish I knew the cause of that light." Thus a very common event appears to one from whom the disordering force excited in the spirit circles has not quite passed away. Let that man return to those places, and there again become subject to the strong action of that force, and what confidence can be reasonably reposed in the validity of any visions which he may have there? The most common events may put on the most miraculous forms conceivable, and with all integrity, he may testify to their actual occurrence in such forms. No good, but much evil physically considered, is to be expected to the majority of individuals who frequent these circles. Its physical results surely do not, and cannot commend Spiritualism to our high regard.

SECTION II.

TENDENCY OF SPIRITUALISM TO BENEFIT OR INJURE MANKIND INTELLECTUALLY.

The tendency of Spiritualism to benefit or injure mankind intellectually next requires our attention. In this respect, the highest conceivable claims are advanced in its behalf by its advocates. By it, "life and immortality," "things unseen and eternal," all that it concerns us to know, and all that is requisite to gratify a laudable curiosity pertaining to the future state, are rapped out with the most perfect distinctness before our minds. Under the tuition and guidance of "the spirits," fallen humanity is, at length, to be led out wholly from the dark and gloomy regions of ignorance, error, and superstition, to a limitless millennium of mental light and spiritual illumination. Our purpose is to bring the validity of these high claims to the test of a rigid examination. To have any claims to our regard, and especially to the high regard demanded for it, it must first of all present a *reliable source of information* pertaining to the objects which it professedly reveals. It must also do much for *the advancement of science*, and for *the purification and elevation of our literature.* It is in these three points of light, that we shall consider the subject.

SPIRITUALISM NOT A RELIABLE SOURCE OF INFORMATION.

To us, it is a matter of no little surprise, that those who seem to glory in nothing but discipleship of "the spirits," have never seriously raised the inquiry pertaining to the *reliability* of those revelations upon the assumed validity of which they are shaping their course, and determining their principles of action for an immortal destiny. Had they raised this one inquiry, and carefully applied those laws of evidence which conduct to a right conclusion in regard to it, we venture the assertion, that there is not in the wide world, a spirit circle which would now be visited by any serious inquirers after truth upon the subjects referred to, with the expectation of receiving new and reliable information in regard to these subjects, any more than a circle of known maniacs would be visited for the same purpose.

"The spirits" are presented to our regard as *witnesses.* If they are intelligent, well informed, and truthful witnesses, and we can have evidence of the same, we may wisely and prudently resort to them for information upon subjects on which they may be willing to make communications. On any other condition than the perfect *reliableness* of their testimony, as a source of information, can we be justified, can we be justly freed from the charge of infinite presumption, in basing our belief in regard to the doctrine of immortality, or any other important subject, upon their revelations? Now no form of testimony can be shown to be valid, but upon the following conditions: (1.) The witnesses must be *identified*, that is, we must know *who* are speaking, what are their names, and from whence they come. If it is a spirit out of the body, or in the body, that is giving testimony, we must, we repeat, know *who* he is. (2.) The character of the witnesses for truthfulness and veracity must also be fully established. The testimony of none but *truthful* spirits, known and read of all as such, should, for a moment, be admitted, on such subjects as those under consideration. (3.) Equally well established must be the fact, that these witnesses are *well informed*, and not at all likely to be *deceived*, on these subjects. (4.) While there is the absence of self-contradiction, in the testimony of each witness, there must be a *substantial* agreement among the witnesses generally, on all fundamental facts. Is the testimony of "the spirits," granting that these communications do proceed from them, of this character? Can Spiritualism be shown to present a *reliable* source of information on the high themes and questions of our immortal destiny? We answer, no; and that for the following reasons:—

1. By no possibility, can these witnesses be *identified*. No one can tell, when receiving a communication, from whom it comes, whether it comes from the spirit of man, from an angel, or a devil, much less can he, by any tests which he can apply, determine what *particular individual* is communicating. There is not a solitary test question that ever was put to identify spirits, to which as correct answers may not, and are not obtained, when put to spirits which are in the body, or never existed at all, as to any others. According to the fundamental teachings of Spiritualism, spirits can read our secret thoughts, and give answers to purely mental questions. Suppose we put a question pertaining to a subject unknown to any person that is now, or ever has been on earth, but ourselves, and the particular spirit with whom we are professedly communicating. How do we know but that some devil has taken the true answer directly from our minds, or was present when the event referred to occurred, and thus learned about it, and is now answering in the name of the particular spirit invoked, and that for the purpose of perpetrating some fatal deception upon us, on other subjects? The voice and manner, and even the handwriting of individuals may be and are copied, when it is known absolutely,

that their spirits cannot be communicating at all. There is, then, no actual or conceivable tests by which the witnesses, in this case, can be identified.

2. Equally impossible is it to identify the *character* of these witnesses, supposing them to be spirits. That wicked spirits do inhabit some of the spirit spheres, and do communicate with men, in these circles, accords with the fundamental teachings of Spiritualism itself. No principles or tests have yet been discovered by which we can determine the character or motives of any spirit that has ever appeared in any of these circles. All the tests which spiritualists have ever suggested on the subject, are sustained by no form or degree of evidence, on the one hand, and are most self-contradictory and absurd, on the other. It has been said, for example, that "the pure in heart" will, by an immutable law of spirit communication, draw spirits of a corresponding character into communication with themselves, while corrupt minds will attract corrupt and lying spirits. If this principle really obtains as the law of spirit intercourse, one fact is undeniable, namely, that bad men should, on no account, ever enter one of these circles; for they will thereby become possessed of "seven other spirits" more wicked than ever dwelt in them before, and "their last state be worse than the first." But, then, where is the evidence of the existence of such a law? Nowhere. It is a mere unauthorized assumption brought in to save a desperate cause. Granting that these are truly spirit manifestations, we have not, and cannot have the least evidence, that any spirits but devils have ever appeared in a single spirit circle on earth. There is no escaping this conclusion.

3. Not a solitary spirit has ever communicated in these circles, if any have, who does not present all the

indications of being a most reckless liar, that can be presented by any spirit, in the body or out of it. Take any spirit that can be named, for example, into an orthodox circle, and he will affirm absolutely all the articles of the evangelical faith, and assert, with equal absoluteness, that no spirits but "the father of lies" and his agents, have ever, in any circle, intimated the truth of any opposite sentiment. Change the character of the circle, and on the same spot, the same spirit will deny all that he has previously affirmed, and avow perfectly opposite sentiments. Change the circle a third time, and a hundred times in succession, and this same spirit will reveal himself a stern advocate of all creeds, and of no creed at all, just according to the sentiments of the company in whch he happens to find himself at any given moment. We make these statements without reserve, qualification, or fear of contradiction from any well-informed persons in the community. If these are spirits who are speaking to us, in these communications, we should be blind, and wilfully so, to undeniable facts, and to all the laws of evidence, if we did not brand the whole mass together as reckless liars, and utterly repudiate their testimony.

4. Not only is the testimony of each witness, in this case, thus self-contradictory, but upon no fundamental questions is there harmony among the witnesses themselves. It is impossible to bring "the spirits" to harmonize in their testimony on any such questions. On all subjects we have an endless chaos of contradictory affirmations. How, then, can Spiritualism benefit mankind, by presenting us with a reliable source of information, on any subject pertaining to this world or the next? If we follow "the spirits," we must hold all opinions and doctrines,

and none at all, as true: we must revere the Bible, as a revelation from God, and scorn it, as embodying a mass of "cunningly devised fables:" we must hold the doctrine of eternal retribution, and believe, with equal absoluteness, that all men will be saved: we must entertain the opinion, that at death, "*all* must appear before the judgment-seat of Christ," and that the spirit may wander for centuries, and, for aught that appears, to eternity, in the spirit land, without seeing him at all: we must hold that all evil propensities die with the body, and that the soul becomes perfectly pure, as it enters eternity; and that it enters this state with the very character which it acquired while in the body, etc., etc. Who would regard such discordant revelations as these,—and these are the only revelations of which Spiritualism can boast—a reliable source of information on any subject?

5. The same view of the subject is most fully confirmed by the concessions of leading spiritualists themselves. "The spirits," even according to Swedenborg, who claims the most ample experience upon the subject, "relate things exceedingly fictitious and full of lies. When spirits begin to speak with man," he adds, "man must beware lest he believe them in any thing, for they say almost any thing; things are fabricated by them, and they lie; for if they were permitted to relate what heaven is, and how things are in heaven, they would tell so many lies, and indeed with solemn affirmation, that man would be astonished." He further affirms, that they will personate the characters of others, and make all manner of assertions, good and bad, in their names, so that it is perilous to deal with them at all. The following extract from the New York *Tribune* presents Judge Edmonds's view of this subject.

"But Judge Edmonds and his friends themselves acknowledge that spiritual intercourse is attended by numerous difficulties, and that it is hard to say how much credit is to be given to the communications of mediums. In the first place, the mind of the medium, as he says in the introduction to his second volume, lately published, influences the message — then the state of the atmosphere and of the locality have something to do with it — next, the harmony or discord of the mortals who are present. And, finally, many of the spirits themselves, have a very decided propensity to mischief and evil. Of the latter, he remarks, 'selfish, intolerant, malicious, and delighting in human suffering upon earth, they continue the same, for a while at least, in their spirit home; and having, in common with others, the power of reaching mankind, through this newly developed instrumentality, they use it for the gratification of their predominant propensities, with even less regard than they had on earth for the suffering that they inflict on others. Sometimes it is, with a clearly marked purpose of evil, avowed with a hardihood which smacks of the vilest condition of mortal society. Sometimes its fell purposes are most adroitly veiled under a cover of good intentions.'

"But how are we to know which is which? How are we to know whether the spirits speaking to Judge Edmonds as Bacon and Swedenborg — often speaking arrant nonsense, and never rising above commonplace — are not some of the veriest wretches whom he has, in his character of judge, committed to the gallows? What authority is there in any thing they say, more than in the unsupported dicta of Jack and Gill, or any other inconsiderable mortal? If it be replied, that their assertions are to be tested by our reason, or by the evidences to which we commonly resort in forming opinions, we rejoin that, in that event, — supposing them to be intrinsically worthy of attention at all, — they become simply intellectual or scientific data, and are not authoritative religious revelations. They are testimonies to a new experience of life, perhaps, given under dubious and conflicting circumstances, — are to be believed or not, as one may decide after investigation, — but in no sense veritable or commanding disclosures of spiritual truth. They are at best only assertions; and, until the spirits bring us, therefore, a great deal better credentials than they have yet brought us, or furnish us with better teaching than any they have yet furnished, the high claims put in for them cannot be sustained, and we are compelled to treat them as ghostly old quacks or jokers, — as of the classes spoken of by Swedenborg and Judge Edmonds, who delight either to mystify or poke fun at us, poor mortals; for, as to their cosmogonies and descriptions of heaven, thus far, they seem to us the merest sentimentalities or stupidities, of which we can find scores that are superior any day on the shelves of any library."

We once put the question to one of the greatest, if not the greatest of the spirit leaders in the Western States, whether he did regard these revelations as reliable sources of information on the subjects to which they pertain. He frankly replied that he did not. "There is not a medium on earth," he remarked, "whose communications I would commit myself to." "If their revelations accord," he continued, "with sound philosophy, I believe them. If not, I disbelieve them." "That is," said a friend who stood by, "you believe these communications, when they accord, and disbelieve them when they do not accord with your own philosophy, and that is all. Every man must act upon the same principle, and we are all left just where we should be, in the total absence of all such revelations." The apostle of "the spirits" was silenced, of course, and yet he was devoting his life to one end, — the persuading of the public to hang their eternity upon the validity of these very revelations. We doubt whether an intelligent and honest spiritualist can be found, who would not give the same answer to the same question as that above given; yet he is acting upon the same principle as the individual referred to.

Some individuals, and of these there are not a few, seem to be perfectly aware of the total unreliability of these communications, and yet maintain their faith in them, by mere dint of will. An individual, for example, sent a question to a certain spirit circle, pertaining to a subject upon which he desired to obtain information. The question was attended with this singular statement: that if the answer obtained should finally turn out to be incorrect, it would not, in the least, shake his faith in the doctrine of spiritual communication. This fact, we hazard little in asserting, presents the precise attitude of the minds of almost the entire mass of those who consult and believe in "the spirits," throughout the world. They know that their faith hangs upon revelations whose validity is perfectly unreliable, and yet, by mere dint of will, they continue to believe.

There is one circumstance which has, no doubt, great weight with many, that should not be overlooked in this connection. While all the diversity and contradictions above described, actually obtain in the teachings of "the spirits," yet a manifest and altogether preponderating majority of these responses actually harmonize in respect to certain important questions pertaining to the invisible world. Now here is a very singular assumption, namely, that amid a perfect chaos of conflicting voices, great questions pertaining to our immortal destiny are to be determined by a majority of responses, and that in total ignorance of the character of the respondents, especially when it is well known, that if the majority of the inquirers held the principles of the evangelical faith, the majority of these very responses would be in favor of said principles, and not, as they now are, against them.

Another consideration has still greater weight with other individuals. They are under the firm conviction, that they have had revelations from the spirits of departed friends whose known characters and relations to the inquirers preclude the supposition, that from such sources false revelations can come. Now the reliability of these revelations is utterly annihilated by the undeniable fact, that even they are just as contradictory as those obtained from any other sources. In the wide and endlessly diversified and contradictory catalogue of human opinions, there is not one, the mere doctrine of a future state excepted, — if even this be an exception, — which has not been affirmed and denied with the most perfect absoluteness, by these the most reliable of all spirit revelations. The spirit of the sainted mother of one individual affirms to him most positively the truth of all the fundamental articles of the evangelical faith, together with the solemn affirmation, that all spirit responses of an opposite nature are from the father of lies. Another individual obtains from his sainted mother responses equally absolute, and yet, in all respects, of precisely an opposite nature. These are the undeniable facts of the case, and they leave with us no grounds of doubt in regard to the real reliability of these revelations. Besides, the relations of "the spirits" to men in the flesh, as affirmed by these very revelations, and held by all who put faith in them, preclude totally the possibility of our knowing, or having any adequate evidence that we have, or can have, any specific communications with any particular individuals in the spirit land. "The spirits," we are taught, are witnesses of our external acts, and can read, with perfect accuracy, our most secret thoughts. Hence the responses given in the spirit circles to purely mental questions. Suppose that an individual in one of these circles, inquires if the spirit of his sainted mother is present. That question can be answered by the father of lies as well as by her. Any response to such a question, therefore, is no certain evidence of her presence. A question is now put pertaining to a subject absolutely unknown, as he supposes, to any being but the inquirer, his mother, and God. How does he, how can he know, but that the father of lies was present at the time, as a witness of that transaction, or that that fell deceiver is now reading his secret thoughts, and that from information obtained from one or both of these sources, is giving forth the very responses which the inquirer vainly supposes can come from no being but the spirit of that mother, and all this for the purpose of ultimate deception on other subjects? The doctrine of spirit revelations as given forth by "the spirits" themselves, precludes totally the possibility of our knowing, or having any reliable evidence in regard to the identity of the particular spirits from whom any given responses proceed, even granting the reality of such revelations.

SPIRITUALISM HAS NOT BENEFITED THE WORLD, AS FAR AS SCIENCE IS CONCERNED.

But what has Spiritualism done for the advancement of science? It has, according to its own professions, brought to its aid the great leading minds of the highest celestial spheres, and those minds have carried us over the whole field of scientific research, in respect to the finite and infinite, time and eternity, and matter and spirit. What is the result of this movement thus far? Have "the spirits" revealed to us any new and important facts in any of these great departments of human thought and inquiry, facts to the elucidation of which the great principles of science are to be applied? Spiritualism has revealed no such facts; not one. Have "the spirits" revealed any new and important *tests*, by the application of which truth may be distinguished from error? This is one of the grand consummations of science. Spiritualism, however, has won no laurels whatever in this important field. Have "the spirits" revealed any new principles, or truths of any kind, which may lead the mind forward in the march of discovery? This is what Bacon did while in the body. He discovered and elucidated great principles of science, under the influence of which humanity has been progressing ever since, and will continue to progress, till the end of time. Bacon, after dwelling for centuries amid the illuminations of eternity, has, according to the teachings of Spiritualism, descended from the celestial spheres to instruct humanity once more. What new truth has the spirit of Bacon, or any other spirit, revealed, or even suggested, for the advancement and perfection of science? None at all. We have sounded the depths of these communications for such principles, and have found none. Others have done the same, with the same results.

In no respect is science under obligations to "the spirits." Bacon, when on earth, and in the body, developed, as we have said, great principles, under the influence of which mind has progressed ever since. Dwelling as he has been for two centuries, amid the light of eternity, what should we expect from such a mind, were he now permitted to reappear as the instructor of humanity? Would he not enlarge our vision, open new tracks for scientific research, and develop new principles, or more perfectly elucidate those we already know, and thus enable us to advance onward and upward, in our search for truth? But the Bacon who now stands before us, as one of the celestial spirits, instead of enlarging our vision, needs to enter some of our primary schools, there to sit among children, and learn the very first principles of science. The same remarks are equally applicable to the entire circle of spirits who are speaking to us, in these new revelations.

The spirits are continually harping upon human progression, and require us, as a means to this end, to yield ourselves to their exclusive and absolute guidance. They then reveal thoughts and ideas, in dwelling upon which progression can result in but one direction exclusively, towards degrading superstition, mental imbecility, and idiocy. That divine revelation which Spiritualism would supplant, while it says almost nothing on this threadbare theme, reveals ideas and principles, upon which mind cannot but expand eternally, ever developing in that expansion, higher and higher forms of beauty and perfection. When the great apostle of Spiritualism, A. J. Davis, was in our city, he remarked, that the Mosaic dispensation had its origin in the back of the head, the Christian in the top of the head, and the new dispensation, that of "the spirits," in the front of the head; the first being the dispensation of *force*, the second of *love*, and the third of *wisdom*. When we read that statement, we were forcibly reminded of a fact which occurred in the place where Mr. Davis commenced his career as a "seer and clairvoyant." A young woman in that place became possessed of that form of clairvoyance in which, at all times, she could see and describe the internal structure of the human system, with all the accuracy of science, and could name the parts affected with disease, and describe their appearance. After listening to a discourse from a certain speaker, she remarked, that the mass of brains on one side of his head was much larger than that on the other, and that on one side, there was a spot about as large as a dollar where there were no brains at all. We were forcibly impressed with the thought, that if Spiritualism has its origin in the front of the head, there must be in all foreheads where it originates, and takes up its abode, spaces much larger than a dollar where there can be no brains at all, or any thing else which can sustain the weight of scientific truth, or of any great thoughts of any kind. Trophies in the field of science, and human progression, Spiritualism has yet to win.

SPIRITUALISM ITSELF UTTERLY WANTING IN ALL THE CHARACTERISTICS OF A TRULY SCIENTIFIC MOVEMENT.

But while Spiritualism has made no additions to science, it is itself, as an intellectual movement, utterly void of all the characteristics of true science. There never was a movement in which there was a greater carelessness, in the following fundamental particulars, than in this, namely: in the induction of facts,—in deducing conclusions from facts induced,—and in the assumption of principles. To have introduced this new theory, with any rational hope of obtaining for it a permanent influence over the public mind, its advocates should have been exceedingly careful to have introduced, as the basis of its high claims, no statements of facts but such as are sustained by the most reliable evidence. They should have been equally cautious in the deduction of conclusions, and none the less so, in the assumption of principles. What has been their course in all these respects?

In the induction of facts, let us say, in the first instance, the history of the world does not present a case of greater carelessness and presumption. Their reliable statements, as far as they have any, are now so intermingled with mountain masses of statements which are utterly unreliable, or greatly exaggerated, on the one hand, and which are the grossest fabrications and impositions, on the other, that, by no possibility, can the public distinguish the one class from the other. We will allude to the following statements as illustrations. The first adduced was given in a public discussion held in Cleveland, on Spiritualism, the past winter. During the progress of the discussion Joel Tiffany, Esq., one of the debaters put forward by the spiritualists, called upon J. M. Stirling, Esq., to state some facts. Our extracts are from a pamphlet published by spiritualists themselves.

"Mr. Stirling said, I could stand until to-morrow morning stating cases which have come within my own knowledge, of which none connected had any knowledge. I was introduced to a lady in the cars near Boston, and soon ascertained that she was a spiritualist and a medium. She told me that she at one time received a communication, signed by Robert Rantoul, saying that he had an important matter to communicate. It will be understood that his estate was considerably embarrassed. The communication was as follows: — 'I wish you to go to such a town where my commissioners are, and inform them that there are certain documents which they need, and the possession of which will save the estate a large amount of money.' She said, that having gone to visit these friends, they had saved the estate $ 30,000. I was present in a circle in this city, in which a lady was told that her mother was sick, and wished her to come home immediately. I said to the circle, 'now this will be a good test, for none of us know this.' A few days afterward the lady received a letter informing her of the sickness of her mother, and summoning her home."

By certificates obtained from the father of Mr. Rantoul, and from the two commissioners and the administrator of this estate, it has been proved before the public, that not one farthing has been saved to that estate by spiritualism. The report that $30,000 has been thus saved stands forth as a gross and shocking fabrication. Suppose, however, that the facts had all been found to have been in perfect correspondence with the statements made by Mr. Stirling. This would not justify him at all, in having put them forward as he did, as proof of the truth of Spiritualism. He is introduced to a female in the cars. Of her character, he knew nothing but this, that she belonged to a class who had the highest motives to report themselves as the mediums of the most startling communications. Before any statements coming from such persons were given forth as the basis of such conclusions as were then sought to be established, the individuals above designated should have been written to, and the facts, when presented, given in the most reliable form. The above, however, is a fair example of the manner in which the great leading facts of Spiritualism are obtained and given to the public. Take another statement, given by Mr. Tiffany himself, during the progress of the same discussion.

"I was in a circle in which a communication was received by raps in a language which none of us understood. No one in the circle knew how to separate the letters into words as they were rapped out. They were all joined together. Some thought there was no sense to it, but I was of the impression that there was a connection in it if anybody knew how to divide the letters properly into words. It was afterwards ascertained to be a communication in French, given by a mother to her son, who could not read French. The intelligence, in this case, was not in the circle, nor could any one in the circle have any definite idea or thought that it was an intelligible communication."

Now what did this wonderful communication, as subsequently explained to the audience, turn out to be? The speaker, on a subsequent occasion, affirmed it to have been "a lengthy communication." But what was this lengthy essay, given in French? A young lad was present in the circle who spoke French, and to the spirit of his departed mother, he put a question in that language. The following "lengthy communication," in the same language, was then rapped out, in reply, "My pretty little son." We do not say, that the speaker meant to deceive us, on that occasion. It is not unlikely, that the minds of all in the circle, were so disordered, by the action of the odylic force, that they could not distinguish a long from a short communication. We adduce this case for this one purpose, to show that the real facts of Spiritualism, as far as they exist, are by the carelessness of its advocates, to use no more offensive term, so intermingled with those which are sheer fabrications or utterly exaggerated, that the one class cannot be distinguished from the other. Myriads of illustrations are at hand to establish the same conclusion. Reports which have gone abroad of what has occurred in the spirit circles are the most unreliable sources of information conceivable.

Equally careless have spiritualists shown themselves in respect to the *conclusions* which they have deduced from these facts. Individuals, for example, place themselves around a table, and call upon "the spirits" to move the object. The object is moved accordingly. Without inquiring at all, whether the same phenomena may not be produced in the same circumstances, when "the spirits" are not invoked, the sweeping inference is drawn, that the truth of Spiritualism has been demonstrated. What a leap in logic does such a conclusion imply! Because a table, when certain conditions are fulfilled, follows the movements of our hands or bodies, what real basis can we find in such a fact for the conclusion, that some disembodied spirit must have hold of the object, and be pushing or dragging it about the room? Other objects begin to perform some crazy antics, and we are called upon to infer that the room about us is filled with spirits. We may justly apprehend, if men continue long to reason thus, that posterity will say, that in our day, logic, if nothing else, "had fled to brutish beasts, and men had lost their reason." The following wonderful incident, originally published in the *Cincinnati Times*, is now going the rounds of the papers, as one among the many new proofs of the divinity of Spiritualism. We give the account entire, that our readers may receive the full impression of the great, and as Spiritualists would have us believe, decisive fact presented.

"Visiting the 'Home of the Friendless' yesterday we gathered the following particulars in relation to a wonderful cure lately performed there by a 'healing medium,' or a spiritualist. It is certainly a wonderful occurrence, and we give it as a matter of news, without expressing any opinion upon the spiritual theory, which has so many ardent believers in the United States.

"A short time ago Frances Jane Price, a native of this city, and an orphan, in very destitute circumstances, came to the 'Home of the Friendless' for assistance.

"She is seventeen years of age, and had been, previous to the occurrence, in the city infirmary, a poor, sick, friendless creature. For *eleven years* the sight of one eye had been entirely lost, and a celebrated physician of this city had pronounced it beyond remedy. Another physician had given it as his opinion that she had the consumption, and in decided terms predicted that her days were few. She was confined to her bed at the 'Home,' it was suggested by some persons who felt interested in her case, to call in Mr. H——, a gentleman of this city, who through some mysterious power, has been lately performing several wonderful cures.

"Mr. H., in company with Rev. J. H. Fowler, accordingly called on the sick girl, whom they found in a very weak condition, scarcely able to sit up. Mr. H. seated himself by her side, took her hand, and after making few 'passes' over her head and neck, pronounced that her lungs were in no manner affected; that they were very susceptible but yet perfectly sound. He then continued his manipulations a short time, and without giving one particle of medicine, or leaving any prescriptions or directions, took his leave. From that the girl commenced improving. Her cough stopped at once, and she appeared stronger. Mr. H. came the next day, and repeated his 'passes' over the girl's head and neck, and took his leave as before. Strange to relate, a dim, pale light began to appear in the eye, which for eleven years had been as rayless as a stone. It increased slowly, but surely, to the astonishment of every one in the house, and to the great joy of the poor girl. Again Mr. H. performed his manipulations, and stronger grew the eye, until its sight was *perfectly restored!* And this cure was performed within the space of eight days. Not only was the eye rendered perfect, but the girl was restored to good health, and has left the 'Home' for a place in the country.

"All the above statement is well authenticated and true. Every person in the 'Home' is acquainted with the circumstance, and can testify to the condition of the girl when she entered and when she left. Mr. and Mrs. Cathel, the superintendents, will also give affidavits, if necessary, of the remarkable cure performed. They were not believers in Spiritualism, and at first looked upon the efforts of Mr. H. with much doubt. However, they must believe their own senses, and in such a plain and simple case it is difficult to be mistaken. Who can tell whether, if Mr. H. had not been called to attend the girl, she might not have languished in partial blindness, or under the pressure of her sickness, been shrouded for the tomb?

"People interested in spiritual matters will find in this incident ample materials for wonder and investigation."

Now we are expected, by spiritualists, to deny the fact

here adduced, or to admit the truth of their theory. To our minds, however, this case lays the basis for the following undeniable conclusions: —

1. We have here the evidence of the presence and action of a very powerful *physical* cause, and absolutely none whatever of any *ab extra* spirit agency. Had this individual made precisely the same "passes" over persons in a normal, physical state, he would have put them into a deep magnetic sleep, those "passes," as none would deny, or imagine the contrary, in such cases, developing and revealing the action of an exclusively physical cause. In connection with the same "passes" over another individual in a totally different physical state, another and different class of exclusively physical phenomena is developed, namely, a gradual, though rapid change from a state of disease to that of health. We have the same evidence of the presence and action of an exclusively mundane and physical cause in one case, that we have in the other, and in neither case have we the most distant indication of the action of an *ab extra* spirit cause. There is not a single feature of the case upon which a ray of light is thrown by the supposition of such a cause.

2. This exclusively physical cause which is so strongly developed in this fancied "healing medium," has very strong *medicinal* qualities, and may be employed, with great efficacy, in certain forms of disease. A man of undoubted Christian character, who formerly resided in Poughkeepsie, N. Y., and who utterly repudiates the claims of Spiritualism, had, if he has not now, precisely the same power that this "healing medium" has, and has performed, to us at least, as wonderful cures. We called a short time since upon a clergyman possessed of very strong mesmeric power.

We found him unable to leave the bedside of a sister of his who was afflicted, at the time, with terrible cramps and convulsions. When he would lay his hand upon her stomach, she would lie as quiet as an infant. The moment he would remove his hand, the convulsions would commence again. Yet this man, while performing such wonders, utterly repudiated the whole system of Spiritualism.

3. Persons in health peril their well-being physically and mentally both, when they subject themselves to the action of this cause, and that for the undeniable reason, that what is medicine to the sick, is poison to persons in health. Such are the conclusions undeniably deducible from this case. Yet we are expected to find in it, an immovable rock on which to base the high claims of Spiritualism. The conclusions of spiritualists, in their reasonings from their facts to their inferences, are invariably of this character. There is no connection whatever of antecedence and consequence between them.

A similar want of scientific care has characterized this entire movement, in the *assumption of the principles.* The whole movement has, for example, been based upon one grand error, namely, the assumption, that if the leading facts set forward by the spiritualists were admitted, the theory itself is established. Now this assumption ought to have received, at the outset, a most careful and rigid examination. But no such examination was ever given it. Never were men more confounded than were the spiritualists in Cleveland, when they were told, at the commencement of the discussion above referred to, that their facts were admitted, and their conclusion deduced from them denied, and that on this single point, we should join issue with them. For such an issue, they were not at all prepared. The connection between their facts and conclusion they had never examined. Had they carefully compared their facts with others equally well authenticated, which result from exclusively mundane causes, they would have perceived clearly, that they had no facts which were not perfectly similar and analogous to those which result from such causes, and consequently none which present the least positive evidence of an *ab extra* spirit agency. Under the influence of the assumption under consideration, Professor Ware, of Philadelphia, became a spiritualist. Professor Faraday had made certain experiments to prove that tables are moved by means of the pressure of the hands upon their surface. If he had established this fact, he would have annihilated all evidence in favor of Spiritualism, as far as this class of facts is concerned. Suppose he had failed to do this, it by no means follows from hence, that Spiritualism is true. If tables are not moved by muscular pressure, it by no means follows that spirits do it. There is in such a fact no ground whatever for such an assumption. This, however, was the assumption of Professor Ware. He, consequently, having proved by the most decisive experiments, that tables are not moved by mediums, through this one means, became a spiritualist throughout.

The same remarks are equally applicable to all the basis principles on which this movement rests. Not one of them can sustain a rigid scientific examination, for a single hour. Spiritualism has not only not made any contributions to science, but has, from its origin, in its process of self-development, violated all the principles of true science.

SPIRITUALISM HAS DONE NOTHING TO IMPROVE THE LITERATURE OF HUMANITY.

But what have "the spirits" done for the benefit of humanity, in the department of literature? Have they elevated the tone of thinking and utterance among us? Have they shadowed forth, through the creations of the imagination, the beautiful, the true, and the good, in more perfect and sublime forms than we had before? The elements of thought entering into the productions of the "spirits" ought surely to be altogether of a higher order, and these elements should be blended into higher forms of beauty and perfection, than characterize mere mundane human productions. The spirits have tried their hands in almost every department of literature, such as music, poetry, fine writing, and even painting. As high as the celestial spheres are above the earth, so high should be their productions above those of men in the flesh. Is it so? Are "the spirits" better poets, better painters, better composers in music, and better writers, than our Miltons and Shakspeares, our Raphaels and Angelos, our Haydns and Mozarts, and our Burkes and Irvings? Unless they are, no credit is to be awarded them in the department of literature. On the other hand, their productions tend most powerfully to degrade and debase humanity, by degrading and debasing our conceptions of immortality. Now we affirm, without fear of contradiction, that the plane of thinking and utterance presented by Spiritualism, is not only not above, but far below, that of humanity in this mundane sphere. For ourselves, we would hardly be willing to "loose, though full of pain, this intellectual being." Yet we would infinitely prefer annihilation to an eternity with "the spirits," if Spiritualism has given us a true revelation of the thinking and acting which obtains among them. We do not say, that no examples of good poetry, and fine writing, may, in instances very few and far between, be found in the spirit productions. But we do say, that their general, and almost exclusive character is such, that humanity ought to be ashamed of them, if they were presented as the productions of men in the flesh, and in a normal mental state.

SECTION III.

MORAL TENDENCY OF SPIRITUALISM.

The moral tendency of Spiritualism now claims our attention. As far as this department of our subject is concerned, we have no hesitation in affirming, that the spirits have revealed no *new* moral principles of any kind. Nor have they disclosed any new applications of principles already known. They have disclosed no new sanctions to the idea of duty, nor have they encircled it with any new and more attractive motives to obedience. Before any utterances even professedly came to us from "the spirits," we had a system of morality absolutely perfect in itself, and equally universal in its applications, a system illustrated, exemplified, and commended to our regard by the instructions and example of one who knew perfectly "what is in man" and what fallen humanity needs, and in whose character every conceivable and possible form of virtue is visibly embodied in absolute perfection, a system, too, enforced upon us by motives and sanctions of infinite and eternal weight; a system, finally, to which absolutely nothing can he added, and from which nothing can be taken away, without visibly marring its beauty and perfection. Spiritualism comes in professedly as a higher light, to supplant "that dearest of books that excels every other," the only book that embodies this divine system of moral legislation. Yet every principle of duty which it does enforce, it copies, and very poorly too, from this rejected volume. At the same time there is intermingled in the moral teachings of "the spirits" principles of the most pernicious tendency. Let us consider a few facts and examples which tend to reveal and expose the moral tendency of Spiritualism: —

1. The known character of a large portion of the mediums, to say the least, does not present the system to our regard, as tending to any moral good. If spirits are communicating to us, in these manifestations, they must know the character of their mediums, being not only able to witness their external acts, but to read their secret thoughts and purposes. If men in the flesh are known by the company which they keep, spirits must be known by the mediums through whom they voluntarily communicate. Spirits cannot preserve a character for moral purity, when they will continue to communicate with us, through persons whose character we and they know to be bad, and nothing can be of a worse moral tendency, than for circles to sit around such persons, with the idea, that through them, communications are being received from spirits inhabiting the celestial spheres. The spirits surely have not been very careful to manifest their regard for moral purity in the selection of their mediums. One such individual, for example, they will never communicate through, excepting when he is drunk, and then they are ready to use him for that high purpose. Others, in some cases, are known to be so morally impure as to exclude them

totally from virtuous society, excepting when virtuous individuals gather around them in these circles, as the favored mediums of "the spirits." One of the grand themes of spiritualists is the moral corruptions of the church and ministry. They themselves, however, have not the effrontery to insinuate, that the spirit of God dwells with and communicates to men, through persons thus corrupt. Yet these very men are loudly calling upon us to encircle mediums more depraved than they dare represent the church to be, and to encircle these persons for the purpose of communing through them, with the pure spirits from heaven itself. Nothing can be of a worse moral tendency than such associations.

2. The character of "the spirits" themselves, as they stand revealed before us, renders all our imaginary intercourse with them, as our intellectual and moral teachers and guides, of the most pernicious moral tendency. When we select for ourselves teachers and guides whom we know to be morally corrupt, or when we remain blind to the moral corruptions of such persons, after their character stands revealed to us, we are subject to the most debasing and pernicious moral influence conceivable. What is the moral tendency of Spiritualism in this one respect?

In general, we would remark, that *not one of "the spirits" bears the marks of even common honesty among men in the flesh.* There is not one of them who, when put to the test, will not make *false assertions* in respect to subjects in regard to which real spirits must know the truth, that will not *profess* absolute knowledge when their answers reveal them as profoundly ignorant, and will not make positive assertions when real spirits must know that they are only guessing with a perfect uncertainty in regard to the result, and all this in circumstances in which they must be aware of the fact that their falsifying will infallibly be detected. Now common liars, even among men, are not in any way guilty of such flagrant conduct. While, therefore, it would be very hasty in us to say, "that all men are liars," it is using very mild language indeed to say that all "the spirits" cannot be any thing else. What should we think of men who should be constantly making the false utterances which "the spirits" are in all spirit circles throughout the wide world?

There is one certain characteristic of conscious quackery and mountebankism which "the spirits" possess so preëminently, as to mark them infallibly as deceivers and hypocrites of no ordinary character. We refer to their continuous harping upon one theme, *human progression*, and to their absolute promises of leading lost humanity out of all its mazes of darkness, error, and superstition, into one universal millennium of light, knowledge, purity, and blessedness, and then revealing nothing for this end but what real spirits cannot but know to be the most senseless puerilities conceivable, — puerilities in the presence of which, as they affirm, that great central light of our moral being, the Bible, is to be thrown into a deep and permanent eclipse. Now we affirm without fear of contradiction, that such facts infallibly mark "the spirits," supposing these communications to proceed from such, as deceivers and hypocrites of no ordinary character. The Bible, while it utters hardly a syllable upon the subject of progression, evinces most infallibly the divinity of its origin by revealing eternal principles, truths, and realities, in dwelling upon and harmonizing with which, universal mind cannot but eternally expand and progress in beauty and perfection. "The spirits" talk endlessly of human progression, and then present themes upon which the mind cannot dwell without progress in one direction exclusively, namely, hopeless puerility, if not idiocy. Now if these are real disembodied spirits which are giving forth these communications, and especially if they are the personages they affirm themselves to be, then we affirm that they cannot but be aware of the downward tendency of their communications, as contrasted with their own promises and professions in regard to them, and that consequently they stand revealed in them as self-conscious deceivers and hypocrites of the grossest kind.

3. The moral character of these communications, those we refer to which are now being given forth, and which, according to Mr. Adin Ballou, one of the oldest and most distinguished spiritualists in the country, is but the beginning of what is yet to be revealed, and but the faint foreshadowing of what is yet to be done among us, on the authority of these revelations, — the moral character of these latter-day revelations, we say, leaves us no ground to doubt the character of the spirits, supposing them to be the authors of these revelations, on the one hand, and of the moral tendency of Spiritualism, on the other. We will give a single extract in illustration, an extract from a work of high authority, entitled, "Astounding facts from the spirit world, witnessed at the house of J. A. Gridley, Southampton, Mass." Mr. G. is represented as an eminent physician. A large portion of this work, as we are informed, first appeared in the New Era of Boston. When we providentially met with this production and obtained a loan of it for examination, we called at the office of the *Spiritual Telegraph*, New York, and inquired whether it was regarded as a genuine revelation from "the spirits?" We were told in reply that it was. Yet they did not

hold tnemselves responsible for the truth of the statements made, as the same diversity of opinion prevailed among "the spirits" as among men in the flesh. This work, however, was one of the spirit productions which they were accustomed to sell. We shall defile our pages with as short an extract from it as possible, and yet give the idea of the revelation of "the spirits" to which we refer. After saying that "no good and advancing spirits below the fifth degree have aught to do with the sexual relation in any sense whatever," "the spirits," after affirming that in this degree "the male is generally and naturally positive to the female," that the former "can readily fill" (communicate the higher or spiritual life to) "the negative" (the female) "by contact," and that "the generative organs" "are the vehicles through which the spiritual life is often, though by no means always, disposed to flow," they proceed to say, that in this higher circle "any positive spirit has free access to any negative spirit where there is affinity — that though the male may have a female companion who is constitutionally adapted to be to him a better help-meet on the whole than any other, and so generally accompanies him, yet the latter has no jealousies and knows no exclusiveness, that she is glad to have the life of God increased in any way, and anywhere — that the same liberty will erelong be given to men on earth," etc. Now if these are real spirit voices, and we have no evidence that any of these revelations come from "the spirits," if these do not, then we hesitate not to say, that they are none others than "devils damned" who are here speaking to us. And the fact that "the spirits," supposing them to be spirit revelations, cannot but be aware that such revelations are proceeding from their midst to corrupt still further fallen humanity, and do not thunder forth their united reprobation of these sentiments, and of those who utter them, fully implicates them in these morally desolating abominations. We read, that in ancient times, men sometimes "harbored angels unawares." Until "the spirits" free themselves from all participation in these revelations, which they would have done ere this, had they been morally pure, it is quite evident, that we cannot harbor them without harboring devils, and that while we know who and what they are.

It may be said in reply to the above, that spiritualists, as a body, have never adopted these sentiments, but have rejected them. This is not denied. Yet they have accepted the work avowing them as a truly spirit revelation, and have, as such, commended it to public regard and patronage. What would even spiritualists say, if a leading Christian library was advertised for public sale, a library embracing a single volume containing such sentiments? The fact that "the spirits" on the one hand, and spiritualists on the other, have not openly repudiated the book, and its authors, holding up both alike to universal reprobation, is sufficient evidence of the downward tendency of the system.

4. The very circumstances in which persons meet in these circles, tend most powerfully to generate precisely such moral feelings and sentiments. For ourselves, we are not at all surprised at the above revelations. We long since believed and affirmed that they would proceed from this very source, and have only wondered that they have not made their appearance earlier. We affirm that meeting in these circles is adapted to generate influences and tendencies which naturally prompt to such sentiments and to corresponding actions, and finally to draw from "the spirits" a similarly licentious

morality; the immutable law of their teachings being to sanctify by their authority the sentiments, whatever they may be, of the circles which entertain them as teachers and guides. For men and women to get together in circles, and there, that spirits, they know not whom, and coming they know not from whence, may take the most complete control of their mental and physical powers, divesting themselves as far as possible of all independent thought or purpose, tends to but one result, to banish rational thought, and to impart to the sensual in man the most full and controlling development, and finally to prepare the mind to receive the most senseless puerilities as the perfection of wisdom, and the most licentious principles and sentiments as the highest and purest morality.

This we affirm to be the certain *tendency* of this mission of "the spirits," a tendency in which their moral character, supposing them to be real substantialities, is being distinctly unmasked. For ourselves, we would as soon inhale the malaria of our brothels and pest-houses as a means of moral and physical health, as subject ourselves to the teachings of "the spirits" as a means of intellectual and spiritual growth and development.

SUMMARY STATEMENT OF THE TENDENCIES OF SPIRITUALISM.

Spiritualism, then, we regard, with very few and slight exceptions, as, in its fundamental tendencies, "evil, and only evil continually," and that for the following reasons, among others: —

1. With the exceptions named, its medicinal effects in a few forms of disease, it tends to no form of good to humanity, physical, intellectual, or moral.

2. Subjection to the influences generated in these circles, very strongly tends to a great, and in many instances, fatal derangement of the physical system of those in health, and to a corresponding derangement of their mental powers.

3. While it tends to unsettle our faith in a revelation absolutely sufficient and reliable in regard to all questions pertaining to human duty and destiny, Spiritualism induces a reliance, for information on the greatest of human concernments, — questions pertaining to God, duty, immortality, and retribution, — upon sources the most unreliable and deceptive conceivable.

4. It tends to abstract and withhold our regard from all that is really great, beautiful, true, and good, and to generate an absorbing interest in the most childish subjects, and the most puerile and senseless forms of thought.

5. It tends, in the strongest manner, to degrade and limit the action of the human mind, by giving to these senseless puerilities the greatest influence over it, in consequence of inducing the belief, that they are the high forms of thinking descended to us, from the high intelligences of the universe. Nothing but this one idea, — the origin of these spirit productions, — has saved them hitherto from the universal contempt and ridicule of the world; and this is what imparts to them their great power to degrade and debase human thinking just as far as these productions become objects of public interest.

6. It presents, while it tends to nothing good, the greatest facilities for artful and unprincipled men and women to practice the grossest and most dangerous deceptions upon the public, and holds out to such persons the most persuasive motives to perpetrate such

criminalities. To gain the greatest celebrity and influence, individuals of this class must become mediums of the most wonderful manifestations, physical and mental. Hence, the so frequent resort to deception and imposition, on the part of mediums, and there is no place so favorable to the perpetration of such crimes as the spirit circles.

7. While Spiritualism has already begun to develop the worst and most debasing moral principles that the seethings of human depravity have yet thrown upon the surface of society, the intrinsic tendencies of the system renders it certain, that this is but the beginning of what is yet to be.

8. The influences naturally and necessarily generated in these circles, tend ultimately, with an unerring certainty, to secure an open and *unblushing* conformity to those principles.

Such is an honest statement of an honest estimate on our part, of the real tendencies of this system, as it now stands before the public. We leave the portrait to speak for itself.

CHAPTER III.

MISCELLANEOUS TOPICS.

A FEW topics of a miscellaneous character, but which have an important bearing upon our present investigations, have been reserved for a distinct and separate consideration, in the present chapter. The principles which we have elucidated, will be found to be quite extensive and important in their applications. Through them, many facts which have hitherto appeared utterly mysterious and inexplicable, admit of a ready and consistent explanation. We will specify a few of these facts, as examples: —

SECTION I.

SPECIAL FACTS CONNECTED WITH SPIRITUALISM.

There are a certain class of what may be denominated special facts connected with these spirit manifestations, facts upon which very special dependence is placed by spiritualists, in establishing the claims of their theory, and which consequently demand a particular notice, before closing our discussion of this subject. Speaking mediums, for example, will sometimes copy the manner and voice of persons they never saw, persons now dead. Writing mediums copy, in a similar manner, the handwriting of such individuals. Individuals, in these circles, and after having been subject to the influences there developed, have peculiar *tactual* impressions, as of individuals taking them by the hand, or grasping, or affectionately touching their limbs, etc. In other instances still, spirits stand revealed apparently in visible form to mediums and others, and, as it seems to them, hold audible conversation with them. Finally, some mediums speak and write in languages with which they are totally unacquainted. Now we affirm in general that no argument can be legitimately deduced from such facts, their reality being admitted, in favor of Spiritualism, for the obvious reason, that precisely similar facts occur from known mundane causes. Here, as we have already observed, lies the great error of spiritualists in all their facts and reasonings. They have entirely overlooked the fundamental and undeniable principle, that they must adduce facts which never result from the action of exclusively mundane causes, before they can infer, as even probable, the conclusion of an *ab extra* spirit agency in the production of any phenomena in the world around us. Let us more particularly examine the different classes of facts above referred to.

COPYING THE VOICE, MANNER, AND HANDWRITING OF INDIVIDUALS.

In regard to the class of cases in which mediums imitate more or less accurately, the voice, manner, and handwriting of persons they have never seen, we remark, that no argument can be adduced from such facts in favor of Spiritualism, for the following reasons: —

1. In the spirit circles themselves, these phenomena do occur, when no spirits at all, and especially the spirits supposed, can be present. The case cited above, which occurred in Cleveland, is a very striking and conclusive example of this class of facts. The manner, voice, and forms of expression of the young man are quite peculiar and unique; yet they were all so perfectly imitated by a total stranger, and that a female, that it seemed to his mother that her son stood directly in her presence, that son at the same time being not dead, but alive. No one also will have the credulity to suppose that the medium, a young lady in Boston, imitated the handwriting of her cousin, through the influence of the spirit of that individual, or of any other disembodied spirit. That which is done without the presence and

agency of spirits, can never, without a violation of all the laws of correct reasoning, be adduced to prove their presence and agency.

2. These same phenomena occur under the influence of exclusively mundane causes, being the not uncommon facts which attend the action of the odylic force, as developed in cases of mesmerism and clairvoyance.

3. It would be an exception to the law which controls the action of this force, an exception for which no account could be given, did these facts not occur in connection with these manifestations, supposing spirits to have no connection with them.

TACTUAL IMPRESSIONS.

Precisely similar remarks apply to all the facts coming under the class of *tactual impressions.* The mother referred to, as soon as she came under the influence of the force developed in the spirit circle, had the same sensations that she would have done, had her hand been grasped by some friend in affectionate salutation; yet no spirit was there. A gentleman who had had great experience of the action of this same force, told us that on waking from sleep at one time, a sleep which occurred after he had been subject to the strong action of that force, all consciousness with him was confined exclusively to his right arm. He at first honestly supposed that his own body was that of another person lying by his side, and when he took hold of his own left hand, he supposed he had grasped that of another individual. These tactual impressions are, of almost all others, of the least weight in favor of Spiritualism. If just such impressions were not experienced in these circles, by those who subject themselves to the influences there generated, the facts of Spiritualism would be more unaccountable than they now are. If these impressions are conclusive for the presence and agency of the spirits of men as the cause of such phenomena, the sensations of persons in delirium tremens, and when affected with other forms of disease, are equally conclusive for the presence and agency of the spirits of serpents crawling over and encircling their bodies.

SEEING SPIRITS.

But spiritualists proclaim, that mediums and others have, at times, what seems evident to them at least, a direct and immediate *vision* of spirits, of their form, size, and complexion. That they have such visions, we have no disposition to doubt or deny. The question for us to decide is, are these visions valid for the reality of their supposed objects? That they are not, we argue from the following considerations: —

1. Many of these visions are of such a character, as to preclude the supposition, that they can be real perceptions of objects external to the organism of the percipient himself, and this class of visions must be held as valid if any are. Judge Edmonds, for example, affirms, that the spirits which he has seen are from three inches to twenty feet in height, the largest that he has seen being a majestic and well-proportioned female twenty feet high; that he has seen spirits who have been eighteen thousand years in the celestial spheres, and yet retain the form of monkeys, while others have hoofs and horns, such as he has seen in pictures. This is what he stated on his western tour, the past year, and his visions are just as palpable and valid as those of any other medium or spiritualist. Any persons who credit

such visions as these, we shall not stop to argue with. They are entirely beyond the reach of reason and logic both.

2. Precisely similar visions occur, when we know absolutely, that spirits are not seen at all, because the spirits which do appear, if any do, are actually alive, and in the body, and at great distances from the percipient, when the visions occur. We shall hereafter, in another connection, adduce a very striking case of this kind, a case in which a mother when wide awake saw the spirit of her son, was addressed by him, and spoke to him in reply, and yet neither that spirit, nor any other was present at all, as an object of vision, the son being at that very moment alive, and about sixty miles distant from the mother. The perception, in this case, was as distinct and palpable, as in any that can be named. The mere fact, that persons appear to themselves to see spirits, is therefore no certain evidence, that spirits are present, as objects of perception.

3. Precisely similar and equally distinct and palpable visions are well known to attend certain forms of disease, and also the action of certain medicinal substances introduced into the physical system, and that when no one has the folly to suppose, that spirits are present as objects of perception. We have only to refer to the journals and productions of medical science to find the most abundant and absolute verification of the above statements. How absurd and unphilosophical is it then, to refer to this same kind of visions as proof of the presence and agency of spirits in these so called spirit manifestations!

4. It is perfectly common for persons, under the action of the very force developed in the spirit circles, to have visions perfectly distinct and palpable of objects

which have no existence whatever. The mesmeric and clairvoyant subject for example, sees a meeting-house, a mountain, lake, ocean, or river; a man, angel, or devil; a serpent, a centaur, or spirit, and all with the greatest possible distinctness, just in accordance with the mere *imaginings* of the mesmerizer. On the supposition, therefore, that spirits have no connection whatever with these so called spirit manifestations, it would be an exception to a general law, an exception for which no account could be given, if precisely the visions under consideration did not constitute a somewhat prominent portion of the leading phenomena of Spiritualism. Of the validity of its high claims, they present not the least shadow of evidence.

SPEAKING AND WRITING IN UNKNOWN LANGUAGES.

There are no higher claims set forward by Spiritualism, than those which pertain to the asserted fact, that mediums, in some instances, speak and write, in languages with which they are totally unacquainted. This class of spirit phenomena demands of us, therefore, a somewhat particular notice. In regard to such phenomena, we remark: —

1. That a very large portion of them, a vast majority in our judgment, are mere impositions originated for purposes of deception. We have carefully traced out not a few of these cases, and have found that those who originated them were "liars from the beginning." A very devoted spiritualist in Cleveland, for example, told us, that he once had a medium in his family who claimed to speak various Indian languages. At length, some natives came to the city belonging to three different tribes. He invited them to his house, that they

might converse with the spirits of their ancestors, through the medium referred to. The spirits, who had been speaking before, however, were all dumb, as soon as the strangers appeared. A gentleman informed us, a short time since, that he was once present at a meeting in a town in northern Ohio, where a distinguished medium, a female, was "bewitching the people with her sorceries," professing to preach to them under the immediate inspiration of the highest spirits from the celestial spheres. At the close of her harangues, she was accustomed to astonish her auditory, by speaking to them in "unknown tongues," generally in Indian. This gentleman, after listening awhile to such utterances, himself gave utterance to forms of senseless gibberish, as in a similar language. The pythoness responded, and quite a lengthy dialogue was held between them. She informed the audience that the stranger was speaking in one Indian language, and she in another, but that she perfectly understood all he said. They very earnestly solicited the stranger to interpret what had passed between him and the speaker. He replied, that he would attend their meetings the next day (Sabbath) when they might, perhaps, hear again a similar conversation. At the close of the spirit discourse, the next day, the dialogue was resumed, and continued at great length. The audience became importunate for an interpretation of what was passing before them. The stranger at length disclosed to them the fact, that though the medium had affirmed to them that he was speaking in one language and she in another, and that she perfectly understood his meaning, he had not uttered a word, in any language, nor had he given utterance to a single thought, in all that had passed between himself and her, and that he now unmasked her before them as a wilful liar and deceiver. It is a well-ascertained part of the known trade of a large portion, if not a majority of mediums thus to lie and deceive, and no field presents such facilities for the perpetration of such impositions, as this "speaking with tongues" in the forms in which they practise it, a form wholly unlike that presented in the Scriptures of truth. Those, therefore, are miserable dupes who suffer themselves to be led away by such shallow devices.

2. A large portion of these cases, also, are monstrous exaggerations of very trifling occurrences, which in themselves present no difficulties whatever, and, above all, no indications of the presence of spirits. As an illustration, we would refer to "the lengthy communication" in French given forth in a circle in Cleveland, a sublime and wonderful essay, as we were given to understand, but which, when literally translated, expressed the great thought, "My pretty little son."

3. Other communications of this class are found to be given forth in no language whatever, but to be constituted of English words with terminations of foreign ones, which the mediums had heard before without understanding their meaning. In illustration, we present the following fact, which is related by a writer in the *North American Review*.

"In matters other than where opinion is involved, there may be traced the same subjective element. We recently received from a medium of transparent ingenuousness and singleness of character, certain metrical productions which she said were written through her hand by the spirit of John Milton. Two of them were in English verse, in sentiment highly devout, though misty and dreamy, in style and rhythm certainly not beyond the capacity of the medium in her normal state, though she said she was not in the habit of writing verse. The third kind our correspondent said was in Latin, to her literally an unknown language, and she requested a translation. It was inscribed "A Latin Sonnet." But it was not a sonnet, and was not in Latin, nor in any language with which we are conversant, yet it had throughout a Latin sound, and the terminations were Latin. Now the father of this medium had for years received into his family boys fitting for college, and others unfit to remain in college. She had undoubtedly heard in her youth a great deal of Latin read and repeated, and the so called sonnet was evidently composed of sounds and fragments that had lingered thus long in her memory, to be reproduced in this written dream.

4. Other cases are found to be simple remembrances of utterances which the mediums had before heard, without understanding the same, remembrances precisely similar to what occurs in other instances. Mr. Coleridge, for example, gives an account of a young girl in Germany, who had always labored as a domestic, who in her last sickness repeated whole sentences from the Greek, Hebrew, Arabic, and Syriac Scriptures. On examination, it was found, that these very passages she had heard a learned clergyman read when resident in his family. Many instances of a similar kind have occurred. Their occurrence, therefore, in connection with these mediums, is no proof whatever of the presence and agency of spirits.

5. It is a well-known and not at all uncommon fact, that individuals, under the influence of the very force generated in these circles, will understand persons when reading or speaking in languages which the former do not understand, and will reply to the latter in their own

language. We have already adduced cases of this kind, and need not repeat them here. That precisely similar phenomena should appear in these circles, therefore, is no more than should be expected, and their appearance is no evidence whatever of the interposition of spirits.

Now we affirm that no case of speaking with tongues has ever occurred in connection with this spirit movement, that does not properly and really belong to one or the other of the classes above named. Of all the claims ever set forward in behalf of Spiritualism, this, to our minds, is among the most shallow and presumptuous, coming nearer than any thing else almost, to a justification of its opposers, in affirming the whole movement to be nothing but a deliberate imposition upon the public.

FACT WITNESSED BY J. G. WHITTIER, ESQ.

The following fact witnessed by J. G. Whittier, Esq., as naturally presents itself in this connection, perhaps, as any other, and demands a passing notice. Mr. W., on one occasion, asked a medium if she could read the contents of a paper which he would fold up, what was written being inside, and placed under her hand. She expressed the belief that she could do it. Mr. W. then retired from the circle, and placing himself where no one could see his motions but himself, wrote upon a slip of paper the word "Truth," and having folded up the paper, with the word inside, returned and placed the object under the medium's hand. The medium, her hand covering the paper all the while, and after she had waited, as in deep thought, a few moments, slowly repeated the letters, s-r-u-t-h. That is not right, says

Mr. W. Try again. Again and again, the same letters were repeated. On being assured, that she was wrong, her reply was, "That is the way I read it." On opening the paper, Mr. W. found that, by a mistake of his own, the letter T had been written so as to resemble that of S. On this fact, which spiritualists would no doubt claim as a great triumph of their theory, we remark:—

1. That the medium, in this case, most evidently had a *direct and immediate vision* of what was in the paper referred to. This was what she affirmed to be true, and of its truth she was unquestionably distinctly conscious.

2. This case presents not the least conceivable degree of evidence of the presence and agency of disembodied spirits, as its cause. The individual under the undeniable influence of a physical cause, had a direct vision of a physical object, the letters referred to. How could spirits, if they were present, help the vision of this individual, or cause that physical force to induce it? Minds constituting the circle could not, by their thoughts, feelings, and acts of will directly induce such vision in the medium, or cause the force acting in her organism to do it. How, then, could disembodied spirits unconnected with that organism, induce, by their thoughts, feelings, and acts of will, (the only way in which they could produce such results, if at all,) such vision in her, or cause the force referred to, to do it? To us, it is a matter of no little wonder that such facts are referred to spirits out of the body, or to any force out of, and unconnected with, the organism of the medium, as their cause, not a ray of light being thrown upon the facts by such a supposition.

3. Precisely similar perceptions, and those far more

mysterious, are well known to result from the action of this force, in other circumstances. Dr. Wayland mentions the case of a Miss Reynolds, of Springfield, Mass., who, when deeply blindfolded, and shut up in a dark room, could even then read the finest print. Others have been known to read sentences when the paper on which they were written were encased in lead. All these things have been done in relations where no one could imagine even that spirits caused the perceptions. How, then, can such a perception as this be adduced as proof of the truth of Spiritualism?

4. This case presents another very clear instance in which an individual is at the same time what is called a medium, and also a clairvoyant, and while it proves the identity of the clairvoyant and spirit phenomena, it also explains the manner in which new information is sometimes brought into these circles, and that unconnected with spirits. The same influence, a mere physical cause, which enabled this medium to read that paper, might enable her to report, in some instances, facts which lie at any distance beyond the vision and knowledge of any one present, and her visions might be embodied in some communication given forth as from spirits.

5. This case, we remark finally, presents very strong evidence against the claims of Spiritualism; because if such a fact may occur, and we have shown that it did occur, without the agency of spirits, any other phenomenon of Spiritualism may occur without such agency. This is undeniable.

SECTION II.

SPECIAL FACTS WHICH REQUIRE A PARTICULAR EXPLANATION.

There are a class of what may properly be denominated special facts which individuals not fully convinced of the truth of Spiritualism, have met with, and by which, while rejecting the theory for what they are compelled to regard as sufficient and incontestable evidence, yet presents no little embarrassment to their minds. Take the following from Rev. Charles Beecher's "Review of Spiritual Manifestations." "Thus in a circle the table addresses itself to a young man, A. B., and says, 'I met you in Rome. George Inman.' A. B. remembers no such person. The table is asked to assist his memory, and replies, 'Cigars — not burn.' Yet A. B. remains oblivious, nor can any of his friends who travelled with him recall any person of that name, nor any incident suggestive of incombustible cigars." On subsequent occasions this individual was annoyed with a repetition of the same communications, without at all, as it would appear, reviving in his mind a remembrance of the person or circumstance referred to. The appearance, and the conclusion of the spiritualist here is, that there is a spirit present who is vainly endeavoring to induce a recollection of himself in the person present, and that when the name, person, and incident suggested can none of them be recalled. We have two remarks to make in regard to such a case: 1. Until the circumstances of time and place are recalled, we should hold the whole affair to be a mere fiction framed and designedly introduced by the medium, or some one present, for purposes of deception, or a spontaneous creation of the imagination of A. B. himself, or of some other individual present. The repetition of the communication after its first introduction presents no mystery at all. It is, on the other hand, just what should be expected. The very strangeness of the communication would fix it upon the mind so firmly that no other result could be anticipated. 2. Should the remembrance of the person and facts, with the circumstances of time and place, be subsequently recalled, then we should say, that in our experience, to say the least, the fact is very common indeed, for the remembrance of real scenes to recur to the mind, in just such broken and disjointed fragments as these. Some name is suggested, and then some fact, or *vice versa*, each perfectly isolated from any real scene that we can, at the time, recall. The case, then, in whatever light it is viewed, presents no indications whatever of the presence of spirits.

In another instance, a gentleman put a question of this kind to the spirit of a friend with whom he was professedly communicating: "Have I, in my possession, a token of affectionate remembrance which I received from you?" The answer was, "Yes," and an object was named which accorded with the recollection of the inquirer. "Have I any other such token?" Answer, "Yes." Not recollecting any such object, he specified a number of articles. When the term "book" was pronounced, there was an affirmative response. Subsequent reflection verified the communication, though, at the time, he could not recall the fact that such a token had ever been received by him from that individual. Here is the appearance, to say the least, of one mind attempting, and with final success, to revive in the mind of another what is to the latter a forgotten fact, and the mind accomplishing this object a disembodied spirit. "How," we were once asked, "do you account for such a fact as that, in accordance with your theory?" Our answer to such an inquiry is at hand. When the first inquiry was correctly answered, an undefined impression rested upon the inquirer's mind, that this was not the only object of the kind that he had received from that friend, and this impression occasioned the asking of the second question, Have I any other such token? This impression would attach to the term "book," the instant it was pronounced, though some time might elapse before the fact of the gift would become an object of distinct recollection, and this was all that was requisite to induce the rap indicating that the right object had been named. There is no difficulty whatever, in accounting, in accordance with the known laws of mind, for such a fact, without supposing at all the interposition of spirits as its cause.

A case which we adduced in the progress of our investigations, prepares the way for a clear and satisfactory explanation of the communication which a friend received, that a daughter whom he supposed to have been in France, was in London, a case which represents a class of facts in Spiritualism demanding explanation. The case was that of Prof. A., who asked the spirit of a deceased sister to specify the given name of their father, and another and different name was given, that of their brother. The professor had just before been putting questions concerning the brother, and his thoughts instantly reverted to him from the father, as soon as the question referred to was put. This would have made no difference, had the spirit of the sister been really responding. As it was, this recurrence to the brother occasioned the response that was received. So our friend had just asked the spirit of his deceased wife, to designate the present locality of their eldest daughter, and the correct answer, London, was given. The question next put, was, where is the daughter next younger? The mind of the inquirer, as in the case of the Professor, instantly and very naturally recurred to the object just before named, and this occasioned the response that was received, a response which *happened*, in this case, to be right. The unexpected answer, from its unexpectedness, would be present to the inquirer's mind, whenever the question was repeated, and this would occasion a repetition of the same response. This to our mind is the true account of this case. Multitudes of surprising revelations are unquestionably thus obtained. The one, in a thousand, that happens to be right, is put down to the credit of Spiritualism, and the nine hundred and ninety-nine wrong ones set aside as of no account.

We once heard an advocate of Spiritualism, in a public meeting, give the following case, as demonstrative proof of the truth of his theory. An individual asked the spirit of a deceased friend this question: What was your age at the time of your death? A certain number was given, which did not accord with the recollection of the inquirer. On his way home, however, as he passed by the city cemetery, he saw upon the gravestone of that friend the precise number given in the spirit circle. The speaker, in this instance, instead of proving his own theory, betrayed his ignorance of the well-known laws of mind. In the memory of the inquirer were two impressions in regard to the age of that friend, the one particularly thought of when he put the question, and that which he, no doubt, had often seen before on the tombstone. After putting the question, the latter was suggested, and occasioned the response, and that without becoming an object of distinct remembrance, as the former was, nothing almost being more common than such forms of recollection.

SECTION III.

PHENOMENA OF DREAMING, AND PREMONITIONS OF FUTURE EVENTS.

There are cases in which persons in sleep seem to have a direct and immediate vision of objects at a great distance from them. A case of this kind has been recently reported in the Cincinnati papers, as having occurred in that city. A lady who had a very endeared brother in California, as she fell asleep, saw him in his log cabin rise suddenly and very carefully from his bed, and having girded on his weapons, look with an intense gaze at a certain opening in the wall at the head of his bed. Soon a hand holding a dagger was seen passing in through that hole, and passing on silently till the point of the weapon was directed to the spot where the brother had been lying down, a deadly thrust was given. The brother, in the mean time, with a single stroke with his bowie knife, completely separated the arm from the body without. A terrible cry was heard, and the brother, rushing out of the cabin, dragged in the body of the assassin, who was in the last agonies of death, in consequence of having stabbed himself with his other hand. Such, in substance, was the vision which was related by the sister the next morning, and subsequently became a matter of interesting conversation among her friends. A few weeks subsequent, she received a letter from her brother, revealing to her the fact, that on the very night in which she had the vision, the identical scene, in all particulars, as it then presented itself to her mind, actually occurred in his cabin. Whether this is an authentic case or not, and we see no reasons whatever to call in question its authenticity, facts of a precisely similar character do arise, and this case may consequently be taken to represent the class. Shall we regard this as a mere accidental coincidence, or an actual vision of what did occur? We take the latter supposition. How shall we account for the facts on that supposition? The brain of the sister, as we suppose, during sleep, came under the influence of the odylic force, and at the same moment happened to be in odylic rapport with the scene referred to, or more correctly, perhaps, with the brain of the brother. A vision of the scene, on that supposition, could not, from the nature of this force, but have occurred. This perception would have occurred, had the individual been awake or asleep. The distance of the scene from the percipient made no difference whatever. In all ages, dreams of this kind have sometimes occurred, and in all cases, excepting when supernaturally induced, unquestionably from this cause.

We take the following case from "Rogers' Philosophy of Mysterious Rappings:" —

"Rev. Joseph Wilkins, an English dissenting minister, relating the case of himself, says: 'Being one night asleep, I dreamed that I was travelling to London, and, as it would not be much out of my way, I would go by Gloucestershire, and call upon my friends.' Accordingly he seemed to have arrived at his father's house; but, finding the front door closed, he went round to the back, and there entered. The family, however, being already in bed, he seemed to ascend the stairs and enter his father's bedchamber. He found him asleep; but, to his mother, who seemed awake, he said, as he walked round to her side of the bed, 'Mother, I am going a long journey, and am come to bid you good-by;' to which she answered, 'O, dear son, thou art dead!' This, understand, was but a dream, to which this gentleman at the time attached no importance.

"He was, however, greatly surprised, when, soon after, he received a letter from his father, addressed to himself, *if alive*, or, if not, to his surviving friends; begging earnestly for immediate intelligence, since they believed him dead. For that on such a night (that on which their son had his dream) he, the *father*, *being asleep*, and *Mrs. Wilkins*, *the mother*, being awake, she had distinctly heard somebody try the fore-door, which being fast, the person had gone round to the back, and there entered. She had perfectly recognized the footstep to be that of her son, who ascended the stairs, and, entering the bedchamber, had said to her, 'Mother, I am going a long journey, and am come to wish you good-by.' Whereupon she had answered, 'O, dear son, thou art dead!' Much alarmed, she had awakened her husband, and related what had occurred, assuring him that it was not a dream, for that she had not been asleep at all.

"Mr. Wilkins remarks that this singular circumstance took place in the year 1754, when he was living at Ottery; and that he had frequently discussed the subject with his mother, with whom the impression was even stronger than on himself. *Neither death nor any thing else remarkable ensued;* and he had no idea of a journey."

To us, the explanation of this fact, whose authenticity cannot properly be doubted, is quite easy and manifest. When two minds, or rather brains, happen to be in strong odylic rapport, the mental states of one are reproduced in the mind of the other. Distance of locality makes no difference whatever. In this case, the brains of the mother and son were in this relation, and hence the vision of the latter in a dream became an object of perception to the former when awake, just as the *imaginings* of the mesmerizer become perceptions in the mind of his subject.

In the same manner the brains of two individuals, when both are asleep, and at a great distance from each other, may come into odylic rapport with each other, so that the mental apprehensions of one may thereby be reproduced in the mind of the other, and thus each have the same vision or dream at the same moment. We received, a few days since, from a gentleman whose testimony no one acquainted with him will doubt, a statement of an affecting fact of this kind which occurred in his own experience. When a youth, he had a pair of twin brothers whom he most tenderly loved. At length one of them died. His heart was then intensely entwined around the other, little Fredy, as he called him. At one time, when he was some fifteen or twenty miles from home, employed as a clerk in a store, he had in his sleep the following vision. He thought, that at night he approached the front door of his father's residence, and on attempting to open it, found it fastened. He then went round to the back door and entered into a large kitchen, in a remote corner of which was a recess where his parents were accustomed to sleep. The room, as he thought, was at the time lighted up by a small fire which was still burning. As he entered the room, his mother extended her arms towards him, and exclaimed, O William!

As he came to her, and they were locked in each others' arms, she said to him, Fredy is dead! They then wept together, while the arms of each were encircling the other, for a long time, till, from excess of grief, he awoke, and found his pillow drenched with tears. About one o'clock in the afternoon of that day, his cousin drove up to the door. As they met, the young man exclaimed, I know what you have come for. Fredy is dead. Yes, was the reply. Fredy is dead, and I have come for you. After he had been home a little while, his father said to him, Your mother had a very singular dream last night. She thought that you came to the front door, and finding it fastened, you came round by the back door, and entered our room. As you entered, she extended her arms towards you, and exclaimed, O William! You came to her, and as each was encircled in the other's arms, she said to you, Fredy is dead, and thus embracing each other, you wept together for a long time. The same identical vision had, as nearly as it could be ascertained, at the same time, passed before the mind of the mother and the son, though they were separated at a distance of some fifteen or twenty miles from each other. People, if they choose, may call such events mere chance coincidences. We judge differently. We think that there must have been, at the moment, a medium of communication between those two minds, the very one of which we are treating, a medium so relatively developed between them, that the thoughts of the one were reproduced in the other. To us such facts which, in some instances, do characterize human experience, admit of no other explanation.

ANALOGOUS FACTS OF COMMON OCCURRENCE IN EVERY-DAY LIFE.

An invisible force which pervades all nature around us, and whose influence we are constantly experiencing, may not be recognized as present at all, excepting in its most powerful and startling occurrences. Of this, electricity may be alluded to as an example and illustration. Our physical system is no doubt continuously pervaded by electric currents, as is nature in its entireness all around us. Many events, also, are continually occurring around us, indicative, to the careful observer, of its presence and action. Its presence, however, is not distinctly recognized, till we witness some of its more startling phenomena, as in the thunderstorm. The same holds true of the odylic force. All nature is instinct with its presence and influence, and we are continuous spectators of its ordinary phenomena. From all the forces in nature, we think that it is distinguished by this one striking peculiarity. The *direction of its activity*, the proper conditions being fulfilled, *is as mental states, and is determined by the same*, and this, too, while, as an attractive and repulsive force, it acts with great power upon all other objects in nature. For ourselves, we believe, and we suggest this for the consideration of scientific men and of the public generally, — we believe, we say, that in the human organism, it is the medium of voluntary muscular action, as well as of sensation. There must be in that organism some such force, a force which, while its own action accords with mental states, and is determined by the same, controls, also, in consequence of its peculiar properties, the muscular system, and thus becomes the immediate cause of all voluntary motion in the physical organization. This we believe to be none other than the odylic force of which we have been treating. When it is not sufficiently, or when it is excessively developed in that system, we then have the various forms of cramp and convulsions, and also nervous developments. When developed in certain relative degrees in the organisms of two or more individuals, then the mental states of one are reproduced in the minds of the others. Where people are much together, in the ordinary intercourse of life, as in families, it becomes spontaneously developed between them to such an extent, that they are often thinking each others' thoughts, or the thoughts of one are reproduced in the minds of the others. The father, for example, when sitting in the family circle, gives utterance to a certain thought. Nothing has been said before to lead to it, or to suggest it to any one. Yet the mother and others remark, "I was just thinking of that very thing myself." Such facts occur so frequently, and in such connections, as to preclude the supposition that such identity of thought, among so many persons, at such moments, is the result of mere accident. There must be some hitherto unrecognized medium of intercommunication, by which the thoughts of one mind are reproduced in others. The hypothesis before us gives us such a medium, and thus explains such phenomena. An individual with whom we were once familiar, has been separated from us for years, and for a long period has been totally out of our thoughts. He, at length, returns to our neighborhood, we knowing nothing of the fact. As he comes within a certain distance of us, he suddenly and inexplicably becomes to us an object of distinct thought and remembrance. When he comes into our presence, we inform him that we were just before thinking about him, though he had not been in our minds before for years. Of more frequent occurrence are such facts, in common experience, relative to individuals who have been separated but short periods from each other. The common recognition of such facts among all classes of community, has, as is well known, given rise to the old, and somewhat vulgar maxim, that "the devil is always near when we are speaking of him." The maxim reversed would, no doubt, be more true, to wit, we are speaking of him, when he is near, and for that reason. Facts which are so general, and so uniform in their character, in human experience, must, as we judge, have a common cause, and that cause must be something else than mere chance coincidence. We think that cause to be this. When individuals come into the vicinity of each other, the odylic relations between them not unfrequently happen to be such, that the thoughts of one are reproduced, to a certain, but limited extent, of course, in the mind of the other, and thus the thoughts of one are turned to the other. Thus we have these common facts of human experience. A moment's reflection will convince the reader, that there is nothing incredible in such a supposition. The dog, for example, passes along where his master and many others had passed hours or days previous. The animal immediately distinguishes the track of his master from all the others, and thus traces him out. Such facts necessitate one of two conclusions. Either something passed from the organism of the master to the objects upon which he trod, and remained there till, and no doubt after, the time referred to, or owing to peculiarities of physical state and constitution, a cause in that organism developed in the objects touched, a peculiar force not developed to so great an extent before, and this force passing from the organism to those objects, or by contact of the organism developed in those objects, was the cause of the peculiar effect upon the animal, an effect by which the latter was enabled to follow the track of the former, and trace him out. Of the truth of one or the other of these suppositions, there can be no doubt. Now if a mere momentary contact may produce effects from which such results arise, is it at all incredible, that from the organisms of individuals, when in a certain vicinity to each other, and when certain conditions are fulfilled, influences should go forth from one to the other, by which common sensations shall be induced in the minds in those organisms, sensations through which the same thoughts shall be induced, at the same moment, in each mind alike? To us nothing is more reasonable than such a supposition, and nothing more accordant with the analogy of known facts in the world around us.

PREMONITIONS OF FUTURE EVENTS.

There are cases in which individuals have premonitions of coming events, premonitions which can hardly be regarded, with a show of reason, as accidental creations of the imagination which, by mere accident, happen to be true. We need not specify cases. It is enough to say, that they have been matters of more or less frequent occurrence, in all ages of the world. A gentleman, for example, had a vision of the shipwreck of a vessel on the coast of Hindostan, a shipwreck in which his own son was lost. Months subsequent to the vision, the events foreshadowed, all occurred in exact accordance with the vision referred to. Yet the father was at the time in utter ignorance of the scenery where the event occurred, and of all the facts of the case. If our view of the nature and action of the odylic force be correct, the occurrence of such foreshadowings is no great mystery, but an event which is to be expected as a matter of occasional experience in the history of the race. When the brain happens to be in odylic rapport with the *causes* on which the occurrence of any particular event depends, the mind then has a vision of such events, however future, for the same reason that when in the same relations with distant objects it has a vision of the same. No person has as much reason to expect any such events, in his own experience, as he has to expect to die from a stroke of lightning. Yet their occurrence in instances few and far between, in the experience of some individuals in a nation, should not be a matter of wonder nor disbelief. Such, we are free to say, is our view, after a careful examination of facts.

SECTION IV.

PHENOMENA OF GHOST SEEING AND HAUNTED HOUSES.

Had the son, in the case above stated, died in connection with that dream, as it no doubt has happened in other instances of a similar nature, who would have doubted that the spirit of that individual had appeared to his mother? Yet undeniably no ghost did appear in this instance. The fact, then, that the spirit of one person is thought to appear to another individual, just at the time of the death of the former, or at any other period, is no certain indication at all that any spirit whatever is present as an object of vision. The vision may have been, and must, till we have positive proof to the contrary, be held to have been a mere mental hallucination occasioned by the fact, that the brain of the person dying happened, at the time, to come into odylic rapport with that of the subject of the vision. The fact, too, that persons have visions as of spirits, when no spirit can be supposed to be present, is also to be assumed as proof, that *seeing* spirits is no evidence that spirits are present as objects of vision. One class of persons take certain medicines, others have certain forms of disease, and others spend a certain time in particular localities. In each case alike similar visions, as of spirits, occur. In the two former instances, no spirits are supposed to have been present, as objects of vision. Why should we suppose them present in the last? Nothing is more contrary to all the laws of scientific induction, than such a supposition. There is known to exist a force in nature, which, when developed to a certain extent in the brain, induces visions as of spirits, ghosts, etc. All such visions, therefore, are to be attributed to the action of such cause, until facts occur necessitating a different supposition. We have then a clear and distinct explanation of the phenomena of ghost seeing, which have troubled the world so much in past ages, and are beginning to trouble it again in the present. Wherever and from whatever cause the odylic force is developed unduly in the human brain, just such visions are from time to time to be expected, and when they do occur, we are, from the effect, to infer the presence of the cause. The fact that persons *speak* to the apparition, and seem to receive answers, does not alter the case at all; because just such facts do occur, when no spirits are present, and the action of the force which occasions the vision equally accounts for such facts also.

What are haunted houses and places of a like character, but localities in which this same force is so developed that persons of peculiar temperament remaining in them for certain periods, become so affected with it, that these forms of phenomena are induced, that is, visions as of spirits are occasioned? We have not yet read or heard of a haunted house all the facts connected with which may not be most fully and perfectly accounted for by a reference to this one cause. The spirits there seen, and the sounds and voices heard, are no more external to the minds and organisms of the percipients, than what the mother above referred to saw of and heard from her son was external to her mind and organism.

There is one other view of this whole subject also, that should not be overlooked in this connection. It is not at all strange, but a matter to be expected, that phosphorescent, and other luminous vapors should, from time to time, arise from graveyards and old, forsaken, and dilapidated and decaying buildings, and that in and near some such places, individuals of peculiar physical constitutional temperament, should very quickly, in many instances, have the odylic force developed in their organisms. A number of most efficient causes of ghost seeing here present themselves, causes sufficiently efficient to account for such perceptions, in the total absence of all corresponding objects, that is, real visible spirits. Any such luminous substances rising in the night time, in the form of columns, as they most naturally do, would of necessity, to the terrified imagination of the beholder, appear as a human body wrapped in a winding-sheet, the form in which ghosts almost, if not quite invariably appear. It is the opinion of some philosophers also, who have carefully investigated the subject, that the odylic force developed in such localities, sometimes, in ascending from the earth, spontaneously assumes a form somewhat like that of the human body, and in that form, becomes visible to individuals present, especially if the same force is developed in their organisms. Then the same force in such organisms often occasions visions as of such objects, when nothing is perceived external to the organism itself. It is well known also, that this force, as developed in particular localities, is attended with the very noises, jarring of surrounding objects, and movement of heavy bodies which are witnessed in haunted houses. All these causes combined are abundantly sufficient to account for all the phenomena of ghost seeing and haunted houses with which the world has, from time to time, been troubled, without the supposition of spirit presence. All such phenomena differ fundamentally from the "angel visits" recorded in Scripture. The latter were intelligent manifestations made to answer important ends. The former are unintelligent manifestations bearing the very characteristics they would bear were they just what we have represented them to be. As such, then, we regard them, having assigned causes abundantly adequate to account for their existence, as such phenomena.

SECTION V.

WITCHCRAFT, FORTUNE TELLING, MANNER IN WHICH MYSTERIOUS EVENTS ARE COMMONLY TREATED.

There are two points of light in which the phenomena of witchcraft may be considered, namely, — the leading facts set forth by those who, in past ages, have believed in such theory, — and the conclusions which have been deduced from these facts. Hitherto, there has, for the most part, been supposed to be a necessary connection between the facts and the conclusion. Hence, those denying the latter, have generally ignored the former as mere illusions, and that without examination. Let us suppose, that each of these questions be considered by itself, without any reference to the other, and that we commence with a candid and careful examination of the evidence that exists of the reality of many of the leading facts adduced by Cotton Mather and his associates, for example, in regard to the subject. We venture the opinion, that few facts of the past will be found to be sustained by higher and more valid evidence than these. Our fathers will be found to have erred, not in regard to the facts many of them, to say the least, but with respect to the conclusions which they deduced from those facts. It will also be found, that there was, in all respects, the same connection between their facts and conclusions, that there is between those of Spiritualism now. We have precisely the same evidence of the agency of devils in the phenomena of Salem witchcraft, that we have of that of the disembodied spirits of men, in the so called spirit phenomena. If our fathers erred in their conclusions, two millions of people, the number asserted by spiritualists to hold their theory in this country, at the present time, have shown themselves to be not more wise; for the same identical phenomena, physical and mental, were presented to reveal and prove the presence and agency of devils in one instance, that are or can be adduced to reveal and prove that of the disembodied spirits of men, in the other. Are physical objects now moved with and without physical contact, and that in accordance with intelligence? So they were then. Have we now various mediums through whom intelligent communications are obtained, as from the spirits of men? Through various mediums, equally intelligent and mysterious revelations were given forth, as from devils then. The witch could do then all that the medium can do now. We are just as sacredly bound to admit the *mere facts* of Witchcraft as we are to admit those of Spiritualism, and have just as high and sacred reasons for rejecting the conclusions of the believers in each alike.

One test which our fathers sometimes applied, in determining who were and who were not witches, will be found to be not so deserving of ridicule, as has been supposed. We refer to the custom of putting individuals into sacks containing lead or stones, and then placing them upon water to see whether they would float, or sink to the bottom, the former class being held as real witches and the latter not. We learn that the body of Frederica Hauffe would float upon water like a cork, and that it was very difficult to get it beneath the surface. For the same reasons, the bodies of witches, that is, of those in whom the odylic force was to a certain extent developed, would thus float upon the surface of water. There, too, was an error, not in regard to facts, but in respect to conclusions to be deduced from such facts. Nor do we suppose, that there is any ground whatever for the assertion so commonly made, that those who, in such trials, sank to the bottom, were left to perish there. They were unquestionably rescued by the spectators, and all arrangements were made for that purpose.

Nor, in our judgment, do our fathers deserve at all, the ridicule and censure heaped upon them by partial and prejudiced historians, for their so called persecutions of witches. What were the real facts of the case? The witches, in the first place, *professed* to be in league with devils, and exercised their strange power as from them. Then they performed such mysterious, and apparently supernatural feats, that there appeared to the public no way of accounting for the facts, but by admitting the claims set forward by this class of persons. They became the sources of great depravity and corruption, as well as objects of corresponding fear and terror in the community. Our fathers supposing, and most honestly too, that there was a necessary connection between the facts which they knew and could not but know to be real, and the truth of the professions of the witches, under that knowledge and conviction proceeded against persons making such professions, and executed upon them what was then believed to have been required in the word of God, in such cases. We believe, that there is not the least reason for sympathy with those who were making such professions, or that their sufferings were beyond their guilt. Those who profess to be in league with devils, and perform, of choice, acts which can be accounted for according to existing light and knowledge, upon no other supposition but that such professions must be true, have no reason to complain, if they are treated according to their professions and acts. On the other hand, we are equally confident that our fathers, in what they did in the case, acted "in all good conscience before God" and man too, that they deserve of their posterity, pity for their mistakes, and commendation for their zeal, misdirected though it happened to have been. That the innocent, in some instances, suffered with the guilty, we have no doubt, and this should be and is a matter of deep and unfeigned regret.

If the theory which we have been endeavoring to establish be admitted, the phenomena of witchcraft wears no longer the veil of mystery. Connect with the so called spirit phenomena of our day, the idea of an origin from devils, let our mediums simply believe themselves under a corresponding influence, and let that sentiment be entertained by those who visit these circles, and we should have all the phenomena of Salem witchcraft over again, and that without change or modification. Spiritualism and witchcraft are the exclusive results of a common cause. The phenomena of each are to be explained upon precisely the same principles. The facts in both cases alike are real, and the conclusions equally false, the conclusions, we mean, that the facts are the result of an *ab extra*, and not of an exclusively mundane, cause. It would be interesting, did our space permit, to draw at length the parallel between the physical and intellectual manifestations attending these two movements, the one under the assumed control of devils, and the other under that of the departed spirits of human beings, and show how perfectly, with this one exception, they correspond with each other. This, however, is not necessary. All that is now required is to designate the cause of such phenomena, and to show how they may all be explained in the light of such cause.

BEWITCHING PERSONS AND OBJECTS.

In all cases of witchcraft, the belief appears to have obtained, that the witch, or wizard, as the case might be, had the power to produce upon certain persons and objects, certain preternatural effects, on account of which such persons and objects were said to have been "bewitched." The following extracts from Mr. Rogers contain a sufficient number of cases to present an illustration of the nature of this power, cases cited by him from C. Mather, and the "Night Side of Nature."

"Nicholas Desbaro, in Hartford, Conn., having unjustly detained a chest of clothes belonging to another man, the former became wonderfully tormented at his own house by various poundings and other phenomena, such as we have already noticed, as the unaccountable movement of various things about his house. 'And it endured for divers months,' says Rev. C. Mather; 'but, upon the restoration of the clothes thus detained, the troubles ceased.' *

"It is astonishing to notice the numerous well-authenticated cases of the same character to be found everywhere, — confined to no particular age or country, though occurring only in particular localities. We have the account of one of this kind having occurred in Portsmouth, N. H., in 1683, at the house of George Walton. He, it seems, was suspected and charged by a woman with having unjustly 'detained some land from her;' after which, for quite a period, his house was strangely beset with unaccountable disturbances, all of them representing revengeful passion, in the destruction of property, and dismal noises. He also found the same thing to meet him not only at home, but even in particular localities away from home.†

"Another singular case related is that of 'Mr. Philip Smith, aged about fifty years, a son of eminently virtuous parents, a deacon of the church in Hadley, Mass., a member of the General Court, a justice in the county

* Mather's Magnalia, B. VI., p. 69. † Ibid.

court, a selectman for the affairs of the town, a lieutenant of the troop, a man of devotion, sanctity, gravity, and, in all that is honest, exceeding exemplary. Such a man was, in the winter of the year 1684, murdered with an hideous witchcraft that filled all those parts of New England with astonishment. He was by his office concerned about relieving the indigence of a wretched woman in the town, who, being *dissatisfied* at some of his just cares about her, expressed herself to him in such a manner that he declared himself thenceforward apprehensive of receiving mischief at her hands.' *

"This expectation, on his part, of receiving mischievous influences from this woman, was sufficient, if the local conditions of mundane force were favorable, to cause his disturbance by the cerebral action of the woman in reference to him or his house.

"Accordingly we find, that soon after having fallen ill, with a derangement of the brain, he incessantly talked of the woman, and of her ghost in his room; and his 'gallipots of medicines' would be 'unaccountably emptied. Audible scratchings were made about the bed, when his hands and feet lay wholly still, and were held by others.' There was an *appearance* of lights sometimes on the bed. The bed would be unaccountably shaken, as in other cases we have mentioned. Amid these strange occurrences the man died; and 'divers noises were also heard in the room where the *corpse* lay, as the clattering of chairs and stools, whereof no account could be given. This was the end of so good a man. And I could,' continues Mather, 'with *unquestionable evidence*, relate the tragical death of several good men in this land, attended with such preternatural circumstances.'"

* Mather's Magnalia, B. VI. p. 70.

28

"Baron Dupotel relates the following,* which occurred at Rambouillet, in the month of November, 1846.

"Some travelling merchants called early one morning at the door of a farm-house, belonging to a man named Bottel, and demanded food; which the maid-servant gave them, when they left. A while after, one of the party returned, and demanded more, which being refused, the man showed resentment, uttered threats, and turned away. The same night, at the supper table, the plates began to dance, and roll off the table. The girl, going to the door, and chancing to place herself *just where the pedler stood*, was seized with convulsions, and a whirling motion. The carter, who was standing by, laughed at her, and out of bravado placed himself *on the same spot*, when he felt almost suffocated, and was so unable to command his movements that he was overturned into a large pool in front of the house. Upon this, they rushed to the curé of the parish for assistance; but he had scarcely said a prayer or two, before he was attacked in the same manner, and his furniture beginning to oscillate and crack as if it were bewitched, which exceedingly frightened the poor people. After a time the phenomena intermitted, and they hoped all was over; but presently it began again, and this occurred more than once before it wholly subsided."

The question which here arises is this: How was this strange power exerted by the witch? We are all aware, that when the magnetic force is developed in one rod of iron, this rod then has the power of developing the same force in other rods with which it is brought into certain relations. So with objects in which the odylic force is developed. They have the power, when

* See Night Side of Nature, p. 384.

brought into certain relations to other objects, to develop in them the same force. This is especially true of this force when developed in the human organism, more particularly when the mind of the subject is intensely excited, and above all, when the whole attention and energy of the mind of such persons become concentrated upon some particular person or object. Thus the intense excitement of the travelling merchant, in whom this force was unquestionably very strongly developed, that intense excitement, we say, excited the action of this force in his organism to such a degree as to develop it also in the objects immediately beneath and around him. The organisms of other individuals, who came into the immediate vicinity of those objects, and especially into the place where he stood, became so charged with that force as to experience the terrible effects described. So with persons and objects upon which the attention of the witch, in a state of terrible excitement, became concentrated. In them the same force thus became developed, and consequently became the cause of the strange phenomena which followed. When the force was thus relatively developed between the witch and such person or object, she had the power to direct its action, in many important respects, at will. On this principle, the drummer of Tedworth could play upon his drum, though at a distance from it. So the witch could inflict many terrible injuries upon her victims, and thus became the terror of the community around. Under the mistaken apprehension that it was satanic power which such persons exercised, our fathers inflicted upon them retributions not undeserved for their real crimes.

FORTUNE-TELLING.

The common supposition is, that fortune-tellers are deliberate impostors, who, while they are in a normal state, and know themselves to be thus, profess to be possessed of a supernatural foresight of future events. For the most part, we have no doubt that this is the case. We are fully convinced, however, that this practice or art, has its basis, in some instances, in an abnormal physical and mental condition of the professed seer, a condition induced by the odylic force, and in which the subject, the fortune-teller, sustains precisely the same relations to the individual present, that the mesmeric or clairvoyant subject does to the mesmerizer. After the accustomed ceremonies have been gone through with, the fortune-teller goes into a manifestly magnetic condition, in which he or she speaks, as if a new power and influence had obtained full control over him. Soon the secret thoughts of the inquirer are disclosed, and facts in his history utterly unknown, as he fully believes, to any being on earth but himself. In the midst of these, there are incoherent predictions of things future, predictions which, in but very few instances are realized in any form, but in some very distant and solitary cases very strikingly fulfilled. The power manifested in revealing things secret, in regard to the past, inspires the inquirer with confidence in regard to the predictions of things future. Here we have another instance, or form, in which the thoughts of one person are transferred to the mind of another through the action of odylic force. A friend of ours, for example, a lady, once as she was at a distant place from that of her own residence, visiting from house to house, called at the residence of an individual of this class. She had never seen that person before, and was equally certain of being a total stranger to her. Finding that she was in the presence of such a person, our friend determined to satisfy her curiosity by seeing for herself what such an individual can do. After the usual ceremony of shuffling cards, etc. were gone through with, the fortune-teller evidently, our friend being acquainted with such manifestations, went into a magnetic condition. Soon she stated, among other things, that she saw the husband of the stranger in a *warehouse*, apparently examining it, (he had gone on that errand at that very time,) that one of her children was affected with a peculiar form of disease, and described with perfect accuracy his motions when under its action, and then, among many other things, related facts in the past history of our friend, which she was perfectly certain no one on earth knew but herself. One prediction, very indefinitely stated, was uttered, which came to pass. "There," says the fortune-teller, after a while, "the influence has passed from me, I can say no more." Who does not see here the results of known mesmeric, or odylic relations between these individuals; relations in which the thoughts and remembrances of one are transferred to the mind of the other? A lady in Boston recently told us of a similar interview which she once had with a fortune-teller in that city, an individual probably now alive. Our informant, whose word will not be doubted by those knowing her, was born and educated in the State of Maine, where her parents now reside. To the fortune-teller she was a total stranger, and from the circumstances of the case, she felt the most undoubted assurance, that her visit was totally unexpected, and that she was to the individual called upon, an unknown and total stranger. When the proper conditions were fulfilled, the leading incidents of this stranger's life, from her childhood up, the peculiarities of her character as a child, special facts in her past history, utterly unknown as she fully believes to any one on earth but herself, the peculiarities of the past and present residence of her parents, and of the scenery about the same, they having removed to another part of the State from that where her childhood and youth were spent, all these things were detailed with the most astonishing minuteness and accuracy, and with a lifelike vividness, in the presence of which she seemed almost to live the past over again.

Of the leading facts pertaining to a celebrated character of this class, who lived in Paris during the early part of the present century, our readers are very probably aware. The name of the individual has escaped us. This, however, was true of her, — all who visited her, from whatever parts of the kingdom or world they came, were astonished, (and her fame drew vast multitudes from all parts to consult her,) and not unfrequently confounded by the minute and specific revelations of their past history, which they would receive through that pythoness. In her case, there would be equally strange revelations in regard to the future, and other facts unknown to her visitants; she, no doubt, while in a magnetic state, being a very powerful clairvoyant. Such facts accord with the history of many fortune-tellers, the world over. The manner in which their revelations, in regard to the past history of utter strangers resorting to them, are obtained and given forth, is quite obvious. In the magnetic or odylic state into which they are introduced by the various ceremonies performed, the remembrances of persons present in regard to their past history, are, through the action of this power, and by virtue of its nature and relations to mind, reproduced in the mind of fortune-tellers, and given forth by them, on the same principles that A. J. Davis uttered the present thoughts of the lady in magnetic communication with him. Equally manifest is the manner in which revelations pertaining to the future commonly are obtained and given forth, through such individuals. The visitant has in his mind, visions and plans in regard to the future. Social, and especially domestic connections may be formed, desired or intended with specific individuals, or with imaginary personages imaged forth in the mind in conformity with the heart's beau ideal. In the presence of the fortune-teller, and in anticipation of such revelations, these plans and persons, real or imaginary, are of course suggested to the inquirer. Through his or her mind, they are reproduced in that of the pythoness, and by her given forth as revelations communicated by higher powers to her mind. It is thus, no doubt, that the image of the person with whom conjugal relations are afterwards consummated, are sometimes presented as prophetic enunciations to the inquirer, and by him or her ever after regarded as proof of a real prophetic foresight in the fortune-teller.

MANNER IN WHICH MYSTERIOUS EVENTS ARE COMMONLY TREATED.

Whenever mysterious events appear, and when inferences unfriendly to truth are drawn from them, the friends of truth are too apt, instead of acquainting themselves with the facts of the case, and thus becoming enabled to speak intelligently upon the subject, to deny the facts altogether, and that without examination, and at the same time, to treat the whole subject with silent contempt, as wholly unworthy of their notice. To our minds, no course of procedure can be more unwise than this, especially among the teachers of our holy religion. They certainly should be able to speak intelligently upon all subjects which, in the public mind around them, bear upon the cause of truth and righteousness. Ignorance, in such cases, renders the religious teacher an object of contempt, on the part of the opposers of the truth. It utterly annihilates also his power to benefit all who believe the facts ignored.

Nor does the evil stop here. The opposer of truth finds an excuse for ignoring altogether the great question of the divine origin of Christianity, and without examination denying its facts, and finds this excuse in the manner in which his facts and arguments are treated. We cannot ask men, with any rational hope of being heard, to listen with candor and wakeful interest to our facts and arguments, unless we listen, with the same candor and interest, to theirs.

By the same course also, the friends of truth are sometimes found treating with contempt great facts, and the most legitimate deductions from the same, as in the case of geology and other kindred sciences, when they first unlocked their priceless treasures to the world. The friends of truth must ever regard themselves as bound to admit facts, however mysterious, when their reality is affirmed by valid evidence. On no other condition can they fully exemplify the love of universal truth required by the gospel which they profess, or require men to admit the facts which lie at the basis of the claims of Christianity to a divine original.

SECTION VI.

THESE SO CALLED SPIRIT MANIFESTATIONS AND SCRIPTURE MIRACLES. BEARING OF OUR PREVIOUS DISCUSSIONS UPON THE DOCTRINE OF A GENERAL AND PARTICULAR PROVIDENCE. CONCLUSION.

Spiritualists everywhere claim, that these so called spirit manifestations are attended with facts which have the same marks of being miracles, that the great facts recorded in the Bible do. Indeed, it is now put forth, unblushingly, that this movement is attended with the same kind of supernatural events that Christianity was, events, too, resulting from the very same cause; and that no one can repudiate the claims of Spiritualism, without being bound, in consistency, to repudiate those of Christianity. It is of no little importance, then, that we clearly distinguish these manifestations from real miracles, those recorded in the Bible especially.

What then is a real miracle, and what especially are the characteristics of the affirmed miracles recorded in the Bible? A real miracle, we reply, is *an event wholly unlike and unanalogous, in its essential characteristics, to any event resulting from mere mundane causes.* A miracle that can properly be used as a *divine* attestation of the truth of any proposition or doctrine, must be an event of such a character, that its occurrence can be accounted for, but by a reference to a direct and immediate interposition of *creative power*, and must sustain such relations to that proposition or doctrine, that the reality of the event cannot be admitted without admitting such proposition or doctrine as a divinely attested truth. Now we affirm the above to be the precise character of the so called miraculous events recorded in the

Scriptures. Such also is the relation of those events to the Scriptures, that the reality of the former cannot be admitted, without admitting the divine origin of the latter. All this is undeniable, as we shall show, in Part III. of this treatise.

What, on the other hand, is the character of these manifestations? There is not one among them, as we have seen, whose existence and entire characteristics may not be accounted for, by a reference to purely mundane causes, and which is not perfectly similar and analogous in all its elements and features, to events which do result from such causes. All these manifestations, in the next instance, may be admitted, and with the most absolute logical consistency, the claims of Spiritualism to an *ab extra* spirit origin denied.

We will contrast a few miraculous phenomena revealed in the Bible, with some claimed to be of a similar character connected with Spiritualism. We will begin with the leading miracles. It is well known that there are certain peculiar forms of disease which can sometimes almost instantly, and at others in very short periods, be cured by the imagination, or certain medicines. There are others which cannot be affected by such causes. Of the former class exclusively are the healing phenomena of Spiritualism. The latter class are among the most prominent miracles revealed in the Bible. The healing medium, by his passes, may, through the imagination of the subject, or through the medicinal influence of the odylic force thus excited in the patient, effect certain forms of cure. Over other diseases he has no power for good. Then he may make as many passes as he pleases over a corpse, and he can never reanimate it with a living soul. He can make no approach whatever towards restoring to a maimed person his lost limb. Yet these last are among the most prominent of "the mighty works" performed by Christ and the sacred writers. The healing power of the medium has no efficiency excepting in the case of a few diseases. That exercised by Jesus Christ had an equal and absolute efficacy in respect to all diseases of every kind. In connection with this fact, he did what the medium can make no approach whatever towards doing, that is, restoring lost limbs to the maimed, and raising the dead to life. The power, then, which originated the Scripture miracles, supposing them to have occurred, differs not in degree, but in kind from that claimed in behalf of Spiritualism.

The same remarks are equally applicable to the spirit of prophecy. Suppose that we have two classes of predictions, each one hundred in number, and relating to events which lie equally beyond the reach of mere human foresight. Of one class but one in the whole hundred is fulfilled in any form. Of the other, not one in the hundred fails in any particular. What higher evidence can we have, that the intelligence which originated the latter class differs, not in degree, but in kind, from that which originated the former? the one being possessed of the most infallible, and the other of the most erring foresight. Such, precisely, is the character of the predictions recorded in the Bible, and those put forward by spiritualists to sustain the claims of their system. The latter class bears all conceivable marks of a mere human, and the former of a divine origin, the one indicating an origin from intelligence omniscient and absolutely infallible, and the other from one most limited and fallible. In all respects the miracles of Scripture stand in absolute contrast to the so called mysteries set forth by the advocates of Spiritualism.

The advocates of Spiritualism claim, that the miracles performed by mediums should rank, we repeat, with those recorded in the Bible. To bring the subject to a still further test, let this class of persons advance to one of our granite mountains, and after making their passes over the surface of the flinty rocks, see if that mountain, at their bidding, will open its sides and send forth floods of water sufficient to quench the thirst of three millions of people, together with their countless flocks and herds. Let these same individuals then approach the Ohio or Hudson river, and making their passes over the same, see if at their bidding the waters thereof will divide and stand in heaps on either side, while the people pass over dry shod, and subsequently roll on as before. And finally, let them turn to the sun in the heavens, and see if on making their passes over his face, he will stand still for a season, or go "ten degrees" backward. When mediums can perform wonders even analogous to these, then, and only then, their mighty works may claim a rank among those recorded in the Bible. In the midst of these great events, there are some of course, which might or might not be the immediate result of creative power. These standing by themselves could not be claimed as miracles, and could never, if they did stand thus alone, be appealed to as proof of the divine origin of Christianity. It is this last class exclusively, forms of healing, for example, which may result from miraculous interpositions on the one hand, or from mundane causes on the other, that Spiritualism copies or can copy.

Let us apply to these two classes of facts the principle of science to which we referred in a former part of this treatise, to wit, that when a given class of facts exist, and we know that a part of them is produced exclusively by one given cause, and that this cause is in itself adequate to the production of the whole, and therefore, to account for their occurrence, we are bound to refer them, in their entireness, to that one cause. Of the miraculous events recorded in the Bible, we know absolutely, that none of these great central facts can have been the result of any cause but the direct and immediate interposition of creative power, and that this cause is perfectly adequate to account for all the rest. Admitting those facts to have occurred, we are required, therefore, by the universal and immutable principles of science to ascribe the whole together to this one exclusive cause. Of the facts of Spiritualism, on the other hand, we know with equal absoluteness, that a part of them are the exclusive result of purely mundane causes, that these causes are perfectly adequate to account for all the rest. By the same principles of science, therefore, we are bound to attribute all these facts to these causes. Thus it is, that the facts of Spiritualism can be compared to Bible miracles, only on the principle of contrast. This is the only relation that these two classes of facts do or can sustain to each other.

BEARINGS OF OUR PREVIOUS INVESTIGATIONS UPON THE DOCTRINE OF A GENERAL AND PARTICULAR PROVIDENCE.

The idea very extensively, and almost, if not quite universally obtains, at the present time, that all effects in the external universe around us, miracles excepted, occur in perfect accordance with the action of fixed and immutable material laws; that at the creation every particle of matter had its particular position assigned it relatively to every other; that all subsequent effects in the material universe, are the necessary and necessitated results of the mutual action and reaction of all such particles, in accordance with the immutable laws of attraction and repulsion, of chemical affinities and of the vital forces; and that consequently, each material event is a link in a chain of necessary causes and effects, and can, by no possibility, excepting through a miraculous interposition of creative power, be otherwise than it is. Suppose, that with that view distinctly in mind, we are about to kneel in prayer, and that the object of the prayer is to secure the occurrence of some particular event in nature, rain in time of drought, or the restoration of a sick friend to health, for example. What effect is this view of the facts of the universe likely to have in exciting or suppressing a spirit of prayer for the objects named? Is it a view adapted to excite in us the belief that prayer "avails much" for the attainment of such objects, and consequently to excite in us sentiments of hope and the exercise of earnest, fervent, and humble but confiding and persevering importunity? According to the view before us, the sick man has a certain amount and form of disease, from which he can recover but through a certain process, a process which cannot be shortened or protracted by our mental states. The drought, too, is the necessary result of the combined action of the entire particles of matter constituting the material universe, and must continue till removed by such action, action which can but move on in the line of necessary causation. Prayer, however fervent, can have no avail whatever, to secure the result referred to, unless it avails to secure a miraculous interposition of creative power, an event which no one anticipates. In the presence of such a view of the operations of the material universe, the mind can no more have faith in the availing efficacy of prayer to secure such results, than it can believe, that the same thing can, at the same time, exist and not exist. This view also, almost of necessity, will extend itself in our minds, from the material over the movements of the moral and spiritual universe. While we regard the one as controlled, in all its movements, by fixed and immutable laws of cause and effect, laws the results of which prayer can have no avail to change, we shall hardly fail to regard the moral and spiritual universe, as governed by similar laws, laws whose results are equally beyond the availing efficacy of prayer. Prayer, in the presence of such a view of the material, moral, and spiritual universe, may remain as a mere form, and in no other state can it well remain. It will not avail to change these results to inform us, that God foreseeing, at the beginning, the prayers of his people, arranged the current of events so that they should accord, in important particulars, with prayer. From the nature of the case, such an arrangement could reach such contingent events but in a very general and limited manner. It is, in itself also, a view of providence in no way adapted to call forth "effectual and fervent prayer" for *specific results*, the form which prayer generally ought to assume. The actual results of this view of providence are precisely accordant with the above presentation. Prayer made for any such results as we are speaking of, is, and no one will deny the fact, little more than a form, and as a form even, it exists to a very limited extent. The spirituality of the church is, in our solemn judgment, being "spoiled through philosophy."

If we turn from this cold and cheerless view of providence to the Scriptures, we find not only a want of correspondence, but a total and irreconcilable opposition between it and their most positive teachings, on this subject. According to such teachings, God is ever with us, as "a very present help in trouble," perplexity, and want, able and ready to respond, by specific providences, to our individual and specific necessities, and filial requests, and that equally in regard to the demands of our physical and spiritual natures. All alike stand revealed, as equally appropriate objects of prayer, objects in respect to which special and specific answers are alike and equally to be anticipated. There can be no doubt on this subject.

If we retire from the Bible and the philosophy of providence under consideration, into the depths of our own moral and spiritual being, we shall find every principle and demand of that nature in fixed and immutable correlation to the former, and in opposition to the latter view of providence. We wander through nature in a state of cheerless orphanage, till God is present to us, in all the movements of providence, in the very parental and special relations revealed in the Scriptures. Now we take the ground that the real providence of God, in the movements of the material creation, accord with the teachings of the higher philosophy revealed through the Scriptures and the moral and spiritual nature of humanity, and not with the teachings of the material philosophy before us, a philosophy which, as we shall see, has taken into the account but a *part* of the material forces of nature, and therefore fundamentally errs in its teachings pertaining to the procedures and laws of divine providence in the material universe.

As preparatory to the elucidation of the subject before us, let us, for a moment, contemplate the physical organism of man. In and connected with this organism, two distinct, and, in some respects, opposite classes of purely physical forces, are continuously operating. There are the vital and chemical forces sustaining the organism itself, and producing all the phenomena of circulation and nutrition, and the attractive and repulsive forces, including all the particles thereof, and holding the organism itself, like any other ponderous body, in connection with external nature. Then in the same organism, there is, as we have seen, another force which, in accordance with mental states, acts upon the muscular system, and becomes thereby the medium of voluntary motion, and may, consequently, not inappropriately be denominated the will-force.

Now this will-force, (the odylic force, as we have seen,) not only pervades the human organism, but all nature, too, and through it, as we have also seen, when the proper conditions are fulfilled, the most astonishing effects may be voluntarily and intentionally produced upon surrounding objects. We will, for example, that the hands of individuals in magnetic communication with us, shall be immovably fastened to the table or other objects, or that their fingers shall remain interlocked, so that they cannot draw them asunder, and these results, all the possible efforts of those individuals to the contrary notwithstanding, — these results, we say, follow in accordance with our wills. Either these events were the result of direct miraculous interpositions, or there is in all nature around us, the very force of which we are speaking, a force through which such voluntary results may be produced, the facts themselves, the reality of which cannot be denied, admitting of no other explanation. It is a first and universal principle of science, that the government of God over the material universe, (that being the only department of creation of which we are now speaking,) shall accord with the nature of *all* the forces actually existing therein. If there are — and none doubt the fact of their existence — forces in nature which act in fixed and immutable accordance with the laws of attraction, repulsion, chemical affinity, etc., then we should expect to find a class of events, like the movements of the heavenly bodies, for example, events which move on in changeless antecedence and consequence, and which prayer can never avail to alter. If, on the other hand, there is in nature another and different force, a will-force of immense power, and influence over all other material objects, a force whose action is controlled by mental states and directed by the same, then the immutable laws of science would require us to suppose, that another class of effects are continuously occurring around us, effects which are the results of successive and immediate acts of divine volition through this very force, — effects immediately produced as existing and special exigencies require, and which are no more to be regarded as miracles than the other class referred to. As thus acting in and controlling nature, God would ever be present to us, as accessible by prayer, and as the immediate and special "rewarder of them that diligently seek him." Healing mercies, rain in times of drought, sunshine in long-continued storms, and "present helps in *all* times of trouble," might be expected in answer to special prayer, and this without the mind being chilled and repelled from a throne of grace by the idea of an immutable concatenation of causes and effects throughout nature, a concatenation which nothing but miracles can avail to break or to alter, miracles which no one believes prayer would avail to secure in our behalf. To this one view of providence, a view in accordance with which special prayer for specific blessings may receive specific answers through events which would not otherwise have occurred at all, and this without miracles, and in full and perfect accordance with God's ordinary method of controlling events in the world around us, — to this one view of providence, we say, a view which also accords with the entire teachings of inspiration on the subject, and the immutable demands of our moral and spiritual nature, philosophy itself, we believe, is now advancing, and the faith of the church will erelong not be "spoiled through philosophy," but confirmed by its teachings. The proposition that God governs the universe, "not by special, but by general laws," we utterly disbelieve, when presented as the exclusive view of providence. We equally repudiate the universal proposition that he governs the universe not by general, but by special laws. We think that in the order of providence, both principles are harmoniously blended. Events falling exclusively under the first class of laws are not objects of prayer, and are never so presented in the Scriptures. Those, on the other hand, falling under the second class, are such objects — events the current of which God, without miracles, may, in the exercise of his sovereign wisdom and love, continuously vary in adaptation to the continuously varying necessities and filial requests of his creatures, just as the acts of the earthly parent vary to meet the ever-changing wants and affectionate petitions of his children. This view of Providence, which certainly accords with the teachings of inspiration, and the demands of our moral and spiritual natures, will yet, we think, stand revealed as the only one which philosophy itself permits.

CONCLUSION.

Such is Spiritualism. We have examined its high claims, and found them empty and vain. We have handled the spirits and found them absolute insubstantialities. We have scrutinized the facts set forth as the basis of the system, and found them wholly mundane in their character, and presenting no evidence whatever of a super-mundane origin. Our aim, in all our investigations has been a far higher one than the mere overthrow of a dangerous and insinuating system of delusion and error, namely, in the first instance, to lay the foundation for a full and satisfactory explanation of certain mysterious facts in nature and the experience of humanity, facts which have been in all ages very fruitful sources of superstition, religious delusion, and unbelief, and in the next place, to prepare, as far as may be done, in such a connection, for a better understanding of the ways of Providence on the one hand, and of the real claims on the other, of that divine revelation which constitutes the last and only hope of fallen humanity. Our reasonings and deductions thus far will speak for themselves, and we leave them to the candid judgment of the reader, earnestly bespeaking a careful examination of the subject next in order.

PART III.

EVIDENCE THAT THE SCRIPTURES ARE GIVEN BY INSPIRATION OF THE SPIRIT OF GOD, AS CONTRASTED WITH THE EVIDENCE, THAT THE SPIRIT MANIFESTATIONS ARE FROM THE SPIRITS OF MEN.

CHAPTER I.

ARGUMENT FROM EXTERNAL MIRACLES.

THE term miracle we have already defined. It represents exclusively a class of events fundamentally dissimilar and unanalogous, in all their essential characteristics, to any effects resulting from the action of any purely mundane cause or causes, a class of events whose existence and characteristics can be accounted for, but by a reference to the direct and immediate interposition of creative power, as their exclusive cause. To our mind, it is self-evident, that nothing but miracles, that is, effects which can result from the action of no finite causes, can properly be appealed to, as evidence of the divine origin of Christianity, or of any other religion. If we look at the record itself, its prophetic enunciations, or its system of moral precepts or doctrines, or to the great facts that stand around it, external miracles, we must find that which could not have originated with man, or from any finite cause or causes, before we find "the footprints of the Creator," "footprints" which can properly be adduced as evidence that "all Scripture is given by inspiration of God." Our conviction is, that the divine origin of Christianity is absolutely affirmed by the three classes of miracles above indicated, namely, external events,—prophetic enunciations,—and Christianity itself considered as an effect for which an adequate cause must be assigned. To each of these departments of evidence a separate chapter will be assigned, with the titles,—argument from external miracles,—argument from prophecy,—and argument from internal evidence. The argument from the class first named will be elucidated in the present chapter.

Every reader will agree with us in the assumption, that "the incorruptible God" has never performed, and never will perform a miracle, in attestation of the reality of that which is unreal or untrue. A religion really and truly attested by divine miracles must, therefore, be admitted as true. Without further introduction we will advance directly to a consideration of the great facts set forth in the Scriptures, in attestation of the divine origin of Christianity. In discussing this subject, two important questions will occupy attention,—the nature and bearing of the facts referred to, supposing them to have occurred,—and the evidence which exists of their actual occurrence.

SECTION I.

NATURE AND BEARING OF SCRIPTURE FACTS CLAIMED AS MIRACLES, SUPPOSING THEM TO HAVE OCCURRED.

In discussing any important subject, the question which first of all arises pertains to the nature and bearing of the facts which lie at the basis of all our conclusions. If we admit their actual occurrence, do they, or do they not, sustain the conclusions deduced from them by those who set the facts before us? Are they of such a nature, that the question of their occurrence or non-occurrence can be determined by testimony, etc.? Of this character are the questions which arise under the present section, in which we are to discuss the nature and bearings of the great facts which are asserted by its advocates, to stand around Christianity, and affirm its divine origin. The Christian argument may be thus expressed. No religion attested as true, by divine miracles, can be false. Christianity, and it alone of all religions on earth, is thus attested. It therefore must be of divine origin. In regard to this argument, we now invite special attention to the following considerations:—

1. If we admit the reality of the facts under consideration, we must also admit, in all its length and breadth, the conclusion before us, the divine origin and claims of Christianity. The reason is obvious. These great facts must be regarded as real divine miracles, and nothing else. They have none of the characteristics of any effects which owe their origin to any exclusively mundane cause or causes. On the other hand, they have all conceivable characteristics of real, miraculous interpositions of creative power. If we suppose them actually to have occurred, as related in the sacred volume, no one will or can doubt the divine origin of Christianity. These facts stand out solitary and alone in their own exclusive grandeur and sublimity, as being, in all their fundamental elements and characteristics, totally dissimilar and unanalogous to any effects resulting from any known or unknown natural causes in the universe around us. They not only lift their summits in-

finitely above all such effects, but stand in the relation to them of total dissimilarity and opposition. As we walk up and down in their midst, we perceive, in all their essential characteristics, nought but the sublime footprints of creative power, as their exclusive origin and cause. We may refer, in illustration, to the great events narrated by Moses and the prophets, such as the plagues of Egypt, the passage of the Red Sea, and of Jordan when overflowing all its banks, the giving of the "fiery law" at Sinai, the feeding of three millions of human beings for forty years, by bread from heaven in the wilderness, the opening, on two different occasions, of the flinty rock, when simply smitten, in the name of the Lord, by the shepherd's crook, and the issuing from those fissures of floods of water sufficient to meet the wants of all those famishing millions, together with their countless flocks and herds; the standing still of the sun and moon, at the bidding of Joshua; the preservation of Daniel in the den of lions, and of his three associates in the furnace of Nebuchadnezzar; together with "the mighty works" affirmed to have been performed by Jesus Christ. No one will pretend that these are the effects of any finite causes in the world around us. No one will pretend to adduce similar or analogous effects as resulting from such causes. No one will deny that such events, if they did occur, were real miracles, and owe their origin to no other cause than the direct and immediate interposition of creative power. Nor will any one deny, that these great events sustain such relations to Christianity, that if admitted to be real, they present absolute proof of its divine origin and authority. We can, by no possibility, separate the facts from the conclusion deduced from them, and we are necessitated to deny their occurrence, or admit that conclusion.

2. The second remark to which we would invite very special attention is this: Such is the nature and character of these great facts, that those who were present at the time when they are affirmed to have taken place, could, by no possibility, have been *deceived in regard to the fact of their occurrence or non-occurrence.* The truth of this proposition in undeniable. Facts of a certain character may, in some instances, appear to be to us what they are not. In other cases, this is impossible, and this is the exclusive character of the great events under consideration. Three millions of people, for example, cannot honestly have supposed themselves to have passed through the Red Sea, as related by Moses, unless they actually had done it. The same number of persons could not have really and truly believed themselves to have passed the river Jordan dry-shod, when it was overflowing all its banks, and when the waters stood in heaps on each side of them, unless this event actually occurred in their history. Similar remarks are equally applicable to the other great events referred to, and especially to "the mighty works" ascribed to Jesus Christ. Whatever may be true of certain other events, no persons of common intelligence, whether civilized or savage, can be present when such events as these are affirmed to occur, and be honestly mistaken in regard to the fact of their occurrence. Hence we remark, —

3. That all who affirmed themselves to have actually witnessed the occurrence of these events, were deceivers, liars, and hypocrites of the grossest character, that ever appeared on earth, unless these great facts actually did occur. We cannot possibly avoid this conclusion, or affirm that the language expressing it is too strong. The alternative is forced upon us, and we cannot escape it, to admit the occurrence of the facts under considera-

tion, and with that admission, affirm the divine origin of Christianity, or to brand every individual, whoever he may be, who affirms himself to have witnessed the actual occurrence of any of these great events, as a most gross and perjured deceiver.

SECTION II.

PROOF OF THE ACTUAL OCCURRENCE OF THESE EVENTS.

This brings us to the second department of our subject — the evidence of the actual occurrence of the great facts which, as divinely attested witnesses, affirm the divine origin of Christianity. The proposition which we here lay down, and shall proceed to establish, is this: The evidence in favor of the actual occurrence of these events is exclusively of that kind which never does and never can deceive, which never does, and never can stand around a non-reality, and affirm its actual existence or occurrence. The truth of this proposition we argue from the following most decisive considerations: —

1. There is an *antecedent probability* of the highest kind, in favor of the actual occurrence of these, or facts of a similar character, during the past history of our race.

Any events have the highest antecedent probability in favor of their occurrence, which perfectly accord, in their essential characteristics, and in the circumstances of their affirmed occurrence, with the known character of God, and his immutable relations to humanity, and with the great facts and analogy of his previous acts of providence and creative power, as developed by the teachings and demonstrations of science. What are the teachings and demonstrations of science bearing upon this great question? They are these, — that all the great facts of creation, from its commencement to its final consummation, owe their origin exclusively, not to the action of natural laws, but to the direct and immediate, or miraculous interpositions of creative power. To such interpositions, every leading race of animals and vegetables owes its existence. In respect to the vegetable kingdom, no power or law exists in nature to originate a seed, but through a plant; or a plant, but through a seed of the same or similar genus. How can the oak be produced, for example, but through the acorn, or the acorn, but through the oak? Throughout the wide domain of the animal kingdom, also, a law equally universal and absolute obtains, namely, that by no natural law can an animal be produced, but through the prior union of two individuals of the same or similar genus. These are the immutable laws of nature, or nature knows no laws. Yet science has demonstrated with equal absoluteness the fact, that the time was, when no animals or plants of any kind, nor any embryos from which such creations now originate, had an existence on earth. To what then did the first plant, that stands at the head of each species in the vegetable, and the first pair that stands at the head of each race in the animal kingdom, owe its origin? To a miraculous interposition of creative power, and to nothing else. The following statement of Professor Agassiz presents us the results of all the facts and demonstrations of science bearing upon this subject, and that in accordance with the united conviction and testimony of scientific men throughout the wide world, a conviction the validity of which is undeniably affirmed by all the facts and deductions of geology, and denied by none of them.

"It is necessary," says the Professor, "that we recur to a cause more exalted, and recognize influences more powerful, exercising over all nature an action more direct, if we would not move eternally in a vicious circle. For myself, I have the conviction that species have been created successively at distinct intervals, and that the changes which they have undergone during a geological epoch are very secondary, relating only to their fecundity, and to migration dependent on epochal influences."

Humanity, then, and all other orders of organized existences owe their origin to miraculous interpositions of creative power. No fact in nature is or can be more evident than this. Now, if God created man by a miracle, a fact which we must admit or deny the absolute demonstrations of science in regard to all the great facts of creation, is it not most reasonable to suppose, that he would interpose by miracles, should it be necessary for the highest interests of humanity, and especially to prevent its remediless ruin? And these are the very reasons for which the great facts recorded in the Bible are affirmed to have occurred, that is, to open to fallen humanity the vista of immortality, to recover man from the ruins of sin, and restore to him the hope and the possibility of attaining to eternal life. These great events, as all will admit, or none others of the kind have occurred since the creation of man. In view, then, of the analogy of creation and providence, of the character of God and of his relations to man, together with the known and undeniable condition of humanity, the balance of probability is infinitely in favor of the actual occurrence of miracles since man was created, and consequently in favor of the great facts which, as divinely attested witnesses, are affirmed to stand around Christianity, and assert its divine origin. In arguing for the real occurrence of these events, we are not arguing in favor of that of improbabilities, but of events which bear upon their broad foreheads all the indications of the highest probability. Our second argument is this: —

2. It is infinitely more reasonable to admit the reality of the great facts under consideration, than it is to affirm what, in that case we must do, of Moses, and the prophets, of Jesus Christ and the apostles, of the whole multitude of their immediate followers, and of all the sacred writers, namely, that they were all, without exception, deliberate deceivers, and impostors of the grossest character. Either these events really occurred, or they all knew when they affirmed their reality, that they were affirming what was false. There is no escaping this conclusion. The facts, as we have seen, were of such a nature that misapprehension in regard to their occurrence or non-occurrence, was an absolute impossibility. Those, then, who testified, as original witnesses to their actual occurrence, were intentional deceivers, or the events referred to actually occurred. Individuals who deny the facts, and yet admit the integrity of the witnesses, must show how honest and intelligent minds can honestly suppose themselves to have witnessed just such events, when no such thing ever occurred. This they may do, if they can do it, in either of these two ways or both together. (1.) They may show, upon truly scientific principles, how just such errors may occur with honest and intelligent minds; so that we may induce similar misapprehensions in ourselves and others. Or (2.), they may themselves actually induce similar misapprehensions in a corresponding number of individuals similarly circumstanced, and of similar mental capacity and cultivation. No individu-

als, we venture the affirmation, will ever attempt the accomplishment of either of these objects; and that for the obvious reason, that all are and must be aware, that it would be attempting an absolute impossibility. If, on the other hand, an individual should deny the facts before us, and assert, as the only alternative left him, the hypocrisy of Christ and the other witnesses referred to, he would, if not regarded as beneath contempt, meet and most justly meet with the deep reprobation of the universe. For ourselves we never met with but one individual who had the hardihood and effrontery to impeach the moral character of Jesus Christ, and he is the only consistent infidel that we ever did meet with, there being no conceivable absurdity greater than this, to admit the perfection of his moral character, and then deny the divinity of his mission, or the divine origin of the Scriptures. Either Jesus Christ is the crowning impostor of earth, or his mission was divine, and his religion from heaven. We dare not assert the former, and therefore, as the only conceivable alternative left us, admit and affirm the latter. For ourselves, we have no confidence whatever in the real moral honesty of the men who are fulsome in their eulogies of the character of Christ, and then deny the divine origin of that religion which he proclaimed as from heaven.

Similar remarks apply equally to the sacred writers generally. Their deep sincerity, honesty, and integrity, are so manifest in all their writings, that no man can, by any possibility, impeach their integrity and retain his own. Yet, by no possibility, can he show how they could have been any thing else than the grossest impostors and deceivers that ever cursed the earth, if the great facts to the reality of which they bear testimony never occurred. No possible alternative is left us, consistent with moral integrity in ourselves, but to admit the facts, and with that admission the necessary conclusion, that Christianity is of divine origin. We hesitate not to affirm to every reader, that he cannot maintain internal moral integrity and come to any other conclusion.

3. The *amount* of testimony existing on this subject, that is, the *number* of witnesses testifying to the actual occurrence of these great facts, is wholly incompatible with the assumption, that they never occurred. Its existence, on the other hand, can by no possibility be accounted for, but upon one supposition, the actual occurrence of the facts referred to. That a few individuals should unite, for interested motives, in the propagation of known falsehoods, is quite conceivable; though it is not conceivable that *such* individuals as Moses and the prophets, and Jesus and the Apostles, should do it. However this may be, it is not even conceivable that whole nations should, with absolute unanimity, join together for any such purpose. How stands the case in regard to the facts before us? In regard to the miraculous events recorded in the Old Testament, we have the united testimony of the entire Jewish nation living at the time, to the reality of their occurrence. We have also the unbroken testimony of that entire race since those periods, to the reality and universality of the *belief* among them, of the real occurrence of these events, at the time and under the circumstances related. In this respect this nation sustains precisely the same relations to these events that ours does to the facts of our past history. Our ancestors then living unitedly testified to their occurrence. Historical records made at the time, and an unbroken

tradition since, have handed them down to us, as actual occurrences. Our forms of government, s ate and national customs, annual festivals, and national monuments, all have such relations to those events, that the existence of the latter can be accounted for, but upon the supposition of the actual occurrence of the former, all together constituting a form of evidence which never does and never can deceive, and which distance of time can never weaken or invalidate. Precisely similar relations does the Jewish nation, together with all their historical records, traditions, national monuments, and usages, sustain to the events under consideration, and no one can show why this evidence should not be regarded as just as valid for the actual occurrence of these events, as that presented by this nation is for the facts of our past history.

Let us now turn to the great events recorded in the New Testament. Who are the witnesses to their occurrence? They are the following: the sacred writers themselves, — the entire mass of primitive converts, — multitudes of early apostates from the faith, — the whole Jewish nation, — and the entire pagan population of Palestine, of whom there were vast multitudes. The testimony of the first two classes was direct and absolute. They had been eye-witnesses to the things whereof they affirmed, and the fact that they unitedly laid down their lives in defence of the gospel, evinces absolutely the honesty of their convictions of the reality of these great events. We must bear in mind, also, that they could not possibly have been mistaken, in regard to the truth or falsehood of their testimony. Can we suppose that such vast numbers of individuals would lay down their lives in testimony to the reality of that which they knew absolutely never occurred, and where, from the nature of the case, no conceivable motives existed to induce them to become Christians but the reality of these events? The other three classes must be admitted to be very important and credible witnesses, inasmuch as they could not but be aware of the deception which was being perpetrated upon the world, had these events not occurred, and they had every conceivable motive to unmask the imposition. Nothing, therefore, but the deepest conviction of the reality of these events could have induced them to testify to their occurrence.

There is one characteristic of the testimony of these three classes which demands our special attention, *that of their silence.* When any very startling events are affirmed to have occurred, events which all have the highest conceivable motives to deny, if they did not occur, and when no one can possibly be mistaken in regard to the fact of their occurrence or non-occurrence, the total absence of all denial among all classes of community, is the highest and most positive testimony which that community can give to their actual occurrence. It shows, that in the united judgment of all, the evidence of their occurrence was so palpable and overwhelming, that it could not be invalidated. Now while the great facts of which we are speaking, were held before the world as having occurred in the presence of all the classes under consideration, no apostate, Jew, or Pagan, can be shown to have denied their actual occurrence as affirmed by Christians. Would they not have done it, had they not known that their occurrence could not have been denied?

On the other hand, all these classes together unitedly admitted the occurrence of these events. We find such admissions in the Jewish writings of the highest authority among that people. In the epistles of Pilate and other Roman governors also, formal records of these events were contained. This is evident from the fact, that the early Christian writers were accustomed to appeal to those very epistles as existing in the archives of the Emperors, and as containing the records of these events. The early Christians never had any controversy with their opponents in regard to the question, whether the mighty works ascribed to Jesus Christ were actually performed in their midst. How shall we account for such testimony, the reality of which cannot be denied? It can be accounted for, we reply, but upon one exclusive supposition, the actual occurrence of these events, and the consequent divine origin of Christianity. Those millions of people, Apostles, Christians, apostates, Jews, and Pagans, never did unite in thus testifying to what they all knew to be false, which they did do, if these events never occurred. The opponents of Christianity never have met this argument, and we are well persuaded they never will do it.

4. We shall fail to do full justice to this department of our subject, if we do not make some special remarks upon the *nature and character* of the evidence under consideration. In every possible respect, it bears the clearest marks of the highest conceivable credibility. It is the testimony of *enemies*, drawn from them contrary to all their worldly interests, principles, and prejudices, and can be accounted for but upon one supposition, the firm and immutable conviction, that these events had actually occurred, and were attended in their occurrence with such palpable evidence, that it could not be resisted nor invalidated, a conviction, also, which could by no possibility be induced but by the actual occurrence of the events themselves. Every convert to Christianity was originally its enemy, and

became, in the very act of conversion, an apostate from his former religion, and the religion of his ancestors, and thereby not only rendered himself infamous in public estimation, but subjected himself to the most intolerable sufferings and persecutions. Nothing but the deepest and most immovable conviction of the reality of the great facts under consideration, and the consequent truth of Christianity, can account for the numberless conversions which occurred under such circumstances.

In regard to apostates, we must distinguish between a renunciation of Christianity, and a denial of the reality of the miracles on which its claims to a divine origin were based. Had these events not occurred, they must have known, and have been fully informed of the cheat which was being perpetrated upon the world. Every conceivable inducement also pressed upon them to unmask the imposture, had it existed. The fact that they renounced Christianity without, in a single known instance, denying its miracles, is the highest demonstration of the fact, that in their judgment, those great events could not be denied. No other conceivable supposition can account for their silence on this subject. Their testimony, then, bears the marks of the highest credibility.

In regard to the Jews, these great events were everywhere, as they well knew, being proclaimed, as having occurred under their direct and immediate observation. They were held up to the world as opposing Christianity with a full knowledge of the reality of the facts on which its claims to a divine origin were based. They, moreover, based the claims of their own religion on the evidence of its miracles, and stood publicly committed before the world to the principle, that none but the true religion is or can be attested by such evidence. Of all religions on earth, we remark finally, none were held by them in such utter detestation as Christianity. How shall we account for the fact, that under such circumstances, they never denied the reality of the great events under consideration, on the one hand, and that they positively admitted their occurrence, as affirmed by Christians, on the other? No explanation of such conduct is possible, but upon the fact that they knew absolutely that these events, as affirmed by Christians, had occurred under such circumstances that their reality could not be denied.

The relation of the Pagan inhabitants of Palestine to those events was such, that they could not have been ignorant of the real facts of the case. It was a part of the business of their rulers to acquaint themselves fully with the character of all important events which were occurring among the people, and especially in their large assemblages, whenever occurring, assemblages in which these events are affirmed to have occurred. If these events had not taken place, as related and affirmed by Christians, their pagan rulers could not but have been aware of the imposition which was being perpetrated upon the world, and would have unmasked the imposture to the reprobation of mankind. Instead of this, they not only did not deny these facts, but admitted them, and themselves positively testified to their actual occurrence. If such testimony as this can deceive us, we may safely affirm, that nothing on earth or in heaven can be established by testimony. Such testimony, however, never does and never can deceive. The claims of Christianity, therefore, to a divine origin, rest upon an eternal and immovable rock.

5. The argument drawn from the *rapid and wide-*

spread extension of Christianity, in the era of its first development, should not be overlooked in this connection, an extension in which, notwithstanding the unparalleled opposition and persecutions which it encountered, it advanced onward from the smallest and apparently most contemptible beginnings, with such resistless power that, in less than three centuries from the era of the crucifixion, it ascended the throne of the Cæsars, and became the established religion of the then civilized world. How can this strange event be accounted for? Upon one supposition only, the deep, universal, and immovable conviction, in that age, and throughout the Roman empire, of the reality of the great facts under consideration. The extension is admitted and detailed by Gibbon. The existence, depth, and universality of this conviction, is also admitted and affirmed by him, and assigned as one of the main causes of the power and progress of Christianity, and none will call in question the truth of his statements on this subject. Now we affirm that it is no more impossible to account for the universal belief of the world in the reality of our Revolution, on the supposition that it never occurred, than it is to account for the existence of the conviction under consideration, on the supposition, that the great events to which it pertains never took place. We may challenge the world to assign any other adequate cause for the existence of this conviction, but this one. The opposers of Christianity never have done it, and they never will do it, and that for the obvious reason that the thing is impossible. These great events, then, did occur, and Christianity is from God.

6. We remark, finally, that we must admit the actual occurrence of the facts under consideration, and with

that admission affirm the divine origin of Christianity, or, to be consistent, we must deny the validity of all evidence of a historical kind, in regard to any past events whatever. On this topic we remark: (1.) That the authenticated records of any nation or people, are to be received as valid for the reality of the leading facts which they relate, unless there are reasons of the greatest weight of an opposite character. This is a universal principle pertaining to historical records of every kind. (2.) The historical records of the Jews and Christians, the Scriptures, records containing the account of these great events, are as well authenticated as are those of any other nation or people on earth. This is undeniable. (3.) Hence, no reasons whatever can be assigned why we should credit the historical records of any nation on earth, and deny the reality of the great facts attested as real in the historical record of Jews and Christians, that is, in the Scriptures. All history of every kind must be held as utter fable and fiction, or the validity of these records must be admitted for the reality of the great events under consideration, and, consequently, for the divine origin of Christianity. We know very well that the opposers of Christianity will never meet this argument.

Such is a bare specimen of the nature and force of the Christian argument for the divine origin of our holy religion, as far as this one department of evidence is concerned. We again affirm, without fear of contradiction, that this is a kind of evidence which never does and never can deceive. We leave the argument upon the conscience of the reader. Let him weigh it, decide and act upon it, with a solemn reference to the coming revelations of his approaching destiny.

CHAPTER II.

ARGUMENT FROM PROPHECY.

THE reader is well aware of the fact, that a large portion of the Bible consists of professedly divinely inspired predictions pertaining to events lying in the future, at the time when these predictions were uttered. No one will doubt, that these predictions, supposing them to have been uttered prior to the events to which they pertain, were uttered either by inspiration of the Spirit of God, and consequently in their fulfilment encircle the Scriptures, as divinely attested witnesses of their divine origin, or else that they are the result of mere human foresight and sagacity.

There are but three ways in which the human intelligence, unaided and unguided by wisdom and foresight higher than its own, can even conjecture what shall occur in the future. The first is this: When all the causes that are operating or will operate to produce a given result are fully known, the result, by a calculation of the force and direction of the action of such causes, may be predetermined. The calculation, in such a case, is purely mathematical, and the conclusion certain. Such is the character of all astronomical calculations. The second is, when men reason from mere precedent, conjecturing from what has occurred in the past, what will be in the future. Here we find ourselves in the region of uncertainty, the greatest events in human experience often turning upon purely accidental circumstances and occult causes, which no human sagacity could have foreseen, or even conjectured. Hence the total uncertainty of human foresight, in the wisest of men, is proverbial. The last class of human predictions are mere imaginings of what may be, with a supposition merely that it will be. Such suppositions, or guesses, are generally wrong, and are yet, in instances few and far between, verified by the actual occurrence of the events referred to.

Prophetic predictions originating from the inspiration of the Spirit of God, and bearing the evidences of their divine original, must stand, in all their essential characteristics, at an absolute remove from each of the classes of human predictions above named. They must be of such a nature as to be wholly out of the sphere of calculations from cause and effect, or from precedent, together with those of preimagined probabilities or possibilities. Their fulfilment also must be absolutely universal and perfect, thus indicating their origin from infinite wisdom and foresight. Predictions of this character, vast in number, and relating to an endless diversity of events which no human foresight could even conjecture, and yet all fulfilled in their exact time, and in absolute perfection, we all know can originate but from the infinite and eternal mind who sees the end from the beginning.

Our object, on the present occasion, will be to show, that such is the precise character of the prophetic predictions recorded in the Scriptures, predictions which thus, as divinely attested witnesses, stand in the midst of its sublime revelations, and affirm their divine origin.

SECTION I.

PREDICTIONS RECORDED IN THE OLD TESTAMENT.

In accomplishing our object, our first remarks will have a special reference to predictions recorded in the Old Testament. On this subject, we remark:—

1. These prophecies were uttered and recorded many centuries before most of the events to which they relate, and long periods before hardly any of them occurred. Four considerations render the truth of the above statement perfectly evident: (1.) The writings containing these predictions have ever been received among the Jews, as the productions of the very persons to whom they are now referred, namely, of prophets who lived at the periods named in the books themselves, periods centuries antecedent to most of the events foretold. (2.) No evidence whatever exists against the testimony of this nation on this subject. No period in their history subsequent to the affirmed time of the prophets can be named when these writings did not exist among that people, and when, for the first time, they were introduced. (3.) At periods long prior to the occurrence of most of the events predicted, these writings were translated into other languages. The Septuagint translation, for example, containing all these books, was made about three centuries prior to the birth of Christ. (4.) They were then translated as ancient writings, which had most of them for centuries previous existed as sacred books among the Jews. No further evidence surely is required to sustain the above proposition.

2. The prophets had before them, at the time they uttered these predictions, no examples whatever of the rise and fall of nations and empires, from which they

could form even a conjecture of the fate of those then existing around them. The nations also to whom their prophecies pertain, existed, at the time, in all their strength and glory, presenting the appearance of an immortal youth, with no indications whatever of a near or remote decay and dissolution, especially of a destruction in any *specific form.*

3. The nations and cities are *very numerous* whose destiny is foretold with great particularity in these prophetic writings, nations and cities, for example, such as Assyria, with Nineveh as its capital, Babylon, and the Chaldean empire, Persia, Greece, Egypt, Syria, and its capital Damascus, Tyre and Sidon, and Philistia, Edom, Ammon, and Moab, with their respective capitals, Petra, Rahab, and Heshbon, and Israel and Judah, with their capitals, Samaria and Jerusalem, etc. With all the particularity of history, we find the destiny of these illustrious cities, nations, and empires, mapped out in these wonderful writings.

4. While a large number of different writers give forth predictions in respect to the destiny of these cities, nations, and empires, while some of these writers speak particularly of that of most or all of them, others of a less number, and some of but one or two, and while some predict particulars not mentioned by others, the predictions of all together blend perfectly into one harmonious unity of description and representation, with the total absence of all contradiction. We are quite safe, in affirming that no one has yet pointed out, if any has ever attempted it, a single contradiction in all or any of these numerous predictions proceeding from so many writers, writers living at great distances of time, located in widely different circumstances, and of natural talents and intellectual attainments equally diverse and unequal.

5. While the destiny of all these cities, nations, and empires is mapped out with great minuteness and particularity, in these prophetic writings, that of each one was to be *peculiar to itself* and widely diverse from all the others. The predictions pertaining to any one would not be at all applicable to any other. This is one of their most striking peculiarities. Let us consider a few of them as examples of all the others. We are all aware that the Assyrian empire was to be subverted by the Persian and Babylonian, the Babylonian by the Persian under Cyrus mentioned by name, and this last by the Grecian, which after the death of its first king, was to be divided into four, and none of these come to the heirs of that monarch, and finally out of one of these four kingdoms, another and small one was to rise from which the greatest calamities were to descend upon the Jewish nation. Of the nation last named, one part, (the ten tribes,) were to be carried captive to Assyria, and the other, (Judah and Benjamin,) to Babylon. After remaining seventy years in captivity, the latter portion were to be resettled in their own land, after which all distinction of tribes among the whole Israelitish nation was to cease. About five hundred years of mingled prosperity and adversity, mercy and judgment were then to intervene, when, subsequent to the death of "Messiah, the Prince," the nation itself, as a civil State, was to be blotted from existence, and to remain "scattered and peeled" among all nations, till "the fulness of the Gentiles should come in." Tyre, Philistia, Edom, Ammon, Moab, etc., were to be utterly and permanently annihilated as nations, and Egypt, after going into captivity for a certain period, was to be restored again, but was never to regain its nationality. Such are some of the general features of these predictions.

Let us now descend still further to a consideration of a few particulars. The army of Assyria was to be destroyed while engaged in a bacchanalian revel. "While they are drunken as drunkards, they shall be devoured as stubble fully dry." Nahum 1 : 10. Nineveh its capital was to be destroyed by successive catastrophes; first by a flood, then by fire, and then by being sacked by its enemies. Nahum 1 : 8. 3 : 15. Its destruction was to be utter and final. Its "affliction was not to rise a second time," but it was to "become a desolation," a "place for beasts to lie down in." Nahum, 1 : 9. Zeph. 2 : 13, 15. "Babylon, the golden city, the glory of kingdoms, the beauty of the Chaldees' excellency," was, after its armies were defeated in the field, to be taken by Cyrus, while its inhabitants were revelling in drunkenness and debauchery, and captured for two reasons, — the drying up of the river that ran through the midst of it, and the providential opening, at the same time, of the brazen gates which guarded the entrance to the city from the banks of that river. Isa. 45 : 1. Jer. 50 : 38. 51 : 36. After being successively plundered, it was to be wholly desolated, and never again inhabited. The Arabian caravans were not to pitch their tents, nor were the shepherds to fold their flocks in it any more. On the other hand, it was for a period to become the dwelling-place of wild beasts; then its palaces and habitations were to become the abode of owls, dragons, serpents, vipers, and doleful creatures. Subsequently, it was to become "pools of water," in which the sea-fowls were to swim and utter their cries. Last of all, it was to become a "burnt mountain." Isa. 13 : 19. 14 : 22, 23. Jer. 51 : 13–43. Egypt was to go into captivity for a season, and on its return was never again to lift itself up among the nations. On the other hand, it was to become "the basest of kingdoms," and to be ever after ruled by foreign princes and not her own. Ez. 29: 15. 30: 13. Of Tyre, the then centre of commerce for the civilized world, we have the following predictions: "And they shall destroy the walls of Tyrus, and break down her towers: I will also scrape her dust from her, and make her like the top of a rock. It shall be a place for the spreading of nets in the midst of the sea." Edom also was to "be a desolation," as when God overturned Sodom and Gomorrah, and such a desolation as to be utterly uninhabited. "No man shall abide there, neither shall a son of man dwell in it." Jer. xlix. and elsewhere.

We have given the above simply as examples. No prophet appears as a copyist of any other. Yet, while one often predicts what is not referred to by others, when speaking on the same subject, no contradiction, we repeat, appears among them, but a perfect unity of design and representation. At the same time, how particular and specific are their statements. How peculiar is the destiny marked out for each people, nation, or city, and how diverse from that of every other. We never find prophecies of desolations in general, but always in specific and peculiar forms.

6. This leads us to remark, in the next instance, that at the time when these prophets lived and wrote, no events conceivable, seemed of less likely occurrence than those to which these predictions refer. All these kingdoms existed, as we have already said, in all the plenitude of their power and glory. Every city referred to was the abode of untold wealth, and surrounded with the most impregnable defences that could be erected by the art of man at the time. Nineveh, according to Diodorus Siculus, was surrounded by walls

sixty miles in extent, one hundred feet high, and so thick that three chariots could go abreast upon them. It had fifteen hundred towers at proper distances in the walls, each tower being two hundred feet in height. Within were every means of defence, and provisions to sustain a siege to any length of time. The walls of Babylon were three hundred and fifty feet high, and eighty-seven feet in thickness. Outside of these was a ditch of great width and depth, and always filled with water. Its gates were all of brass, and were opened but in the daytime. It was garrisoned within by numerous armies, and so provisioned that it could not be straitened by being besieged from without. How utterly improbable was it, that cities which for ages had stood thus "proudly preëminent" amid surrounding nations, and against which no force then existing on earth could have any apparent power, would, ere a few centuries were past, become utter and perpetual desolations. So of all the other objects of the prophetic predictions under consideration. Upon mere calculations of worldly experience and observation, those who gave utterance to such predictions must have appeared as madmen, rather than as speaking by inspiration of the Spirit of God.

7. Yet, we remark finally, not one of these strange utterances failed of its full and complete accomplishment. The prophet had said of Assyria, that when its army was "drunken as drunkards, they should be destroyed as stubble fully dry." Accordingly, Diodorus Siculus relates, that "while all the Assyrian army was feasting for its former victories, that those about Arbaces (king of the Medes) "being informed by deserters of the negligence and drunkenness in the camp of their enemies, assaulted them unexpectedly by night,

slew many of the soldiers, and drove the rest into the city." "In the third year of the siege," he further informs us, "the river being swollen with continual rains, broke down the walls of Nineveh for twenty furlongs." The king then "built a large funeral pile in the palace, and, collecting together all his wealth and his concubines and eunuchs, burnt himself and the palace with them all; and the enemy entered the breach that the waters had made, and took the city." Thus, according to the sayings of the prophets, it was destroyed, first by the drunkenness of the army, then by water and fire, and finally by being sacked by the enemy. Its destruction also was complete and perpetual. Modern science is now developing, from the bowels of the earth, where that proud monument of ancient greatness once stood, the demonstrations of prophetic foresight in Israel's divinely inspired seers. With the manner in which, in perfect accordance with prophetic prediction, Babylon was taken and plundered by Cyrus, the reader is no doubt familiar. Defeated in one or two battles without, the Chaldean army took refuge within the walls and defences of the city, which the conqueror referred to proceeded to besiege. Learning that on a given night the whole city would be given up to feasting and revelry, he succeeded, by means of trenches, canals, and an artificial lake which he had excavated, in draining, on the same night, the Euphrates, which ran through its centre, so as to leave the channel dry for the introduction of his army into the heart of the city, where, as he expected and as the prophets had foretold, they found the gates which guarded the entrance from the channel into the streets, left wide open.

Thus Babylon was first taken and plundered. For

a long period, however, though successively plundered, it retained much of its royal magnificence, being made the capital of the Macedonian empire, under Alexander. When Seleucia, however, became the capital of the eastern portion of that empire, after its division, the nobility and wealthy portion of the people of Babylon followed the royal family to the former city. These in time were followed by the entire population, and Babylon became desolated of all its inhabitants. Subsequently, one of the latter kings of Persia, in the fourth century after Christ, converted it into a chase to keep wild beasts for hunting within its walls. Ages rolled on, and by the falling in of the roofs of houses, the decay of vegetation, etc., it became the abode of serpents, vipers, and poisonous reptiles, so that, according to an ancient writer, no one could approach excepting in winter, within half a league of it. In a subsequent age, by the change of the channel of the river, much of the city was overflowed, and became "pools of water," in which, as predicted, the sea-fowl makes its appearance. Now the curtain falls over this devoted city, and for centuries it remains concealed from the vision of civilization, till modern travellers visit the place where "the beauty of the Chaldee's excellency once stood." We wish to know whether one more prediction has been fulfilled. Babylon was to become a "burnt mountain." History records no occurrence whatever in which such a prediction could be fulfilled. Israel's seer, however, has said that it should be so, and what do modern travellers find there? In approaching the place, a high mound lifts its form to view, a mound constituted no doubt of the ruins of the ancient temple of Belus, or the tower of Babel, now composed, in the language of another, of "immense fragments of brickwork of no determinate figures, tumbled together and converted into solid vitrified masses," masses "completely molten." "The heat of the fire," says Sir Robert Ker Porter, "which produced such amazing effects, must have burned with the force of the strongest furnace; and from the general appearance of the cleft in the wall, and these vitrified masses, I should be induced to attribute the catastrophe to lightning from heaven. Ruins by the explosion of any combustible matter would have exhibited very different appearances." Again he says, "the falling masses bear evident proof of the operation of fire having been *continued* on them as well after they were broken as before, since every part of their surface has been so completely exposed to it that many of them have acquired a rounded form, and in none can the place of separation from its adjoining one be traced by any appearance of superior freshness, or any exemption from the influence of the destroying flame." So much for the relations of prophetic foresight to this once proud mistress of the world, who boasted in the pride of her vainglory saying, "I shall be a lady forever; I am, and none else beside me; I shall not sit as a widow, neither shall I know the loss of children." Let us now turn in other directions. The voyager, as he sails up the Mediterranean, approaches at length the site of ancient Tyre, "the crowning city, whose merchants were once princes, and whose traffickers the honorable of the earth," and what does he now behold there? A mass of naked rocks from which even the dust has been totally scraped off, and upon which a few miserable fishermen are drying their nets. Egypt, disrobed of all her former greatness, deprived of her nationality, and ruled over by foreign despots, has stood for eighteen centuries, the "basest of kingdoms," as a monument visible to all the world, of an unearthly and superhuman foresight in those ancient prophets. We need not speak of Israel and Judah, of Edom and Moab, and Ammon and Philistia, and other nations and their proud capitals. From one hundred to one thousand years prior to the full occurrence of the great events predicted, the destiny of all these nations and cities were definitely marked out with an astonishing particularity, and where each was to be subject to a series of catastrophes altogether peculiar to itself, and diverse from that of all the others. Yet not one of all these endlessly multiplied and diversified predictions has failed of its full and complete accomplishment, and that in every particular, the least as well as the greatest. Yet every solitary event predicted had the greatest conceivable antecedent probability against its occurrence. Nothing in the previous experience of these or other nations could have suggested, even to the wildest imagination, the peculiar destiny of any one of these cities or nations. What must we think of this strange foresight in these wonderful men? We affirm that but one cause can be conceived of adequate to the production of such results, and that is the cause assigned in the Scriptures themselves, namely: "For the prophecy came not in old time by the will of man: but holy men of God spoke as they were moved by the Holy Ghost." The cause which originated these predictions possessed not only a foresight of the future, but one that has all possible characteristics of absolute infallibility. By a reference to the known powers of the human mind, we cannot account for the mere existence of the ideas expressed in those predictions, much less for the relations of infallible foresight which they sustain to the events to which they relate.

SECTION II.

NEW TESTAMENT PREDICTIONS.

Of the numberless predictions recorded in the New Testament, we select but two as examples of all the others. The first is found Rev. iii. 10, and pertains to the church of Philadelphia. "Because thou hast kept the word of my patience, I also will keep thee from the hour of temptation, which shall come upon all the world, to try them that dwell upon the earth." This one city, or rather the church in it, was to be preserved amid the sweeping desolations which were to overwhelm all the others. How has that prediction been fulfilled? Let an infidel historian tell us. Speaking of this and the other cities containing the seven churches of Asia, Gibbon makes the following statements: "In the loss of Ephesus, the Christians deplored the fall of the first angel, the extinction of the first candlestick of the Revelation: the desolation is complete, and the temple of Diana, or the church of Mary, will equally elude the search of the curious traveller. The circus, and three stately theatres of Laodicea, are now peopled by wolves and foxes. Sardis is reduced to a miserable village; the God of Mahomet, without a rival, is invoked in the mosques of Thyatira and Pergamos; and the populousness of Smyrna is supported by the foreign trade of the Franks and Armenians. Philadelphia alone had been saved by *prophecy or courage*." "Among the Greek colonies, and churches of Asia, *Philadelphia is still erect: a column in a scene of ruins*." How happened it, that the eye of the Revelator fell upon this single church and marked it out as the only one which was to be preserved in the midst of the surrounding desolations? The individual that will entertain the sentiment, that this is an instance of unaided human foresight, shows an equal want of candor, and ignorance of what is and is not possible to man.

The second prediction to which we will refer, we will place before the reader, by presenting the attempt of an arch.enemy of Christianity to prove it false, by the accomplishment of what Christ had said, should not then be accomplished. Christ had predicted, that the temple and city of Jerusalem should be trodden down by the Gentiles, "till the fulness of the Gentiles should come in." Julian the Apostate, when Emperor of Rome, resolved to prove that prophecy false, by rebuilding that temple, and restoring it to its ancient splendor. This he resolved upon about three hundred years after its destruction. He accordingly turned the resources of the empire to the accomplishment of that object. The following is Gibbon's account of the effort, and of its final result. The minister Alypius "received an extraordinary commission, to restore, in its pristine beauty, the temple of Jerusalem, and the diligence of Alypius required and obtained the strenuous support of the governor of Palestine. At the call of their great deliverer, the Jews, from all the provinces of the empire, assembled on the holy mountain of their fathers; and their insolent triumph alarmed and exasperated the Christian inhabitants of Jerusalem. The desire of rebuilding the temple has in every age been the ruling passion of the children of Israel. In this propitious moment the men forgot their avarice, and the women their delicacy; spades and pickaxes of silver were provided by the vanity of the rich, and the rubbish was transported in mantles of silk and purple. Every purse was opened in liberal contribution; every hand claimed a share in the pious labor; and the commands of a great monarch were executed by the enthusiasm of a whole people."

"Yet on this occasion, the joint efforts of power and enthusiasm were unsuccessful; and the ground of the Jewish temple, which is now covered by a Mohammedan mosque, still continues to exhibit the same edifying spectacle of ruin and desolation.

"Perhaps the absence and death of the Emperor, and the new maxims of a Christian reign, might explain the interruption of an arduous work, which was attempted only in the last six months of the life of Julian. But the Christians entertained a natural and pious expectation, that in this memorable contest, the honor of religion would be vindicated by some signal miracle. An earthquake, a whirlwind, and a fiery eruption, which overturned and scattered the new foundations of the temple, are attested, with some variations, by contemporary and respectable evidence. This public event is described by Ambrose, Bishop of Milan, in an epistle to the Emperor Theodosius, which must provoke the severe animadversion of the Jews; by the eloquent Chrysostom, who might appeal to the memory of the elder part of his congregation at Antioch; and Gregory Nazianzen, who published his account of the miracle before the expiration of the same year. The last of these writers has boldly declared, that this preternatural event was not disputed by infidels; and his assertion, strange as it may seem, is confirmed by the unexceptionable testimony of Ammianus Marcellinus. The philosophic soldier, who loved the virtues without adopting the prejudices of his master, has recorded, in his judicious and candid history of his own times, the extraordinary obstacle which interrupted the restoration of the temple of Jerusalem.

"Whilst Alypius, assisted by the governor of the province, urged with vigor and diligence the execution of the work, horrible balls of fire breaking out near the foundations, with frequent and reiterated attacks, rendered the place, from time to time, inaccessible to the scorched and blasted workmen; and the victorious element continuing in this manner obstinately and resolutely bent, as it were, to drive them to a distance, the undertaking was abandoned. Such authority should satisfy a believing, and must astonish an incredulous mind."

Such is the record and testimony of the infidel historian. We leave it to speak for itself. The authority and facts adduced do satisfy the believing, and should they not more than astonish the incredulous mind? Should they not induce in him the apprehension, if not the unshaken conviction, that beneath the system of Christianity lies the rock of eternal truth, and that the superstructure raised upon that rock is nothing else than the handiwork of God himself? In the strong-hold based upon that rock, may we not safely take refuge for eternity?

Such is prophecy, as it appears in the Scriptures of truth, and such is its fulfilment. We might with almost as much show of reason affirm absolute omniscience of the prophets, as to affirm that they were illuminated by any other cause than Omniscience itself, in the predictions recorded in Scripture, — predictions which, now verified by their most minute and absolute accomplishment, stand in the midst of its high revelations as divinely attested monuments and witnesses of the divine origin of Christianity. We might have multiplied examples to any extent. What we have adduced, however, is sufficient for our purpose. We affirm, that such predictions as these do not attest the truth of that which is unreal and untrue. In their midst, the Bible, that "dearest of books, that excels every other," stands before us as nothing else than the divinely attested word of God, and as such, as a light shining in upon our darkness, a "light to which we do well to take heed, till the day dawn, and the day-star arise in our hearts."

All these divine predictions, however, are not yet fulfilled. Some refer to what is yet to be in the future history of our race. Others extend our vision beyond the circle of time, and indicate what shall be the connection of present character and deeds with the events of that eternal future, long after "the sun shall be turned into darkness, and the moon into blood." Every foretold event of the past has taken its place in exact accordance with these predictions. Is the connection between these same hitherto infallible predictions and what yet remains to be accomplished, less indissoluble? "Heaven and earth will pass away, but my word," says the Author and spirit of prophecy itself, "shall not pass away."

CHAPTER III.

ARGUMENT FROM INTERNAL EVIDENCE.

EVERY production of an intelligent agent will bear somewhere upon it the indications of the character of its author. Whatever is strictly human in its origin, will present the characteristic imperfections of humanity. Whatever, on the other hand, is really and truly of divine original, will have pencillings upon it which the mind will perceive could have been drawn but by the finger of God. All will admit, at the outset of our remarks, that the Scriptures are either human or divine in their origin. If they are exclusively of man, they will present the characteristic imperfections of humanity, and of humanity in the particular *era and circumstances* in which they were written. But if they are of divine original, the production itself, when wisely and candidly contemplated, will present the most absolute demonstration of the divinity of its origin. We here lay down this proposition, which we shall proceed to establish, that there are two great volumes that God has written, the book of nature and the book of inspiration, that each bears equally the most absolute indications of a divine original, and that it would be just as unreasonable to suppose that man is the author of the one as of the other. The author of the former, we know perfectly, must be possessed of all the attributes involved in the ideas of absolute infinity and perfection. On the other, we perceive with equal distinctness the pencillings of the same infinity and perfection. The mind cannot entertain a greater absurdity than to ascribe the origin of the universe of matter and mind, to any finite cause. An absurdity not less gross, as we purpose to prove, is involved in ascribing the Bible to man as its originator and exclusive author.

It is not easy for us to set limits to the possible attainments of humanity. Yet there are some things which no one hesitates to affirm, as impossible to man. We know absolutely, for example, that no untutored savage could originate the Paradise Lost. Above all, we know absolutely, that twelve such savages did not, and could not, each, without knowing at all what either of the others were doing, write one of the twelve books of that great production, the twelve books thus separately written, possessing an absolute unity of conception and arrangement, and all together constituting one perfectly harmonious whole. Equally manifest is it, that no twelve men of any degree of mental cultivation, could thus independently and undesignedly produce the separate parts of any such work. Suppose that twelve men had, in this or in a similar manner, originated such a production, each writing perfectly independently of all the others, and in absolute ignorance of what they were doing, and yet the productions of each should fall in with those of all the others, so as to constitute one grand, sublime, and perfectly unified whole, having all possible indications of being the production of some one mind, a mind which comprehended the whole together with all its parts, and originated and adapted each part accordingly. We should conclude in that case, with the most undoubting certainty, that each and all these twelve individuals acted under the guidance of some such mind in what they produced, and that they were but instruments in its production, thinking and writing only as they were moved by this one mind, and that in accordance with his thoughts and purposes. On no other supposition could the existence of a production originated through such diverse instrumentalities be possibly accounted for.

The above supposition presents a faint illustration of the indications which we have in the Scriptures themselves, that the multiplied writers who composed the different parts of the same, were all under the guidance of some one all-controlling, all-unifying intelligence, out of and infinitely above their own. The thoughts presented, are infinitely above the possible reach of the human intelligence in any age, especially in those in which the Bible was written. At the same time, there is among them all an absolute unity of conception and representation impossible to such a number of minds, each acting independently of, or even in intentional concert with the others, on any subject whatever, and above all on the high themes treated of in the sacred volume. Such thoughts, and such a unity of conception and representation in regard to the same, as obtains among the sacred writers, we hesitate not to affirm is just as impossible to man, unguided by an intelligence out of and above himself, as the creation of a world. We will now proceed to illustrate the thought here expressed by a reference to a few examples.

1. We will begin with the *idea of God* as developed in the Scriptures. Let us first contemplate the harmony and identity of this idea with that revealed in creation. We know perfectly, as we have already said, that the author of the universe of matter and of mind must possess all the attributes involved in the ideas of absolute infinity and perfection. This is the identical being revealed to our contemplation in the Bible, with this difference only, that in the latter, Divinity, in all the

infinity of his perfections, stands revealed in absolutely perfect adaptation to the known and acknowledged necessities of universal humanity, humanity in all ages and in all circumstances. The following are the fundamental characteristics of this idea as shadowed forth in the sacred volume. (1.) It is absolutely perfect in itself. No conceivable attribute belonging to an absolutely infinite and perfect mind is wanting, and each attribute, as there revealed, is absolutely perfect in its kind. No element can, by any possibility, be added to or taken from this great and all-overshadowing idea as here developed, without marring its beauty and perfection. (2.) This infinite and eternal being here stands revealed in full and absolute adaptation to the known and acknowledged necessities of universal humanity, in all ages, and in all circumstances actual and conceivable. The idea of God, as here given, is not only absolutely perfect in itself, but equally perfect in its adaptation to the known necessities of fallen humanity. (3.) While the sacred volume is made up of the productions of from forty to sixty writers, to say the least, and while the idea of God is the grand and all-absorbing theme of them all, there is among them, without exception, an absolute unity of conception and representation in regard to it. No one writer affirms of God what is denied by another. No one, by any representation, mars the perfection of the idea in itself, arrays it in any other light than that of perfect adaptation to the condition and wants of man as a sinner, or breaks, in the least degree, the absolute unity of conception and representation of it under consideration. (4.) No man, nor any number of men, in the era in which the sacred writers lived, nor in any preceding age, had made any approach toward the perfect conception and representation of this great truth, which obtains among the sacred writers. Out of this one circle, humanity, in all its researches, had not attained to a conception of the divine unity, much less to that of the infinity and perfection of God. (5.) Among a similar number of minds, in any age since that era, minds who have attempted to copy the great original, and have taken the sacred writers as their all authoritative guides in doing it, have the same perfection and unity of conception and representation obtained. In this respect the Bible stands alone, lifting its sublime summit to absolute infinity above all human productions.

How came this great idea in these minds? Whence originated its absolute perfection of conception and representation, together with its equally perfect adaptation to the condition and necessities of universal humanity? Whence, above all, this absolute unity of conception and representation of this all-overshadowing reality among these writers, a unity absolutely impossible to humanity on any great subject, and above all, on such a one as this? But one answer can be given to such questions, that that idea came into those minds from a light above humanity, and that in conceiving and shadowing it forth, they were under the supreme control of an intelligence other than their own, an intelligence possessed of an absolutely perfect knowledge of God, on the one hand, and of universal humanity on the other. In the revelation itself, a knowledge absolutely perfect of both alike is demonstrably evinced, a kind and degree of knowledge utterly impossible to man unaided by a power out of and infinitely above himself, and which can pertain to none but the infinite and eternal mind.

Let those who would object to the validity of the above argument show, if they can, a similar perfection and unity of conception and representation among a similar number of writers, similarly circumstanced, on this or on any kindred subject, or indeed on any important subject whatever. If they will not do this, and we are very sure they will not attempt it, let them show us how such attainments are possible to such minds, or to any class of minds under any circumstances whatever, but by the inspiration of the Spirit of God. To our minds, the argument is complete and unanswerable. The fact of the unity and perfection of conception and representation, under consideration, cannot be denied, without a denial of what we all know to be true of the word of God. The occurrence of this great fact is conceivable but upon one supposition, that those in whom it appears were under the guidance of some one all-presiding intelligence out of and above themselves, that is, of the Spirit of God.

2. The character of Christ, as developed in the Scriptures, is a phenomenon also, the existence of which can, by no possibility, be accounted for on but one supposition, that its origin is divine. In the character of Christ two distinct and opposite elements are harmoniously blended, the infinite and the finite, God and humanity. "In the beginning was the Word, and the Word was with God, and the Word was God." "And the Word became flesh, and dwelt among us." In the history of Christ, these two distinct and opposite characteristics are perfectly sustained. There is not a word or an act imputed to Him in the whole circle of the Scriptures, that is unhuman, on the one hand, or ungodlike, on the other. In both relations, his character also is absolutely perfect. Not a solitary defect has ever been found in it. And

this is the only absolutely perfect character that has ever appeared in human form, or that humanity has ever imagined. Those who "see His glory," as revealed in these writings, see humanity in the perfection of beauty, and with equal distinctness, they "see the Father also." This character, in which such distinct and infinitely opposite elements are so mysteriously and harmoniously blended is, in the first place, the theme of the ancient prophets. It is then in formal history portrayed by the four Evangelists, and is finally shadowed forth by other individuals in the epistles of the New Testament. In all these writings there is a perfect unity of conception in respect to the fundamental elements of the character, and no contradictory elements are found in the portraitures drawn in them. This divine portraiture, and the absolute unity of conception in respect to it among those who drew it, are ascribed to one cause in the Scriptures, the inspiration of the Almighty in originating the idea in the minds of the writers, and in guiding them in shadowing it forth. Now if the validity of this explanation be admitted, together with the reality of the character itself, then the existence of the idea, as it appears in the writings under consideration, is accounted for. If this be denied, the following facts are themselves to be explained in consistency with such denial: (1.) the origin of the idea of God becoming incarnate for the object affirmed in the Scriptures; (2.) the blending of the finite and infinite into one character of perfect unity, a unity in which humanity, on the one hand, and deity, on the other, are manifested in absolute perfection; (3.) the existence of such an absolute identity of conception among so many individuals, individuals of such diverse capacities and attainments, and living at different periods of time, and in such variety of circumstances;

(4.) and finally, for the absence of all real contradiction on the one hand, and of absolute unity of conception on the other, in the portraitures which they have all drawn of Him. Now we affirm that these phenomena can never be accounted for, on the supposition that the character under consideration is a fiction, and not a reality, or any other than a superhuman guidance vouchsafed to the sacred writers in portraying it. No individual, by reference to the original powers of the human mind, to the history of the race, or the circumstances of the times, or to all combined, can account for such phenomena on any such supposition, or any supposition other than the absolute validity of the idea of Christ, as developed in the Scriptures. The supposition that ten untutored savages had, without any concert among themselves, each written different parts of Newton's Principia, so that all their productions together constitute one great whole, complete in all its parts, and possessing throughout a perfect unity of plan and arrangement, is far more credible than the dogma that the sacred writers first originated among themselves an absolute unity of idea in respect to such a character as that of Christ, and then preserved an equal identity, in all the portraitures which they all drew of it, when that character was a fiction, and not a reality, and they under no superhuman guidance in conceiving and portraying it. Let ten of the best writers of fiction in existence be selected, and let them be required to take some of the leading characters shadowed forth in the writings of Walter Scott, Di. Vernon, for example, to present them in relations and circumstances new and widely diversified, and to preserve a perfect likeness to the original in the first instance, and an equally absolute unity of portraiture among themselves in the next. Who does not know, that the accomplishment of such an object would be, even to such individuals, an absolute impossibility? How then could a far greater number, mostly of uneducated minds widely diverse in capacities and attainments, living many of them in different times, and under equally diverse circumstances, attain to an absolute unity of conception and representation in respect to such a character as that of Christ? supposing that character to be a fiction, and that they were aided by no power out of themselves in conceiving and shadowing it forth? Nothing short of infinity is impossible to humanity, even in its present condition, if such an object has already been accomplished by men in the circumstances in which the sacred writers lived and wrote. The character of Christ, as drawn in the Scriptures, is, in itself, an absolute demonstration of its validity, on the one hand, and of the inspiration of the sacred writers, that is, of the Scriptures, on the other.

One additional consideration demands special attention in this connection. The writers who have drawn the character of Christ, if what they have recorded of him is not true, were undeniably deliberate deceivers and impostors of the grossest character. Such persons, of all others, never did and never could thus conceive and portray such a character, supposing it not to have been real. Absolute unity of conception and representation could not have obtained among them. Above all, there never did and never could originate in such minds the conception of an absolutely perfect imaginary character. Bad men, impostors especially, would, with infallible certainty, have introduced somewhere into the ideal, some of the elements of their own depravity. That character, with no real original corresponding to it, was never conceived and portrayed by bad men, and it could not have originated with good men, and been presented as it stands revealed in the Scriptures, unless it did represent a reality.

3. The *morality* of Christianity as set forth by the sacred writers, next claims our attention. The following statements, the truth of which none will deny, will set this department of our subject in its true light before the reader's mind. (1.) The system of moral duty revealed in the Scriptures is absolutely complete and perfect in itself. There is no form of wrong actual or conceivable which its principles do not directly and specifically prohibit; nor any form of moral righteousness which they do not as directly and specifically require. You cannot add to, or take from, this system of moral duty a single principle, without marring its completeness and perfection. (2.) This system of moral duty is also equally universal and complete in its adaptations. There is not a condition or relation of humanity, or of any member of the human family, social, civil, or religious, in which the moral principles of Christianity are not an all-sufficient guide, as far as the question of duty is concerned, the only subject with which moral principles have to do. (3.) There is an absolutely perfect unity of conception and representation among all the sacred writers, in setting this complete, perfect, and universal system of moral legislation before our minds. No contradictory principles appear in any of their writings. No one affirms a single principle which any other writer denies. A more perfect unity of conception and representation could not, by any possibility, have obtained, had these entire writings been the exclusive production of some one single mind which had an absolutely perfect knowledge of all conceivable and possible principles of moral legislation. (4.) No system of morality making any ap-

proach whatever to any such forms of perfection appears among any people or nation in the age in which the sacred writers lived, or in any preceding or succeeding age, among any merely human productions. All such systems, on the other hand, are incomplete and self-contradictory in themselves, and in respect to no one principle is there a perfect unity of conception and representation, much less, in presenting a *system of morality itself.* Occasionally, some individuals like Confucius, have announced some one principle of the gospel. In the same connection, however, other false principles are given which pervert and neutralize what of truth has been before uttered. Outside of the Scriptures, and without the circle of their divine illumination, all human productions on such high themes, present nothing but a total chaos of contradictions and absurdities. Within that circle absolute perfection and unity of conception and representation appear, and no form of contradiction whatever. In view of such undeniable facts, permit us to put the following questions: Whence this system of moral legislation? Whence this absolute unity of conception and representation among all these writers, in shadowing it forth, writers living at such wide intervals of time, and in such dissimilar circumstances? But one answer can be given to these questions. Such completeness and perfection, such unity of conception and representation, on such a subject as this, is an absolute impossibility to any such number of men unguided by a power of and above themselves, in any age and in any circumstances, and above all, to the sacred writers, in their age and in their circumstances. The home of this law can be nowhere else than the bosom of God. It can be nothing else than the system of moral legislation which originally lay out before the infinite and eternal mind alone, and these writers, in shadowing it forth, could have been under no other guidance than the eternal spirit of that one infinite and eternal mind. We may safely challenge the world, to account for the existence of the system of moral legislation, as set forth in the Scriptures, on any other supposition.

4. The manner in which *the universal is blended with and expressed in the particular*, is another form in which the finger of God is visible, in the Scriptures. While it is not possible for us to assign, as we have already said, definite limits to the possible attainments of humanity, there are some things which no individual hesitates to affirm to be absolutely impossible to it. We have no hesitation in affirming, for example, that no individuals giving special instruction to a particular people in one age, and in circumstances altogether special and peculiar, could embody a system of instruction, on such high and mysterious themes, as God, duty, and immortality, equally adapted to the entire necessities of universal humanity in all ages and in all circumstances. It is a universal fact that admits of no exception, that forms of thinking humanly derived, and adapted to one age, become wholly unadapted to the human mind in another and subsequent age. Humanity in its childhood, cannot give forms of instruction, especially on the themes referred to, adapted to meet its entire necessities in the era of its manhood. Nothing can be more manifest than this, and nothing more absurd than the opposite idea. All forms of false religion, together with all forms of corrupt Christianity, tend to one result, and have one common characteristic which infallibly marks their origin as human. They gave an expansion to the human mind, and imparted a renewed energy to the human powers in the era of their first development, and

then tended to limit and debase its thinking and activity in every subsequent age. That which was light to humanity in one age becomes darkness to it in every subsequent age. To the truth of this statement there is, and from the nature of the case there can be, no exception. If the Bible is human in its origin, it will have this the invariable characteristic of all merely human productions. Being local in its origin, and originated for one people, and for men in a particular age and in peculiar circumstances, it will be found to be imperfect and incomplete in its system of moral rules and principles, and fundamentally adapted, as the universal source of spiritual knowledge and instruction, to limit thought and retard human progress. If, on the other hand, it was written by the finger of God, and the pencillings of infinity are consequently upon it, we shall find the universal blended and expressed in the particular, in the form above indicated; we shall find writings, originally addressed to, and prepared for a primitive people of a particular age, and in circumstances equally special and peculiar, yet equally adapted to be the light of universal humanity, in all ages and in all circumstances.

What are the facts of the case? In the first place, no writings ever were or can be more local and special in their original design and adaptations. They were addressed to one people, and always with special and almost exclusive reference to circumstances then existing. The Old Testament is wholly Jewish in its original adaptations. The New Testament, the Epistles especially, are constituted of diverse productions called forth exclusively by circumstances occurring at the time. All is local, all addressed to men in a particular age, in circumstances altogether peculiar, and with reference to their special necessities in these circumstances.

Now, while the Scriptures are thus local, thus special in their origin and original design and adaptations, they are equally adapted as the universal light of humanity in all ages and in all circumstances, and in all respects their adaptations are absolutely perfect. In all the circumstances of their existence in every stage of progress, all men alike find the Scriptures as fully and perfectly adapted to all the peculiarities of their ever-varying condition, as if they had been written by the finger of God for that condition exclusively.

The system of moral duty which they reveal, for example, is absolutely perfect and complete in the two respects under consideration, in its specific adaptation as a strictly universal system of moral rules and principles for the people to whom they were originally addressed, in their peculiar and special circumstances, and as a similar system for universal humanity in all ages and in all circumstances. Where is the defect in this system, in any respect actual or conceivable? There is not a form of duty which does or can pertain to humanity in any circumstances, which is not most manifestly demanded, as duty, by the moral precepts of the Scriptures; nor a form of wrong doing which is not with equal manifestness condemned by them. No defect ever has been, or ever can be, found in this system, as a system of universal moral legislation for universal humanity in all ages and in all circumstances.

Equally absolute is the universality of the adaptations of the Scriptures as sources of *spiritual illumination*. Every individual who reads them attentively finds his own character as specifically and minutely drawn out there, his own peculiar necessities as perfectly designated, and all the exigencies of his entire existence as specifically provided for, as if the eye that guided the hands by which they were written, rested down upon him alone, and saw with unerring light through all departments of his being, and with absolute omniscience comprehended all the circumstances of the same. Here are writings prepared for, and addressed to men living two and three thousand years ago, to men in the infancy of the earth, and in reference to the peculiar specialities of their then condition. Yet in these same writings we can read with unerring certainty universal humanity in all ages and in every possible variety of condition. Was it the eye of man that guided the hands that penned those mysterious writings? Was it not the eye of Omniscience itself?

We may mark the adaptation of the Scriptures as being equally perfect in respect to the *law of human progress.* Here are writings peculiarly local, individual, and specific, in their original design and adaptations, yet equally adapted to secure the endless development of universal humanity, in all ages and in all circumstances. The Scriptures are as far in advance of humanity now as they were in the age in which they were written. The Infinite and Perfect, with all the truths and interests of immortality, are so pencilled out there, that under their influence the development of humanity cannot but be endless. There are two great volumes which God is affirmed to have written, the book of nature, and inspiration. Humanity has no more outgrown the one than it has the other. There are still and equally in each infinite depths unfathomed, and infinite heights unascended, and lengths and breadths to which humanity has never yet attained. In each volume alike the pencillings of the Infinite and the Perfect are equally visible.

Now we affirm that the Scriptures themselves contain the most absolute demonstration of their divine original, — that it would be just as absurd to ascribe the production of one of the volumes above named to humanity unaided and unguided by power divine, as the other. If any thing is absolutely impossible to man, to any being of finite capacities, it is the blending of the universal in the particular in the manner in which they are blended in the Scriptures.

5. The train of thought which we have thus far pursued, prepares us to consider another form of internal evidence peculiar to the Scriptures. I refer to what may be called the *experimental* argument. Man is conscious, and cannot but be conscious, of three fundamental facts in regard to himself — that he is, from the immutable laws of his existence, a religious being, requiring some object of worship, and that nothing in that object but absolute infinity and perfection will or can meet the changeless wants of his nature, — that he is a fallen being, and needs subjection to a remedial system to restore him to moral purity and peace, — and, finally, that he is an endlessly progressive being, and needs to be in the presence of realities adapted to draw out his immortal powers, and cause them to expand towards absolute intellectual and moral beauty and perfection forever. In the centre of the human mind, also, is an immutable conviction, that there is a system of eternal truth perfectly adapted to meet, and to meet fully all these conscious necessities of man as a creature and a sinner, that no system of religion can be true which is not thus adapted to the wants of universal mind, and that that system cannot be false which is thus adapted. Now when the mind comes within the circle of the great realities revealed in the Scriptures, it has, and

cannot but have, as they open more and more distinctly upon its vision, the absolute consciousness of their complete and perfect adaptation to meet fully the entire demands of its moral, spiritual, and intellectual nature, in all the respects above named. It knows, and cannot but know, that every principle of that nature is a lie, or that it is in the unveiled presence of nothing but eternal verities. Here is an object of worship possessing the very forms of absolute beauty and perfection which the immortal nature within demands or can demand in such object. Here, also, is a system of moral duty which meets with equal fulness the utmost demands of the conscience and moral nature of universal humanity. Here, too, is a remedial system, which, as the mind cannot but be conscious, meets, with the same completeness and fulness, the immutable necessities of man, as a morally fallen and ruined creature of God. In the midst of the same revelations, also, the mind has an equally distinct consciousness, that it is in the presence of realities upon which its immortal powers may eternally expand towards infinite intellectual and moral beauty and perfection; while in the example and character of Jesus Christ, it will ever be in the presence of an all-perfect example, in conformity to which its own character may ever take on the most complete forms of beauty and perfection of which its nature is, or ever will be, susceptible. Of this absolute correspondence between the great truths which Christianity reveals, and the entire fundamental and immutable demands of our immortal nature, the mind becomes more and more distinctly conscious, the more it dwells upon them, and this immutable consciousness is the highest conceivable evidence that the mind is in the presence, not of sublime and fleeting fictions, but of eternal truth. Who can believe that our immortal nature, in all its laws and susceptibilities, is fundamentally adapted to the unreal and untrue? and that a system of religion which thus meets those laws and susceptibilities, as we cannot but know that none others can, has, or can have, any other foundation than the rock of eternal truth? "He that believeth hath the witness in himself," that is, in the conscious correspondence between what is believed, and the immutable demands of his moral and spiritual nature, he has a continued testimony that what he believes, is and must be true, and this kind of testimony, which is exclusively peculiar to Christianity, which is common to it, with no other religion, or system of sceptical or religious belief, is the highest possible evidence of its divine origin. That great fundamental principle of science that for every demand of sentient existence, there exists a corresponding provision, must be false, or a religion which thus completely meets the moral and spiritual necessities of the universal mind must be true.

6. There is one general remark bearing upon the argument for the divine origin of Christianity, from internal evidence, which should not be passed by, without special notice. We refer to the manifest and undeniable marks of honesty and integrity which everywhere characterize these writings and their various authors, and that without exception. We know perfectly, that if they are thus honest, the Scriptures cannot be from man, but must have been given by inspiration of God. Yet in reading their multiplied writings, we cannot avoid the deep and immovable conviction, that we are in the presence of men of the purest and most unshaken integrity. Not a solitary indication of any opposite characteristic in the writers themselves appears upon a single

page of the Bible. On the other hand, every thing which distinguishes and characterizes the most perfect forms of moral integrity everywhere appears. In following these men we cannot escape the conviction that we are following men who really and truly think themselves leading us in the paths of truth and life, and nowhere else. We know that they cannot themselves be deceived in regard to the facts which they reveal, and are equally impressed with the conviction, that they are not and cannot be intentional deceivers.

Thus it is, that the Bible itself is its own divinely attested witness, a witness whose testimony we cannot misapprehend, and who cannot lead us in the direction of the unreal or the untrue. There stands the Bible, reader, arrayed in all its own unrivalled, unearthly, and unapproachable grandeur and sublimity, encircled everywhere with external divinely attested witnesses of its divine origin, witnesses which by no possibility can thus stand around any thing which is unreal or untrue. There stands the Bible too, with its own all-perfect, all-overshadowing revelations lifting their sublime and awe-inspiring summits infinitely above the actual or possible reach of all human productions. "Walk about our Zion, tell her towers, mark well her bulwarks, and consider her palaces," and then say, if you will risk your eternity upon the supposition, that the Bible is a fiction, that its religion is any thing else than the rock of eternal truth.

CHAPTER IV.

OBJECTIONS ANSWERED.

NOTWITHSTANDING the overwhelming weight of the evidence in favor of the divine origin of Christianity, objections to the supposition of such an origin exist, to a considerable extent, in the public mind, objections which induce not a few to subject themselves to the cold and freezing moral atmosphere of infidelity, and which hold a still greater number of individuals in such doubt and uncertainty on the subject, as to prevent their giving any serious attention to the great questions which hang around that of their own immortality. Our discussions would, therefore, be manifestly defective, in their adaptations to meet the wants of the public mind, were these objections passed by unheeded. Of course, we shall not be expected to meet, or specify every difficulty which is floating on the surface of society, but only such as have the greatest weight, and which involve in their destruction that of all the others.

In approaching this subject intelligently, the question first to be raised and decided, pertains to the nature of these objections, and to that department of the sacred volume against which they are adduced. In answering this inquiry, we remark: —

1. That no one objects to the divine origin of Christianity, on the ground that its claims are defective, so far as the validity of the argument based upon the attestation of miracles is concerned. No one pretends, that if we admit the reality of the great facts adduced by Christians, in attestation of this truth, that they are not real miraculous interpretations of creative power,

and as such place the known and undeniable seal of the incorruptible and eternal God upon the Bible, as his own all-authoritative revelation to man. Nor has any one ever shown, that the evidence in favor of the actual occurrence of these divine attestations is not valid, is not what Christians claim it to be, a kind of evidence which never does and never can deceive, which never does and never can stand around what is unreal or untrue, and affirm its existence and occurrence. So far the Christian argument is really unassailed and truly unassailable.

2. Nor is the objection based upon any want of completeness or force in the Christian argument, as far as the evidence from *prophecy* is concerned. No one will attempt to account for the prophetic predictions found in the Bible, by a reference to any form of foresight possible to man. Nor will he pretend to weaken or modify the argument, by finding a single instance of failure in the fulfilment of those predictions, nor by adducing similar or analogous instances of similar predictions similarly fulfilled, predictions which originated with man. Nor will he attempt to account for these predictions on any other principle than that their origin is from the inspiration of the spirit of God. Here undeniably the Christian argument is perfect and complete in all its parts, and perfectly fundamental in its bearings upon the question at issue. We believe that the world is yet to hear, for the first time, of an objection to the validity of the Christian argument, by a formal attempt upon the prophecies of Scripture, in any of the forms above named, or in any scientific form whatever.

3. Nor does the objection lie against the completeness and force of the Christian argument from *internal evidence* in any of the forms in which it has been pre-

sented to your consideration. No one, we may safely assume, will deny or disprove the *facts* stated, namely, the perfection of the character of God, and of Christ, as developed in the Scriptures, the completeness and perfection of the system of moral duty there presented, nor the absolute unity of conception and representation which obtains among the sacred writers on these high themes. Nor can the absolute adaptations of Christianity as a universal religion for humanity, in all ages and under all circumstances, be objected against, nor the absolute unity of conception and representation among the sacred writers in regard to it be denied. Equally undeniable is the fact of the blending of the universal in the particular in the sense and forms explained in the last chapter, namely, the fact, that forms of instruction given to men in the infancy of the race, and in the lowest stages of mental development, embody and reveal a system of moral legislation absolutely complete and perfect in itself, and equally adequate as such a system, to the entire necessities of universal humanity in all ages and in all circumstances and relations, social, civil, and religious, together with a religion equally complete and perfect in itself, and equally universal and absolute in its adaptations. Nor can it be shown that such perfection of thought on such high themes, and such unity of conception and representation in regard to it, among so many writers thus circumstanced, is not infinitely above the possible reach of so many minds unaided and uncontrolled by some other intelligence out of and above themselves, or in any circumstances actual or conceivable, much less, in the circumstances in which these writings were originated. Equally undeniable is the fact, that the intelligence which originated these wonderful writings did possess a perfect omniscience in regard to God on the one hand, and the character, nature, and wants of man on the other; in other words, that "all Scripture must have been given by inspiration of God." Nor can it be objected, finally, that the sincerity and integrity of these writers is for a moment to be called in doubt. Nor can it be shown how that such integrity can have existed in them, and the facts to the reality of which they give testimony never have occurred. In all these respects there is undeniably no want of completeness or force in the Christian argument, and against none of those impregnable fortresses which lift their awful summits around "the glorious gospel of the blessed God," have its enemies ever arrayed their objections, nor will they ever dare to do it.

4. While the enemies of Christianity have never met the Christian argument, in any of the forms above stated, nor formally arrayed their objections against it, they have never shown how it is possible, that a religion sustained by such evidence, external and internal, can be false, can be any thing else than it claims to be, of divine origin and authority. They do not, and dare not meet the evidence, on the one hand, nor can they demonstrate the want of necessary connection between it, and the conclusion based upon it, on the other. So far Christianity stands out before the world unassailed and unassailable. Every hostile argument falling upon this adamantine rock, the evidence of Christianity derived from the sources under consideration, is broken, and every objection upon which that evidence falls, is, by its overwhelming and crushing weight, ground to powder.

5. Nor will any individuals lay the objections which they urge against the claims of Christianity, by the

side of all the forms of evidence actually existing in favor of those claims, and then affirm, as the result of an intelligent comparison, that in the judgment of honest and enlightened men, those objections ought to outweigh that evidence. Weighed distinctly in the balance against that evidence, they undeniably have no weight or substance whatever.

Let us now advance to a direct consideration of these objections, and see what they are. Like the argument in favor of the divine origin of Christianity, they divide themselves into two classes, external and internal. We will consider them under these two divisions. Of the first class, the following only are worthy of notice: —

OBJECTIONS RELATIVE TO EXTERNAL EVIDENCE.

1. The first that I notice is the celebrated objection raised by David Hume against the possibility of *proving* the actual occurrence of miracles by evidence. The argument may be thus stated, and we give it in all its force. We can only reason on this subject from what we know to be true from experience, that is, from our own personal knowledge of facts. "It is contrary to experience that a miracle should be true, but not contrary to experience that testimony should be false." Miracles, therefore, cannot be established by testimony. Now this argument bears upon the face of it, the grossest error conceivable, in the assertion of facts of experience. It does accord with experience, that *some kinds* of testimony should be false; while there are other kinds which, from experience and observation, we know absolutely, never does and never can prove false; and that, without exception, is the very kind which

affirms the reality of the Christian miracles. The experience of man, from the creation to the present hour, cannot designate a single instance in which this kind of testimony has ever proved false. The objection rests wholly upon an assumption known absolutely to be false. No more, therefore, need be said in regard to it.

2. The objection under consideration exists in the popular mind, at the present time, in a *form* somewhat different to that above stated, a form in which the argument from miracles is intuitively ignored, as unworthy of the regard of thinking men, in this enlightened and progressive age. The objection may be thus stated. All events in the universe, past, present, and future, occur through the exclusive action of natural laws, and can occur from no other cause. Miracles, which imply the suspension of such laws, and the production of effects by an interposition of creative power out of and above nature, and not through or in accordance with natural law, is a natural impossibility, and therefore incapable of being proved by any degree of evidence whatever. Hence it is assumed, that the Christian miracles being absurd, and impossible in themselves, are unworthy of our regard or investigation. In reply to this objection we would invite special attention to the following observations: (1.) The objection rests upon a mere assumption, which has its exclusive basis in sheer ignorance and nothing else, an assumption unsustained by the least shadow of evidence whatever. Let us put the following questions to the objector: How do you, or how can you know, that all events past, present, and future, occur, and must occur, through the exclusive action of natural laws? Where is your proof of the truth of such a principle, — a principle whose truth is neither self-evident, nor affirmed by a solitary fact in

the wide universe. Because some events, all if you please, which fall under your immediate observation, occur through and in accordance with such laws, what proof is that, what shadow of evidence does it afford, that no event ever did, or ever will or can occur but through such laws? (2.) This assumption, as we have already seen, is falsified by the most absolute demonstrations of natural science itself. Every demonstration of such science must be held as utterly false, as we have already seen, if creation, from its commencement to its final consummation, has not been exclusively through the direct and immediate, that is, miraculous interposition of creative power, a power out of and above nature, and itself originating, sustaining, and controlling natural law. (3.) The evidence which affirms the reality of the Christian miracles is a kind of evidence which, as we have seen, never does, and never can prove false. It has all the force of natural law. It will not do, reader, to ignore such evidence, and such demonstrations as these, and attempt to supplant them by mere assumption not self-evidently true, and unsustained by the least shadow of evidence whatever.

3. We now refer to an objection which appears in the form of a general assumption, in regard to all the great events recorded in Scripture. All the statements of Scripture pertaining to the leading events there recorded, are affirmed to be altogether of a mythical, that is, fabulous character, having their derivation from, and bearing but a remote resemblance to, ancient events of no miraculous character whatever. Jesus Christ himself is also affirmed to be not a real historical, but a mythical or fabulous character. So of "the mighty works" ascribed to him, the New Testament record of him and his works bearing no more

resemblance to him as he was, and to the real acts of his life, than the fabled legends in regard to Hercules do to the real acts of his life. Upon this assumption, the leading forms of infidelity, as represented in the writings of such men as Strauss, in Germany, and Theodore Parker of this country, are based, and must stand or fall with that assumption. In reply to this objection, we remark, (1.) That if we admit its validity, the argument from prophecy and internal evidence remains in all its force, unassailable and unassailed, and this alone establishes most absolutely the divine origin of Christianity. (2.) This objection has its basis in a mere assumption, and nothing else, an assumption unsustained by the least shadow of evidence, of any kind whatever. The only evidence that we have of its truth is simply this, and nothing more, namely, Mr. Strauss and Mr. Parker boldly affirm that it is so, and affirm this without any positive evidence whatever to sustain their assertions, and that while their assertions are contradicted by the most weighty and valid evidence conceivable. (3.) All the great events of inspiration, as narrated by the sacred writers, have, in all conceivable and possible respects, absolutely none of the characteristics which distinguish fables from real facts, on the one hand, and every characteristic which distinguishes real facts from fables, on the other. Fabulous statements relate, without exception, either, like the stories of Hercules, to events of a remote antiquity, events seen by those who first recorded them through the veil of the most obscure tradition, a veil, also, which permits the narrators themselves to impart any form, and to put any coloring upon them they please, or to events, like the fabled ascent of Mohammed to heaven, professedly witnessed only by those said to have performed them, and who consequently had the highest motives to exaggerate and deceive. On the other hand, all the great events narrated in the Bible are affirmed to have occurred at definite periods in the history of the peoples among whom they occurred, and that with the eye of nations upon them when they took place, the events themselves being, as we have seen, of such a character that those present at the time could by no possibility have been deceived, in regard to the fact of their occurrence or non-occurrence. Moreover, the historical records of those events were written at the time of their occurrence, and in their very midst, or within the memory of those who were direct and original witnesses of their occurrence, and have, from that time to this, remained as the universally authenticated and absolutely reliable historical records of the peoples among whom they occurred. Here we have the only fundamental characteristics which distinguish real valid history from that which is mythical and fabulous, and real facts from fables; and we must admit the validity of such tests, or pronounce all history of every kind to be nothing but fable.

All will admit, also, that if Jesus Christ be a real, and not a mythical character, and that if the events attributed to him in the New Testament are the real scenes and acts of his life, all the great events narrated in the entire Scriptures are real facts, and not fables. On this subject, permit us to invite very special attention to the following statements, statements the truth of which none will deny: (1.) No mythic or fabulous character is or can be the subject of such prophetic predictions as are recorded of Jesus Christ, in the Old Testament, the very date of his death, for example, being fixed more than five hundred years prior to his birth. (2.) No mythical or fabulous character has full historical records of the great events of his life, events of the highest conceivable public interest and notoriety, and written within the memory of, and published, at the time, in the midst of the millions to whom those events were personally known, as is true of the histories of Christ given by the four evangelists, and all this, while these very records have, from that time to this, been universally received as containing nothing but veritable facts. (3.) The historical records of no mythical character ever were or can be verified by such external testimony as that which stands around those of the four Evangelists in respect to Jesus Christ. The testimony of the Jewish nation, and of Jewish historians, we have already considered. Permit us here to introduce a single Pagan witness, Tacitus, whose history, from which our citation is taken, was written but about thirty years after the death of Christ. According to this historian, Nero, to avert from himself the infamy of having set fire to Rome, accused Christians of having done the deed, and inflicted on them the most cruel tortures. "With this view," he says, "he inflicted the most exquisite tortures on those men, who, under the vulgar appellation of Christians, were already branded with deserved infamy. They derived their name and origin from Christ, who, in the reign of Tiberius, had suffered death by the sentence of the procurator Pontius Pilate." No fabulous statements ever had such confirmations as these. (4.) All fabulous characters, we remark finally, are almost exclusively creations of the imagination. But that of Christ, as we have most abundantly shown already, is, when we consider its absolute perfection, the elements blended into it, and the unity of conception and representation among the sacred writers in respect to it, infinitely above the possible reach of the imagination, in any age, much less in that in which this divine portraiture was drawn, and among such writers as drew it. No reference to the human imagination, or to any of the powers of the human mind, or to all combined, nor to the opinions, expectations, or wants of that age, can account for the mere conception of the character of Christ, as drawn by the sacred writers. To what hopeless straits must infidelity be driven, when its last refuge is the assumption, — an assumption unsustained by the least shadow of evidence, and affirmed to be false by all the tests and principles which do or can distinguish facts from fables, — when its last refuge and only hope, we say, is the assumption that the history of Christ is a fiction.

OBJECTIONS BASED UPON WHAT IS FOUND IN THE BIBLE ITSELF.

We now turn to a consideration of the second class of objections, those based upon what is asserted to be found in the Scriptures themselves. These objections, as we shall see, have no reference to any defect in the morality of Christianity, as far as its principles are applicable to us, to its want of adaptation to man's necessities as a sinner, or to any thing defective in the external or internal evidence, as developed in our previous investigations. All pertain to certain affirmed dispensations of Providence in regard to Jews and Pagans, to facts asserted on divine authority, as having occurred, to certain precepts given to the Jews at that time, and to the application of certain moral principles to them in their peculiar circumstances. Now before any such objections can be urged, we must be certain of the following facts: (1.) That we rightly understand the record itself. Any objections based upon a misapprehension of the sacred text, exposes the ignorance of the objector, and not the error of the Bible. (2.) That we rightly understand all the circumstances of the case. A failure here, may again only expose our ignorance and error, instead of proving the Bible not to be the word of God. (3.) That we rightly understand and interpret the end really and truly aimed at, in the dispensations objected against. Without such knowledge, an act may appear to us very objectionable, which, when seen in the light of this end will, and may appear as a means most wisely adapted to its full and complete realization, and therefore assume the aspect of the most pure and perfect wisdom and benevolence.

These objections, we would also remark, refer, for the most part, to what is found in the Old Testament. In regard to the character of this entire dispensation, we have the opinion of one, let us say, whose opinion is entitled to some consideration, to say the least, and should be well pondered, before we commit ourselves on the subject, "lest haply we should be found fighting against God." Jesus Christ has affirmed absolutely, that this entire dispensation, with all its real principles and teachings, has its exclusive basis in the law of absolute benevolence and rectitude: "On these two commandments hang all the law and the prophets," that is, the entire ancient Scriptures, with all their asserted divine acts, principles, and precepts. What must we think of the professions of men, who affirm themselves to agree with whatever Jesus Christ taught, and yet object fundamentally against what he asserts to be perfect? We will now proceed to consider the objections referred to: —

1. Not a few object to the claims of Christianity, on

account of the *doctrine of retribution*, as set forth in the Scriptures. On this subject, permit us barely to hint the following suggestions: (1.) Remember that you are an interested party, and are very liable to be misled by a state of mind which has two wrong elements in it, — an unwillingness to meet the requirements of Scripture, though seconded by the behests of your own conscience on the subject, — and in that state to entertain the idea, that such unwillingness must be connected with the consequences revealed in the Scriptures. (2.) It looks somewhat like presumption in us, to place difficulties arising in our minds on such a subject against the infinite weight of evidence actually existing, in favor of the divine origin of Christianity, and, consequently, in favor of the truth, that these very retributions, and these alone, measure the actual desert of sin, as seen by that infinite and eternal mind, that cannot err in judgment. (3.) Those who have most profoundly studied the laws and principles of their own moral nature, the claims of God, and of the law of duty, as really revealed in the universal conscience, have come to the united conviction, that these very retributions alone measure the actual deserts of sin. (4.) The most beautiful and perfect forms of moral virtue that have ever appeared on earth, have been generated under these very truths, and others of a kindred character revealed in the Scriptures. (5.) Separated from these very truths, Christianity, as a matter-of-fact, is divested of all really morally renovating and reformatory power. With these considerations, we leave the subject upon the conscience of the reader.

2. Others object to the claims of Christianity, on account of the *doctrine of atonement* as set forth in the Scriptures. On this point, also, we would barely drop

the following suggestions: (1.) If the doctrine of retribution as above indicated is true, a doctrine whose truth cannot be invalidated, that of atonement must be true, or there is no redemption for man. (2.) The idea of atonement, instead of being contrary to reason, as many suppose, is, in fact, the great leading idea that lies upon the conscience of universal humanity, being the greatest element of all religions on earth, that of false forms of Christianity excepted. The presence and pervading influence of this idea is manifest in the sacrifices which characterize all these religions. Now an idea so universal as this must, as the great philosopher Coleridge affirms, have been imparted to man by inspiration, or be in itself so accordant with reason, as to have all the force of a truth of revelation. (3.) In Jesus Christ, this idea which thus lies upon the conscience, and there indicates a fundamental want of universal humanity, is fully realized. (4.) This doctrine thus realized, and this alone, perfectly meets the conscious necessities of universal mind when it has once attained to a consciousness of its actual condition as under sin. Of the truth of this statement, no one under the consciousness referred to, can doubt any more than man can doubt his own existence. (5.) It is only through an implicit faith in the doctrine of retribution on the one hand, and atonement as realized in Christ on the other, that the most perfect forms of moral virtue that ever appeared on earth, have been generated. (6.) Separate these two doctrines from Christianity, and you extract from it all its power really and truly to renovate and to bless fallen humanity. We stop not to argue the truth of these statements. To all who read these facts as they are, their truth is self-affirmed.

3. But a fundamental objection is, in the judgment of some, found in the affirmed divine dispensations in the indiscriminate destruction of the inhabitants of Canaan, on the one hand, and their being supplanted by the Israelites, on the other. To form a right judgment of this, or any other acts of providence, we must first of all know the end for which the thing is done, and its adaptation as a means to that end. The fact that any thing is done, as we have the highest conceivable evidence that the transaction under consideration was under the immediate direction and bidding of Jehovah himself, affords some presumption, to say the least, that the thing done was a wisely adapted means to a perfectly benevolent end, and should render creatures like us, at this distance of time, and ignorant as we must be of all the reasons for the occurrence, to be slow in questioning the Almighty on the wisdom and rectitude of his dispensations. We need to be reminded that there is such a thing as impious presumption, which may ultimately bring upon those who perpetrate it, the terrible rebuke of God himself. We are not left at all in the dark, however, in regard to the end for which the transaction under consideration was ordered, and have some facilities for judging of its adaptations as a means to that end. The end was nothing more nor less than the destruction of idolatry among all nations, together with the numberless crimes and abominations everywhere existing and perpetrated under its influence, and the reintroduction of the lost knowledge and worship of the only living and true God, together with all the virtues and external blessings necessarily resulting from that knowledge and worship. "That my name might be declared throughout all the earth," "that the living may know that the Most High

ruleth in the kingdom of men." This was the exclusive end proposed in this whole transaction. That we may understand its adaptation as a means to this end, consider the following undeniable facts: (1.) Among all nations, the knowledge and worship of the true God was supplanted by those of devils, whose character, without exception, was such, that none could worship them, without imbibing degrees and forms of moral depravity and debasement utterly impossible to humanity under any other influences. (2.) This system of devil-worship was attended everywhere with the most horrid and debasing rites of which we can possibly form a conception. Drunkenness, debauchery, sodomy, degrading bestiality, infanticide, and all forms of human sacrifices, are terms which but faintly indicate the nameless abominations which constituted the fundamental elements of heathen rites and worship in all parts of the earth. By a law of the empire, for example, every matron in Babylon was required to prostitute herself at least once to a stranger in a heathen temple. Everywhere the temples themselves were the very centres of such monstrous immoralities. (3.) Under this system all forms of domestic, social, civil, and religious virtue had hopelessly disappeared. The world had become an aceldema, a visible hell, whose moral aspect could fully satisfy the utmost wish of the prince of darkness himself. (4.) Under the influences then prevailing, and without the most signal and startling interpositions of God himself, there was no hope for the better; but humanity was hopelessly advancing towards worse and worse forms of moral corruption and death. (5.) The land of Canaan was the centre and focus of all these abominations, the common sewer into which all that was degrading and debasing in heathenism itself seemed to run, and there attain its utmost consummation. (6.) To understand the whole subject, also, it should be remembered, that every particular nation had its own guardian divinities, under whose protection it was supposed that all national interests were safe. All parts of nature, also the earth, the air, the ocean, the sun, moon, and stars, were supposed to be under the control of particular deities. Under such circumstances, what is the Most High affirmed to have done? Did he leave humanity to hopeless debasement and ruin? And what if he did destroy a nation already lost to all hope of moral renovation, and destroy that nation to save a world? Who will say that God had not a right to do it, and that the means he did adopt were not best adapted to the great end referred to?

What were the means which the Most High is affirmed in Scripture to have adopted to realize this end? The following: —

(1.) He interposes by the most signal judgments upon old Egypt, for its most degrading forms of heathenism, and universal moral debasement consequent thereon, every judgment being a specific assault upon the religious system then and there prevailing, and most wisely adapted to secure its destruction. (2.) He took from the midst of that nation a people prepared in the best manner possible under the circumstances, and himself went visibly before them, in a pillar of fire by night and of cloud by day, opening a passage for them through the Red Sea, at Sinai, amid the most impressive manifestations conceivable, giving them "a fiery law" which prohibited idolatry in all its forms, and that together with the purest conceivable system of morality, domestic, social, civil, and religious. After feeding them miraculously forty years in the wilderness, and by every possible means preparing them for their high mission, he visibly led them into the centre of the moral abominations of desolation of the whole earth, and there commanded the utter extermination of the people who upheld and perpetrated them, uniting his own visible and all-impressive interpositions for the accomplishment of that command, and all this for one end, to rebuke the world for its crimes, restore to man the knowledge of truth indispensable to his moral restoration, and save lost humanity from hopeless debasement and ruin. (3.) As a still further means to the great end before us, he hung over his own people, after their settlement in Canaan, and that before all nations, the all-impressive enunciation, that while they practised the pure virtues which their divine religion required, they should be the strongest, and that when they should apostatize towards the abominations of the heathen around them, they should be the weakest of all the nations of the earth, and become subject to signal judgments, such as should descend upon no other people, an enunciation which God has most signally verified. (4.) Finally, he hung over all the earth the all-impressive and startling predictions, that he would then proceed to shake all nations, dashing them to pieces as the potter's vessel, till "the living should know that the Most High ruleth in the kingdom of men," and should turn from the worship of devils, and the practice of corresponding abominations, to serve the only living and true God, and to the practice of the virtues which he requires, and the well-being of universal humanity demands, predictions which, as we have seen, he has most impressively fulfilled.

Now we affirm, that in this whole procedure, the end aimed at is worthy of infinite wisdom and love, and the means most wisely adapted to the realization of that end. Nothing but the most startling judgments could at all have broke the slumbers of moral death which pressed upon ruined humanity. Unless God had appeared as he did, at the head of some one nation, he could not effectually have broken the power of national idolatry, as it everywhere existed at the time. All the judgments inflicted through that nation, under the divine direction, were called for in themselves, and wisely adapted to the end for which they were ordered. The indiscriminate destruction of the people among whom all these abominations centered, was the wisest arrangement that could have been adopted at the time, and only adequate to make the proper impression upon the world of God's sentiments and purposes in regard to the abominations for which that destruction was ordered, judgments withheld "till the iniquity of that people was full." Thus to every enlightened and candid mind, God's eternal government must stand approved.

4. We are now prepared to understand that great event so often held up against the Bible, the standing still of the sun and moon at the bidding of Joshua in the valley of Gibeon. The impiety and moral presumption manifest in the form in which this transaction is often held before the public, deserves the deepest reprobation of the universe, namely, that all this was done to enable one nation to murder the innocent and feeble inhabitants of another, and then seize upon their possessions. Had not the very event, let us say, actually occurred, heathenism, in all its forms, would not have received a needful rebuke. According to its teachings, as held the world over, one class of divinities reigned over the earth, and others presided over the movements of the heavenly bodies. God, while asserting, before all nations, his

own exclusive and all-presiding divinity, and while before all he is thundering forth his judgments upon men for having other Gods before him, in testimony of his own exclusive dominion over the entire universe, stops the sun and moon and stars in their courses. This event is just as possible to God, as any other, and how adapted to startle and arouse all nations on earth, and arrest them in their downward course of crime and debasements! Nothing else could have been so impressive a revelation to the nations of God himself, to the exclusion of all others before him, under the circumstances.

5. The transactions recorded in Numbers 22: 22, of Balaam, is not unfrequently held up to ridicule, as too absurd in itself for the supposition that it is true, or occurred under the direction of God. In regard to this transaction, we deem it important to make simply the following observations: (1.) It is well known, that necromancy, soothsaying, etc., attended as they were by ventriloquism and other kindred sources of deception, were among the most powerful of all the sources of influence which heathenism held over the human mind, and that men who excelled in these arts, stood preëminent above all others in public estimation. (2.) Of all men of this class, Balaam, in the estimation of all surrounding nations, was most eminent. So eminent was he, that no heathen doubted that nothing could avert the blessing or curse pronounced by him upon individuals or nations. (3.) For this man to be brought under an influence through which he should, in the presence of all surrounding nations, proclaim the God of Israel to be the only living and true God, and the utter vanity and impotence in his presence of this great central power of heathenism, was to strike the heaviest pos-

sible blow against this system of error and corruption and in favor of the truth that, by any possibility, could have been struck. (4.) Every event here recorded as occurring prior to the appearance of this preëminent prophet of heathenism on Nebo, where, in the presence of surrounding nations, and in the most impressive circumstances conceivable, he proclaims the being, perfections, and all-presiding agency of one God, the God of Israel, and the utter vanity and impotency, in his presence, of heathenism, with all its enchantments and lies, all events recorded as having occurred prior to this, were ordered, we say, as a means to this one great end, and no means conceivable could be more perfectly adapted to that end. At first, Balaam is confounded by the message from Balak to come and "curse Israel." Then comes a solemn prohibition against his complying with the request. Subsequently, he receives permission to go, but under the most solemn charge to say nothing whatever but what God should communicate to him. To secure this result what immediately followed was ordered. On his way the prophet is first startled by unheard of, and to him unaccountable acts in the brute on which he rode. Then his madness is rebuked by a voice coming to him from the mouth of "the dumb animal," a voice whose existence he could account for, by a reference to no acts of ventriloquism which he had been accustomed to practise. Then an angel of God with a drawn sword in his hand, suddenly stands revealed to the terror-stricken necromancer. When prostrate upon the ground, he is told to go on his journey, but to say nothing but what God should bid him say. Thus the great end sought was realized. Taken as a whole, we have here one of the sublimest and most impressive scenes on record. So it must appear to every candid and well-informed mind.

6. The standing objection of infidelity next claims our attention. In Deut. 15: 21, the Israelites, it is said, while they are prohibited themselves eating the flesh of animals dying of disease, "that which dieth of itself," they are permitted to give this diseased and tainted meat to strangers, and to sell the same "unto an alien." Here is something which we know never did and never could come from God. Yet it stands in such connection with other Scriptures that they must stand or fall with it. In reply, we would simply add, that in the original there is no word or phrase that in any form answers to the phrase "that which dieth of itself," or which makes any approach whatever to any such meaning. It is a single word, a noun, which receives this rendering, "that which dieth of itself," a word which means simply a *carcase*, a dead body of any kind, and is so rendered in Hebrew lexicons. Literally understood, the Jew is here prohibited eating meat of any kind. Happily we are not kept in the dark in regard to the kind of flesh referred to. In Exodus 22: 31, the Jew, for purely ceremonial reasons, is prohibited eating the flesh of any animal that has been "torn (killed) by a wild beast." In Lev. 7: 24, and 17: 15, he is prohibited eating "that which dieth of itself, *or* that is torn by wild beasts." The original literally and truly rendered is, *a carcase, namely, that which is torn by wild beasts*, the object of the second clause being to define and limit the meaning of the first. In these passages the Jew is told what he may *not* do with such kind of meat. In Deut. 15: 21, he is told what he *may* do with it, the kind of carcase referred to having been defined, the one word simply is used. For ceremonial reasons exclusively, the Jew was not permitted to eat such flesh himself. As it was just as

wholesome in itself as any other, however, he was told that he might give it to the stranger, or sell it to the alien; as benevolent a precept as could have been given. It is in this light exclusively that that dispensation throughout appears, when rightly comprehended. There is nothing in it of which God has reason to be ashamed, or which Christ, with absolute truth, could not affirm to have been, in the circumstances, an infallible application and embodiment of the law of perfect rectitude and benevolence. For ourselves, when we hear individuals scoffing at that sacred dispensation, or impeaching the character of God as therein revealed, we are free to say, that we entertain little respect for their moral judgments, or moral character; for nothing but the absence of moral principle in us, can induce a want of appreciation of what is wise in legislation, perfect in morals, and sublimely venerable in truth.

We are obliged, for want of space, to omit one entire chapter, a chapter *on the genuineness and authenticity of the Scriptures.* We know whereof we affirm, and what we are able to prove, when we say, that all that infidelity has said against the Bible, in this respect, is just as false as the utterances of A. J. Davis which we have exposed in Part I. Our motto, reader, is, "the Bible, the whole Bible, and nothing but the Bible," as an all-authoritative revelation from God. We receive the whole of it as coming to us from the heart of infinite wisdom and intelligence. And, reader, when you stand in the unveiled presence of that infinite and eternal One, as you soon will, our solemn conviction is, that you will find yourself wholly unable then to present an adequate reason for not having received that book as God's only all-authoritative revelation to man, and as "the light to your feet and the lamp to your path" in your journey to immortality, and that if you have ever uttered a scoff, or an irreverential sentiment against that book, and have not deeply repented of the same, you will then cover your face with shame under the righteous frown and reprobation of the moral universe. Byron penned a sentiment worthy of all regard, when he wrote on a blank leaf of his pocket Bible the following lines: —

"Within this awful volume lies
The mystery of mysteries.
Ah, happy they of all our race,
To whom our God has given grace,
To read, to mark, to learn, to pray,
To lift the latch and force the way.
And better had they ne'er been born
Who read to doubt, or read to scorn."

PART IV.

CLAIRVOYANT REVELATIONS OF EMANUEL SWEDENBORG.

WE have the following reasons, among others, for subjecting, in the present treatise, the professed revelations of the individual above named to a sufficiently careful and rigid criticism to develop their real merits: —

1. They undeniably belong to the very class of developments which were the subject of criticism in the first two Parts of this work.

2. These pretended revelations are now being very diligently urged upon public regard, on account of this very fact. Mr. Bush, for example, has published a work of 288 pages, the exclusive object of which is to disclose the relations of these revelations to Mesmerism. The following extract from this work will give the case as now presented to the public by the advocates of Swedenborgianism among us.

"The indubitable facts of Mesmerism are affording to the very senses of man a demonstration which cannot be resisted, that *Swedenborg has told the truth of the other life.* The denial of his claims has now to encounter something more than the intrinsic character of his statements. It must meet, and, in order to be successful, must overcome, the strong array of *facts* planted around it by the progress of mesmeric discovery. These facts are intuitively seen to connect themselves indissolubly with the whole tissue of Swedenborg's relations, as to the laws and phenomena of the spiritual world. The result is inevitable. *If Mesmerism is true, Swedenborg is true.* Can the further inference be resisted, that if Swedenborg is true, he is a divinely commissioned messenger from heaven to man? It avails not to say in reply, that his revelations may have been merely mesmeric, and consequently are no more authoritative than those elicited from persons in ordinary magnetic *extase.* We have already shown that his state differed from that of ordinary mesmeric subjects, — that while there are certain points of resemblance and relation between them, his psychological condition was distinguished by peculiarities which elevated it immeasurably above theirs. The repetition of our proofs on this head will be unnecessary here. We content ourselves with the simple affirmation, that it is impossible to deny, on intelligent grounds, that the higher mesmeric phenomena fall into the same category with the revelations of the Swedish seer, and that the truth of the former establishes that of the latter."

3. If we admit the validity of these revelations as now commended to the world by their advocates, we must hold, and that for no other reason than the simple word of this one man, that a part of the Bible was given by inspiration, and a part, about one sixth of the Old, and one half of the New Testament, the Acts, and *all* the Epistles, was not thus given. This we are to hold, when we have all the evidence, Swedenborg's testimony aside, that the parts rejected were thus given, that we have that the others were.

4. The main and almost exclusive interest which that portion of the Holy Writ which is left us, is to possess

in our minds, after receiving these revelations as divine, is to be derived from the new meaning which we are now to attach, and that simply because Swedenborg says we must, to the words of Scripture, a meaning arbitrarily attached to them, and which they have no adaptations whatever to convey. The *literal* meaning of the Bible, we are taught, that is, the Scriptures, when explained according to the laws of language, is often self-contradictory and false, contrary to valid history and true science, and of an immoral character and tendency. It is only when we come to the higher and spiritual meaning which Swedenborg was commissioned to reveal, that we find real and absolute truth, truth self-consistent and eternal. The great interest, then, which the Scriptures should possess, and will possess, the validity of his claims being admitted, the interest which, with all his followers, they do in fact now possess, is to attach almost exclusively to this new and higher meaning. Yet this one all-absorbing meaning, the words of Scripture have no adaptation to convey. We will give a single illustration, Swedenborg's explanation of 1 Samuel chapters v. and vi., which contain the account of the retention of the ark for a season in the land of the Philistines, and its being sent back by them. " The Philistines represent," he says, "those who exalt faith above charity; which was the occasion of their continual wars with the Israelites, who represent those who cherish faith in union with charity. The idol Dagon is the religion of those who are represented by the Philistines. The emerods are symbols of the appetites of the natural man, which, when separated from the spiritual affections, are unclean. The mice, by which the land was devastated, are images of the lust of destroying, by false interpretation, the spiritual nourishment which the church derives from the word of God. The emerods of gold exhibit the natural appetites, as purified and made good. The golden mice signify the healing of the tendency to false interpretations, effected by admitting a regard to goodness. The cows are types of the natural man, in regard to such good qualities as he possesses. Their lowing by the way expresses the repugnance of the natural man to the process of conversion. And the offering them up for a burnt-offering typifies that restoration of order which takes place in the mind, when the natural affections are submitted to the Lord." * Who, from any correct laws of interpretation, could ever have dreamed that God intended to represent by two cows "the natural man in regard to such good qualities as he possesses," and by the lowing of these cows "the repugnance of the natural man to the process of conversion?" The words have no adaptation whatever to convey such an idea. The same holds equally true of every other spiritual idea which this revelator affirms to be expressed by the words of Scripture. Yet, if we receive him as our guide, our interest in these ideas thus arbitrarily attached to the words of Scripture, will become the almost, if not quite exclusive source of interest with us, in the Word of God.

5. As a natural and necessary consequence, the Bible, as originally given to man, will in human estimation, be thrown into a deep, dark, and permanent eclipse; while the so called revelations of Emanuel Swedenborg will take its place, as the only revelations with which we have any deep concern. Among the Swedenborgians, as the world cannot but know, this result has followed already, and it will universally follow, should

* True Chris. Religion, § 203.

this religion prevail. This, we say, is practical infidelity in regard to the Bible, as God gave it to man.

6. We see nothing in these ideas thus arbitrarily attached to the words of Scripture, that indicate to us that they have a natural, or can have a divine right thus to take the place of this great central source of moral and spiritual illumination to fallen humanity. On the other hand, we see very little in these ideas which do not tend most powerfully to veil from our vision humanity as it is and must become, in order to be prepared to meet the exigencies of the coming future, to neutralize the efficiency of the glorious Gospel of the blessed God, in the work of human moral renovation, and finally, to degrade and debase our ideal of God and immortality.

7. For ourselves, we could not make any approach towards receiving these revelations, without becoming utterly infidel in our notions in regard to the whole Bible. In that case, we must hold that all the evidence that now exists, or ever has existed, for the divine origin of those portions of the Scriptures which we are required to reject, the Acts, and all the Epistles of the New Testament, for example, is totally invalid and deceptive. But no higher, nor any other evidence exists for the divine origin of any other part of the Bible. If the Christian argument fails in one case, it fails in the other. It does totally fail and deceive, in one case, according to Swedenborg. The same identical evidence cannot but fail and be deceptive, therefore, in both cases alike, and we have no divine revelation to the words of which Swedenborg's spiritual ideas can be attached. This is the necessary consequence that we must adopt, before we can even look at the claims of Swedenborg. If the Christian argument is valid, for

the divine origin of any one book of the New Testament, it is equally valid for that of all the others, and Swedenborgianism, from the beginning to end, is a delusion. What evidence, for example, can be offered for the inspiration of Luke in writing his gospel, that would not affirm, with equal absoluteness, his inspiration, as the author of the book of Acts? What evidence exists for the inspiration of John, in writing the Gospel and Revelation, that does not affirm with equal absoluteness his inspiration, as the author of his epistles? But one alternative is left us, we maintaining logical consistency, and that is to reject Swedenborg, or become throughout infidels. We cannot be infidels, and therefore we must repudiate wholly the claims of Swedenborg.

8. The time, in our judgment, has now arrived, when the real claims of this self-assumed divine revelator, may be set with such distinctness before the public mind, that they will be duly appreciated.

Without further introduction, we shall now proceed to lay before our readers our reasons, some of them, for regarding the claims of this individual as an inspired revelator, utterly false and vain, and his system, taken as a whole, as nothing but delusion and error. We regard him as, like Frederika Hauffe, simply a clairvoyant, whose visions were to him real, but were the exclusive subjective result of an abnormal odylic physical and mental state, and utterly void of any claims to objective validity, or to be thus regarded by us. That his revelations are utterly void of all claims to validity, and that they should be held by us as untrue, we argue from the following considerations: —

1. These professed revelations belong exclusively to a class which the unvarying experience of mankind in

all ages, have found to be an utterly unreliable and deceptive source of information. "*If Mesmerism is true*," says Mr. Bush, "*Swedenborg is true*." Suppose we state the proposition in a somewhat different form, namely, if Mesmerism is a *reliable* source of information, Swedenborg is a true and reliable revelator. If, on the other hand, Mesmerism is an unreliable and deceptive source of information, then we should be guilty of infinite presumption in placing confidence in the revelations of Swedenborg; for the two classes of phenomena have a common origin, and must have common characteristics. Now clairvoyant revelations, Swedenborg's aside, have never, in a solitary instance, stood revealed to the world as thus reliable,—as any thing else than the most uncertain and unreliable source of information conceivable. The clairvoyant, in all instances, is subject to visions, the vast majority of which are untrue, with exceptions very few and far between correct, while the subject is utterly void of all capacity to distinguish the true from the false. This is the immutable law which characterizes them in all forms of development in which they have ever appeared, in any age of the world, or in any nation on earth. No man can intelligently read the life and experience of Swedenborg, without being convinced, that his revelations are exclusively from this one source. To regard them, therefore, as a reliable source of information, is as presumptuous as it would be to expect a suspension of the natural laws of the universe, and that without a miracle. Judging from the immutable law which characterizes these phenomena, the probability that any one of his visions pertaining to the other worlds, or to a future state, is true, is not as one to a hundred, while the probability that they are generally true, is not as one to millions. He certainly is very unwise, who accepts such sand-banks, as the rock of eternal truth.

There is one fundamental fact which characterizes this class of phenomena, that should not be overlooked in this connection. The only objects lying beyond the compass of ordinary vision, in respect to which the perceptions of the clairvoyant are ever found to be true, are mere physical facts, with which he happens, at the moment, to be in odylic rapport. Whenever he attempts to reveal general truths, truths especially pertaining to objects lying beyond this mundane sphere, then his visions become utterly lawless and unreliable, and we might show that, from the nature of the case, it could not be otherwise. The history of the world, we believe, presents us with not a solitary exception to this statement. Now it is in this very sphere, where clairvoyance has ever, without exception, utterly failed, that the visions of Swedenborg as a clairvoyant are found. The probability, therefore, is as infinity to unity against their reliability.

2. The fundamental principle of science to which we have alluded on other occasions, that of *sufficient reason*, demands the assumption that the visions of Swedenborg are mere mental hallucinations, having an exclusively subjective origin without any corresponding realities. When we have ascertained that a part of a given class of facts owe their origin exclusively to a certain cause, and that this cause is fully adequate to the production of all the rest, we must refer them all alike to such cause, or we abandon the fundamental principle on which all scientific deduction is based. Let us apply this fundamental principle to the visions of Swedenborg. Of the manner in which these visions commenced, together with the exclusive ground of con-

fidence which the subject had, that he was a divinely commissioned and authoritative revelator, the following extract from Dr. Pond's "Swedenborgianism Reviewed," will present us with a clear and authenticated account.

"In the spring of 1745, an event took place, which was regarded by Swedenborg (and is so regarded by all his followers) as the most important in his whole life. He professed to have had his spiritual senses opened, so that he could look directly into the invisible world, and converse with departed souls, angels, and demons, as freely as with men here on the earth. But the account must be given in his own words. 'I have been called to a holy office, by the Lord himself, who most graciously manifested himself in person to me, his servant, when he opened my sight to the view of the spiritual world, and granted me the privilege of conversing with spirits and angels.'* Again: 'I can sacredly and solemnly declare, that the Lord himself has been seen of me, and that he has sent me to do what I do; and for such purpose, he has opened the interior part of my soul, which is my spirit, so that I can see what is in the spiritual world, and those that are therein; and this privilege has now been continued to me for twenty-two years.'† To another friend, who inquired how and when it was, that he was enabled to see what was done in heaven and hell, he gave the following answer. 'I was in London, and one day dined rather late by myself, at a boarding-house, where I kept a room, in which at pleasure, I could prosecute the study of the natural sciences. I was hungry, and ate with great appetite. At the end of the meal, I remarked that a vapor, as it were, clouded my sight, and the walls of my chamber

* Letter to Dr. Hartley. † Letter to Dr. Oetenger.

appeared covered with frightful creeping things, such as serpents, toads, and the like. I was filled with astonishment, but retained the full use of my perception and thoughts. The darkness attained its height, and soon passed away. I then perceived a man sitting in the corner of my chamber. As I thought myself entirely alone, I was greatly terrified; when he spoke and said, 'Eat not so much.' The cloud once more came over my sight, and when it passed away, I found myself alone in the chamber. This unexpected event hastened my return home. I did not mention the subject to the people of the house, but reflected upon it much, and believed it to have been the effect of accidental causes, or to have arisen from my physical state, at the time. I went home; but in the following night, the same man appeared to me again. He said, 'I am God, the Lord, the Creator and Redeemer of the world. I have chosen thee to lay before men the spiritual sense of the holy word. I will teach thee what thou art to write.' On that same night, were opened to my perception the heavens and the hells, where I saw many persons of my acquaintance, of all conditions. From that day forth, I gave up all mere worldly learning, and labored only in spiritual things, according to what the Lord commanded me to write. Daily he opened the eyes of my spirit to see what was done in the other world, and gave me, in a state of full wakefulness, to converse with angels and spirits." *

It is undeniably evident that Swedenborg, in his own mind, based the validity of his commission, as a divine revelator, upon that of the supposed visions of God which he had on these two occasions. It is equally evident that he expected that the world at large would thus

* See Robsam's Memoir of Swedenborg, in Hobart's Life, 214.

receive him on the assumed validity of the same visions. To these visions he himself appeals before the world, as the basis of his high claims. "I can sacredly and solemnly declare," he says, "that the Lord himself has been seen of me, and has sent me to do what I do." Suppose that we can show, that by the fundamental and immutable principles of science, we are required to hold these visions as merely mental hallucinations which had an exclusively subjective origin, without any corresponding object whatever external to the mind. Then we should be sacredly bound to hold all his other visions as nothing else but hallucinations of this exclusive character; for the latter sustain such relations to the former, that they must be placed together under the same class or category. This is undeniable. Now, these very assumed visions of God are presented to us by the author himself, as a part of a class, all the rest of which were and could be nothing but mere mental hallucinations without any corresponding objects of real perception, and the cause which produced the latter is equally adequate to originate the former, in the total absence of such objects. Prior to these visions, it should be borne in mind, that according to the express testimony of Mr. Wesley, and the celebrated Dr. Hartley, one of Swedenborg's intimate personal friends, and earliest followers, "he was seized with a fever, attended with delirium." Subsequently, when in London, after eating an immoderate dinner, and retiring to his room, he had a vision in which the walls of his chamber, to use his own language, 'appeared covered with frightful creeping things, such as serpents, toads, and the like.'" Shall we suppose that there were real "serpents, toads, and the like," on the walls of that chamber, on that occasion? We should be guilty of voluntary and reckless self-dementation, if we should, for a moment, entertain such a thought. We think, that even the most self-abnegating followers of our revelator, will not show themselves so idiotic as to pretend that there were upon those walls any real objects corresponding to his perceptions on that occasion. Here, then, we have a cause developed, and in active efficient operation in the organism of this individual, a cause which did induce distinct visions as of external objects, when no such external objects existed. In immediate connection with these identical visions, there is the appearance of a man "sitting in one corner" of the same room. Is not the cause which produced the other visions, in the absence of all corresponding objects external to the organism of the subject, equally adequate to produce this one vision in the absence of any such external object? But one answer can be given to this question. Every principle of science, then, requires us to hold this vision as nothing but a mental hallucination occasioned by the peculiar abnormal physical condition of the subject himself. The same cause which originated this vision, to which no corresponding object was present, was equally adequate to reproduce the same vision after Swedenborg had returned to his home. Thus far, we cannot follow the immutable laws of scientific deduction, without regarding ourselves as in the exclusive presence of mental and physical hallucinations, and of nothing else. Yet we have here the beginning and the end of Emanuel Swedenborg's commission and authority as a divine revelator.

These undeniable hallucinations also have such a connection with his subsequent visions, that we are bound to suppose, that they are all of the same exclusive character. The same night after this second assumed vision of God occurred, "were opened to my perception," says Swedenborg, "the heavens and the hells, where I saw many persons of my acquaintance, of all conditions." Nothing which demands the supposition of the presence and action of any new cause yet presents itself. The same reasons which require us to suppose the first visions to be nothing but hallucinations, demand that we attribute the same character to these, and so of all that follow. No object corresponding to any of them is required to account for its occurrence, or any of its characteristics. The immutable laws of science, therefore, prohibit our referring any of these visions to such objects as their cause, and to present these visions as any evidence whatever of the reality of such objects.

3. A respect, also, for the known character of God, every attribute of his nature, demands of us, that we attribute precisely such a character, and none other, to these professed revelations. Who does not know, that if God was about to reveal himself to man, and that for the high purpose of introducing a totally new dispensation, he would not, under such circumstances, connect the visible manifestation of himself, with undeniable hallucinations, in the same percipient, and so connect the two, that the immutable laws of science would demand, that the same character of utter unreliability, and mental illusion, should be ascribed to each? If we can affirm, with absolute certainty, any thing whatever of God, we can affirm, with the same certainty, that a real revelation from him to man has never come to us in such connections. The visions of Emanuel Swedenborg are not from God, and he was never divinely commissioned to take from our hearts a part of the divine word, and to nullify the rest by veiling them behind a new revelation.

4. The same conclusion is forced upon us by the known and exclusively *subjective* character of these entire revelations. What are Swedenborg's "heavens and hells" but Swedenborg himself, turned inside out, that is, the exclusive reflections and external embodiments of his own previous mental states? Any philosopher who should fully acquaint himself with the previous history and character of this individual, with the leading direction of his thoughts and feelings and sentiments, on all subjects, social, civil, philosophical, and religious, would predict, with perfect certainty, that if he should ever become the subject of odylic mental hallucinations, and that if these should be connected with the illusion that he was a divinely commissioned revelator to man, precisely these and none others would be the leading character of his visions, supposing that not one of them was valid for any corresponding reality. In his previous life, it is well known, that he was disappointed in an affair of the heart, in consequence of which "conjugial and scortatory love" became with him, the all-pervading element of his mental existence; and this is the central element of Swedenborg's visions of immortality. While in heaven, he attends a wedding of course. All his ideas in regard to the sexual relations are turned over and over, with a disgusting familiarity, in his intercourse with female angels. His heart comes fully out here, and it stands revealed to us combined of elements with which we have no desire to become further acquainted. His hells, too, are eternal brothels, in which nearly if not quite every fallen spirit there is "permitted to keep one mistress." "Conjugial love," he tells us, "is the very sphere of heaven." This single statement indubitably indicates the exclusively subjective origin of his visions.

Swedenborg, also, entertained certain peculiar notions in regard to the trinity, justification, etc. In heaven, he is permitted to attend church, on a certain occasion. The preacher, to whom, of course, such an illustrious personage as our visitant is introduced, stands revealed, as a devoted Swedenborgian, the object of the discourse being to set his hearers right on these special themes. The entire theological discourse of heaven is exclusively upon the very themes with which his mind had been previously exercised.

Swedenborg, finally, had peculiar philosophical conceptions pertaining to the universe of matter and mind, and of their peculiar relations. His "heavens and hells" are exclusively constructed in perfect accordance with the principles of that philosophy. On all subjects alike, the highest intelligences of heaven knew just what he knew, and nothing more and nothing less. Swedenborg heard no "unspeakable words" in heaven. The table, at a dinner party which he affirms himself to have attended with the Almighty himself, was spread with the very "sweet cakes and condiments," wines and beverages, with which his appetites had been previously delighted. The dresses, too, of the Prince, his grandees and courtiers, each to "their breeches and stockings," were patterned after his previous ideas of beauty and perfection. All in heaven and hell move in this one circle, and take exclusive form from this one mundane pattern. Now we say, that we cannot have higher evidence, that any visions are exclusively subjective and mundane in their origin, than we have in such undeniable facts as these, of the exclusively subjective origin of Swedenborg's pretended revelations, together with the fact, that none of them have any claims whatever to take rank, but among other mental illusions and hallucinations which arise in the human mind, in certain abnormal conditions of the physical organism.

There is one very striking feature of these revelations, that should not be overlooked, in this connection, as presenting very nearly, if not quite demonstrative evidence of their exclusively subjective origin, and of their utter want of any claims to objective validity. We find Swedenborg's heaven pervaded throughout with reflections of his peculiar prejudices and antipathies against persons who had previously lived. How hardly all persons get along there who, however honest and excellent in their character, morally and religiously considered, happened to differ on any question of doctrine from this our revelator, especially if they held the doctrine of justification by faith. Luther, for example, "is still in the world of spirits, which is in the midst between heaven and hell, where he sometimes undergoes great sufferings," and all for one reason exclusively, that he has not yet given up the doctrine of justification by faith. Poor Melancthon, for the same reason, is shut up in a cold stone chamber, "clothed in a bear-skin, by reason of the cold, because faith without charity is cold." Towards Calvin our revelator at first seemed quite well disposed, giving him, in 1763, a place "in a society of heaven." Subsequently, however, he seems to have become the object of Swedenborg's peculiar dislike. Hence we find him at one time with a company of Predestinarians shut up in a dark cavern underground. Then he is companioned with a company of simpletons who are without ideas on any subject. Next, after residing for a time in a certain governor's house, we find him "in a house occupied by harlots, where he remained some time." Now he is in an infernal cavern, where "they are forced to work for their victuals, and are all enemies one to another. Here they do evil one to another to the extent of their power, and this is the delight of their life." Now when we see a professedly divine revelator's vision of immortality thus dotted all over with reflections of his own peculiar personal theological piques and prejudices, we should close our eyes to all the laws of cause and effect, if we did not read here the exclusively subjective origin of these revelations; and we venture the affirmation, that not even Mohammed's visions are so fully charged with these infallible indications of subjective origin, as those of Emanuel Swedenborg.

5. We find in these revelations such palpable *errors and misstatements* in regard to *things visible and known*, as to render all confidence in his revelations, in respect to "things unseen," infinitely presumptuous. We will specify two or three cases, as examples. He professed to have perfect knowledge of the solar system, so perfect that he could describe minutely the inhabitants of all the planets, their manners, customs, modes of life, and character. If he had such a range and accuracy of vision, could he not tell us correctly of the number of planets of which the system itself is composed? Certainly he could. Suppose we find him asserting, as absolutely true, what science has demonstrated to be false, and that in regard to great and palpable facts? If he thus errs in regard to what we do know, should we not infer, that he is not to be received as a safe and authoritative guide, in regard to what we do not know? Now he asserts absolutely, that of all the others connected with the solar system, "the planet Saturn is the furthest distant from the sun," and that this is the reason why it is furnished with "a large luminous belt." Did God teach him to make such

a statement? If he did, then inspiration itself is not a reliable source of information. If he did not, we have no evidence whatever, that in any of our seer's revelations, he was taught of God what to write, and if he was not thus taught, all these revelations are to be held as illusions and nothing else. The following extract from Dr. Pond presents another of our revelator's disclosures in regard to things about which the world has since become informed.

"Swedenborg taught that, in his time, a new gospel or revelation was being made to the Africans, 'which, having commenced, goes from its region around, but not yet to the seas.' These enlightened Africans 'despise foreigners coming from Europe, who believe that man is saved from faith alone.'* In another of his works, Swedenborg introduces the same subject as follows: 'Such being the character of the Africans, there is at this day a revelation begun among them, which is communicated from the centre round about, but does not extend to the sea-coasts. They acknowledge our Lord as the Lord of heaven and earth, and laugh at the monks who visit them, and at Christians who talk of a threefold divinity, and of salvation by mere thought. I was informed *from heaven*, that the things contained in the doctrine of the New Jerusalem concerning the Lord, concerning the Word, and in the doctrine of Life, are now revealed, by word of mouth, by angelic spirits, to the inhabitants of that country.' Of these people it is further said, that though 'permitted by their laws to take several wives, they nevertheless have but one. Strangers from Europe are not freely admitted among them; and when any, especially if they are monks,

* True Chris. Religion, § 840.

penetrate into the country, they inquire of them what they know; and when they relate any particulars concerning their religion, they call them trifles which are offensive to their ears. And then they send them away to some useful employment; and in case they refuse to work, they sell them for slaves.' "*

None of Swedenborg's revelations, it should be borne in mind, are more absolute in their affirmations, or attended with higher evidence of a divine origin. "I was informed *from heaven.*" This is the affirmed source of his information. Now the whole revelation is, from beginning to end, a baseless fiction, the exclusive result of mental hallucination, and his followers will not dare deny it. If his visions thus grossly and palpably falsify real facts in regard to this earth, what but infinite presumption would induce any individual to place the least reliance upon them, when they pertain to facts in distant planets, or the future state?

In the following extract from Swedenborg's writings, we have another revelation equally absolute, equally important, and equally false. It pertains to a book affirmed to have been written by Enoch, to be "the most ancient Word," and that from which Moses copied the first eleven chapters of Genesis, and other parts of his writings.

"'Concerning this ancient Word,' says Swedenborg, 'which had been in Asia before the Israelitish Word, it is permitted to relate this news, that *it is still reserved there among the people who live in great Tartary.* I have conversed with spirits and angels who were thence in the spiritual world, who informed me that *they possess the Word*, and that *they have preserved it from ancient*

* Continuation of Last Judgment, § 76 – 78.

times, and that *they perform their divine worship according to this Word*, and that it consists of mere correspondences. They said that in it is the book of *Jasher*, mentioned in Joshua 10: 12, 13, and in 2d Samuel 1: 17, 18; also that with them are the books called *The Wars of the Lord;* and the *Enunciations*, mentioned by Moses, Numbers 21: 14, 15, and 27–30. And when I read to them the words which Moses had taken thence, they looked to see if they were there, and found them. In conversing with them, they said that they worship Jehovah, some as an invisible God, and some as visible. They further told me that they do not suffer foreigners to come among them, except the Chinese, with whom they cultivate peace, because the Chinese emperor is from their country; also that their country is exceedingly populous, beyond that of almost any other; which is quite credible, from the wall of so many miles which the Chinese built, to protect their country against invasion from them. Moreover I heard from *the angels*, that the first chapters of Genesis, which treat of the creation, and of the first ages of the world up to the time of Noah and his sons, are also in that Word, and that they were copied thence by Moses.' "*

Now we have just as much reason to believe the affirmations of the sacred books of the Hindoos, that somewhere between their country and Tartary there are mountains some six or ten thousand miles high, and that the succession of day and night is occasioned by the sun's passing around those mountains, as we have to put confidence in the above vision. We have, on the other hand, just about as much reason to discredit the one story as the other. This whole country was, during

* True Chris. Religion, § 279.

all the middle ages, covered by Christian churches. For centuries, too, it has been traversed by Romish missionaries. Yet no such books, and no such people, have been found or heard of there. Of the non-existence of such a book, and of such a people, Swedenborgians, also, are well persuaded, or they would long since have obeyed the positive injunction of their revelator, to "seek for it [the book] in China." What revelation coming from this individual can we properly place confidence in, if not in the above? Nothing can mark any communications as mental hallucinations, if these do not those of Emanuel Swedenborg. The very first vision he had was exclusively of this character, and we then find all the others so mingled with these, that we should violate every principle and law of scientific deduction, if we did not class them all together under this one category. We might adduce other examples equally to our purpose, and that, in any number that could reasonably be desired. The above, however, which are perfectly fundamental in character and bearing, are sufficient.

6. We now adduce the *intrinsic absurdity* of Swedenborg's interpretation of the sacred text, as demonstrative evidence, that in such interpretations, he was never "taught of God," nor acted under a divine commission. Suppose that God wished to specify and represent such good qualities as man in his natural state possesses, on the one hand, and "the repugnance of the natural man to the process of conversion," on the other. Who in his senses, can believe, that he would take two cows yoked in a cart, to represent the first idea, and the lowing of those cows to represent the other? Lowing is always expressive of desire and not of repugnance, and is the last symbol conceivable at all adapted to express

the idea here attached to it. Take the following explanation of 2 Kings 2: 24, containing the account of the destruction of forty and two children, by two she bears. "Elisha," says our divine revelator, "represented the Lord as to the word. Baldness signifies the word devoid of its literal sense, thus not any thing." [A very important idea that, and how aptly the bald head of a prophet represents it.] The number forty-two signifies blasphemy. And bears signify the literal sense of the word, read indeed, but not understood." So hereafter when we meet with the number forty-two, we are to connect with it the idea of blasphemy, and when we think or hear of two she bears, we are to connect with them the idea of the "literal sense of the word, read indeed, but not understood." How clear and impressive these two ideas become when connected with such symbols! How worthy of the spirit of inspiration! Let us suppose further, that God wished to represent this idea, "the understanding in the spiritual man," on the one hand, and of the will of the same on the other. According to Swedenborg he took this sublime method to do it, namely, the penning of this sentence, "male and female created he them," the term male signifying the understanding, and that of female the will. The term marriage represents the union of understanding and will in such a man. Again, God wished to express to man this idea, "the knowledge of all things relating to faith and love." According to our revelator, he made use of the following phrase to accomplish that object: "The second river Gihon which encompasses the land of Cush." We will not multiply examples. We have yet to meet with any thing in the Celestial Arcana which does not degrade and debase all our sacred and venerating ideas and sentiments in regard to God, when we suppose that He is the author of such senseless monstrosities. We must remember, that no new truths at all are to be found here, as far as any real truth is presented. All that we meet with is simply and exclusively this, that known truths are arbitrarily connected with symbols which have no adaptation whatever to represent them, and are thus placed in new to be sure, but in totally unnatural, and thereby ridiculous and debasing associations. In the name of the common sense of the universe, we would ask, of what benefit can it be to us, to have any known and important truth associated in our minds, for example, with the bald head of a prophet, the number forty-two, two she bears, or the lowing of a pair of cows yoked in a new cart? And here lies the exclusive merit of Swedenborg's Celestial Arcana. It adds not a particle to our stock of real knowledge, but simply, we repeat, places truths already known in unnatural associations. When we are told, for example, that the sentence, "of the tribe of Reuben were seated twelve thousand" — "signifies wisdom derived from celestial love, with them who are there," we obtain no clearer conceptions of that form of wisdom than we had before. We have no new symbol at all adapted to represent it. The idea which we had before has been placed in a new, but unnatural, and thereby debasing association. That is all. And here, we repeat, lies all Swedenborg's merit as the revelator of the affirmed spiritual signification of the sacred word. When any man presents himself to us, as divinely commissioned, to generate such associations, we shall assume, that the pretence itself is absolute proof that the professed revelator is either void of understanding, beside himself, or a deliberate impostor.

7. The next remark to which we invite very special attention is this. The known character of God renders it impossible, that Swedenborg's fundamental representations in regard to the Scriptures can be true, and consequently, that any of his professed revelations can be worthy of confidence. We hold this truth to be self-evident, that if God should give a revelation to man, he would not suffer the records containing the same, to be given in such relations to others not of divine original, that the former can, by no possibility, be distinguished from the latter, and that in all respects, there should be the same evidence of the divine origin and authority of one class, as of the other. Equally evident is it, that he would not give such revelation in a form adapted to mislead, in important particulars, even the honest mind, and all this, while the only meaning of the word with which humanity has the most deep and vital concern, is utterly veiled from the possible vision of man, and kept so, in regard to a majority of the sacred books, for thousands of years, and in respect to all, for more than sixteen centuries. All this, and more too, is true of God, in regard to his own revealed word, according to the fundamental teachings of Swedenborg. God's own inspired writings were originally given in such connections with many others not inspired, that, by no possibility, could the one class be distinguished from the other, while the real vital meaning of the portion given by inspiration was utterly veiled from the possible knowledge of humanity, and remained so for ages. We are shut up to the alternative to believe all this of God, or to reject the claims of Swedenborg as a divinely commissioned revelator. We take the latter position, and do so with no fear whatever of erring in our deductions.

8. We now advance to a consideration of an objection against the claims of our revelator, an objection about which there can be no mistake. Swedenborg's *fundamental ideas of a future state can, by no possibility, be true.* His entire philosophy of that state must be false, and can no more be true, than the proposition, that the same object can, at the same time, exist and not exist. According to the fundamental principles of Swedenborg, the soul, on its entrance into eternity, ceases wholly to exist in any relations to time or space. To the souls in that state, there are no such realities, time and space having relation exclusively to material objects, and to mind only when in the body. Angels, the disembodied spirits of men, have not, and cannot have, even the ideas of time and space in their minds. There is there nothing but *states* of mind. "The angels," he says, "cannot have any idea of time, but in its place an idea of state." Again, "times in the word signify states." So in regard to space and the idea of it. "Although all things," he says, "in heaven appear in place and in space just as in this world, still the angels have no notion and idea of place and space." Similarity of state, and that alone, constitutes nearness among spirits, and dissimilarity of states, separation or distance. "Those," he says, "are near to each other who are in a similar state, and those at a distance who are in a dissimilar state." It is upon this one principle exclusively that the inhabitants of heaven and hell are separated from each other, and different societies are formed in each. In heaven and hell alike, nothing whatever exists but the mind and its states. Yet the mind there has perceptions as of external objects, just as it does in this world. The reason is, that mental

states are seen by the mind, as objects external to the mind itself. If the mind thinks of any object, in that thought the object is present to the mind, as an object of external perception. Yet the object has no real existence out of the mind itself. "From this cause also it is," says our revelator, "that in the spirit world one is exhibited as present to another, if he only intensely desires his presence, for thus he sees him in thought, and puts himself in his state; and conversely, that one is removed from another, as far as he is averse to him." If every inhabitant of the spirit world should, at the same moment, intensely desire the presence of of the same individual, he would be equally present to each, and equally able to communicate with each, in the same instant of time. So of all other objects of thought. "In heaven," he says, "there appear mountains, hills, rocks, rivers, castles, altogether as in this world." When the thought is turned with desire upon an object, that object is present, we repeat, to the mind, in that thought, as something external to it. If the mind thinks of some particular truth, as purity, virtue, innocence, some object will instantly appear as external to the mind, a flock of sheep, of lambs, or a rose, for example, symbolizing that truth to the mind. As objects thus present to the mind as external to it, correspond to its own interior states, the world, the universe in which each individual has an apparent dwelling-place will be as his interior states. Each one really and truly makes his own heaven or his own hell. To minds in the same states, the same realities will be present in the same forms. Minds, in different states, will not only exist as encompassed by different realities, but the same objects will appear to them in totally different and opposite forms.

To the inhabitants of heaven, for example, those in hell, he says, appear as clothed in the most frightful forms conceivable, while to each other, they appear in forms of perfect comeliness and beauty. All the above ideas are fully developed in the great work of Swedenborg, " On heaven and hell," especially in the articles " Concerning time in heaven," and " Concerning space in heaven." Swedenborgians, we think, will do us the justice to admit, that we have truly represented the teachings of Swedenborg on these subjects, and have put no false coloring whatever into the picture. They will also admit, that these views are so entirely fundamental in his entire system of doctrines in regard to a future state, that if they are demonstrated to be utterly false, and their truth an absolute impossibility, that entire system must be held as a delusion throughout. Hence we would invite very special attention to the following remarks upon what may properly be denominated Swedenborg's philosophy of a future state, a philosophy which must be true throughout, or his entire revelations in regard to the spirit world must be held, as nothing but a congeries of mental hallucinations. We here repeat the proposition with which we commenced our remarks under this head. This philosophy can no more be true, than the same object can, at the same time, exist and not exist. This we affirm for the following reasons: —

(1.) The *states* of spirits in the spirit world, as well as of minds in this, must be *successive*, one to another. From the nature of the case, it cannot possibly be otherwise. These states are in fact successive, according to the express teachings of Swedenborg himself. " All things," he says, " have succession and progression in heaven as well as in this world." Now *succession supposes time*, and that as the *necessary* condition of its occurrence. This is an absolutely necessary truth, it being utterly impossible for the mind even to *conceive* the opposite as true, any more than we can conceive of an event without a cause, or of the annihilation of space. If the *states* of spirits in the spirit world sustain the same relations to time that they do in this, then the mind itself sustains the same relations to time in the one world that it does in the other, and the revelations of Swedenborg are throughout nothing but mental illusions. Mind does sustain the same relations to time in the spirit world that it does in this; for its states in both alike and equally are successive, and consequently do and must sustain the same identical relations to time. The revelations of Swedenborg, therefore, must be false. We feel quite safe in the assertion, that by no possibility can there be a mistake about this argument. We once presented the argument to Professor Bush, after he had presented to us Swedenborg's philosophy of a future state in the precise form above presented, and presented it as the crowning glory of the system. To us he appeared perfectly confounded. He made no attempt whatever to meet the difficulty, but simply expressed the belief, that he should be able to do it at some future time. We now present the argument to him once more, and before the world, ask him to renounce Swedenborg, or relieve his revelations from the difficulty above presented, together with those involved in the propositions next to be considered.

(2.) Our second remark is, that mind in the spirit world, not only sustains, in fact, the same relations to time that it does in this, but has and must have, from the immutable laws of its intellectual nature, the same *idea* of it in the one state that it has in the other. Its states in each alike not only sustain the same relations to time, but are with equal distinctness recognized, in each alike, as successive. From the nature of the mind it cannot be otherwise. They are recognized by the mind as successive in each state alike and equally, according to the express teachings of Swedenborg himself. He tells us that angels often conversed with him about their past and present experiences, representing them as successive, just as men speak of their successive states now while they are in the body. Angels, then, have the idea of succession as well as we do, and in the same form. Now the idea of succession can, by no possibility, be in the mind without that of time. Without this latter idea, the mind could by no possibility conceive of or speak of past and present states. It is a contradiction in terms to suppose the opposite. If angels have the idea of succession, or of their own mental states, as past and present, they must of necessity have the idea of time, and the revelations of Swedenborg can, by no possibility, be any thing else than a mass of illusions. They have, and must from their nature as rational beings have, and according to the express teachings of Swedenborg himself, they do have, the idea of succession most distinctly developed in their minds. They must, therefore, have the idea of time, and we should be guilty of absolutely infinite presumption, did we not regard Swedenborg's professed revelations as nothing but a mass of mental hallucinations. To us it is a matter of wonder, that Swedenborg, even in the state of hallucination in which he was, should have made such a fundamental mistake, as he undeniably has, in this instance, a mistake which renders it absolutely impossible that his visions as of eternity should be true. He has visions as of angels.

He converses with them about their past and present experiences in the spirit world, and he finds that they converse on such subjects just as minds in the body do; that angels, in short, have ideas equally as distinct of succession as men have. Yet the latter, he affirms, have the idea of time, while the former can, by no possibility, have it at all, and that when they once had it, that is, when they were themselves in the body, and still have ideas which cannot exist in any mind, in any world, without that very idea which he says they cannot possibly have at all. Swedenborg's system would not be more demonstrably false, had he asserted and introduced the dogma as a fundamental element into his system, that angels have the idea of time, they having the idea of succession, and that men, though equally with the angels they have the latter idea, do not, and cannot, by any possibility, have the former.

(3.) Swedenborg's revelations, we remark, in the next place, cannot possibly be true, and his followers will not deny this, if angels have, and must have, not only the ideas of succession and time, but also those of *place* and of *space*. Yet the immutable laws of mind, and Swedenborg's own revelations, render it demonstrably evident, that angels do and must have these last two ideas as well as the former ones. They have the idea of themselves as real existing beings. This none will deny. Now rational minds cannot have the idea of itself as existing, without connecting with that idea, that of existing *somewhere*. Mind cannot put to itself the question, What am I, and it cannot have the consciousness of existing at all, without putting this question, it cannot put to itself the question, we say, What am I? without, with it, putting another, namely, *Where* am I? The ideas of existence, and whereness, are necessarily connected in the mind, and it must cease to be rational at all, before the former can be in it, without the latter. Then angels, even according to the express revelations of Swedenborg himself, have the ideas of *form*, and of *body*. They appear to themselves, as he affirms, as in bodies, dwelling in houses, inhabiting cities, and passing from place to place, just as they did, when in this world. "As often as I have spoken with angels face to face," he says, "so often have I been with them in their habitations. Their habitations are altogether like the habitations on earth, which are called houses, but are more beautiful; in them are parlors, rooms, and bedchambers, in great numbers; there are also courts, and round about are gardens, shrubberies, and fields." In the same connection, he tells us that he has "several times spoken with angels" about their habitations, and told them, that among men "scarcely any one would believe that they [the angels] have habitations and mansions," and that the angels express their wonder "that such ignorance reigns at this day in the world" and "chiefly in the church." Angels, then, according to the express revelations of Swedenborg himself, have just as distinct ideas of form, of body, and of the relative positions of different bodies as men in this world have. Yet he tells us that the latter have, and the former have not, and cannot have, any idea whatever either of *place* or of *space*. Now body supposes space, and the idea of the former can, by no possibility, be in any rational mind, without that of the latter. It is just as much of a contradiction to say, that the idea of body, and of mind in body, dwelling in houses surrounded "with gardens, shrubberies, and fields," houses, too, constituted of "parlors, rooms, and bedchambers, in great numbers," it is just as much of a contradiction, we say, to affirm, that such ideas are in rational minds in any world, and that the ideas of space and of place are not, and cannot be in the same minds, as it would be to say, that body does not suppose space, or that the same thing can, at the same time, exist and not exist.

Then Swedenborg affirms, that he obtained information from angels pertaining to facts and localities in this world, information which they never could have conveyed, had they not had distinct apprehensions of succession and time, and also place and space. They gave him, for example, he says, and as we have already shown that he says, specific information in regard to facts as occurring in Africa and Tartary, and at specified periods, as in the time of Enoch, before the flood. Now if they have and can have no ideas of time, or of place or space, how could they thus speak of particular localities, and of events as occurring there, and at specific and relative periods, in the history of our race? No intelligent being can give an intelligible expression of an idea that is not and cannot be in his mind. Angels, according to Swedenborg himself, can and do converse intelligently and intelligibly concerning successive events, events, too, as occurring at specified periods of time, and of material objects as existing in specific localities in space. According to his express teachings, therefore, they do and must have distinct apprehensions of time and succession, and of place and space.

The argument, under the present head, stands thus. Swedenborgianism must be false, if mind in the spirit world does exist in the same relations to time and space that it does in this, or if it there has, or can have, even the *ideas* of time, or of place, or of space; for Swedenborg has affirmed absolutely that none of these things can be true of mind in that world, and has so constructed his entire system, that it must be false, if any of these things are true. Again, Swedenborgianism cannot possibly be true, unless mind, in the spirit world, does exist in the same relations to time and space, and has the same, or similar ideas of them, that it does sustain and possess in this life; for he declares absolutely, that its states, and all things else, "have succession and progression in heaven;" that angels have apprehensions of such states and all other things, as successive and progressive, of particular events as occurring at specific periods of time, and of objects as having form and relative position, and as existing in specific localities in place and space; none of which could be true, unless the mind there has, in fact, the same relations to time and space, and has the same ideas of succession and time, and of place and space, that it has here. Swedenborgianism, then, is as demonstrably false, as the proposition that the square of the hypothenuse of a right-angled triangle is equal to the sum of the squares of its two sides, is demonstrably true, and we are no more liable to err, in affirming the former, than we are in affirming the latter.

(4.) Admitting Swedenborg's philosophy of a future state to be throughout true, we are bound, by the fundamental principles of that philosophy, we remark finally, under this head, to reject utterly all his specific visions and revelations, as having no validity whatever for facts as they are in that state, or for what we ourselves may expect to see or experience, when we enter it. According to the fundamental principles of that philosophy, what a mind sees there, that is, the appearances around it, depend wholly upon its interior states, and are determined by the same. To minds in different states, even the same objects put on not only different, but totally opposite appearances. Suppose that Swedenborg did enter the spirit world, and has correctly reported the visions which *he* had there. That is no certain evidence that *we*, when there, shall have any visions even analogous to his. To him conjugial love was the very centre and sphere of heaven. Every angel and devil that we may meet with, may affirm absolutely that "in the resurrection, they neither marry nor are given in marriage," and that all Swedenborg's visions on the subject are the sheerest illusions conceivable. When in a certain locality he heard noises proceeding from certain miserable habitations, noises like "gnashing of teeth." On entering, he found multitudes of wretched beings who had held, while on earth, the doctrine of justification by faith, etc., engaged in fierce and angry disputes on the subject, and that their voices had constituted the discordant sounds which he had before heard. To us those very habitations may appear as "a sea of glass mingled with fire." Those multitudes, too, may appear to us, as standing upon that sea, with the harps of heaven in their hands, while their voices may sound to us, as the notes of that everlasting song that "makes melody in the ear of God." Instead of finding Luther and Melancthon and Calvin where he saw them, we may meet them in "buildings of God, houses not made with hands, eternal in the heavens;" while Emanuel Swedenborg, for rejecting and contemning the doctrine of atonement and of justification by faith, we may find in the lowest hell that can be found there. We also may find the Dutch, the Germans, the English, etc., in no such localities as he assigns them to, and all because his visions of them grew out of his peculiar states relative to them, and we may be in relative states the opposite of his. If Swedenborg's philosophy, we repeat, is true, and we have seen that it cannot but be false, then, by the fundamental principles of the system, his visions are of no value whatever to us, excepting as matters of idle curiosity.

9. We now approach a department of this subject which we would gladly pass over in silence, did the interest of morality permit. What we here say, will be penned in sorrow, not in anger. We refer to Swedenborg, as a *moral revelator.* If he errs here, we may know absolutely, that his revelations are not, and cannot be from God; and here we affirm, he fundamentally errs, and errs just where all false religions do, in giving principles or permissions which *mar the purity of the domestic relations.* One fundamental error in regard to mind and morals both, we impute to him, on the authority of Dr. Pond, we not now having the specific articles containing the error before us. Our revelator teaches, that conscience in man, is wholly the result of education, and pertains to him only in this world, that in the spirit world, mind is without a conscience, and suffers nothing through it. If mental science has now established any truth whatever in regard to mind, it has established this, that conscience is not a creature of education, but a changeless and undying attribute of rational mind. Any professed revelation built upon the opposite supposition, not only cannot be from God, but must be of most dangerous and pernicious tendency, making all moral wrong nothing but violations of conventional rules among men, and not as it is, a violation of the will of God, and of eternal and immutable rules of rectitude. No inspired

man, we may safely say, ever made such a fearful misstep in his morals and philosophy both as this.

But what are the moral rules to which he, as a professedly divine revelator, attempts to educate the conscience? Here we find him as fully accommodating to human lust, as the most licentious could ask. We hesitate not to say, that the conscience of our revelator, if a creature of education, took its principles wholly from the most corrupt maxims of a corrupt court, and that, under the influence of the form of inspiration to which he was subject, its moral principles received no modification for the better. For the regulation of the life of the young man who has strong sexual propensities, and is not able to keep a wife, he says, expressly, "*keep a mistress*," and urges upon him various philosophical and ethical reasons for so doing. If he has formed the intention of marrying an individual, he may, to "initiate her into the friendship of love," "cohabit with her as a mistress," "if he does it, with the constant intention to make her a wife."

His principles are equally accommodating, and accommodated to the lust of the husband after marriage. He is not permitted to cohabit with a wife and mistress at the same time. But if the wife has certain vitiated states of the body, such as fevers, leprosies, cancers, fainting, epilepsy, rupture, etc., then without any crime or fault on her part, or any want of devotion to him, he may totally separate himself from her, and while he has no divorce, and keeps her in his own house, he may "have another woman in keeping," and thus in the presence of his agonized wife and family, raise up a herd of bastards, as the companions and fellow heirs of his legally begotten children. If we have used strong language, in this last sentence, it is because facts, as they are, could not be expressed without it. The above are but specimens, and by no means the worst, of what this professedly divine revelator has uttered, on these and kindred subjects. It is no reply to say, that the things referred to are not required, but merely permitted to prevent greater evils. The permission makes action in accordance with it a sacred duty, as soon as the circumstances referred to arise. If it is right, in the circumstances named, for the individuals referred to to "take a mistress," then they are in conscience bound to do it, when in their honest judgment, the less evils would arise from their doing, than from their not doing it. There is no escaping this conclusion. The following, then, are among the necessary results of his principles on this subject: (1.) It is not only permitted to individuals, but is a sacred duty for them, in the circumstances named, to "keep a mistress," and parents, as he instructs them, may be bound to furnish such for their sons. (2.) The relation of mistress is an honorable, and in itself virtuous relation, and should exclude the persons occupying it, from no position or associations in society, which they would otherwise occupy. If it is honorable in one party, and Swedenborg affirms it to be, it cannot be dishonorable in the other, and should not be so regarded or treated in society. (3.) If it is proper in parents to allow their sons, and Swedenborg says it is, to keep mistresses, it is equally proper in parents to furnish daughters to be kept as such. This is undeniable. (4.) One of the best means of preparing daughters to occupy the position of wives, is to have them first fill, with their future husbands, the sphere of mistresses. Thus they may be, in the language of our revelator, "initiated into the friendship of love." These are the necessary deductions from the principles of this professedly divine revelation, and consequently what, if his claims be admitted, must be received as "taught of God." We will not trust ourselves to say what we really think on this subject; but will barely add, that we no more believe that God ever authorized this man to speak in His name on this, or any other subject, than we believe that He expressly authorized and commanded Judas to betray his Master with a kiss.

10. We are now, we remark, finally, prepared to understand the bearing of Professor Bush's tests by which the question of Swedenborg's inspiration is to be decided. "The truth of his mission is to be established by the truth of his message and by that only."

"We must rely," he says again, "upon internal evidence," etc. We have shown, we think, demonstrably, that the system of Swedenborg can, by no possibility, be true. We therefore, on the authority of the above principles, draw the necessary inference, that he was not and could not have been an inspired revelator, and that we should be guilty of infinite presumption, if we should receive him as such.

Before concluding our remarks, it may be important for us to notice the reasons urged by the friends and followers of our revelator in favor of his high claims, reasons aside from internal evidence. They are like the following: (1.) He was a man of preëminent natural powers, and of corresponding eminence in science. (2.) He revealed facts unknown to any living persons, or unknown to any on earth but the inquirers, and had visions of objects beyond the reach of the senses. He revealed, for example, to the Queen of Sweden, a communication which passed between her and her brother before his death, and which she was sure she had never communicated to any person living, and to the widow of the Dutch envoy in Stockholm, the existence and location of an important document of which she was ignorant. When three hundred miles from Stockholm once, he told that a fire was then raging in that city, and at length said, " thank God, the fire is extinguished, the third door from my house." All was found to have occurred just *when* and *as* he stated. Then, it is affirmed, that he had direct and open visions as of the spirit world, and held immediate conversation as with spirits distinctly revealed to him. We readily grant the reality of the facts before us, as their authenticity cannot reasonably, we judge, be questioned. Yet the facts throughout make an entirely opposite impression upon our mind from what they do upon those of his followers. 1. In the known principles of his philosophy, together with the known states of his mind, we see throughout the patterns after which all his visions of a future state took form. His visions are not patterned after things in heaven, but all things in his heavens are patterned after things preëxisting in his mind. His philosophy, etc., gave form to his visions of heaven. This philosophy, as we have shown, can by no possibility be true, and therefore his visions of heaven must be false. 2. From the previous eminence of Swedenborg in science, we infer, with the most undoubting conviction, that while receiving and constructing his visions, he must have been, as to these, in an abnormal mental state. On no other supposition can we account for the palpable contradictions that he has introduced into his system. When he tells us, for example, that " all things are successive and progressive in heaven," that angels converse upon them as such, and then relate events as having occurred at *definite periods* of the past; that they perceive external objects as having definite relative localities, and then reveal to him facts as existing in definite localities on earth; and then affirms, that angels have, and can have, no ideas of succession and time, or of place and space, that by times they mean states, that with them "by length is meant a state of good, by breadth a state of truth, and by height their discrimination according to degrees," we say that it is very difficult for us to see how a well-balanced scientific mind should put together such palpable and absolute contradictions on the same page. We thence infer that, at the time, the mind of Swedenborg had, as far as these revelations are concerned, lost its balance, and could not have been thinking and writing under the guidance of inspiration. 3. From the particular facts above referred to, the nature and cause of this abnormal state is distinctly revealed to our mind. Swedenborg was undeniably a clairvoyant, and his visions were the exclusive result of an abnormal mental and physical state, occasioned by the permanent development in his organism of the odylic force. All his visions become perfectly intelligible, in regard to their origin and character, when this fact is taken into the account in connection with his known preëxisting philosophical views, and other mental states, and render certain the exclusively subjective origin of those visions. 4. We remark, finally, that the conclusions which Swedenborgians deduce from his apparently preternatural visions impress us, not with the conviction that those conclusions are valid, but with the singular absence of logical and scientific procedure in their deductions from such facts. They ought to take into the account the undeniable fact, that precisely similar disclosures of facts unknown to inquirers, and equally distinct and palpable visions of spirits and other objects, when no such objects are present, attend the action of the very force developed in the organism of Swedenborg, and that when nothing preternatural attends or controls its action. We have before us multitudes of facts precisely similar to those attributed to him. Some years since, for example, a circle existed in Cincinnati, who professed to have, through a clairvoyant, immediate intercourse with the dead, and visions of the future state. A pastor of one of the Presbyterian churches in that city, now president of a western college, told them, that if they would reveal to him certain facts known to himself alone pertaining to his father, who had before died in New Hampshire, he would admit that they were in connection with preternatural sources of information. Those very facts were detailed to him with perfect accuracy, and that as from the spirits, and he concluded that he was in the presence of satanic agency. The character of the circle, as subsequently revealed, rendered it certain, that no preternatural agency of a higher order than the satanic could have been there. We could also cite any reasonably required number of cases in which objects in unknown localities have been revealed, to parallel any and all of Swedenborg's, belonging to this class. As for his visions, as of spirits, we know very well that jugglers, in all ages, have, in some instances, been able to induce in spectators equally palpable visions of absent living persons. A case of this kind will be found in the following extract from Dr. Leonard Woods on Swedenborgianism: —

"I would not undertake to disprove the authenticity of the stories related of Swedenborg. And what then?

In all ages wizards and witches have said and done things seemingly preternatural, and very astonishing. You remember the story of the Witch of Endor. And in Lane's Travels in Egypt, feats of Egyptian jugglers are related which are as wonderful as what Kant relates of Swedenborg. On one occasion a juggler was required to bring to view the image of a man in France, whom it was certain that he never saw, and that he could have no suspicion to whom the person making the request referred. After some incantations, the juggler plainly showed the form of the French officer intended, lame of one leg, and wearing a peculiar badge of military honor. The party who made the requisition on the juggler, was struck with as much consternation as was the queen in the case of Swedenborg."

In this case we have a distinct, present vision of a living person then in a distant kingdom, and we are now able to explain the manner in which this vision was induced. By means of the incantations, etc., the traveller was brought into odylic rapport with the juggler. On the same principles as the clergyman induced in a medium in the case described, a mental vision of a tree the like of which she had never seen nor heard of before, the thought of the traveller was first, no doubt, reproduced in the mind of the juggler, and through him finally again produced as a vision of the object referred to, in the traveller's mind. We think that it was upon this principle, that the vision of Samuel was induced in the mind of Saul. We could also adduce authentic cases in which individuals have had visions as of, and communications as with, spirits, visions just as distinct and palpable as any of Swedenborg's, when the persons having them had no idea that any spirits at all were present, and when facts showed that they were right in their apprehensions. How illogical, then, to reason from the fact, that Swedenborg had such visions, to the validity of the same!

Probably we should not finally dismiss this subject, without an expression of opinion in regard to the character of the two great clairvoyant revelators, A. J. Davis and Emanuel Swedenborg. We agree with the public generally, in regarding the latter as honestly *supposing* himself a divinely commissioned revelator, while he was utterly deceived in that supposition. In regard to the former, we would say, that we have never, since we first read the work which we have reviewed, had a doubt, that the mind or minds which produced the introduction to that work, and the note on page 130, was or were the real author or authors of the whole production. The identity of style throughout precludes, in our judgment, any other supposition. Then we subsequently learned, as we have stated, that Davis, as a matter-of-fact, had the peculiar power, when in the magnetic state, of uttering, just as they would, the thoughts of those with whom he was in odylic communication. We then learned, on the authority of Mr. Bush, that the class of persons from whom these very thoughts were likely to proceed, were, while he was giving forth his "divine revelations," always with him, and never suffered him to be alone. The individual, also, who first introduced Davis to the mysteries of clairvoyance, and who has had very good opportunities to know, has said, that Davis was not the real author of a dozen pages of this work. Our authority is Rev. J. H. Smith, then of Poughkeepsie, and now pastor of a Baptist church in Buffalo, N. Y. There, an individual who affirms himself to have been with Davis at the time, and to know the facts, and who is believed to be a reliable witness, affirmed to Willard Sears, Esq., of Boston, that Davis, in the production of this work, was simply a medium through whom other men's thoughts were uttered. We leave the above facts and statements to speak for themselves, and our whole work to the candid judgment of the reader.

END.

www.ingramcontent.com/pod-product-compliance
Lightning Source LLC
LaVergne TN
LVHW020923110826
845150LV00004B/754
9781425554248